Douglas B. Miller and Loren L. Johns, Editors

BELIEVERS CHURCH BIBLE COMMENTARY

Old Testament
Genesis, by Eugene F. Roop, 1987
Exodus, by Waldemar Janzen, 2000
Leviticus, by Perry B. Yoder, 2017
Numbers, forthcoming
Deuteronomy, by Gerald Gerbrandt, 2015
Joshua, by Gordon H. Matties, 2012
Judges, by Terry L. Brensinger, 1999
Ruth, Jonah, Esther, by Eugene F. Roop, 2002
1-2 Samuel, by David Baker, *forthcoming*
1-2 Kings, by Lynn Jost, *forthcoming*
1-2 Chronicles, by August H. Konkel, 2016
Ezra-Nehemiah, by Steven Schweitzer, *forthcoming*
Job, by Paul Keim, *forthcoming*
Psalms, by James H. Waltner, 2006
Proverbs, by John W. Miller, 2004
Ecclesiastes, by Douglas B. Miller, 2010
Isaiah, by Ivan D. Friesen, 2009
Jeremiah, by Elmer A. Martens, 1986
Lamentations, Song of Songs, by Wilma Ann Bailey and Christina A. Bucher, 2015
Ezekiel, by Millard C. Lind, 1996
Daniel, by Paul M. Lederach, 1994
Hosea, Amos, by Allen R. Guenther, 1998
Joel, Obadiah, Nahum, forthcoming
Micah, Habakkuk, Zephaniah, by Dan Epp-Tiessen and Derek Suderman, *forthcoming*
Haggai, Zechariah, Malachi, by Patricia Shelly, *forthcoming*

New Testament
Matthew, by Richard B. Gardner, 1991
Mark, by Timothy J. Geddert, 2001
Luke, by Mary H. Schertz, *forthcoming*
John, by Willard Swartley, 2013
Acts, by Chalmer E. Faw, 1993
Romans, by John E. Toews, 2004
1 Corinthians, by Dan Nighswander, 2017
2 Corinthians, by V. George Shillington, 1998
Galatians, by George R. Brunk III, 2015
Ephesians, by Thomas R. Yoder Neufeld, 2002
Philippians, by Gordon Zerbe, 2016
Colossians, Philemon, by Ernest D. Martin, 1993
1-2 Thessalonians, by Jacob W. Elias, 1995
1-2 Timothy, Titus, by Paul M. Zehr, 2010
Hebrews, by Estella Horning, *forthcoming*
James, by Sheila Klassen-Wiebe, *forthcoming*

1-2 Peter, Jude, by Erland Waltner and J. Daryl Charles, 1999
1, 2, 3 John, by J. E. McDermond, 2011
Revelation, by John R. Yeatts, 2003

Old Testament Editors
Elmer A. Martens, Mennonite Brethren Biblical Seminary, Fresno, California
Douglas B. Miller, Tabor College, Hillsboro, Kansas

New Testament Editors
Willard M. Swartley, Anabaptist Mennonite Biblical Seminary, Elkhart, Indiana
Loren L. Johns, Anabaptist Mennonite Biblical Seminary, Elkhart, Indiana

Editorial Council
David W. Baker, Brethren Church
W. Derek Suderman, Mennonite Church Canada
Christina A. Bucher, Church of the Brethren
John R. Yeatts, Brethren in Christ Church
Gordon H. Matties (chair), Mennonite Brethren Church
Jo-Ann A. Brant, Mennonite Church USA

Believers Church Bible Commentary

Leviticus

Perry B. Yoder

HERALD PRESS
Harrisonburg, Virginia

Library of Congress Cataloging-in-Publication Data
Names: Yoder, Perry B., author.
Title: Leviticus / Perry B. Yoder.
Description: Harrisonburg : HERALD PRESS, 2017. | Series: Believers church Bible commentary
Identifiers: LCCN 2017032395 | ISBN 9781513801636 (pbk. : alk. paper)
Subjects: LCSH: Bible. Leviticus--Commentaries.
Classification: LCC BS1255.53 .Y63 2017 | DDC 222/.1307--dc23 LC record available at https://lccn.loc.gov/2017032395

Scripture quotations, unless otherwise indicated, are from the *Holy Bible, New International Version®, NIV®*. Copyright ©1973, 1978, 1984, 2011 by Biblica, Inc.™ Used by permission of Zondervan. All rights reserved worldwide. www.zondervan.com. The "NIV" and "New International Version" are trademarks registered in the United States Patent and Trademark Office by Biblica, Inc.™ Other versions briefly compared are identified with Abbreviations.

© 2017 by Herald Press, Harrisonburg, Virginia 22802. 800-245-7894.
    All rights reserved.
Library of Congress Control Number: 2017032395
International Standard Book Number: 978-1-5138-0163-6 (paperback);
    978-1-5138-0246-6 (ebook)
Printed in United States of America
Cover by Merrill R. Miller
Interior design by Merrill R. Miller and Alice Shetler

All rights reserved. This publication may not be reproduced, stored in a retrieval system, or transmitted in whole or in part, in any form, by any means, electronic, mechanical, photocopying, recording, or otherwise without prior permission of the copyright owners.

21 20 19 18 17   10 9 8 7 6 5 4 3 2 1

To Moshe, who taught me

And Elizabeth, who sustained me

Abbreviations

*	The Text in Biblical Context (in Contents)
+	The Text in the Life of the Church (in Contents)
//	parallel passages in the New Testament Gospels
ABD	*The Anchor Bible Dictionary.* Edited by David Noel Freedman. 6 vols. New York: Doubleday, 1992.
ANET	*Ancient Near Eastern Texts Relating to the Old Testament.* Edited by James B. Pritchard. 3rd ed. Princeton, NJ: Princeton University Press, 1969.
AT	author's translation
BCE	before the Common Era (= BC before Christ)
BDB	Brown, Francis, S. R. Driver, and Charles A. Briggs. *A Hebrew and English Lexicon of the Old Testament.* New York: Oxford University Press, 1952.
CAD	*The Assyrian Dictionary of the Oriental Institute of the University of Chicago.* Chicago: The Oriental Institute of the University of Chicago, 1956–2006.
CE	Common Era (= AD, after Christ's birth)
CEV	Contemporary English Version of the Bible
cf.	*confer*, compare
ch(s).	chapter(s)
DBI	*Dictionary of Biblical Interpretation.* Edited by John Hayes. 2 vols. Nashville: Abingdon, 1999.
DCC	*Dictionary of the Christian Church.* Edited by F. L. Cross and E. A. Livingstone. 3rd ed. Peabody, MA: Hendrickson, 1997.
DCH	*Dictionary of Classical Hebrew.* Edited by David J. A. Clines. 9 vols. Sheffield: Sheffield Phoenix Press, 1993–2014.
ed(s).	edition; editor(s)
e.g.	*exempli gratia*, for example
EJ	*Encyclopedia Judaica.* Edited by Cecil Roth. Jerusalem: Keter, 1972.
emph.	emphasis
EN	Explanatory Notes
Eng.	English
esp.	especially
et al.	*et alia*, and others
etc.	*et cetera*, and the rest
Gk.	Greek
HALOT	*The Hebrew and Aramaic Lexicon of the Old Testament.* Ludwig Koehler, Walter Baumgartner, and Johann J. Stamm. Translated and edited under the supervision of Mervyn E. J. Richardson. 4 vols. Leiden: Brill, 1994–2000.
Heb.	Hebrew

ibid.	*ibidem*, in the same place
i.e.	*id est*, that is
KJV	King James Version of the Bible, 1611
lit.	literally
n	note: e.g., 45n2 = page 45, note 2
NEB	New English Bible, 1970
NET	New English Translation, 2005 (lumina.bible.org)
NIDB	*New Interpreter's Dictionary of the Bible.* Edited by Katharine Doob Sakenfeld. 5 vols. Nashville: Abingdon, 2006–2009.
NIV	New International Version, 2011
NJB	New Jerusalem Bible, 1990
NJPS	Tanakh: The Holy Scriptures: The New Jewish Publication Society Translation according to the Traditional Hebrew Text, 1999
NLT	New Living Translation of the Bible, 2013
no.	number
NRSV	New Revised Standard Version, 1989
OT	Old Testament
REB	Revised English Bible, 1996
SAW	*Spiritual and Anabaptist Writers.* Edited by George H. Williams and Angel M. Mergal. Library of Christian Classics. Philadelphia: Westminster, 1957.
s.v(v).	*sub verbo*, under the word(s)
TBC	The Text in Biblical Context (in the commentary)
TLC	The Text in the Life of the Church (in the commentary)
v(v).	verse(s)
vol(s).	volume(s)
Webster's	*Merriam-Webster's Eleventh Collegiate Dictionary*, 2003

Pronunciation Guide for Certain Transliterated Hebrew Consonants

ʾ	(not pronounced)
ʿ	(not pronounced)
ḥ	ch (Scottish *loch*)
ṣ	ts
ś	s
š	sh
ṭ	t

Contents

Abbreviations 8
Pronunciation Guide 9
Series Foreword 15
Author's Preface 17

Introduction to Leviticus 21
A Book of Worship and Life 21
Why Leviticus? 22
    God Is Gracious 23
    God Is Holy 24
    Ethics Matter 24
    God Is Present 25
Leviticus Is about Being God's People 25
Reading Leviticus Helps Us Understand the New Testament 26
Ritual Texts 27
A Road Map to Leviticus 30
The Method of This Commentary 32
The Essays 33
Using This Commentary 34

PART 1 (1:1–15:33): RITUALS FOR GOD'S PRESENCE
1A (1:1–7:38): Sacrificial Rituals 39
Introduction, 1:1-2a 41
Rituals for Pleasing God: The Whole Burnt Offering, 1:2b-17 .. 44
Rituals for Pleasing God: The Grain Offering, 2:1-16 50
Rituals for Pleasing God: The Peace Offering, 3:1-17 55
    * Words and Ritual 58
    * Sacrifice for Jesus and the Early Church 59

+ Grace and Worship 60
+ Prayer as Sacrifice 61
Forgiveness Rituals: Inadvertent Sins, 4:1-35 62
* Forgiveness 70
+ In Praise of Negative Commands 71
Forgiveness Rituals: The Penalty Offering, 5:1–6:7 73
* Forgiveness and Relationships 81
+ The Elements of Public Worship 82
Priestly Instructions for Sacrifice, 6:8–7:38 84

1B (8:1–10:20): Inauguration of Worship 93
The Installation of the Priesthood, 8:1-36 95
The Dedication of the Sanctuary, 9:1-24 101
A Tragic Act of Worship, 10:1-20 104
* The Apparent Violence of God 108
* Dynasty and Temple 110
+ Specialized Functions and the Rest of Us 112

1C (11:1–15:33): Rituals for Purity 114
Rituals for Food Impurity, 11:1-47 118
Birthing Rituals, 12:1-8 123
Rituals for Blemishes, 13:1–14:57 126
Rituals for Reproductive Impurities, 15:1-33 137
* Individual Impurity but Social Consequences 142
* Requirements for Entering God's Presence 143
* Jesus and Paul on Ritual and Social Implications 144
+ The Relevance of Purity 145

PART 2 (16:1–17:16): A HINGE
The Day of Cleansing, 16:1-34 152
* What Is Sin? 160
* The Effects of Sin 161
* Getting Rid of Sin 161
* Sin as Understood in the New Testament 162
+ Forgiveness Rituals and Purification Rituals 163

Why Blood Has Power of Removal, 17:1-16 166
* Eating Blood 171
* The Noachian Laws 172
+ Eating Blood in the Early Church 172

PART 3 (18:1–27:34): LIVING IN LIGHT OF GOD'S PRESENCE
3A (18:1–22:33): Holy Living 178
Forbidden Sexual Practices, 18:1-30 179
   * The Law Gives Life 185
   * Paul and the Law 186
   + Latent Anti-Semitism 187
   + Leviticus and Jesus 187
   + Practicing Christians 189
Holiness in Daily Life, 19:1-37 191
   * Love Your Neighbor 203
   + Love for Each Other 204
Holiness as Obedience, 20:1-27 206
   * Is Israel Special? 210
   * Sexual Prohibitions 211
   + The Significance of Sexual Prohibitions 212
Holiness for Priests, 21:1–22:33 214
   * Holy Things, Holy People 221
   * New Testament Holiness and Ethics 222
   + Holy Places and Holy People 223

3B (23:1–25:55): Holy Time 226
Celebrating Religious Festivals, 23:1-44 227
   * The Festivals in the Bible 234
   + Festivals and the New Testament 235
Duties and a Case of Blasphemy, 24:1-23 237
   * Homicide and Capital Punishment 241
   + Humans as the Image of God 243
The Sabbatical and Jubilee Years, 25:1-55 246
   * Was the Jubilee Ever Practiced? 256
   * The Jubilee Idea 257
   * Social Justice and Mission 258
   + The Use of Resources 259

3C (26:1-46): The Promise and Danger of Covenant 261
   * Curses and Covenant 268
   * Covenant and Continuation 268
   * Jews and Christians 269
   + Jews, Gentiles, and Christians Today 270

3D (27:1-34): Addendum: Vows, Dedications, and Tithes ... 272

Outline of Leviticus 279

Essays 287
    Aaron 287
    Anointing 287
    Atonement 288
    Atonement as Transfer 291
    Atonement in Christian Thinking and Leviticus 292
    Bearing/Removing Iniquity or Sin 294
    Blessings and Curses 295
    Calendar 295
    Cleansing Offering 297
    Covenant 298
    Cut Off 299
    Forgiveness 300
    Hebrews and Leviticus 300
    Holy and Holiness 302
    Jubilee Year 304
    Law 304
    Leadership 306
    Levites 306
    Literary Style 306
    Noachian Covenant 307
    Plain-Sense Interpretation 307
    Pure 309
    Radical Reformation and Mennonite Use of Leviticus 310
    Ransom 312
    Sacrificial System in Leviticus 313
    Scapegoat 316
    Sin (see TBC on Lev 16, p. 160) 317
    The Tabernacle 317
    Taboo 318
    The Traditional Western Method of Exegesis 318
    Worship and Ethics 320
    Yahweh 321
Map of Palestine for Leviticus 322
Map of the Ancient Near East for Leviticus 323
Bibliography 324
Selected Resources 333
Index of Ancient Sources 336
The Author 343

Series Foreword

The Believers Church Bible Commentary series makes available a new tool for basic Bible study. It is published for all who seek more fully to understand the original message of Scripture and its meaning for today—Sunday school teachers, members of Bible study groups, students, pastors, and others. The series is based on the conviction that God is still speaking to all who will listen, and that the Holy Spirit makes the Word a living and authoritative guide for all who want to know and do God's will.

The desire to help as wide a range of readers as possible has determined the approach of the writers. Since no blocks of biblical text are provided, readers may continue to use the translation with which they are most familiar. The writers of the series use the New Revised Standard Version and the New International Version on a comparative basis. They indicate which text they follow most closely and where they make their own translations. The writers have not worked alone, but in consultation with select counselors, the series' editors, and the Editorial Council.

Every volume illuminates the Scriptures; provides necessary theological, sociological, and ethical meanings; and in general makes "the rough places plain." Critical issues are not avoided, but neither are they moved into the foreground as debates among scholars. Each section offers "Explanatory Notes," followed by focused articles, "The Text in Biblical Context" and "The Text in the Life of the Church." This commentary aids the interpretive process but does not try to supersede the authority of the Word and Spirit as discerned in the gathered church.

The term *believers church* has often been used in the history of the church. Since the sixteenth century, it has frequently been applied to the Anabaptists and later the Mennonites, as well as to the Church of the Brethren and similar groups. As a descriptive term, it includes more than Mennonites and Brethren. *Believers church* now represents specific theological understandings, such as believers baptism, commitment to the Rule of Christ in Matthew 18:15-20 as crucial for church membership, belief in the power of love in all relationships, and willingness to follow Christ in the way of the cross. The writers chosen for the series stand in this tradition.

Believers church people have always been known for their emphasis on obedience to the simple meaning of Scripture. Because of this, they do not have a long history of deep historical-critical biblical scholarship. This series attempts to be faithful to the Scriptures while also taking archaeology and current biblical studies seriously. Doing this means that at many points the writers will not differ greatly from interpretations that can be found in many other good commentaries. Yet these writers share basic convictions about Christ, the church and its mission, God and history, human nature, the Christian life, and other doctrines. These presuppositions do shape a writer's interpretation of Scripture. Thus this series, like all other commentaries, stands within a specific historical church tradition.

Many in this stream of the church have expressed a need for help in Bible study. This is justification enough to produce the Believers Church Bible Commentary. Nevertheless, the Holy Spirit is not bound to any tradition. May this series be an instrument in breaking down walls between Christians in North America and around the world, bringing new joy in obedience through a fuller understanding of the Word.

—*The Editorial Council*

Author's Preface

Writing this commentary has been a substantial journey. The journey began by becoming acquainted with Leviticus and the scholarly literature written about it. Pleasantly, my journey began at a time when a revolution was taking place in understanding the sacrificial rituals in Leviticus, especially the "sin offering." This development was sparked by the work of Jacob Milgrom, which challenged at least some if not many traditional assumptions. Milgrom's work caused a flourishing of scholarly debate and discussion, beginning in the 1980s and extending into the first decade of the twenty-first century. The new developments and the resulting debates made this part of the journey exciting. Now, at journey's end, we are in the "beyond Jacob Milgrom" phase of study.

Besides suggesting new ways of understanding certain rituals in Leviticus, this debate necessitated focusing on the wording of texts, what was happening in these rituals, and the concepts conveyed by them. For me this was a refreshing development, since earlier scholarly debate seemed more concerned with classic topics like the history of the book's development and redaction, its dating, and its audience. The debate about the relationship between Leviticus and other literature in the Bible, like Deuteronomy, seemed unending, as were the questions about its character. Is it a utopian document like we find at the end of Ezekiel (chs. 44–48)? Was it the result of a struggle among the priests, Ezekiel representing one faction and Leviticus another? Was it a grab for power and control by the Jerusalem priesthood late in Israel's history? Or was it an early work, thus assuming local shrines to which people could bring their sacrifices? All answers to these questions are to some degree speculative, and it seemed to me that these questions are not the most significant ones for a layperson. Rather, the first need is for a simple understanding of *what is actually in the text*, as well as reflection on how our understanding of these texts has changed since Milgrom's work and the ensuing debate.

My first goal in writing, then, was to focus on Leviticus as Leviticus—making clear as carefully as I could what the text is saying and what happens in what is described. This approach, I hoped, would give readers new understandings and perspectives grounded in the text itself. Focusing on the text and its explication would, as a bonus, give my interpretive comments a concrete grounding (although any understanding is to a degree subjective).

Milgrom's work also challenged long-held beliefs about important theological topics that found expression in Leviticus. Atonement and purification are now understood differently than what had been traditionally assigned to them. The question about the function of blood in sacrificial rituals was an especially significant part of the debate. For Christians, above all, these debates challenged cherished beliefs that were supported by previous interpretations and suppositions. Thus evolved the second goal of this commentary: to set out these new understandings and to show how they represent what is in the text as well as to point out what has been assumed but is not in the text. This is why there are three essays on atonement in the essay section at the end of the commentary.

These two goals lent themselves to an interpretive journey following in the footsteps of an interpretive tradition called plain-sense interpretation (*peshat*), which has its roots in medieval Jewish interpretation and was adopted by some Christian scholars as they became acquainted with Hebrew and with their Jewish colleagues—thus the essay "Plain-Sense Interpretation" as well as "The Traditional Western Method of Exegesis."

I had a companion on this journey: my editor, Dr. Douglas Miller. His patience with me as I struggled to express myself, his suggestions of what needed explanation or a better explanation, and his constructive critical comments have left their imprint on most pages of this commentary, which is better and wiser because of his guidance. His contribution was all the sweeter because as his teacher I was able to help him along the way, and now as my editor he was able to return the favor. Life has few greater joys for a scholar.

I was also aided by the comments of Dr. Wesley Bergen, who read the commentary with a careful eye for my wording as well as my thinking. He made helpful suggestions for additional work as well as others. At many points I have profited from his comments, and the

Author's Preface

result is a stronger commentary. In addition, I profited from the insights of Diane Zaerr Brenneman into the content and message of this commentary. Her comments were both challenging and affirming, and she was especially helpful in polishing the TBC and TLC essays. I am indebted to her and thankful for her contribution. I am also grateful for the work of the staff at Herald Press, especially the fine editing of David Garber, whose meticulous reading and suggestions have made the text clearer.

The first article of any kind that I wrote was for a church magazine in about 1963. It grew out of my first Bible class with Dr. Moshe Greenberg on Deuteronomy. Its title, as I recall, was "Leviticus and the Christian." My work ever since has been indebted to him as a teacher and as a person of integrity. My life has been richer for my acquaintance with him.

My wife, Elizabeth, has also contributed to this work. As a professional copyeditor, she read through the manuscript, checking my references and bibliography. Yet with all this help, any errors in this work are fully my own.

I thank God who has brought me to this place.

—*Perry B. Yoder*
Ely, Minnesota

Introduction to Leviticus

Perhaps you can picture yourself deep in the desert with the people of Israel. Moses, the revered leader, has come down from the mountain, a near-catastrophic rebellion against him has been averted, and the covenant between the people of Israel and Yahweh their God has been established.

The tabernacle has been built. God's presence has descended from Mount Sinai and is present in the tent outside the camp. What comes next? What will happen now that God's presence is so near as to be visible?

Moses and the people must now ask: How can we live in the presence of this holy God in the days and years ahead? The book of Leviticus addresses this question, answering it in very practical detail. In this answer we find out a great deal about the character of God, about worshiping God, and about living with God.

A Book of Worship and Life

Leviticus begins as a book of worship. In fact, the book's English title means "of the Levites," that group of Israelites who assisted with worship matters (see Num 18:2), although interestingly they are rarely mentioned directly in the book that bears their name (for the Hebrew title of Leviticus, see discussion at 1:1). When God comes to Israel, the Israelites must learn how to worship a God who is very near and present. These instructions occupy the first seven chapters of Leviticus and give directions for the rituals of worship. The worship rituals begin with voluntary offerings (chs. 1–3), offerings brought willingly from goodness of heart, and then turn to obligatory offerings, those required because of sins committed (4:1–6:7).

The Israelites must also know and practice the requisite rituals for purity before entering the tabernacle courtyard and coming before God. God is holy, and only those who are pure may come before the presence of the holy. Rituals for restoring purity are found in chapters 11–15. Chapter 16, the Great Day of Cleansing (Day of Atonement), concludes the presentation of the public worship rituals.

Realms	Holy (tabernacle)	Common (the camp)
Ritual States	Pure	Impure

This chart illustrates the dynamic relationship between holiness and purity in Leviticus. The Israelite camp is divided into two areas, or realms: the holy area of the tabernacle and the common area, which includes everything else. Likewise, people live in two states: purity and impurity. Becoming impure, as we shall see, is a normal, daily occurrence. However, before entering the realm of the holy, a person must perform a ritual for the restoration of their purity. Once pure, the person may leave the area of the camp and enter the holy realm. Thus in the common area we find both pure and impure people. But in the holy, only pure people are allowed (see the diagram in Milgrom 1991: 616).

Besides the normal worship rituals, we also find rituals carried out by the priests to maintain worship, such as the daily entirely burnt offering to ensure a continuous fire on the altar, rituals for the installation of the high priest and the regular priests, and rituals for the inauguration of worship. These rituals are found in chapters 6:8–9:24 *[Leadership, p. 306]*.

The holiness of God affects how the Israelites must live. Instructions for holy living are given in chapters 18–22 and 25. Chapter 23 sets Israel's calendar of holy festivals, times when Israel comes together in special ways to worship God. The use and function of the special "furniture" in the tabernacle is given in chapter 24 *[The Tabernacle, p. 317]*. See the diagram on page 35.

Why Leviticus?

But what about Leviticus now, when there is no longer a visible sign of God's presence? Today, sanctuaries of worship do not seem to be holy places that demand great respect on our part. The sense of the holy has been diminished in Western societies and in our secular lives. Nevertheless, there are excellent reasons why Leviticus should be read and studied today. First of all, Leviticus teaches us important characteristics of God in relationship with humankind.

God Is Gracious

From Leviticus we learn above all that *God is gracious.* Leviticus reveals a God of extravagant grace—by human standards an irresponsibly gracious God. Indeed, God's grace is so shocking in Leviticus that it may be hard for us to accept. That just isn't the way God should be! God, we sometimes think, must be more judgmental.

With all the sacrificial slaughter commanded in Leviticus, you might think God to be a very angry and judgmental God—a God needing to be supplicated, pleased, or appeased at every turn by fearful, trembling worshipers. Surprise! In Leviticus, God is never angry! God may be angry in Exodus (22:24; 32:10-12) or in Numbers (1:53; 11:1, 10, 33), but never in Leviticus. The possibility that God could become angry in the future for disobedience is considered (only in 10:6; 26:28), but God is not now angry with Israel. Sacrifices in Leviticus are not motivated by an angry or hostile God.

In fact, there is no punishment for sins committed inadvertently. If transgressors become aware of a trespass at a later time, they must act to obtain forgiveness, which their gracious God freely gives to them. But what happens if an Israelite never remembers an inadvertent sin? Apparently nothing! The text of Leviticus is silent. However, on the Day of Cleansing (Atonement), the high priest performs rituals that cleanse the tabernacle from *all* the sins of the people. All the sins and impurities are loaded onto a goat, which is expelled from the tabernacle and from the camp. The slate, so to speak, is wiped clean. Israel and God can begin again in the new year (16:16-20). Is there any other depiction of God that is more generous and gracious?

The God who every year wipes away the sins of the past is a friendly God. This God is not a bookkeeping deity ready to pounce on the sinner. This God blesses the Israelites, and they return the favor by wholeheartedly offering sacrifices whose only ritual purpose is to please their God (chs. 1–3). These are the sacrifices of people who feel happy with God, not threatened.

In chapter 26, however, we do find punishments that God initiates when Israel breaks their covenant, or contract, with God. Israel had accepted a covenant with God willingly, and even had a night in which to think over their decision (Exod 24:3-8). In accepting God's contract, they also pledged their obedience to its terms. If the people deliberately break this agreement, turning their back on God, they will be penalized for breach of contract. These contract penalties, or punishments, do not occur because God is angry. Judges in a courtroom are not necessarily angry with those they sentence. Nevertheless, they command punishment for those convicted.

Surprisingly, after punishment for breach of contract, God will still keep the covenant made with Israel. Punishment for breaking a contract does not annul a contract any more than a late payment abolishes a contract for a loan. Even when Israel does not want to maintain their agreement with God, God does not write them off. Instead, God declares, *I will not reject them or abhor them so as to destroy them completely, breaking my covenant with them* (Lev 26:44). God chooses to forgive instead: *I will remember the covenant with their ancestors whom I brought out of Egypt* (26:45). After punishment, Israel will continue to experience God's grace, which seemingly is timeless.

God Is Holy

Although a God of unlimited grace, *God is* also *holy*. The first section of Leviticus (chs. 1–10) emphasizes holy things and places (6:17, 25-30 [Heb.: 6:10, 18-23], etc.). These chapters prepare for the coming of a holy God. These preparations culminate when *the Presence of the* LORD *appeared to all the people, and* Fire *came forth from before the* LORD *and consumed the burnt offering and the fat parts on the altar. And all the people saw, and shouted, and fell on their faces* (9:23-24 NJPS).

The holy God is now in Israel's midst, and the accent shifts to the holiness of the people. Because of God's holiness, *You are to sanctify yourselves [make yourselves holy] and be holy because I am holy* (Lev 11:44 NET). The holy God requires a people who are seeking holiness.

Ethics Matter

God is the source of holiness, and God has chosen to make Israel holy: *I the* LORD *make you holy* (Lev 20:8 NJPS; cf. 21:8, 15, 23; 22:9, 16, 32). However, the Israelites are responsible to maintain their holiness: *Consecrate yourselves and be holy, because I am the* LORD *your God* (11:44; 20:7). God's holiness necessitates a certain way of life on the part of the people: *Be holy because I, the* LORD *your God, am holy* (19:2). How do the people Israel sanctify themselves? By keeping the regulations and instructions given by God for being holy. The people's holiness, or sanctification, depends on following the instructions provided for holy living (20:7, 26; 21:5-6, 8). Obedience is the way of holiness, and this holiness is about a relationship between a holy God and a holy people [Worship and Ethics, p. 320].

God Is Present

Israel has a history with God as a gracious and holy God. They have experienced deliverance from slavery and God's care and guidance in their desert journey from Egypt to Mount Sinai. At Mount Sinai they experienced God's presence as fire, as thunder, as clouds, and even as a voice. Then God's presence descends from Mount Sinai and enters a tent outside the camp. God keeps coming closer to Israel.

Now, in Leviticus, God's presence moves into the very midst of Israel. When Israel moves, the tabernacle of God's presence will move with them. This continuing presence of God introduces a new reality. God has journeyed from a mountain to a shrine in the camp. Everything has changed: *You shall put the Israelites on guard against their uncleanness, lest they die through their uncleanness by defiling My Tabernacle which is among them* (Lev 15:31 NJPS). Israel now lives in God's continuing presence.

But the presence of this holy God is both a boon and a hazard. As we learn in Leviticus 10:1-2, God's holiness must be respected. It is one thing to disobey a holy God; it is another matter to violate the holiness of this God. God's holiness matters, and respecting God's holiness forms the basis for both worship and life. In Western society, having largely lost the sense of awe for God's holiness, Leviticus can prod us to think about a God who is holy and about what is lost when we lack a sense of awe for the holiness of God [Holy and Holiness, p. 302].

Leviticus Is about Being God's People

A second value of Leviticus is that it helps us understand what it means and how to be God's people. Leviticus makes sense of the five books of Moses. There is a chasm between the end of Exodus and the beginning of the book of Numbers. In Exodus, God commands, "And let them make Me a sanctuary that I may dwell among them" (Exod 25:8 NJPS). This goal is fulfilled in the last few verses of Exodus (40:34-38) and on into Leviticus, when God's presence enters the tabernacle in the midst of the camp, and Israel enters into a new relationship with God. Numbers begins with this new reality (1:1). Genesis and Exodus lead up to Leviticus. Numbers and Deuteronomy lead away from God's presence and revelation at Mount Sinai as Israel leaves for Canaan. Leviticus represents the pinnacle.

To miss Leviticus is to miss not only the coming of the new reality but also the formation of Israel into God's people. How is Israel to become "a kingdom of priests and a holy nation" (Exod 19:6)? The answer is the purpose of Leviticus. It explains what this means by instructing Israel about how to worship God and how to live as God's people. Leviticus is the crucial turning point in the first five books, transforming Israel into a people of God.

This transformation is important for all who would become God's people. In 1 Peter 2:9 the verses from Exodus 19:5-6 are applied to the early church: "You are a chosen people, a royal priesthood, a holy nation, God's special possession, that you may declare the praises of him who called you out of darkness into his wonderful light." The rules for becoming and being a holy people found in Leviticus are still relevant for God's people today.

For a discussion of some additional themes in Leviticus, see the essays at the end of this commentary.

Reading Leviticus Helps Us Understand the New Testament

Leviticus is valuable for those who wish to better understand the New Testament. It gives us the plain sense of items, expressions, and practices that are referred to symbolically and metaphorically in the New Testament. Understanding how objects like an altar were used and why a ritual was practiced can place New Testament references to them in a new light. For example, to say that Jesus was tabernacled among us (John 1:14) recalls the presence of God that in Leviticus came to earth and dwelt in the tabernacle.

Knowing Leviticus may also challenge us to look below the surface of texts we take for granted. For example, John the Baptist says, "Look, the Lamb of God, who takes away the sin of the world!" (John 1:29). If this verse refers to the scapegoat, then we might expect the text to read, "Behold the *goat* of God, who takes away the sin of the world." On the other hand, if the scapegoat of Leviticus *is* referred to as a "lamb" in this quotation, this expression by John the Baptist does not refer to the death of Jesus, since in Leviticus the scapegoat did not die! But the use of "lamb" does give the passage a sacrificial connotation. In the ritual of forgiveness for sin, what did the blood applied to the altar do? Read on!

Leviticus also provides helpful background on understanding such concepts as purity and holiness. For writings such as those by Paul, Leviticus shows us how these topics may have been understood in the early church. This in turn can show us their significance for the formation of churches.

Ritual Texts

Most of the texts in Leviticus are ritual texts (Lev 1–16, 22–24). Ritual texts are a special type of text, and they immediately raise interpretive questions. So what is a ritual? The definition of what constitutes a ritual is difficult and has led to complex and abstract definitions that have varied over the past two centuries and from scholar to scholar. In this commentary, two assumptions are made about rituals. First, a ritual is composed of fixed actions or words having a set order. A ritual is *performed*. It takes place only when its words are spoken and the proper actions or gestures are made by the appropriate people.

Second, a ritual is performed to achieve some end. The act of doing a ritual is *performative*—that is, the performance of a ritual causes something to happen. For example, in a marriage ritual the statement "I now pronounce you husband and wife" causes the couple to become husband and wife. The outcome of a ritual is the reason it exists and why it is carried out. (See Bell; Klingbeil; Bibb; Frevel and Nihan: 3–10. Bergen uses ritual theory to apply rituals in Leviticus to our contemporary behavior.)

Ritual texts are different from the description of rituals in narrative texts. In stories, for example, laypersons could offer sacrifices, as Manoah, Samson's father, did: "Then Manoah took a young goat, together with the grain offering, and sacrificed it on a rock to the LORD" (Judg 13:19; see Watts 2011). The case is similar in poetic and metaphorical usages where they are the application of sacrificial terminology and action to another realm. Psalm 51 teems with examples. In verse 2, for instance, the psalmist requests, "Wash away all my iniquity and cleanse me from my sin" (Ps 51:2). This verse uses the language of a purification ritual found in Leviticus 11–15. Here it is applied to forgiveness, which requires neither washing nor purification in Leviticus.

What Is a Ritual Text?

Obviously, reading a ritual text in Leviticus does not perform a ritual. Neither do the texts describe the enactment of a ritual, except in the cases of chapters 8 and 9 (and perhaps 16). Nor do these texts represent all the details necessary to perform a ritual. The text of the ritual using a burnt ox (Lev 1:1-8), for example, has gaps. The crucial matter of specifying who slaughters the ox in verse 5 is unclear. The text implies "he," which can refer either to the priest or to the layperson. The NET makes a decision: *[the one presenting the offering] must slaughter the bull.* The brackets indicate what has been added. Other translations make no decision by simply putting the clause in the passive, *the bull shall be slaughtered* (NJPS, NRSV), letting the reader make the decision: priest, layperson, or perhaps either is acceptable.

The next ritual step is even less clear: *The priests shall bring the blood and splash it against the sides of the altar.* How and in what way do they collect the blood, and how do they splash or dash it against the sides of the altar? Do they use a ladle and take blood from a container for splashing, or do they splash blood from the container directly upon the altar?

Perhaps our best illustrative model would be a recipe. Normally a recipe lists the major ingredients and the amount to be used. It will also tell what to do with them—chop, grind, grate, and so on—and when to use them. It may give instructions for cooking the dish: covered or uncovered, baking temperature, and length of cooking time. What a recipe provides is the basic structure for the actual performance of cooking or baking something. It is not a video of someone performing the recipe, nor is it a description of what tools are used or all that is done during the performance.

So also the rituals in Leviticus. Like recipes, rituals need the right person(s), the right equipment, and the right ingredients. In Leviticus there are normally two participants in a ritual: a priest and someone who requests the performance. The necessary equipment must be available, such as an altar, and the necessary ingredients for performing the ritual. The different ingredients have different roles or functions. In rituals for pleasing God, both grain and a fragrance are necessary ingredients (ch. 2). The grain with the perfume added is burned, making a pleasing odor for God. The remaining grain provides food for the priests.

In structure, these ritual texts follow the form of case law: when this happens, then you do this. When someone comes with the offering of an ox for a whole burnt offering, then you do this. If it is a sheep or a goat, then you do that. (Compare the case of the slave laws found in Exod 21:2-11 with Lev 1:1-8 *[Law, p. 304]*).

Why follow a recipe? Because if you want to bake a chocolate cake, you find a recipe for a chocolate cake. If you follow the recipe for a chocolate pie, you will not end up with a chocolate cake. So also in Leviticus. The ritual, the recipe, is performed by those who know how to do it—the priests—and by the one initiating the ritual, who seeks its desired outcome. In this sense, ritual texts are also legal texts: their recipe must be followed to reach the desired results.

Silent Rituals

The most striking aspect of the rituals in Leviticus is that they are performed in silence. The priests say nothing; the layperson says nothing. Everything happens in gestures: the layperson lays a hand on the head of an ox but says nothing. The priest dashes the blood of the ox against the altar but utters not a word. Although we find indications of both words and actions in the ritual texts from surrounding cultures, and something similar may have been the case in Israel (see discussion of Psalms in TBC for ch. 3), such verbal aspects are not indicated here.

This silence makes the meaning of the gestures in these rituals uncertain. The interpretation of ritual gestures is not found in the text but is supplied by the interpreter. For example, in 1:5 the layperson lays a hand on the head of an ox. What is happening here? What is being done? The text is silent. Interpreters, of course, have filled this vacuum, and certain explanations have become so traditional that they are taken as obvious. But remember, these explanations are guesses. We have no evidence from the ritual texts themselves explaining why the one bringing an ox places a hand on its head when delivering it to the priest. (For the seminal work on silence in the priestly sanctuary, see Knohl.) While this gesture has been commonly construed to transfer something from the person to the animal, in the commentary to Leviticus 1:5 a different explanation will be given.

Although no words are given for the gestures of a ritual in Leviticus, the text does say what a ritual accomplishes. For the whole burnt offering in chapter 1, for example, the outcome is *an aroma pleasing to the* LORD (Lev 1:9). From this outcome we infer intention—someone brings a whole burnt offering in order to produce this aroma to please God. Other intentions have been suggested or taken as fact, but a plain-sense interpretation follows what the text actually says.

In this commentary, since ritual outcomes are stated, the rituals in Leviticus are named according to their outcome. In chapter 1 the ritual produces an aroma that pleases God. These we will label "rituals for pleasing God." All the rituals in the first three chapters of Leviticus have this goal: they are different ways of pleasing God. By contrast, the rituals in chapters 4 and 5 have forgiveness as their goal.

Terminology

A *gesture* refers to an individual action within the ritual and is named according to its description. For example, the ritual for pleasing God in chapter 1 begins with the layperson placing or leaning a hand on the head of their animal. This gesture could be termed "the leaning-hand gesture." This is awkward but has the advantage of being descriptively accurate. Whatever we believe this gesture *does* should fit the reason for the ritual, which is known.

A gesture may have different meanings in different rituals. The interpretation of a gesture should fit the type of ritual in which it occurs. This leaves great latitude for explaining what placing a hand on the head of an animal does in chapter 1. But it does exclude explanations that are incompatible, unneeded, or fit the outcome of a different ritual. In the Explanatory Notes to chapter 1, we point out that a traditional explanation such as transferring a person's sin to the sacrificial animal does not suit the purpose or the context of this gesture in its ritual context.

Ritual ceremonies like the inauguration of priests into the priesthood (ch. 8) are composed of a series of rituals and gestures strung together. They are a composite of various rituals: when done alone, each would have its own reason for being performed. Ceremonies may also contain their own distinctive gestures and rituals. A good example is chapter 16, the ceremony for the Day of Cleansing. As almost the final act of this ceremony, we find the ritual of a goat being led into the wilderness in order to carry away all the sins of the people. This elimination ritual is unique to this particular ceremony. Likewise, the high priest placing both hands on the goat and saying a prayer are unique gestures occurring only in this elimination ritual.

A Road Map to Leviticus

The following outline presents the overall structure of topics in Leviticus. The book is usually divided into two parts. Chapters 1–16 are devoted to the rituals of worship. These rituals end with the Day of Cleansing ceremony in chapter 16. Chapters 17–27 form the second half, with its major emphasis on holiness in life.

However, chapter 17 appears to be more closely related to what precedes it than to what follows. This chapter, in fact, ends with a purification ritual for eating impure food, a ritual like those found in chapter 11. Chapter 17 also has a strong link to the sacrificial ritual in chapter 3, the peace offering, by requiring all butchering to be done in the form of a peace offering. It seems best to consider chapters 16 and 17 as forming a hinge between two parts of the book. The first fifteen chapters are about worship at the tabernacle. Chapter 18 begins the instructions for holy living. The Day of Cleansing, chapter 16, with its rituals of purification, is the capstone of the first fifteen chapters, while chapter 17 explains why blood has its cleansing power.

Outline of Leviticus	Chs.
Part 1: Rituals for God's Presence	**1–15**
1A: Sacrificial Rituals	
Voluntary offerings	1–3

Obligatory offerings
      Forgiveness rituals (4–5)
      Instructions for priests (6–7)
	4–7

1B: Inauguration of Worship	
Installation of the priesthood	8
Dedication of the sanctuary	9
A tragic act of worship	10
1C: Rituals for Purity	
Food	11
Birthing	12
Blemishes	13–14
Reproduction	15
Part 2: A Hinge	**16–17**
2A: The Day of Cleansing	16
2B: Why Blood Has Power of Removal	17
Part 3: Living in Light of God's Presence	**18–27**
3A: Holy Living	
Forbidden sexual practices	18
Holiness in daily life	19
Holiness as obedience	20
Holiness for priests	21–22
3B: Holy Time	
Celebrating religious festivals	23
Duties and a case of blasphemy	24
The Sabbatical and Jubilee Years	25
3C: The Promise and Danger of Covenant	26
3D: Addendum: Vows, Dedications, and Tithes	27

(See Douglas 1999; Warning; Zenger. A more complete outline is found at the end of the commentary section.)

The Method of This Commentary

Like an argument or interpretation, it's a rare text that has only one interpretation. Different understandings of a text are possible, although not all are equally probable. How a text is understood depends in large part on the interpreter's goals, which can determine what evidence is considered relevant or important and how it is weighted. Goals matter as much in this commentary as in any other.

This commentary tries to present a plain-sense interpretation of Leviticus *[Plain-Sense Interpretation, p. 307]*. Since Leviticus was written in Hebrew, this commentary begins with the Hebrew text, explaining how it may be understood. Translations are useful since they also represent differing interpretations of the Hebrew text. However, a translation may or may not reproduce the plain sense of a text. The New English Translation (NET) of Leviticus is very helpful in this regard. It adds informative footnotes explaining why its translators understood a passage or a word as they did. (See NET notes on the first several verses of chapter 1, for example.) Reference to NET and its translation notes is an easy way for readers of English to become aware of interpretive questions and the different answers given by the translations. Readers are encouraged to use these notes, which can be found online at bible.org/netbible/.

A question to constantly keep in mind when evaluating a translation or commentary is, Given the audience, goal, and context of Leviticus, would this interpretation have made sense? This criterion aims to exclude anachronistic understandings, interpretations assigned to a text long after it was written. Such understandings do not fit the envisioned audience of the text, its apparent goal, or its suggested context. Rather, these proposals belong to the history of interpretation of Leviticus, which often serves to caution us as we engage the text (Lienhard).

Of course, the book or scroll of Leviticus likely was understood differently at different times within the biblical period itself. However, within that period we have little or no historical evidence for changes in its interpretation. This has much to do with the nature of the material itself. These are set out as instructions for rituals that the priests would supervise and perform. If this were an instruction manual for the priests at Jerusalem, we would not expect it to be widely known or even important for most people. If Leviticus is utopian literature of how the priests wished things were, we would know even less. The placement of Leviticus in the wilderness gives a very spare context for its understanding. What we can know, however, is that at a certain point it became Scripture, providing the basis for Jewish practice, and that its interpretation was disputed, for example, in the Mishnah and Talmud. At this point we can surely speak of later interpretations that go beyond the plain sense of the text.

This does not mean that metaphorical, symbolic, and typological uses of Leviticus are invalid. The use of "tabernacling" for the presence of Jesus is a metaphor for illustrating the meaning of Jesus' presence (John 1:14 Gk.). It can be likened to the presence of God in the tabernacle in Leviticus. However, such is a *use* of the text, not an explanation of its plain sense.

My own perspectives influence my judgment concerning the meaning of Hebrew words and texts. The questions I ask are, What are the relevant data to be drawn from the text, and what are the possible interpretive conclusions to be drawn from them? Which conclusion is most likely or probable within the goal and context of the text? An illustration of this methodology can be found in *Seeing the Text: Exegesis for Students of Greek and Hebrew* (Schertz and Yoder). A different and more prevalent methodology is discussed in the essay *Traditional Western Method of Exegesis [p. 318]*. (On the history of interpretation, see Lienhard; in the believers church tradition, see the essay *Radical Reformation and Mennonite Use of Leviticus, p. 310*.)

The Essays

Besides the commentary proper, this volume contains supplemental essays, gathered at the end of the commentary in a section titled "Essays" and cited throughout the work for those who wish further explanation of a given topic. In addition, other essays are attached to the commentary after certain chapters or blocks of material. These are labeled "The Text in Biblical Context" and "The Text in the Life of the Church." In TBC essays, similar texts may be discussed as well as the impact of a text on the rest of the Bible. For example, the notion of purity in Leviticus is important to Paul and is illustrated and commented on in a TBC essay for chapter 15. The TLC essay that follows discusses the relevance of this understanding of purity for the life of the church. Further, since Paul and Acts represent an early example of using a text in the church, Paul and Acts may be discussed in this section as well.

However, no attempt has been made to document all the ways Leviticus has been *used* or *applied* by later biblical authors. It seems more appropriate for commentators on the work of a later biblical author to explain their author's particular use of ideas found in Leviticus. The use of "tabernacle" in the gospel of John (cited above) is an example. Why did John use "tabernacle"? What might it have meant to Jews in the first century CE or to his supposed audience? The present essays begin with Leviticus and play it forward to show the impact of Leviticus on later writers rather than how later writers have applied Leviticus for their own purposes. (For how Leviticus has been understood in the believers church tradition, see the essay *Radical Reformation and Mennonite Use of Leviticus, p. 310*.)

Using This Commentary

This commentary is written with an audience in mind, an audience that has some familiarity with the Bible but little with Leviticus itself. It is an audience more familiar with the New Testament than with the Old Testament, more familiar with later theological interpretations or uses of Leviticus than with its plain sense.

It is not written for scholars or for those who want extensive discussion of some passages. For readers who want more information, three valuable reference works are frequently cited in this commentary. The first is *The New Interpreter's Dictionary of the Bible* (*NIDB*), which is recent and extensive; however, other Bible dictionaries may also be helpful. The other two are commentaries. The work by John Hartley (1992) is scholarly but not overwhelming for the more advanced reader. It represents a more traditional point of view. The other is Jacob Milgrom's three-volume commentary on Leviticus, which is used here somewhat like a Bible dictionary. For example, rather than try to determine the identity of the clean and unclean animals in Leviticus 11 (the translations differ), reference is made to Milgrom's discussion of the arguments for the differing identifications. This way tedious detail can be avoided when it is not significant for most readers, yet a source is provided for those who do want the extra detail.

Since the 1970s, Jacob Milgrom's work on Leviticus has produced a watershed in the interpretation of Leviticus and the priestly material more generally (see commentary on ch. 4 and the essay *Atonement, p. 288*). Post-Milgrom studies and scholars may be divided into three loosely defined groups: those who follow Milgrom but make modifications to his thinking (e.g., Gilders 2004); those who agree with Milgrom's basic findings but do not agree with all the conclusions he draws (e.g., Sklar 2008); and those who simply disagree with Milgrom (e.g., Kiuchi). This commentary belongs to the first group, which explains the frequent references to Milgrom's commentary. For a brief overview of Milgrom's work and its further extension or clarification, see the introduction (xii–xvi) and also

Introduction to Leviticus

articles in Gane and Taggar-Cohen. This commentary will provide further comments and illustrations of Milgrom's importance.

Because Leviticus was written in Hebrew, its Hebrew terms will be discussed from time to time. Such words are transliterated: presented by using the English alphabet. An example would be *kipper* (atone, expiate, purity), which has been translated in a variety of ways even within the same verse by the same Bible translation. In such cases, to ensure the reader knows that the same word, *kipper*, is being discussed regardless of translation, I will give the Hebrew word in English letters.

The standard translation used for quotations from the Bible in this commentary is the New International Version (NIV). This is not because it is necessarily the best translation, although it is a good one, but because it is readily available and is the translation of choice for many readers. Quotations from the NIV will have no attribution. Quotations from other translations are marked accordingly, such as NRSV (New Revised Standard Version), NJPS (Tanakh, the New Jewish Publication Society version), and NET (New English Translation). Also, AT indicates the author's own translation and sometimes represents a more literal or more consistent rendering. When Hebrew versification differs from that of English versions, it is added within parentheses, or square-bracketed if the reference is already within parentheses—for example, Leviticus 6:1-7 (5:20-26); 6:8-30 (6:1-23).

These other translations are used to illustrate wordings preferred to those of the NIV or to illustrate the various ways in which a text may be understood. The Explanatory Notes provide a rationale for preferring one understanding above another.

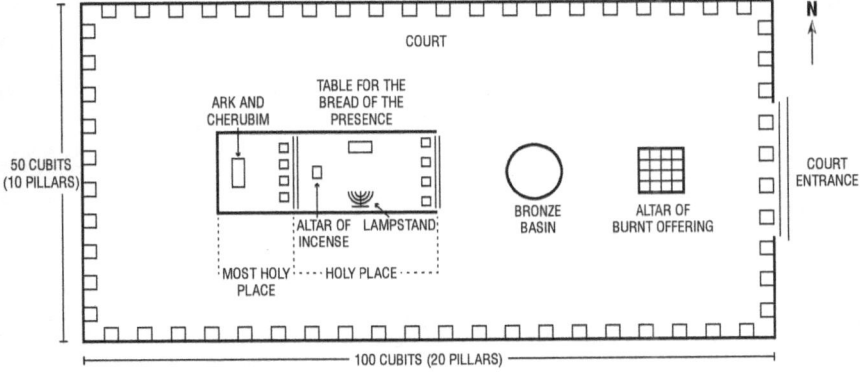

The drawing depicts the tabernacle as described in the Hebrew Bible. See a discussion of the tabernacle among the essays [*The Tabernacle, p. 317*].

Part 1

Rituals for God's Presence

Leviticus 1:1–15:33

OVERVIEW

The first fifteen chapters of Leviticus are about worship at the tabernacle. Chapters 16 and 17 serve as a hinge to the final major section, which is devoted to holy living (chs. 18–26, with ch. 27 as an addendum). The Day of Cleansing, chapter 16, with its rituals of purification, is the capstone of the first fifteen chapters, while chapter 17 explains why blood has its cleansing power.

OUTLINE FOR PART 1
Sacrificial Rituals, 1:1–7:38
Inauguration of Worship, 8:1–10:20
Rituals for Purity, 11:1–15:33

Leviticus 1:1–7:38

Part 1A
Sacrificial Rituals

OVERVIEW

The rituals in Leviticus are sacrificial rituals using either animals or grain. Their presentation begins with voluntary rituals—the person freely chooses when and what to offer. The purpose of these actions is to please God. As seen from Leviticus 7:11-35, these sacrifices may be brought to provide meat, to thank God, or to pay a vow. Their purpose is *not* to bribe God to act in the future on behalf of the one bringing the offering but is a response to what God has already done.

Why place these voluntary rituals first? This order assumes that the worshiper has a positive relationship with God and offers a sacrifice with a glad and willing heart. Indeed, the worshiper wants to bring joy to God. The first acts of worship listed in Leviticus are those that allow the worshiper to give thanks to God and to please God through worship.

The voluntary rituals are found in chapters 1–3.

- Rituals with a whole animal sacrifice, 1:2b-17
- Rituals with a grain sacrifice, 2:1-16
- Rituals with a peace sacrifice, 3:1-17

The rituals in the second group are obligatory: the person has no choice but to perform them. The text specifies when they must be performed and the offering that is required. The obligatory rituals in 4:1-6:7 end with the statement that the worshiper is forgiven. These rituals are remedial, restoring a previous state.

The rituals in the third group (6:8-7:36) are directed to the priests and concern their daily obligatory sacrifices (6:8-18) and instructions for their coming inauguration (6:19-23). The priests also receive additional instructions (6:24-7:21) concerning the obligatory rituals already mentioned in 4:1-6:7. At the end of this section, additional explanations and supplemental information (7:22-36) are addressed to the people concerning the voluntary rituals in chapters 1-3, particularly with regard to the priests and their share in the sacrifices.

Taken by subject matter, the voluntary offerings begin and end this larger block of material. In this way the voluntary rituals form "bookends" around the obligatory rituals *[Literary Style, p. 306]*. We can arrange this structure schematically, in this pattern:

A Voluntary Offerings, 1:1-3:17
   B Obligatory Offerings, Lay and Priestly, 4:1-7:21
A' Voluntary Offerings, 7:22-36

The summary verses in 7:37-38 bring this section of sacrifices to a close.

(TBC and TLC on chs. 1-3 appear in the section on ch. 3.)

OUTLINE FOR PART 1A

The Voluntary Offerings, 1:1-3:17
   1:1-2a   Introduction
   1:2b-17   Rituals for Pleasing God: The Whole Burnt Offering
   2:1-16   Rituals for Pleasing God: The Grain Offering
   3:1-17   Rituals for Pleasing God: The Peace Offering
The Obligatory Offerings, 4:1-7:36
   4:1-35   Forgiveness Rituals: Inadvertent Sins
   5:1-6:7   Forgiveness Rituals: The Penalty Offering
   6:8-7:36   Priestly Instructions for Sacrifice
Retrospective Summary of Sacrifice, 7:37-38

Leviticus 1:1-2a
Introduction

PREVIEW

The book of Exodus ends with a question mark. God had promised Moses that after the completion of the tabernacle, God would meet him there and give him "all of my commandments for the Israelites" (Exod 25:22 NRSV). At the end of Exodus we find that the tabernacle had been built and was now shrouded with a cloud and filled with God's presence. Moses did not dare to enter it (Exod 40:35). How was God's promise to Moses to be fulfilled? The first verse of Leviticus addresses this problem: *And [God] summoned Moses* (AT).

Beginning a book with the word *And*, as well as a verb without a stated subject, is awkward in English. The English translations resolve this problem by omitting the *And*, then supplying *the* LORD as a subject for the verb. These changes obscure the fact that the beginning of Leviticus assumes and continues the book of Exodus.

In ancient times, Scriptures were written on scrolls. These scrolls could comfortably contain only a certain amount of material. The book of Isaiah, for example, was about as much text as would fit conveniently on a single scroll. Think of all the rolling and unrolling needed to find a particular passage. The material in the Torah, the first five books of the Bible, was divided among five scrolls, leading to the later title in Greek, Pentateuch, which means "five scrolls." Leviticus was the third scroll. The first verse of Leviticus indicates that this scroll continues the scroll of Exodus and presupposes its ending.

OUTLINE
Title, 1:1a
Location, 1:1b
Commission, 1:2a

EXPLANATORY NOTES

Title 1:1a

In the Hebrew text of the Pentateuch, the book of Leviticus is named after its first word, which means "to call out, summon." In ancient times, scrolls were named after their first word or words. Genesis, for example, was named "Beginning." If we were to imitate this practice in English, the name of Leviticus would be "Summoned."

In the book of Exodus, God had summoned Moses four times. The first time was at the burning bush at Mount Sinai (Exod 3–4), where God commissioned Moses to lead God's people out of Egypt. The second and third times were when Moses and the Israelites arrived at Mount Sinai (Exod 19:3, 20). There Moses was summoned to declare to the Israelites that if they obeyed God's commands, they would be God's people, a kingdom of priests (Exod 19:5-6), in effect, a commissioning of the people. The final time God summoned Moses, he was to ascend into the cloud shrouding Mount Sinai in order to receive the commandments of God (Exod 24:16). Each of these passages represents a key event. The summons of Moses in Leviticus 1:1a thus indicates that an important message from God will follow.

Location 1:1b

God summons Moses to the tent of meeting. God will no longer speak to Moses on Mount Sinai: the cloud of God's presence has come down from the mountain and taken up residence in the tent of meeting. God now speaks to Moses from the tent and in full view of the people.

The coming of God to God's people is a revolutionary development. God is no longer out there on top of a mountain, hidden by a cloud. God is present just outside the camp. God's new location necessitates the central question of Leviticus: How do God's people live in the light of God's presence?

The terms "tabernacle" (*miškan*) and "tent of meeting" (*'ohel moʿed*) are used interchangeably in Exodus (see 40:34). Leviticus, however, uses "tent of meeting," as here, with four exceptions.

"Tabernacle" occurs in 8:10, the consecration of the shrine; in 15:31, the summation of the laws of purity; and in 17:4 and 26:11, which precede the promise *I will walk among you and be your God, and you will be my people* (v. 12). The use of the word "tabernacle" in these four passages seems to give them an air of solemnity and importance [*The Tabernacle, p. 317*].

The word translated *meeting* has the nuance of a place of meeting and of a time or date to be kept. Putting these two connotations together, the tent was the place where Moses would keep his appointments with God.

Commission 1:2a

Having summoned Moses, God commissions him to relay the following words to all the people. While verse 1 looks back to Exodus, verse 2 looks forward to what will follow: *Speak to the Israelites and say to them*. This commissioning statement completes the link between the end of Exodus and the beginning of Leviticus.

(TBC and TLC appear in the section on ch. 3.)

Leviticus 1:2b-17

Rituals for Pleasing God: The Whole Burnt Offering

PREVIEW

How do we begin to worship God? Where do we start? Leviticus begins with rituals for pleasing God. This unadorned beginning reminds us that worship begins with God and our relationship to God, and not with ourselves. The ritual instructions given in Leviticus are formulated as if they were case law *[Law, p. 304]*. In Hebrew, case laws begin with an "if" or "when" (*ki*), which introduces the general case: "*When* you buy a male Hebrew slave, he shall serve six years, but in the seventh he shall go out a free person, without debt" (Exod 21:2 NRSV, emph. added). But what if his master gives him a wife and they have children? Do they also go free in the seventh year as well? Such subcases are introduced by "if" (*'im*) (see Exod 21:1-4).

When anyone among you brings an offering is the general case. Three subcases follow in verses 3, 10, and 14. First comes the ritual using a herd animal; second, an animal from the flock; and third, a bird. The cases begin with the most costly, an animal from the herd, and end with the least costly, a bird. This is a graded offering. Everyone, regardless of economic status, could voluntarily offer a sacrifice to please God.

The distinguishing characteristic of the whole burnt offering is that it is wholly given over to God and, except for the hide, is entirely burned on the altar. The priest retains the hide. The worshiper gains nothing from the sacrifice.

OUTLINE

Introduction, 1:2b-c
    1:2b   Audience
    1:2c   General Case
Whole Burnt Offerings, 1:3-17
    1:3-9   Cattle
    1:10-13   Sheep or Goats
    1:14-17   Birds

EXPLANATORY NOTES

Introduction 1:2b-c

1:2b Audience

When anyone among you brings an offering to the LORD. Moses, having been summoned to the tent of meeting, is now given instructions for the sacrificial rituals. These instructions are addressed to the entire Israelite people, both men and women. Elsewhere in the ancient Near East, laws regulating temple rituals were not common knowledge but remained in the hands of religious specialists like priests (for sources, see Milgrom 1991: 143-44). In Leviticus, however, we find these instructions addressed to all Israelites. This "all" who might bring a sacrifice includes women (12:6) and even sojourners, the Gentiles who reside in the community (17:8; 22:18). Specialists were a necessary and integral part of these rituals, but the entire community heard the instructions for them.

1:2c General Case

The sacrifice brought is called an "offering" or "gift" (*qorban*). The gift may be an animal, as here in chapter 1; a grain offering, as in chapter 2; or even gold or silver (Num 31:50; 7:13). Since obligatory offerings are usually termed a "sacrifice" (*zebaḥ*; e.g., 4:10, 26, 31 NJPS, NET; but NIV, *offering*), the use of the term "gift offering" may reinforce the notion that these animals were brought by choice.

Whole Burnt Offerings 1:3-17

1:3-9 Cattle

The first subcase is a whole burnt offering of a herd animal. Some have translated the Hebrew word ʿolah as *whole offering* (*burnt offering*, NIV). We will label it a *whole burnt offering* because the animal's carcass is wholly consumed by fire on the altar: it is wholly given over to God. This distinguishes the whole burnt offering from the peace offering in chapter 3, in which the meat of the offered animal is retained by the one offering the sacrifice.

The first step is to choose an animal. The herd animal must be a male without a blemish (v. 3). It may be that males were more expendable than females for the continuation of the herd. The word "unblemished" is the opposite of blemished. What constitutes a blemish is spelled out in 22:21-25. If worshipers choose to bring an offering to please God, they are not to use it as an opportunity to cull their herd.

Interpreters differ in their understanding of the last phrase of verse 3. The NIV translates *so that it will be acceptable to the* LORD (also see NET and note), meaning the animal is presented so that it can be accepted as a legitimate offering for God, having no blemish. The NRSV and NJPS read *for acceptance on your/his behalf*, which could mean the animal is presented so that it will be accepted for the sake of the worshiper. In this context it seems best to follow the simpler interpretation of the NIV and read *The layperson shall present it for its acceptance before the* LORD (v. 3b AT). The selected animal is brought into the courtyard and presented before the altar as a suitable animal for a sacrifice to God. The ritual (vv. 4-9a) has the following elements:

1. First, we find a gesture that probably indicates a claim of ownership (v. 4a). The reason for this assumption is that comparative cultural studies suggest the meaning "This is my sacrifice." (For more information on "hand leaning," see the discussion in Milgrom 1991: 150–53). The sacrifice must belong to the one offering it in order for it to be accounted as their sacrifice. This ritual action should not be confused with placing both hands on an animal and having words spoken over it, as in 16:21. There, Aaron's actions are part of an obligatory ritual of elimination in which the goat is not sacrificed but rather is turned loose outside the camp to bear away (eliminate) the sins of the community. Here, by contrast, the ritual is entirely voluntary: it is offered by a layperson, no words are spoken, and the goal is pleasing God [*Aaron, p. 287*].

The phrase *to make atonement for you* (v. 4b) employs the word *kipper* (to make atonement/expiation, i.e., to wipe or wipe away) with voluntary offerings, a usage not found elsewhere in Leviticus. The goal of these rituals is to please God, not to gain forgiveness from sin. As we will see in chapter 4, the goal of the rituals for sin is explicitly forgiveness. Neither the noun "sin" nor the verb "to sin" is mentioned with the voluntary offerings in chapters 1–3. Only with the obligatory offerings for sin do we find "sin" or "to sin" (Lev 4 and following). (See the Preview to chapter 4 for the marked change in vocabulary between chs. 1–3 and 4, as well as *Atonement as Transfer*, p. 291.)

However, we do find whole burnt offerings occurring with an obligatory ritual for sin. In one case the whole burnt offering, the offering of the two birds in 5:7-10, is a part of an offering necessitated by sin. Two birds are brought. One becomes an "expiation" offering, and the other, offered right after it, becomes a whole burnt offering (5:7-10 below). As is the norm, the whole offering comes *after* expiation for sin is made (see 8:16-18; 9:7-12, 22). Thus the whole burnt offering is not intended to remove sin and obtain forgiveness. Rather, it is an offering that comes temporally after forgiveness and expresses the joy of the one being forgiven. The sequence of rituals set out in the text of Leviticus is not necessarily the sequence performed in actual practice.

2. The animal is now slaughtered (v. 5a). The one presenting the sacrifice evidently kills the animal. The verb "slaughter" is also used in 2 Kings 10:7, where it refers to the killing of seventy men whose heads were then placed in a basket. Perhaps this verb has the nuance "to cut at the throat, decapitate." The blood from the animal is then collected by the priests in a container and brought to the altar and dashed on it (Lev 1:5b). Here the blood is offered back to God because, having life, it is sacred. This, as we shall see, is the point of chapter 17. Thus, in all offerings the blood must be disposed of properly.

The hide of the animal is removed and the animal butchered (1:6 AT). After the dashing of the blood, or perhaps beginning after the collection of the blood, the animal is skinned, perhaps by the layperson. The deposition of the skin is not prescribed here. However, we learn from 7:8 that the officiating priest retains the hide for his labors. Once the hide is removed, the animal is cut into pieces and placed on the altar by the priest.

3. The priest then places fire on the altar and arranges wood over it (v. 7). This action is chronologically out of place. The priests

prepare the altar by placing wood on the altar fire that is kept burning day and night (6:9). They build up this eternal fire while the layperson is skinning and butchering the sacrificial animal. The pieces of meat and the rest of the animal are then placed on the altar (1:8, 9a). The word translated *fat* (NIV; *suet*, NRSV) is a rare word in Hebrew, occurring again in 8:20. It may refer to the fat around the kidneys. Next, the entrails and legs are washed and placed on the altar (1:9a). The washing was done earlier so that all parts of the animal can be placed on the altar simultaneously.

4. Finally, the priest turns the whole into smoke (v. 9b). This action concludes the ritual. Turning the whole offering into smoke makes explicit that all parts of the animal in their entirety, excluding the hide, are completely consumed by the fire and thus turned into smoke.

What results does this ritual obtain? Some translations interpret it as *an offering by fire of pleasing odor to the* LORD (NRSV). However, it is better translated *It is a burnt offering, a food offering, an aroma pleasing to the* LORD (NIV). Milgrom has argued that the Hebrew word for "fire" in this context cannot mean "fire (offering)," because it also refers to offerings that are *not* burned (Milgrom 1991: 161–62). For example, in Leviticus 24:7, 9 it is used of the bread of display, and in Numbers 15:10 it refers to a wine offering. He suggests instead the translation *food offering*, which is the meaning of its cognate in Ugaritic, a language closely related to Hebrew. (However, *DCH* retains "fire offering.")

This food offering gives off *an aroma pleasing to the* LORD. The first word in the Hebrew means "aroma" or "smell." The second word is more uncertain. It is a verbal form having the sense of "to please, make glad," as in Proverbs 29:17. With one exception (Lev 4:31), this phrase represents the positive outcome of the voluntary rituals in chapters 1–3. The goal or result of these rituals is God's enjoyment or pleasure.

1:10-13 *Sheep or Goats*

The second case, the offering of a goat or sheep, follows the same template as that for the offering of a herd animal. Two steps are not mentioned—the placing of a hand on the animal and the skinning off of the hide—and one detail is added: the place of slaughter is specified more closely (1:11a). This place was previously defined as *before the* LORD (v. 5). Here we find *at the north side of the altar* (v. 11).

1:14-17 Birds

In the third case, two species of bird are mentioned: turtledove and pigeon. There is no mention of the requirement that they be male and without blemish. We might think that since the sacrifice of a bird was an offering given by the poor, the regulations would make it as easy as possible for them to make such an offering.

In this ritual, the layperson does not participate in any of the ritual actions. The text does not even mention the bringing and handing over of the birds to the priest. The priest brings a bird to the altar, pinches off its head, places the head on the fire, and turns it into smoke (v. 15a). The blood from the body is squeezed out on the side of the altar (v. 15b). The bird is gutted, and the priest tears the bird's carcass apart by the wings but without severing it into parts (v. 17a), then places it on the altar. It is burned up and produces a smoke pleasing to God (v. 17b).

(TBC and TLC appear in the section on ch. 3.)

Leviticus 2:1-16

Rituals for Pleasing God: The Grain Offering

PREVIEW

Not every sacrifice needed to be an animal or have shed blood. Instead of an animal, flour or baked goods could be offered to please God. This sacrifice is called a grain offering or a meal offering. Olive oil was used to moisten the flour, and in some cases frankincense was added to provide a pleasing odor. Unlike the whole burnt offering, the priests would retain a portion of the grain offering for their support. Again, the person bringing the offering has no gain from it.

The legal case style continues from chapter 1. The first type, the uncooked or raw grain offering, is introduced by *when* (*ki*) and has only a single case. The second type, the cooked grain offering (vv. 4-10), represents a new set of cases and is introduced by *when* (*ki*) and its two subtypes by *if* (*'im*) in verses 5 and 7. At the end of the chapter, in verses 14-16, we find *if* introducing instructions for the ritual of the firstfruits of grain. Formally, the firstfruits offering forms a subtype of the cooked grain offering (the *if* depending on the *when* in verse 4). (On the legal style, see the essay *Law*, p. 304.)

The firstfruits grain offering is separated from the other grain offerings by the instructions given in verses 12 and 13. These verses separate the preceding voluntary grain offerings from the mandatory firstfruits offering. (For their mandatory status, see Exod 34:22, 26.) As a mandatory ritual, the firstfruits offering fulfills an obligation, so a statement of pleasing God does not follow it. The mandatory offering of the firstfruits offering was apparently placed at the end of the voluntary grain offerings because it too was a grain offering.

OUTLINE

The Grain Offering, 2:1-13
    2:1-3   The Uncooked Meal Offering
    2:4-10   The Cooked Meal Offering
    2:11-13   Further Instructions
Firstfruits of Grain, 2:14-16

EXPLANATORY NOTES

The Grain Offering 2:1-13

2:1-3 The Uncooked Meal Offering

The chapter begins with the general case *when a person [nepeš] presents a gift offering [minḥah]*. *Nepeš* (sometimes translated *soul*) indicates a living being and includes a man or a woman; here it should be translated as *person* or *anyone*. The offering is termed *minḥah*, "a gift or present." The Babylonian king sends a *gift* to Hezekiah because of Hezekiah's illness (2 Kings 20:12). On his return to Canaan, Jacob sends a *gift* to Esau (Gen 32:13). In the sacrificial system, however, "gift" (*minḥah*) refers to a sacrifice of grain or a grain product such as flour or meal (see *HALOT*, meaning B). It is normally translated as *grain offering* (NIV, NRSV, NET) or *offering of meal* (NJPS).

The initial *when* (*ki*) signals the beginning of a new set of instructions independent of the cases in chapter 1. However, chapter 3 appears to continue chapter 1 since it begins with *if* (*'im*), which depends on the *when* in chapter 1. Why break up the series of rituals involving animal sacrifice (chs. 1 and 3) with the grain offerings (ch. 2)? Animal offerings were often accompanied by a grain offering (see 9:3-4, 15-17; 14:10, 20, 21). Perhaps because of this close association the grain offering is introduced after the first set of animal sacrifices, separating the animal sacrifices in chapter 1 from those in chapter 3.

In presenting a grain offering, a person must gather the necessary ingredients to prepare it. The grain product used in the raw grain offering is called *solet* ("wheat porridge, groats, finely milled flour," *HALOT*). This flour was used in Solomon's court and illustrated the luxury of his court table (1 Kings 4:22 [5:2]). It could only be dreamed of in a time of hardship (2 Kings 7:1-16). It was milled from wheat, which was twice as expensive as barley: "So a seah of the finest flour sold for a shekel, and two seahs of barley [flour] sold for a shekel" (2 Kings 7:16).

Next, an unspecified amount of oil is poured onto the flour, and frankincense is placed on top of the flour and oil mixture to give the burnt grain offering a pleasant odor. The worshiper brings this mixture to a priest, who will bring the offering to the altar (while this action is not mentioned here, it is assumed; cf. the baked meal offering, v. 8).

A handful of the grain and oil mixture is removed, along with all the frankincense. This handful of meal, oil, and the frankincense is termed an 'azkarah and comes from a verb meaning "remember" or "remind." It is translated *token portion* by the NRSV and NJPS since it seems to function as a part representing the whole. Burning this symbolic amount creates a pleasant aroma for God.

Since part of the flour and oil mixture has been offered on the altar, the remainder is most holy because what affects a part also affects the whole. Being most holy, the remaining offering cannot return to the world of everyday life *[Holy and Holiness, p. 302]*. It must be eaten by priests in a holy place (v. 3).

2:4-10 *The Cooked Meal Offering*

The layperson could choose from three types of cooked meal: the baked, the fried, or the grilled. The first part of the paragraph is devoted to giving instructions for the preparation of each type (vv. 4-7). The instructions for the ritual itself follow in verses 8-10.

If the offering is of baked goods, it may take two forms: unleavened loaves in which the flour has been mixed with oil, or unleavened flat bread that is then spread with oil. Frankincense is missing since portions of these baked goods are to be eaten.

Instead of being baked, the oil and flour mixture could be fried on a *griddle*, a term whose exact Hebrew meaning is uncertain (v. 5). This word occurs in Leviticus only here and in 6:21 (14) and 7:9. In Ezekiel 4:3 it seems to refer to a metal sheet used on top of a stove. This crispy "fry bread" would be crumbled, and oil poured over it (Lev 2:6).

The last alternative is cooking the grain on or in a *pan*. This word only occurs here and in 7:9: *Every grain offering baked in an oven or cooked in a pan or on a griddle belongs to the priest who offers it.* It seems that this grain offering was made in a pan with sides or perhaps a cover and was cooked in or with oil. The NET translates as *deep fried in olive oil*.

Verses 8 and 9 prescribe the ritual for the cooked grain offering. First, the layperson brings the prepared food to the tabernacle and presents it to the priests. As with the raw grain offering, the priest brings the entire offering to the altar and then removes a symbolic portion, which he turns into smoke. As with the raw grain offering, the remainder is now most holy and must be eaten by the priests in a holy place (v. 10).

2:11-13 Further Instructions

These verses contain two general principles for all grain offerings. The first is that none of these offerings may contain a leavening agent. *Leaven* (sourdough) and *honey* must not be used in or with them. There must be no fermentation in grain offered on the altar.

Verse 12 points to an exception to this principle for the offering of choice products: *You may bring them [leavening agents] to the LORD as an offering of the firstfruits, but they are not to be offered on the altar as a pleasing aroma* (emph. added). This clarification allows leavened and sweetened goods to be presented as firstfruits, since they are not placed on the altar (cf. Num 18:12).

The second principle (v. 13) commands adding salt to these grain offerings and continues with the prohibited leaven. Salt, which has not been mentioned previously, must be a part of all grain offerings. This salt is called *the salt of the covenant of your God.* This expression occurs only here. A similar phrase, "a covenant of salt," occurs twice in the Old Testament. This phrase refers to an eternal covenant made between God and the priests (Num 18:19) as well as between God and David (2 Chron 13:5). The meaning of placing salt of the covenant on a sacrifice of a layperson is uncertain.

Verse 13 ends with the clause *add salt to all your offerings.* Was salt to be placed on animal offerings? The word used for offering (*qorban*) certainly includes animals, as in 1:3. The best translation is *add salt to all your offerings* (so NRSV, NIV, NJPS). The NET limits it to just grain offerings: *on every one of your [grain] offerings you must present salt.* This translation assumes that since grain offerings are mentioned in the first part of the verse, they are to be assumed here. However, the structure and punctuation in Hebrew favors the translation *add salt to all your offerings.* Thus the subject of the last clause includes salting the animal offerings as well.

Firstfruits of Grain 2:14-16

The *if* at the beginning of verse 14 indicates a new subcase that hangs from the *when* in verse 8 *[Law, p. 304].* This case concerns "first ripe" (so Num 13:20) or "firstfruits" (as here). It can refer to an offering of bread (Lev 23:17, 20; 2 Kings 4:42), of wheat (Exod 34:22), of whatever is sown in the field (Exod 23:16), or of agricultural produce in general (Num 18:13). Here *firstfruits* refers to a grain offering of grain just ripening (Exod 9:31), roasted or parched by fire and crushed into bits. These groats (*HALOT*), like the previous grain offerings, have oil and frankincense added to them and are brought to the sanctuary.

Although this offering is a *food offering* to God (Lev 2:16), there is no pleasing aroma for God's pleasure. The reason is that while the previous grain offerings have been voluntary, the firstfruits offering is obligatory. For example, a firstfruits offering of the harvest is mandated in Exodus 23:16, 19; 34:22, 26. As we shall see in Leviticus 4, "pleasing God," which occurs frequently with voluntary offerings, occurs only once with obligatory ones.

(TBC and TLC appear in the section on ch. 3.)

Leviticus 3:1-17

Rituals for Pleasing God: The Peace Offering

PREVIEW

Is this chapter redundant? What is the difference between the voluntary offering of animals in chapters 1 and 3? In chapter 1 the whole animal was entirely burned up on the altar. In chapter 3 the meat goes to the person offering it and to the priests. In effect, the Israelites butchered their animals at the altar as a peace offering. Because all animals were to be butchered there (ch. 17), the peace offering replaces secular slaughter. After the blood of the animal for a peace offering is dashed on the altar, a token part of the animal is removed and burned. The officiating priest takes a share (7:34), and the rest is for the layperson to eat and share (7:11-21). In short, in Leviticus, the peace offering is how the Israelites obtained meat.

The name of this offering, *šelamim*, has been translated in a variety of ways (see HALOT and NIDB, s.v. "Sacrifices and Offerings"). The translation *fellowship offering* draws on the fellowship surrounding it. However, we will follow the KJV and NET and use *peace offering*. This term reminds us of the underlying consonants, which also can spell *shalom* (*šalom*), the Hebrew word that can be used for peace.

Chapter 3 continues the legal style of the previous chapters. However, it begins with *if* (*'im*) instead of *when* (*ki*), thus subordinating it to the *when* that introduces animal offerings generally in 1:2. Consequently, the peace offerings parallel the cases of the whole burnt offerings that also begin with *if* in 1:3. While the whole burnt offering was given over entirely to God, the peace offering benefited

55

the layperson offering it. (On the intrusion of grain offering into the sequence of animal offerings, see comments on ch. 2.)

There is no peace offering of birds. Only domestic four-legged animals may be used for the peace offering. (For game animals, see the instructions in Lev 17:13.) The herd animals come first, followed by the flock animals. Each case begins with the introductory *if*, in verses 1, 6, 7, and 12, and each is described in almost identical language. The ritual itself parallels the steps for the whole burnt offering in chapter 1.

OUTLINE
Heading, 3:1a
If Cattle, 3:1b-6
If Flock, 3:7-16
Concluding Prescription, 3:17

EXPLANATORY NOTES

Heading 3:1a

The first word after *if* is *offering* (*zebaḫ*), which is used here for the first time in Leviticus. This word, along with the verb *šaḥaṭ*, may have the connotation of "slaughtering" an animal for meat (note the use of "slaughter," *šaḥaṭ*, in vv. 2, 8, 13 below). The exclusion of secular slaughter (*šaḥaṭ*) for the peace offering is legislated in 17:3-7. Here in verse 3, the word "slaughter" (*šaḥaṭ*) is used again. This wording alerts the reader that chapter 3 is about "butchering" as well as offering.

If Cattle 3:1b-6

If the offered animal comes from the herd, it may be either male or female, but it must be whole and without blemish. In contrast, for the whole burnt offering the animal must be a male (as in ch. 1).

The ritual closely parallels that of the whole burnt offering. It begins with the presenter laying a hand on the head of the animal and then slaughtering it. The priest collects the blood and dashes it on all four sides of the altar. After the animal is butchered, the priest removes the fat from around the entrails, along with the two kidneys and their accompanying fat, and a lobe from the liver. This lobe seems to be a finger-like projection from the liver ("the caudate lobe," *HALOT*) that lies close to the right kidney. The priest must first remove these parts, since these parts belong to God and must not be eaten (vv. 16-17). When the whole animal was burned up, as in chapter 1, this separation was of course unnecessary.

The ritual comes to an end with the priest turning these special parts into smoke. The result, as with the whole offering, is a smoke that presents a pleasing odor to God. (Lev 7:11-34 contains additional instructions and ritual gestures for the peace offering.)

If Flock 3:7-16

Like an animal from the herd, the flock animal—a sheep or a goat—can be either a male or a female. Because of their differences in anatomy, however, the case of the sheep and of the goat need different treatment. The ritual for a sheep is the same as for a herd animal (above) with one exception: *its fat, the entire fat tail cut off close to the backbone* (v. 9) is added to the pieces of fat removed for burning on the altar. After these parts are placed on the altar and turned into smoke, this offering is called *a food offering by fire to the LORD* (v. 11 NRSV, NJPS). No pleasing odor is mentioned.

The ritual for a goat follows the ritual for a herd animal. It too is called a "food-fire offering," and the resulting smoke forms a "pleasing odor." Since this phrase was missing in the case of a sheep, its occurrence here seems to cover both cases of slaughter from the flock.

Concluding Prescription 3:17

This chapter concludes with a prohibition that is valid at all times and in all places: the Israelite must not ingest any blood nor eat any of the special fat. This prohibition against eating blood covers not only domestic animals but also game animals that may be eaten but not sacrificed (Lev 17:13). In all cases the blood must be disposed of properly, because the life of the animal goes with its blood, and life belongs to God alone (Lev 17:10-12).

Here "fat" designates the best, the choicest part of something (*HALOT*). In Genesis 45:18, God promises to the sons of Jacob the best of the land of Egypt where they will eat "the fat of the land," meaning the best of the land's produce. So when slaughtering an animal for food, the Israelite was to offer the choicest parts of the animal to God.

The eating of fat and blood arises here because the layperson, instead of the priest, both slaughters the animal and eats its meat. This taboo against eating blood and fat is stressed for all Israelites whenever they slaughter a four-legged animal. Some things belong to God alone *[Taboo, p. 318]*.

THE TEXT IN BIBLICAL CONTEXT

Words and Ritual

Where are the words? Our worship services are usually filled with words, whether in a sermon or homily or a ritual such as in baptism or communion. But there are no words to accompany the rituals in chapters 1–3 or in any sacrificial rituals in Leviticus. Would there not have been prayers or songs spoken or sung while these ritual actions were carried out? After all, other nations around Israel had words to accompany their rituals. In Leviticus, as Israel Knohl points out, silence rules in the sanctuary. The text gives us only ritual actions, no words.

Why might this be the case? Perhaps it was to limit the opportunity to think of these worship rituals as magical acts. If the right words are spoken and the rituals are performed properly, then the desired result will be assured. Since there are no words, we cannot be certain what the ritual gestures meant during the ritual for a whole burnt offering, for example. We only know that Israelites could do this whenever they wanted to (1:2-3), and the result was a smell pleasing to God.

The book of Psalms, in contrast, has words but no rituals. Although the psalms only allude to rituals, the words are revealing. Consider Psalm 66:

> I will sacrifice fat animals to you
>   and an offering of rams;
>   I will offer bulls and goats.
> Come and hear, all you who fear [revere] God;
>   let me tell you what he has done for me.
> I cried out to him with my mouth;
>   his praise was on my tongue. (Ps 66:15-17)

The sacrificial ritual is prompted by what God has done, but the psalmist also testifies to his motivation: "I cried out to him with my mouth." In addition there are words of praise: "His praise was on my tongue" (Ps 66:17).

Sacrifice and praise are also linked in Psalm 107:22: "Let them sacrifice thank offerings and tell of his works with songs of joy." The audience is exhorted to offer sacrifices and also to accompany them with a joyful song, reciting what God has done. It seems the sacrificial rituals were but one part of what was done at the temple. Another part was singing and praising God for what had happened in history and in life.

These spoken or sung words are placed in the mouths of laypersons, not priests. The words are often cast in the first person and related expressly to the individual's situation. They also assume that an audience is hearing them: "Let me tell you what he has done for me" (Ps 66:16). The ritual actions done by the priest are fixed, but the words of praise and thanksgiving are occasional, fitting a person's particular situation. (On the occasional nature of Israelite prayer, see Greenberg 1983.) In these contexts, whole burnt offerings were a response to God's grace.

It would be helpful to read the sacrificial rituals in Leviticus along with the book of Psalms. Each seems to complement the other. Reading Psalms with Leviticus in mind gives us a different view of a psalm's context. Reading Leviticus along with Psalms shows us that although the ritual might be silent, it could be accompanied by joyful words and a rejoicing audience. Ritual was grounded in the life experiences of the people.

Sacrifice for Jesus and the Early Church

Although the sacrificial system is very foreign to us, for Jesus this was not so. Jesus himself supported the sacrificial rituals at the temple. After healing a leper, Jesus commanded him: "Show yourself to the priest and offer the sacrifices that Moses commanded for your cleansing [purification]" (Luke 5:14).

Jesus did not abolish the sacrificial system or discourage his listeners from bringing their offerings to the temple. Rather, his concern was that they be offered properly, as illustrated by Matthew 5:23-24: "If you are offering your gift at the altar and there remember that your brother or sister has something against you, leave your gift there in front of the altar. First go and be reconciled to them; then come and offer your gift." Jesus assumes that sacrifices will be offered by his followers. Human reconciliation is a *precondition* of the ritual, not its *replacement*.

The temple in Jerusalem was the meeting place for the earliest Christians, who regularly went to the temple. Paul went to the temple for purification and to offer vowed sacrifices (Acts 21:24-26). These early Christians were well aware of the rituals taking place in the temple.

When Gentiles entered the church, these ritual practices were called into question. Did Gentiles need to offer these sacrifices? Did they need to follow the ritual law commanded in Leviticus? We will comment on this issue at various places in the commentary, but for now the short answer is that most of the ritual law was seen as unnecessary for Gentiles. (See Acts 15 for an example of the early church's debate on this issue.)

After the destruction of the temple in 70 CE, the issue of sacrifice and priesthood became a moot point for both Jews and Gentiles. The book of Hebrews adapted the functions of priesthood and sacrifice for the post-70 era for both Jew and Gentile Christians by spiritualizing the temple and its service, which no longer existed on earth, and by going back to Genesis 14 and claiming Melchizedek for a Gentile priesthood. By this means the author of Hebrews was able to cast Jesus as both an eternal high priest and the final necessary sacrifice for the sins of the people *[Hebrews and Leviticus, p. 300]*. (See *NIDB*, s.vv. "Hebrews, Letter to the" and "Melchizedek.")

A side note: While Hebrews solves the problem of obtaining forgiveness from sin when sacrifices for forgiveness are no longer possible, the sacrifices in Leviticus 1–3 were not given on account of sin, nor was their goal forgiveness. In both Jewish and Christian traditions, thanksgiving became expressed by prayer around the meal table. In this sense, the meal table replaced the altar as the place for giving thanks to God.

THE TEXT IN THE LIFE OF THE CHURCH

Grace and Worship

The voluntary rituals in Leviticus 1–3 assume an already existing relationship with God; they do not create a relationship. After all, the presence of God—who delivered the people of Israel from slavery and who is leading them toward freedom—is in the tabernacle. The freewill sacrificial rituals from this point of view are a "maintenance mechanism." They respond to a relationship and maintain it or strengthen it. These rituals and sacrifices are the first answer to the question, "How ought we to worship the God who is present with us?" The answer: "With joy and thanksgiving!"

These sacrifices, which focus on God, function as reminders of what God has done. Such reminders are needed on a regular basis because forgetfulness wipes away the past. "Your heart will become proud and you will forget the LORD your God. . . . You may say to yourself, 'My power and the strength of my hands have produced this wealth for me'" (Deut 8:14, 17). Lack of historical memory leads one to think, What I have is mine, and I can do with it whatever I want. The ritual of the peace offering in Leviticus 3 provided food for the Israelite and the Israelite's family and kinship group. Thankfulness to God was expressed at this time and served as a continual reminder of God's grace toward them. (Compare the ritual in Lev 7:11-15 and the psalms of thanksgiving.)

Likewise, in our worship we need not only prayers of forgiveness, but also prayers of thanksgiving to remind ourselves that God is the source of our well-being and prosperity. Frequent reminders of this belief are necessary because we are too apt to believe ourselves to be the sole source of what we have and enjoy.

Paul uses the image of a voluntary sacrifice when he exhorts the Christians in Rome to "present your bodies as a sacrifice—alive, holy, and pleasing to God" (Rom 12:1 NET). Pleasing God is what the voluntary sacrifices are about. Offering ourselves to God reminds us of the whole burnt offering that was wholly devoted to God. For us, the "ritual" of discipleship is a way to please God. It is a voluntary response to what God has already done for us. Rather than being disciples out of *necessity*, we *want* to be disciples. Worship should instill a sense of God's grace and a challenge to live in light of God's grace.

Prayer as Sacrifice

The ritual of offering a prayer of thanksgiving at mealtime is our counterpart to the peace offering that provided meat for the Israelite. Praying before we eat signifies that God is ultimately the source of all life and that what we now eat in some sense belongs to God, the giver of all life. "By God's hand we all are fed" is both a simple prayer and a profound one. As Jesus put it, God "sends rain on the righteous and the unrighteous" (Matt 5:45). God is the ultimate source of all fertility. At mealtime it is appropriate to acknowledge this.

The constant temptation is, as it was for Israel, to worship the apparent sources of prosperity as if they were the ultimate source of our well-being. At times some Israelites worshiped Baal, the fertility god of the pagan people around them. Hosea laments, "She [Israel] has not acknowledged that I was the one who gave her the grain, the new wine and oil, who lavished on her the silver and gold—which they used for Baal" (Hos 2:8). For us it might be an economic system or a nation that gives us plenty.

For Paul, like Jews of his time, the original sin is worshiping the proximate sources of prosperity rather than the ultimate one. Worshiping the created rather than the Creator is idolatry, the root of all sin. Other visible manifestations of sin flow from it (Rom 1:23, 25). Likewise for us today, acknowledging that we live from the hand of God is an antidote to the idolatry of attributing our success to ourselves and to the material causes of our prosperity.

Leviticus 4:1-35

Forgiveness Rituals: Inadvertent Sins

PREVIEW

Sin is complicated. We may think sin is sin, but not all sins are equal. Why? Because some sins are deliberate and committed on purpose. Some sins are accidental, and others are done unknowingly. It is the latter type of sin, termed *inadvertent sin* (see on Lev 4:2 below), that is the focus of 4:1-35. Deliberate sin, knowingly and willfully disobeying a command of God, is quite a different matter. These two types of sin are contrasted in Numbers 15:27-30. For inadvertent sins, cleansing (or expiation, which means to wipe or wipe away) may be made and forgiveness received. But for deliberate sins no cleansing can be made by the individual, and no forgiveness is granted. (For further discussion of sin and its removal from the congregation, see TBC for ch. 16.)

In chapter 4 we find rituals for a very specific type of inadvertent sin, the trespass of a negative command. Only with awareness of sin can a person act to be forgiven a sin. The ritual for forgiveness must be performed when the person becomes aware of their trespass.

When people become aware of their accidental trespass, they must perform the appropriate ritual for forgiveness. The ritual and the sacrifice to be offered depends on the status of the person committing the sin and whoever is affected by the sin, whether the whole community or a single individual. Chapter 4 begins with the gravest sin, one committed by the high priest, which leads the entire community astray, and it ends with the inadvertent sin of a single common person.

These rituals are obligatory (Lev 4:1–7:21). The shift from the previous voluntary offerings is underlined by a structural marker, a new introduction—*The LORD said to Moses* (v. 1)—which parallels the heading to the book in 1:1, *The LORD called to Moses and spoke to him*. Likewise, the initial command—*Say to the Israelites* (4:2)—repeats *Speak to the Israelites* (1:2, identical in Heb.). This new beginning is foreshadowed by the ending to chapter 3, which refers to and emphasizes the proper treatment of the blood and fat in the preceding freewill sacrifices (3:17).

Furthermore, the terminology used with the voluntary rituals in the previous section almost ceases. "Food gift" (*ʾiššeh*) occurs fifteen times in the first three chapters but only four times with the forgiveness rituals in 4:1–6:7. Since these offerings are obligatory, they are hardly gifts. "Pleasing aroma" occurs eight times in the previous chapters but here only once (4:31). Forgiveness is the goal of these rituals. These changes in terminology reflect the new conceptual context for the rituals found in 4:1–6:7. For the first time in Leviticus, we encounter the verb "to sin" (*ḥaṭaʾ*), the noun for "sin" (*ḥaṭṭaʾt*), and the verb "to forgive" (*nislaḥ*).

The structure of these rituals is straightforward. Each paragraph, except for the first, begins with *If X sins inadvertently* (AT) and ends with *The priest will make cleansing, . . . and there is forgiveness* (AT). However, the functions of the individual ritual actions are not necessarily clear and will need explanation. The first paragraph, which involves the high priest, is anomalous. The discovery of the high priest's sin is not mentioned, nor does this paragraph end with the purification of the altar and the receipt of forgiveness (see "What Is Sin?" in TBC for ch. 16). The following outline gives an overview of the obligatory laws found in this chapter *[Cleansing Offering, p. 297]*.

OUTLINE

Heading, 4:1-2
Individual Cases, 4:3-35
    4:3-12   The High Priest
    4:13-21   The People
    4:22-26   The Leader
    4:27-35   The Commoner

EXPLANATORY NOTES
Heading 4:1-2

Verses 1-2a repeat the heading in chapter 1, indicating a new beginning and setting the obligatory sacrifices apart from the voluntary ones. The general case is presented in verse 2b: *When anyone transgresses inadvertently one of the commandments that you are not to do* (AT). The opposite of violating a commandment unintentionally is doing so defiantly, brazenly, as in Numbers 15:29-31: "Anyone who sins defiantly, whether native-born or foreigner, blasphemes the LORD and must be cut off from the people of Israel" (v. 30) *[Cut Off, p. 299]*.

The word "inadvertent" is used to designate an accidental, unintended homicide (Num 35:11, 15; "accidental," NIV). The one who sinned inadvertently did not intend to transgress a *negative* command. In addition, not only was there no intention to transgress, but there also was no consciousness that a prohibition had been broken. Not carrying out a *positive* command, not acting as you should, is covered in the next ritual series (ch. 5).

Individual Cases 4:3-35

4:3-12 The High Priest

What if the high priest (the anointed priest) should transgress a negative commandment, thereby *bringing guilt on the people* (Lev 4:3)? Actually, the (grammatically) feminine noun *ʾašmah* (*bringing guilt*) is used here instead of a verb. While assigning a verbal sense to this noun is straightforward in this context, in what follows, both the (grammatically) masculine form "guilt" (*ʾašam*) and the verb "to be guilty" (*ʾašem*) have different senses, depending on their specific context. Consequently, there is some debate about how to translate them, and translators differ in their interpretation. We will note these differences in individual cases below. (For a discussion of the problem, see Hartley: 76-80.)

Because of his sin, the high priest must bring a *sin offering* (v. 3b). The Hebrew noun translated *sin offering* has two different meanings in this verse: *as a sin offering [ḥaṭṭaʾt] for the sin [ḥaṭṭaʾt] he has committed* (Lev 4:3, emph. added). In this translation, the first occurrence gives a name to the sacrifice; the second gives the reason for it. However, should a sacrifice for a sin be called a "sin offering" because it is brought on account of sin, or should it be named for what it actually does in the ritual? In answer to this question, several objections have been raised against the traditional translation *sin offering* and in favor of naming it after its function, which is *cleansing*.

1. The noun *ḥaṭṭaʾt* (sin) also means "purification," as in Numbers 8:7: "sprinkle the water of purification [*ḥaṭṭaʾt*] on them" (NRSV). Translating *waters of sin* would make little sense—the water brings about purification.
2. The verbal form of this noun, *ḥaṭṭaʾt*, also occurs in Leviticus. In the form used (*piel* stem) it means "to sterilize or purify." For example, in 8:15, Moses takes blood from a so-called "sin offering" (*ḥaṭṭaʾt*) and applies it to the altar; thus Moses *decontaminated [sterilized] the altar* (NET). The blood from a *ḥaṭṭaʾt* offering applied to the altar cleanses the altar (see also 9:15).
3. The *ḥaṭṭaʾt* offering functions as a cleansing offering. For example, the new mother is to bring *a young pigeon or a dove for a [ḥaṭṭaʾt]. . . . Then she will be ceremonially <u>clean</u> from her flow of blood* (Lev 12:6-7, emph. added; and often in ch. 16).

Given these uses of a *ḥaṭṭaʾt* sacrifice for purification, we will translate it according to what it does: it "purifies or cleanses" [*Cleansing Offering, p. 297*]. As stated below, *inadvertent* sin requires a cleansing of the altar by a cleansing sacrifice (*ḥaṭṭaʾt*), thereby bringing about forgiveness for the sin committed [*Atonement, p. 288*].

We now move to the ritual for forgiveness (4:4-12). First, in preparation for the ritual, the high priest brings a bull to the entrance of the tent of meeting. As befits such a severe situation, the high priest brings the most expensive animal sacrifice he can bring. The ritual begins, as it does for the voluntary animal offering, with the high priest placing a hand on the head of the animal. He then slaughters it.

Thus far this ritual follows the steps of the rituals for pleasing God in chapters 1-3. With verse 5, however, something new occurs. The high priest collects some of the blood and brings it into the shrine. This is the first entrance of blood into the tent: previously only the courtyard altar had blood placed on or around it. The ritual has three major movements:

1. In the front room of the tent, the high priest dips his finger into the blood. He sprinkles this blood seven times toward or on the curtain that obscures the ark of the covenant from view. He then daubs some of the blood on the horns of the incense altar that was kept in the first room of the tent. This handling of the blood,

daubing, is new with this ritual. (The tent was divided into two spaces by a curtain. The ark of the covenant was in the space behind the curtain.)

2. Leaving the shrine, the high priest pours the remaining blood at the base of the courtyard altar, also a new ritual gesture. The fat, kidneys, and a lobe of the liver are now removed as in the peace offering and are turned into smoke (3:16).

3. All the remaining parts of the bull—the head, skin, meat, and so forth—are carried to a clean place, an ash heap *outside* the camp. There the high priest burns the remains of the animal with a wood fire. The word for "burned" (*śaraph*) is used elsewhere of secular burning, not of sacrificing. This part of the ritual is a "disposal" rite: it gets rid of the remaining parts of a cleansing offering.

The meat of a cleansing offering (traditionally, "sin offering") would ordinarily be eaten by the priests as payment for performing the ritual (6:26, 29 [19, 22]; 7:7). However, in the present case the high priest is implicated in the sin, so he cannot profit from the ritual by eating the priestly share.

In this ritual the high priest sprinkles or daubs blood on three different objects; he sprinkles the curtain in front of the ark, daubs blood on the horns of the incense altar, and pours the remainder at the base of the altar in the courtyard. Pouring the blood at the base of the altar is unique to the cleansing offering. (For the whole burnt offering, the blood would be dashed on the sides of the altar.)

The application of blood to these objects effects a cleansing for them and their areas, restoring their purity. The following reason is given explicitly for the purification rituals: *so that they do not die in their uncleanness by defiling my tabernacle that is in their midst* (Lev 15:31b NRSV). Sin can defile holy areas and objects: *for by sacrificing his children to Molek, he has defiled my sanctuary and profaned my holy name* (Lev 20:3; NRSV, *Molech*). Once purified, the tabernacle and its furniture can continue to serve their proper function *[The Tabernacle, p. 317]*.

4:13-21 The People

In the case of the entire people, the text says that they have sinned inadvertently and *the matter escapes [their] notice* (v. 13a NJPS, NRSV; lit. *be hidden*). The sense here is that after sinning unintentionally, they remain unaware of their fault. The verb "be hidden" occurs again in cases of negligence (5:2, 3, 4; 20:4) where people forget, but only here does "hidden" cover an *unknown transgression* that continues to be unknown for an indefinite time (see comments on 5:2-4).

What happens next in 4:13b? The NRSV translates this *incur guilt*, while the NIV has *they realize their guilt*. Does the text mean their state of being guilty (NRSV), or a coming to the consciousness of their guilt (NIV)? The latter seems to be preferred, since the meaning "incur guilt" for the verb *ʾašem* (to be guilty) does not fit its other contexts in this chapter, where virtually the same formula occurs (vv. 22, 27). Note that the person becomes conscious of their guilt *or* someone makes known to them their sin (4:22-23). From this context it seems that persons come to knowledge in two ways: on their own or when they are informed by another. Rather than an explicit "or" in the present case (v. 13b), we find the conjunction *waw*, a very flexible conjunction having a multitude of meanings, one of which is "or" (*HALOT*, use no. 16 of the thirty uses listed!). Thus the translation *and they realize their guilt, or the sin of which they are guilty is brought to their attention* (vv. 13b-14a AT).

The ritual for the people follows the steps for that of the high priest, with some simplification since the reader can refer to the high priest's ritual to fill in the blanks. The ritual "makes atonement" (*kipper*) on their behalf. This is the first time in Leviticus that the verb *kipper* (make atonement) is used. After this last ritual step, the goal or purpose of the ritual is given (v. 20): the people are forgiven. This is also the first occurrence of the word "forgiven" in Leviticus.

How does the blood make atonement? What does it actually do? (See the essay *Atonement, p. 288*.) Here several points concerning the verb *kipper* (to cleanse, atone) must be noted:

1. *Kipper* is made by applying the blood of the cleansing sacrifice to holy objects or areas. It is never applied to a person.

2. When *kipper* is done to a thing, the translation *atonement* is very problematic. Note the NRSV's translation of Leviticus 16:20: *When he has finished atoning for the holy place and the tent of meeting and the altar...* (emph. added). The *for* is added to the text to enable the translation *atonement*. The text actually reads *atoning the holy place, the tent of meeting, and the altar...* (AT). What does it mean to "atone" a holy place? Thus the NET translates *When he has finished purifying the holy place, the Meeting Tent, and the altar* (emph. added). Things are purified, not atoned.

3. The blood applied to things cleanses them from the effects of the people's sin: *Thus he shall purge [kipper] the Shrine of the uncleanness and transgression of the Israelites, whatever their sins; and he shall do the same for the Tent of Meeting, which abides with them in the midst of their uncleanness* (16:16 NJPS).

Once the altar is cleansed, the person or persons presenting a cleansing offering (*ḥaṭṭaʾt*) are forgiven—literally *It is forgiven to/for them* (4:20 AT). This idiom occurs almost exclusively in Leviticus and in this section (4:20, 26, 31, 35; 5:10, 13, 16, 18, 26; 19:22; also Num 15:25-26, 28). The passive is a divine passive, which means that God is the agent of the action: *It is forgiven them by God* (AT; only God is the subject of the active form of this verb). Once the purity of the holy object is restored and the person or people are forgiven, their access to God is assured.

What is the *it* that is forgiven by God? Is it their contamination of the altar, the deed that contaminated it, or both? Leviticus does not say, because it only uses "forgive" (*salaḥ*) in the passive voice: "is forgiven." If we go outside Leviticus to its related material in Exodus and Numbers, we find Moses asking God to forgive the people their sins and transgressions (Exod 34:9; Num 14:19). In Numbers 14:20, God agrees to do so immediately; that is, God is expected to forgive sin. In Leviticus, then, we assume that God forgives the sin of the people once they have taken care of the effect of their sin.

As shown above, however, sin polluted holy objects, and the people needed to repair the damage caused by their sin (see the comments on Lev 16). In Leviticus, it is the contamination of the altar caused by sin that is cleansed (*kipper*). This contamination must be removed before forgiveness can take place *[Forgiveness, p. 300]*. Just as glass in a window remains transparent even though it is fogged over, its function becomes impaired and needs cleaning to work best. If it is never cleaned, in time it will cease to function as it should. Likewise, *You must keep the Israelites separate from things that make them unclean, so they will not die in their uncleanness for defiling my dwelling place, which is among them* (Lev 15:31).

Since the results of inadvertent sin can only be "cleaned up" once a person knows they have committed a sin, unknown inadvertent sin cannot be remedied. There is also no punishment for them.

4:22-26 The Leader

What happens if a leader or ruler of the people commits an accidental trespass? The ritual has the same outline, with a male goat as the sacrifice, but none of its blood is brought into the shrine. Verses 22b-23 reflect two possible ways the sin becomes known: either the person realizes the guilt on their own or it is brought to their attention by someone else (so NJPS, *or*; contra NIV, *and*; likewise vv. 27b-28).

The "cleansing formula" in verse 26 differs from the one used above (v. 20) in using the preposition *min* (from) in place of ʿ*al* (for).

Most versions do not reflect this difference, translating *for* the leader's sin (emph. added). However, this understanding of the preposition has been disputed. Perhaps it has the meaning "from" (a common meaning for this preposition). The translation would then be *from* his sin (emph. added), and expiation would represent the removal of sin from the person rather than contamination from the altar (Gane). In favor of retaining the usual translation and understanding are the following arguments (Milgrom 2007):

1. The usual translation best fits its usage in 16:16. The priest makes cleansing. In this way he will make atonement for the Most Holy Place *because of* (*min*) the uncleanness and rebellion of the Israelites, whatever their sins have been (see *HALOT* and *DCH*, s.v. "*kipper*"). The sanctuary has become contaminated because of the people. The priest now removes this contamination on their behalf.

2. More often we find the preposition "on account of" (*'al*) instead of "for" (*min*) in the expiation formula: the priest makes expiation *on account of his sin* (Lev 4:3; also 28, 35; 5:6, 13; 19:22). These two prepositions seem to be interchangeable in the context of the forgiveness rituals. Compare 5:6, 10 (*min*) with 5:13, 18; 6:7 (5:26) (*'al*) [Atonement, p. 288].

4:27-35 The Commoner

When common persons accidentally trespass one of the prohibitions, they may choose between offering a sheep or a goat. Two slightly different rituals are given for the two different animals. If they offer a goat, the ritual actions are straightforward, as is the result. However, the use of the phrase *an aroma pleasing to the* LORD (4:31) is anomalous, and its placement here is surprising. This phrase elsewhere expresses the outcome of voluntary rituals, as in chapters 1–3. However, the offerings in 4:27-35 are obligatory, and forgiveness is sought and given. Verses 27b-28 reflect two possible ways that the sin becomes known: either the person realizes the guilt on their own or it is brought to their attention by someone else (so NJPS, *or*; contra NIV, *and*; likewise vv. 22b-23).

In the ritual for the sacrifice of a sheep, we find an additional detail: the priest shall burn the fat of the sheep *on the altar on top of the food offerings presented to the* LORD (v. 35). While the phrase "food offering of the LORD" occurs frequently with voluntary offerings, it is rare with obligatory offerings. It seems that in the case of an individual seeking forgiveness, some of the language used with the voluntary offerings of individuals (chs. 1–3) is also applied to their cleansing offering.

THE TEXT IN BIBLICAL CONTEXT
Forgiveness

God is the only subject of the verb "forgive" (*salaḥ*) in the Hebrew Bible. However, this is not readily apparent in Leviticus, because "forgive" only occurs there in the passive. In this context the text simply says *is forgiven him*, which we understand to mean *it is forgiven* (AT).

However, outside of Leviticus, forgiveness also takes place as a result of prayer. For example, we find prayers of petition, such as "Forgive our wickedness and our sin" (Exod 34:9). Moses intercedes on behalf of the people, praying, "Forgive the sin of this people," and God responds, "I have forgiven them, as you asked" (Num 14:19-20; see also Solomon's plea for forgiveness, 1 Kings 8:50). Indeed, God can forgive someone without being asked. Such is the case of a woman who takes an oath in the name of God, but her husband or father annuls her oath. If this happens, "the LORD will forgive her" (Num 30:8 NRSV, NJPS [Heb. v. 9]; NIV and other translations, *release her*). In these cases the verb "forgive" is active, with God as the subject and the trespass as the object, either stated or implied.

The unlimited nature of God's forgiveness (*salaḥ*) was an important point of development for Jeremiah. In Jeremiah 5, God sees no reason to forgive the people; they are determined to do wrong, to deliberately sin (vv. 1, 7). But God is willing to forgive the people if they change their behavior by turning from their evil ways (36:3). Repentance on the part of the people needed to precede God's forgiveness of their deliberate sin. However, in the "book of consolation" (chs. 31–33), Jeremiah claims in God's name that God "will cleanse them from all the sin they have committed against me and will forgive all their sins of rebellion against me" (33:8). There is no mention of repentance or change of ways; nevertheless, God will forgive their deliberate sin (31:34). Finally, God describes Israel's future as a time when a "search will be made for Israel's guilt, but there will be none, and for the sins of Judah, but none will be found, for I will forgive the remnant I spare" (Jer 50:20).

Jeremiah was active while the temple was still standing and forgiveness rituals were taking place. Yet within his lifetime the temple would be destroyed and the people scattered among foreign nations. For Jeremiah, after their punishment Israel's restoration and forgiveness would rest with God alone. Jeremiah's good news was that God will act to purify and forgive. Even without temple and ritual, in desolation, God's grace and forgiveness will come to Israel.

The concept that God would act to restore Israel is found in Leviticus 26. In this chapter the restoration of Israel depends in part on what Israel does, but their actual restoration depends on God's remembering the contract with their ancestors (vv. 40-45). The word "forgiveness" is not used in chapter 26, but we find the notion of God's restoring Israel even without their undertaking a ritual of forgiveness.

In Jesus' and Paul's time, the temple had been reestablished. Forgiveness rituals were once more being performed. But many Jews were far from Jerusalem and the temple. Even those in Galilee might not be able to undertake the journey and purchase a sheep or goat. In this context, God's forgiveness was not limited to the temple rituals.

Jesus taught his disciples to pray for forgiveness: "Forgive us our sins, for we also forgive everyone who sins against us" (Luke 11:4; cf. Mark 11:25). Prayers of petition for forgiveness rest on our forgiving others. Consequently, Jesus taught that "when you stand praying, if you hold anything against anyone, forgive them, so that your Father in heaven may forgive you your sins" (Mark 11:25; cf. Matt 6:14-15). Forgiveness requires forgiveness of others as a precondition.

Outside of the Gospels, forgiveness and sin are joined only rarely. James declares, "And the prayer offered in faith will make the sick person well. . . . If they have sinned, they will be forgiven" (James 5:15). Forgiveness coming through petition reminds us of Moses's intercessory prayers for the people of Israel (Num 11:2; 21:7).

THE TEXT IN THE LIFE OF THE CHURCH

In Praise of Negative Commands

Leviticus 4 is about transgressing a negative command—doing something you are not supposed to do. While negative commands may be off-putting and may strike us as legalistic, these commands of God are very important in the Bible. After all, eight of the Ten Commandments are negative commands! However, we are more comfortable with positive commands like "Love your neighbor as yourself" (Lev 19:18).

The reason for preferring positive commands is probably that the transgression of a negative command is easier to see than the transgression of a positive command, that is, not doing something you are supposed to do. For example, we feel that a person is more accountable for committing adultery than for not loving their neighbor. Even when formulated in terms of action rather than attitude, "Do to others as you would have them do to you" (Luke 6:31), the command to love your neighbor remains somewhat abstract. However, if the command were formulated in the negative, "Do not do to another what you would not have them do to you," it might become more concrete. We have a rather clear notion of fairness and justice. We know when we have not been treated fairly, and we may well become angry when we have not received justice.

"Don't steal" seems clearer than "Respect others' property." We know what stealing is, but respecting the property of others feels hazier. After all, "borrowing" something to use for just a bit is not stealing, is it? We are more comfortable with a guidebook pointing out possibilities than with a road map giving clear instructions.

Perhaps negative commands are given so that we know how to keep the positive ones. The Ten Commandments are a good example. Bearing false witness, stealing, committing adultery, killing, and coveting—all these transgress the "law of love," so we are commanded *not* to do them. So also with many of the negative commands we will meet later in Leviticus and throughout the Bible. While keeping the negative commands may not totally fulfill the command to love others, they do point out when we have not loved.

Leviticus 5:1–6:7

Forgiveness Rituals: The Penalty Offering

PREVIEW

Clearly, doing something forbidden is a transgression. But is it a sin to *not* do the right thing? Aren't we better off just staying out of things? Chapter 5 has much to say about responsibility both for doing the right thing and for making amends when we have done the wrong thing.

Chapter 5 begins simply: *When a person sins* (NET). This clause introduces cases of negligence. The cases are presented in three parts. Leviticus 5:1-13 continues the speech of chapter 4. The next two parts are each introduced by *The LORD said to Moses* (5:14; 6:1 [5:20]). This gives an "uneven" feel to this section, since 5:1-13 continues the speech of chapter 4, but the subject matter is that of the following speeches.

Several vocabulary items do link 5:1–6:7 with chapter 4. In Leviticus, apart from 23:43, the term "to know" (*yada'*) occurs only in chapter 4 and in 5:1–6:7. This distribution is surprising, since "to know" is a very common verb in Hebrew, as it is in English. Second, the verb "to be hidden, unconscious of" (*ne'lam*) occurs in 4:13 and in 5:2, 3, 4 (and only again in 20:4). Third, "accidental sin" (*šegagah*), the focus of chapter 4, also occurs in 5:15, 18. This word occurs only again in 22:14. However, the concentration of the words "be guilty, culpable" (*'ašem'*) and "penalty offering (guilt offering)" (*'ašam*) sets chapter 5 apart. These words occur only three times in chapter 4, but seventeen times in 5:1–6:7.

The material in 5:1-13 forms a link between chapters 4 and 5. While 5:1-13 continues the speech begun in chapter 4, the subject matter of negligence and the resulting culpability is new. For these sins, a variety of options for a sacrifice are given, ranging from costly to inexpensive. Transgressors presumably will choose a sacrifice according to their financial abilities. However, the text gives no rationale for these "graded" offerings. Contrast this smorgasbord of choices with the prescribed offerings for inadvertent sin in chapter 4.

OUTLINE

Trespass by Negligence, 5:1-13
    5:1-4   The Four Cases
    5:5-13   The Penalty Ritual
Accidental Trespasses on the Divine, 5:14-19
    5:14-16   The Case
    5:17-19   Trespassing Inadvertently
Intentional Trespasses on the Divine, 6:1-7
    6:1-3   Trespasses against God and Neighbor
    6:4-7   The Penalty Ritual

EXPLANATORY NOTES

Trespass by Negligence 5:1-13

5:1-4 The Four Cases

These trespasses result from neglecting to perform a positive duty (Levine: 26–27). In the first case, a person hears an oath but does not step forward as a witness (v. 1). The background for ignoring an oath is perhaps found in Judges 17:1-2. Micah steals money from his mother. Not knowing who took it, she issues a public curse against the thief in the hearing of her son. The son responds with a confession and returns the money to his mother. The mother than blesses him, and he is free from culpability. Our case is different in that the person is a witness but deliberately shirks the responsibility to testify.

The penalty for ignoring this responsibility is that *he will bear his punishment for iniquity* (Lev 5:1 NET). The notion of bearing "punishment for iniquity" also occurs in Leviticus 17:16 NET. The sense of this idiom is to suffer the consequences of one's action (Schwartz 1995). A sin of omission places a person under judgment. To escape this fate, the person must offer up a sacrifice as a penalty.

Next come two cases of forgetting about ritual purification. The first concerns the contraction of an impurity from touching anything unclean other than persons (v. 2). A trespass on the impurity regulations seems out of place in rituals for sin, since contracting impurity is not a sin. (Purity and its restoration are the focus in chapters 11–15. See the essay *Pure, p. 309*, and the Previews to chs. 11–15).

Leviticus 17:15-16 gives a background for this case. A person is impure if they eat meat from the carcass of an animal that died a natural death or was killed by another animal. While Israelites may eat such meat, they must undertake a purification ritual afterward. This ritual is a common and easy one: they must launder their clothes and wash their bodies and wait until evening. When evening has come, they will be clean again. No harm done. *But if they do not wash themselves or bathe their body, they shall bear their guilt* (17:16 NRSV). They knowingly ate from the carcass and knew they were impure but did nothing about it. Now they bear iniquity: they are guilty of a failure to act.

Likewise, in the present case the person knew they were impure but "forgot" to remedy their situation. Perhaps by putting off the necessary ritual in the press of other duties, *it is concealed from him* (5:2 AT). Consequently, *he remains unclean* (AT), and as we know from 17:16, now *they shall bear their guilt* (AT). As a result of not doing the right thing, the person must offer a penalty sacrifice.

The next case is the same except that the source of impurity is another human being (v. 3). The sequence of events assumed for verse 2 seems clearer in verse 3, which may be translated *It is hidden from him, but he had known it and is guilty* (v. 3b AT). (Grammatically, the verb sequence—imperfect verb, a verb of narrative continuation [*wayyiqtol*], and then a perfect verb [*qatal*]—places the action of the last verb in the pluperfect. The person had done something at a time previous to the preceding verb.)

At the time of contracting impurity, the person knew what they were doing—knew they had become impure. But they subsequently forgot to "neutralize" their impurity, and thereby they now bear their guilt, as in verse 1. The translation that comes closest to this construal of the text is the NJPS: *When he touches human uncleanness—any such uncleanness whereby one becomes unclean—and, though he has known it, the fact has escaped him* (v. 3).

The final case, like the first, concerns an obligation connected to an oath (v. 4). A person swears an oath, literally *to do harm or good* (AT). As in the case of ritual impurity, swearing an oath is not improper: "By his name you shall swear" (Deut 10:20 NRSV). Subsequently, however, the obligation to fulfill the oath has escaped the person's attention, and they have not fulfilled it.

5:5-13 *The Penalty Ritual*

A summary statement for the preceding cases is given in verse 5. Whenever anyone who has committed one of these lapses and later realizes their guilt (*'ašem*), they need to take the following steps.

First, as a prerequisite for performing the ritual, *they must confess in what way they have sinned* (v. 5). The confession of sin was not necessary in the case of unintentional sin (ch. 4), but in a case of neglecting to do the right thing, the supplicant must announce their negligence. This confession might also be considered an additional penalty.

The text makes no mention of where this confession is made. The assumption is that as part of the penalty process, the person confesses in public. Milgrom argues that the *necessity* of making a confession is significant for this series of cases. The act of confession, showing publicly a change of heart and taking responsibility for one's actions, allows an intentional sin of negligence to be "converted" to an unintentional one (Milgrom 1991: 301). This allows the sinner to have a cleansing made for them just like that made for the inadvertent sinner of chapter 4 *[Atonement, p. 288]*. Whether failing to remember something is a deliberate sin might be challenged. Perhaps not acting in a timely manner is considered deliberate: they deliberately postponed doing their duty and thus forgot to do it.

After confessing their error, the person must bring a penalty offering (*'ašam*, v. 6). The traditional translation is *guilt offering*. Modern translations, however, render it *penalty* (NIV, NRSV, NET, NJPS). In a similar context, Numbers 5:7-8, *'ašam* clearly means penalty or restitution: "The person shall make *full restitution* for the wrong, adding one-fifth to it, and giving it to the one who was wronged" (Num 5:7 NRSV, emph. added). Beginning in Leviticus 5:14, we have cases of trespass on the holy, which call for a fine in addition to the offering itself. Here we have only the offering itself mentioned without any penalty or fine. Of course, if the person would have done the right thing, no sacrifice would have been needed. The penalty offering here is for disobedience or forgetting to carry out a *positive command or obligation*.

In verses 11 and 12 the penalty offering is identified as being a cleansing offering. In a discussion of the penalty offering in Leviticus 7:1-7, we find this: *The same protocol applies to both the cleansing offering and the penalty offering* (7:7 AT; NIV, *sin offering, guilt offering*). Thus chapter 5 assumes the ritual instructions of chapter 4. But in chapter 5 instructions are needed for birds or grain, because birds or grain were not brought for a cleansing sacrifice in chapter 4. (For further discussion and details concerning the *ʾašam* sacrifice here and in the following passages, see the excursuses in Hartley: 76–80.)

The first choice for a penalty offering is a female from the flock, either a sheep or a goat (v. 6). Although the priest makes expiation on behalf of the individual, receiving forgiveness is not mentioned as the result of this ritual. This lack is covered by the general statement at the end of this unit in 5:13: *They will be forgiven*.

Two birds can be offered instead if the person cannot afford a flock animal. The priest first takes one of the birds for a cleansing offering (v. 8). The priest pinches the nape of the bird's neck without severing the head from the neck. (In 1:15 the head was severed and burned.) The priest then sprinkles some of the blood on the side of the altar. The remaining blood is squeezed out at the base of the altar. The sprinkling of blood sets this sacrifice apart from the whole burnt offering in 1:15. Sprinkling blood and pouring or squeezing it at the base of the altar are the gestures used in the ritual for forgiveness.

Next the priest offers the second bird as a whole burnt offering (5:10). This ritual proceeds according to the instructions in 1:15-17. After this offering, the ritual is completed and the person is forgiven.

Finally, a flour sacrifice may suffice. A tenth of an ephah of fine flour, something over two liters, is presented as the sacrifice (5:11). Neither oil nor frankincense is offered with the flour as in the voluntary grain offering described in chapter 2, where a pleasing odor was the goal.

After the flour is brought to him, the priest takes a handful of the flour as a memorial portion (see ch. 2). He then places it on the altar and turns it into smoke. Thus the priest makes expiation for the person, who is forgiven (5:13). As in the meal offerings of chapter 2, the remainder of the flour goes to the priests.

This series of offerings has been called "the graded penalty offering." The value of the offering, it is assumed, depends on the economic status of the person bringing the offering. Why was gradation allowed for negligence but not for inadvertent sins (Lev 4)? The answer is not clear. Perhaps neglecting to obey a positive command is a less serious offense than trespassing a negative command, even inadvertently.

Finally, we notice that the meal offering is explicitly defined as a cleansing offering in 5:12. Likewise, the result is forgiveness. This equates the meal offering with the preceding animal offerings and the manipulation of their blood on the altar. *Atonement or cleansing and forgiveness do not require the presence of death or blood.* Forgiveness rests finally with the graciousness of God *[Sacrificial System in Leviticus, p. 313]*.

Accidental Trespasses on the Divine 5:14-19

5:14-16 The Case

Verse 14 begins a new speech: *The LORD spoke to Moses, saying* (NRSV). Verse 15 states the case: *When a person violates one of the holy things of the LORD, sinning inadvertently* (AT). We turn again to unintentional sin, the subject of chapter 4. Why isn't this case grouped with those in chapter 4? Evidently trespassing on God's holy things is a more serious crime than the inadvertent sins of chapter 4. Trespass on the holy requires an offering plus a penalty. The verb for trespass (*maʿal*) can mean misappropriating sacred things set aside for God (*DCH*). An example is Achan's action when he encroached (*maʿal*) on what was God's by taking things that had been devoted to God (Josh 7:1-16; 22:20).

For unintentional trespass on the holy, the offender is to bring a penalty offering (*ʾašam*) of a ram of *the proper value* (v. 15). The meaning of the term *ʿerek*, translated *proper value* or *converted* (NJPS, NET, NRSV), is not certain. Its general meaning is "value, valuation" (*DCH*). So we could translate, literally, *according to your valuation* (see ch. 27 for more uses of this term). The ram brought for a sacrifice needed to be worth the equivalent amount of what was damaged or appropriated, as in the NIV quoted above (v. 15). But this does not seem workable. How could people be expected to find a ram that precisely matched the amount of the damages or misappropriation? Another understanding is that the ram could be converted into money (NRSV, NET, NJPS), that is, into sanctuary shekels of silver. But why convert the ram into money since an actual ram was needed for the penalty offering (v. 16)? Baruch Levine and others suggest that the offender could bring either a ram or its value in silver. In the latter case, the money would be used to purchase an appropriate ram for the ensuing sacrifice (30-31). Since temple shekels are required, the offender's payment would be calculated using these rather than normal shekels. Because the temple shekel was of less value than the normal shekel (twenty grains in temple shekels, twenty-four grains in everyday shekels), the one paying for the ram paid less than its normal everyday price.

In addition to the sacrificial animal, the person must make restitution for their wrong by adding a fifth of the value as penalty for the damage or harm done by trespassing on the holy (v. 16). The payment of this penalty comes before the actual ritual and is a prerequisite for it, just as confession comes before the ritual in verses 5-13. The person gathers together the animal and the necessary compensation and gives them to the priest. The priest then makes expiation for the offender with the ram or the penalty offering. The result is forgiveness. How the money is used is not specified.

5:17-19 *Trespassing Inadvertently*

The second (and last) paragraph of the present speech is puzzling. It seems out of place since it concerns an unknown inadvertent sin, as in chapter 4. However, it also concerns a trespass (*ma'al*), as in the previous verses. The text stresses the inadvertent nature of the transgression in 5:18: *an inadvertence that was done inadvertently—he did not know* (AT). But here the person also *bears his guilt* ('*ašam*; v. 17 AT), a phrase that did not occur in chapter 4 with inadvertent sin. Furthermore, as in the preceding case (5:14-16), the person must bring a ram, according to valuation, for a penalty offering (vv. 18-19).

It seems that the person broke a negative commandment; the person did not know this but was bearing culpability for the transgression anyway. Was this a penalty sacrifice for an unknown sin? In the preceding case, as here, the text assumes that the person realizes the harm done—how can one make compensation according to value for an unknown transgression? The clause referring to the bearing of guilt or punishment in 5:1 (e.g., *will be held responsible*, NIV) refers to a deliberate choice, not inadvertence as it does in chapter 4.

Normally a case ends with cleansing and the forgiveness formula. However, verse 19 adds a strong declaration that the sacrifice was an '*ašam*, a penalty offering, because *they have been guilty of wrongdoing against the* LORD. This clause implies that the negligent action was a trespass or misappropriation of sacred things. By this offering, the person makes a penalty payment to the Lord for "damages" caused. The context supports this understanding. There are only two cases in this unit: 5:14-16 and this one, vv. 17-19. The first, preceded by *when*, is a case of trespass on sacred things. This case, verses 17-19, begins with *if* and hangs from the first case. It likely concerns the same type of trespass.

Additional support that this is a penalty payment is found in Numbers 5:6-8, which likewise concerns the crime of trespass (*ma'al*). One person wrongs another. The one doing wrong confesses the sin, then returns the principle plus a fifth to the one wronged. The verb *'ašem* at the end of Numbers 5:7 means "to wrong someone": "give it all to the person they have wronged." In the current text (Lev 5:19), a parallel translation would be *He has certainly wronged the* LORD (AT). A trespass against God or God's holy things, even one caused by negligence, has immediate consequences and needs compensation—here a penalty offering of the necessary value.

In summary, for some reason the person comes to realize what they have done: they have transgressed the holy. Since they have wronged God, they offer a suitable offering. No additional fine is added as in the previous cases, because they were unaware of what they had actually done. (For a variety of explanations of this enigmatic passage, see Hartley: 82; Milgrom 1991: 332-33, 361-63; Levine: 31-32.)

Intentional Trespass on the Divine 6:1-7 (5:20-26)

First, a note on the numbering of verses. While this verse begins a new chapter in most English versions, the Hebrew text does not begin a new chapter until 6:8 in the English text. This difference in numbering can cause confusion in consulting different sources. The Hebrew text presents a better division, since the subject matter of this paragraph continues what has just gone before—trespass on the holy and the penalty offering. Only with verse 8 in English do we have a break—the beginning of a new speech with a new set of instructions addressed to a new audience, the priests rather than all the people.

6:1-3 *Trespasses against God and Neighbor*

The focus of this paragraph is lying or fraud. The crimes are (1) lying about a deposit, a pledge/investment, or a robbery; (2) fraud (*DCH* 1a); (3) lying about the ownership of a found object. All these acts represent a trespass against God, because they all would deny by oath the true facts of the case (v. 3b). Verse 5 extends this list to *anything else about which you have sworn falsely* (NRSV). This specific list provides illustrations of cases in which a person might swear falsely.

These offenses are against God because Israel was commanded to swear only by God's name: "The LORD your God you shall fear; him you shall serve, and by his name alone you shall swear" (Deut 6:13 NRSV). To commit perjury in God's name would be to take God's name "in vain" (Exod 20:7 KJV); accordingly, the NIV translates: "You shall not misuse the name of the LORD your God." Just as the larger unit begins with the subject of an oath (5:1), so it ends with oath taking.

6:4-7 *The Penalty Ritual*

The penalty is that the person must return the object in dispute (v. 4) and pay an additional one-fifth to the owner (v. 5). This repayment plus penalty is done on the *day of his guilt* (AT). The word for guilt, *'ašmah*, occurs four times in Leviticus, two of them in this passage. It may function either as an infinitive "to be guilty" (see 4:3; 6:7) or as the noun "guilt." Here it has been translated variously as *realizes his guilt* (NJPS, NRSV), *is found guilty* (NET), or as a *guilt offering* (NIV). *Realizes his guilt* has the sense that previously the person had not known they were guilty. But since this is a deliberate crime, the culprit knew they were swearing falsely. It seems that for some reason the person decided to make amends. Perhaps a guilty conscience drove them to make things right (Milgrom 1991: 338).

Only after the payment of the principle and the penalty of an additional one-fifth to the wronged party does the guilty person proceed to the sanctuary with his offering. As in previous cases, the wrongdoer brings as his penalty offering a ram or its equivalent value in money. The priest makes expiation for him, and the wrongdoer is forgiven *[Atonement, p. 288]*.

THE TEXT IN BIBLICAL CONTEXT

Forgiveness and Relationships

In the teachings of Jesus we find several statements that support making things right before forgiveness is granted. They may also expand our understanding of the process of forgiveness. As in the cases found in Leviticus 6:1-7, the one seeking to obtain forgiveness through a forgiveness ritual must first make matters right with their fellow (Matt 5:23-24). (Other types of sacrifice, such as a whole burnt offering, do not pertain directly to human relationships and thus do not require such a precondition.)

In Leviticus, the need of the wronged party to grant forgiveness is not required: only God forgives. However, Jesus tells his disciples that they should forgive another not just seven times, but seventy-seven times (Matt 18:22). But thereupon follows the parable of the ungrateful steward whose forgiveness was retracted by his master because he would not forgive others. Our prayer is "Forgive us our sins, *for we also forgive everyone who sins against us*" (Luke 11:4, emph. added). Only as a person practices forgiveness can they expect God's forgiveness. In Jewish tradition, a person must ask for forgiveness three times from their fellow. If the other person evades them or does not forgive them, they no longer need the other's forgiveness in order to receive God's forgiveness. However, a person must forgive if they expect God to forgive them. This demonstrates the importance of asking for and giving forgiveness before expecting God's forgiveness (*EJ*, s.v. "Forgiveness in Talmud and Jewish Thought").

THE TEXT IN THE LIFE OF THE CHURCH
The Elements of Public Worship

Instructions for the public sacrificial rituals have now been given in Leviticus. What may we learn from them and from their sequence here? The first element of worship presented was the expression of praise and gratitude to God through the freewill offerings (chaps 1–3). We have suggested that these offerings are a response to general well-being, a feeling of being blessed by God. As we saw from the Psalms, the peace offering was a focus for joy and praise.

Peace offerings also celebrate important events in the life of an individual, a congregation, or even the nation as a whole. For example, at the dedication of the temple, "Solomon offered as peace offerings to the LORD 22,000 cattle and 120,000 sheep" (1 Kings 8:63 NET). The whole community was included in the great feast provided by these sacrifices. Public events of celebration like this call to mind church or family potlucks. These events might include not only celebrating birthdays or wedding anniversaries but also celebrating and giving thanks for God's blessings in life. Buying a home or celebrating the success of a company or professional endeavor comes to mind. Celebrating such events with thanksgiving to God puts these achievements in proper perspective for the believer.

The obligatory rituals come next. First is the seeking of forgiveness. Churches are composed of mortals who do wrong unknowingly and only later come to realize what they have done. Instead of saying "It's too late now" or "That's water under the bridge," unintended or thoughtless actions need forgiveness.

Where are the people? Only three parties have been involved in the forgiveness ritual: the supplicant, the priest, and God. The supplicant brings the offering, the priest performs the ritual on behalf of the supplicant, and God grants forgiveness. The focus is on God, whose forgiveness is sought. Nothing is said about human relationships until we get to the forgiveness rituals in 6:1 (5:20) and following. In these rituals a penalty is paid to the offended party as a prerequisite to receiving forgiveness. The payment includes not only what was originally taken but also an additional fifth. This ritual gesture of restitution and a penalty must precede the ritual of forgiveness. God's forgiveness is not cheap forgiveness.

A contemporary illustration may help. When someone causes an auto accident, they may say, "I'm so sorry." But this in no way ends the person's responsibility for the wrong they have done, whether deliberately or by inattention. The offending party bears the obligation to make things right. The other person's car must be fixed or replaced and any medical expenses covered. In some cases compensation may be due. The words "I'm sorry" do not magically make right the damage that was done. Neither do they make things right in cases of sin. If we harm others, compensation is needed for God's forgiveness.

Opening worship with praise and thanksgiving to God is good. Confession of sin is often part of a liturgical process in which a generic statement is recited. In other traditions, confession is made in private to a priest. Both practices may ignore the need to make things right. Acknowledging our sins of commission and omission as individuals is difficult. Making things right, repairing as much as possible the damages done, is even more difficult. Just as sin has lingering effects on others, so our responsibility for those affected remains. Sin brings responsibility.

Grace does not make perfect people, but it allows imperfect people to be restored by God's grace and to restore others. Israel's liberation from slavery in Egypt did not make Israel sinless. Rather, God's grace is continuously needed in order that a people saved by grace may continue living in the presence of their gracious God through the forgiveness of their sins and the act of taking responsibility for their sins.

Forgiveness is indispensable because misdeeds, missteps, and trespasses are a part of daily life. Rather than making us discouraged, worship can be a time to acknowledge that we are a forgiven people who continually need forgiveness and also that we are a forgiving people who accept responsibility for our wrongs.

Leviticus 6:8-7:38 (6:1-7:38)
Priestly Instructions for Sacrifice

PREVIEW

What happened behind the scenes? How did the priests keep busy? Did they have obligatory duties? The address to the priests about these matters now begins. The audience changes from the Israelites as a whole (see 1:2; 4:2) to the priests, Aaron and his sons (6:14). The previous instructions were addressed to the entire nation because all Israel was to be familiar with these rituals and know their part in them. However, certain aspects of temple worship pertained specifically to the priests and what happened in the sacred area.

The type of language also changes. Previously the instructions were given in the form of cases—when this is the case, then do this. Here, however, the language becomes prescriptive: this is what you *will* do. This change is indicated already by the introduction, *Command Aaron and his sons* (v. 9a NRSV). The commands that follow are labeled *regulations* (v. 6:9b). This is the first time the word *torah* (regulations) is used in Leviticus.

While this section assumes what has gone before, supplementing or repeating it, it begins with a new ritual that is to take place twice daily, in the morning and in the evening. This is a new type of ritual because it is to be performed each day according to schedule rather than according to the occasion, such as the commission of a sin [*Sacrificial System in Leviticus, p. 313*].

(TBC and TLC appear in the section on ch. 10, which concludes the priestly instructions, further clarification of sacrificial rules for the priest, and the consecration of the priests and tabernacle.)

OUTLINE

The Scheduled Daily Offerings, 6:8-18
    6:8-9a   Introduction
    6:9b-13   The Daily Burnt Offering
    6:14-18   The Daily Grain Offering
The High-Priestly Grain Offering, 6:19-23
Additional Comments on Public Offerings, 6:24–7:36
    6:24-30   The Cleansing Offering for Forgiveness
    7:1-10   The Penalty Offering
    7:11-36   The Peace Offering
A Retrospective Summary of the Section on Sacrifice, 7:37-38

EXPLANATORY NOTES

The Scheduled Daily Offerings 6:8-18 (6:1-11)

6:8-9a Introduction

While verse 6 says *These are the regulations for the burnt offering*, this paragraph assumes the ritual of the whole burnt offering as set out in chapter 1. This ritual is to ensure that a fire is always burning on the altar, day and night. The goal is stated at the conclusion of these ritual instructions: *The fire must be kept burning on the altar continuously; it must not go out* (6:13). The Hebrew word *tamid*, translated *continuously*, has come to be the name of this offering. It consists of two yearling lambs (Exod 29:38-39). Every day one was offered in the morning and one in the evening. The regulations here concern only the morning ritual.

6:9b-13 The Daily Burnt Offering

The term "hearth" (*moqdah*), the location for this perpetual fire, occurs only here in the Bible (v. 9). It is related to the verb translated *burning* near the end of verse 9. Thus the fire is to be kept *burning* upon the *place of burning* (AT). The necessity of a continually burning fire is stressed again at the close of this unit (v. 13).

In preparation for this ritual, the priest dons his linen garments (v. 10). These are perhaps a robe and underpants. The latter are to cover his "nakedness" and extend from his waist to his thighs (Exod 28:42). The ritual itself is outlined as follows:

1. Each morning the priest approaches the altar, removes the ashes, and places them beside the altar.
2. He then changes into different clothes, preparing for duties outside the tabernacle (v. 11).
3. The priest carries the ashes outside the camp and disposes of them in a clean place. This place is referred to in 4:12.

The wearing of linen garments and instructions for the priest to change clothes are noteworthy. Only in chapter 16 are linen garments again mentioned in Leviticus. This happens on Yom Kippur (Day of Cleansing; see ch. 16). On this day, Aaron changes into linen garments at the beginning of the ceremony (v. 4) and takes them off again toward its end (v. 23) *[Aaron, p. 287]*.

These linen garments are only to be worn within the tabernacle and its courtyard. If priestly duties call for service beyond the entry to the courtyard, regular clothes must be worn. In Ezekiel 44:19 the rationale is that these garments are able to transmit holiness to the people.

We are not told where the priests keep these linen garments. On Yom Kippur, Aaron leaves his linen clothes in the first room of the tabernacle (16:23). Ezekiel instructs the priest to leave them in a holy chamber of the temple (Ezek 44:19). The tabernacle, however, did not have such a chamber.

Now that the altar has been cleared of its ashes and they are deposited outside the camp, another day of sacrifice can commence. The ritual of building up the fire for another day has the following steps (6:12): (1) wood is fed into the fire to invigorate it; (2) a regular whole burnt offering is placed on the fire (Exod 29:38-39); and (3) the fat of this offering is burned. The goal of this ritual is stated again: the fire on the altar must burn continuously (Lev 6:13).

6:14-18 *The Daily Grain Offering*

A portion of the regular grain offering has been allotted to the priest by God. In chapter 2, the priest was to burn only a token amount. The remainder of the grain or grain product was the priests'. However, rather than the occasional grain offering of chapter 2, this grain offering was likely the scheduled grain offering mentioned in Exodus 29:40-41 and Numbers 28:4-8. This offering differs from the occasional grain offering in chapter 2 because it is brought by the priest to accompany a whole burnt offering.

The priests are now instructed how to handle their portion. If the offering were of ground grain, they must eat it as unleavened bread (v. 17). Since part of the grain was offered to God, all of this offering is most holy and must be eaten in a holy place, in the courtyard of the sanctuary. Any priest may eat from this offering (v. 18).

The final statement of this paragraph is ambiguous. The most probable understanding is *Whatever touches them will become holy* (NIV, NRSV, NJPS). The idea of contagious holiness is very rare in Leviticus but is also found with the cleansing offering discussed below. Even a garment accidentally spritzed by the animal's blood must be washed in a holy place (v. 27). Likewise, whatever touches the altar is holy (Exod 29:37). Ordinarily, only impurity is contagious. Holiness, on the other hand, is either produced through rituals or acquired through holy living *[Holy and Holiness, p. 302]*.

The High-Priestly Grain Offering 6:19-23 (6:12-16)

The regulations for this offering begin in a unique way. Moses is addressed, but there is no command to repeat these regulations to anyone. Perhaps this is because this grain offering can only begin when Aaron is installed as high priest in chapter 8, since only the high priest may perform this ritual. Like the regularly scheduled offerings discussed above (6:8-18), part of the offering will be presented in the evening and part in the morning (cf. vv. 8-13). This practice will commence after chapter 9, when the tabernacle is dedicated.

For this offering the high priest brings one-tenth of an ephah of flour, about what a person would eat in a day. (The exact equivalent in our measurement system is unknown, cf. *NIDB*, s.v. "Weights and Measures.") Half of this amount will be offered in the morning and half in the evening. This flour must first be cooked on a griddle with oil and divided into pieces, making an offering described as "mixed dough" (*HALOT*). This prepared food offering is then burned whole on the altar. Since it is an obligatory high-priestly duty, the priests do not profit from it. As with the regular grain offering, the result is pleasing to God.

However, this paragraph is puzzling since the offering is brought on the day of Aaron's anointing but is also called continuous (*tamid*). Are there two daily grain offerings: one by the priests described in 6:14-18 and one by the high priest? Some suggest that this was an offering given only on the day of the high priest's anointing. However, the actual offering given upon the anointing of a high priest in chapter 8 differs from these instructions (8:26-28) *[Anointing, p. 287]*. Milgrom argues that this offering is the *daily* offering of the priests. The previous grain offering was brought by a layperson, as in chapter 2 (Milgrom 1991: 389-91). Others argue that this grain offering was not meant to be daily but was only offered on the day when the high priest was anointed. A decision is difficult, but later practice supports the notion of its being a special offering rather than a daily one (Hartley).

After the completion of the ritual, additional features of this grain sacrifice are added (6:22-23). After the death of Aaron, the son who succeeds him will perform this duty (see ch. 8 on priestly ordination and succession). Furthermore, the text stresses that the scheduled grain offering belongs entirely to God. These verses underline what has already been said. The high priest must be clear that unlike the voluntary grain offering of the laity, eaten mostly by the priests, this offering is to be burned whole. To make this point even more emphatic, a general regulation concludes this unit: *every* priestly grain offering is to be burned in its entirety. It is never to be eaten (6:23).

Additional Comments on Public Offerings 6:24-7:36 (6:17-7:36)

6:24-30 The Cleansing Offering for Forgiveness

The focus of this passage is on the disposition of the meat after the ritual of forgiveness (Lev 4). Since only a small portion of the animal, the viscera, is burned on the altar, the meat remains (see 4:26, 31, 35). What happens to this meat? The priest who offers the sacrifice (lit. *makes purification*) eats it (6:26). Since the whole carcass of an animal is too much for one person to eat, the text says, *Any male in a priest's family may eat it; it is most holy* (v. 29). This most holy meat must be eaten in the courtyard of the sanctuary, and only by priests who are in a state of purity. Furthermore, because this flesh is most holy, anything that touches it becomes holy (v. 27a). This is another example of contagious holiness within the holy realm (very rare overall).

But what happens if a garment is spattered by the blood of a cleansing offering? The spot needs to be washed in a holy place (v. 27). As for pots coming into contact with holy meat, if they are made of clay, they are to be broken: they have become indelibly stained with holiness. If they are metal, they must be scoured and rinsed to remove their contracted holiness so they can be reused.

The text has been referring to the cleansing offering presented on the courtyard altar. The matter is different for those sacrifices whose blood is brought into the tent, as with the cleansing offering for the high priest (4:3-12). The flesh of this animal must not be consumed by the priests but must be entirely burned up. The guilty party cannot profit from their guilt. Also, the increased holiness of the place where the blood is placed causes a corresponding increase in the holiness of the animal's meat.

7:1-10 *The Penalty Offering*

The regulations for handling the penalty offering are found in 7:2-5. For the ritual, see chapter 5. The blood of the offering brought for a penalty ritual was to be dashed against the sides of the altar. Previously, in chapter 4, the blood was daubed on the horns of the altar, and the remainder was poured out at its base. We learn here that a ritual of forgiveness may take two kinds of sacrifice, one for inadvertent sins, chapter 4, and one for the penalty offering, as here. The regulations for sharing the meat of this offering and their place of eating are specified. The officiating priest retains the hide, as we find in chapter 1 with the whole burnt offering. He also receives all baked grain offerings. But any dry grain offering or one mixed with oil belongs to all priests equally.

7:11-36 *The Peace Offering*

The regulations for distributing meat from the peace offering found here supplement those given in chapter 3. This unit is divided into three parts. First come regulations for two different types of well-being offering: the vow offering and the thanksgiving offering. These regulations are addressed to the priest. The second part, beginning with verse 22, addresses all Israel. The third part, beginning with verse 28, is also directed to all Israel. These instructions extend and clarify the rules pertaining to the priestly share of the well-being offering. The laity are informed as to what is the priestly share.

The first set of instructions focus on the different motives that might prompt a peace offering (vv. 11-15). If the motive is *thankfulness*, then the sacrifice is a thank offering and must be supplemented with a grain offering. This supplement may take three forms: (1) baked unleavened bread mixed with oil, (2) baked unleavened crackers mixed with oil, or (3) fried unleavened cakes of fine flour mixed and moistened with oil.

The first two grain offerings were prepared in an oven (see 2:4). The third, made of fine flour, was mentioned in 6:14. These cakes would be fried in a pan or on a griddle. In addition to these forms of unleavened bread, leavened bread may also accompany a thanksgiving sacrifice (7:13; but would not be placed on the altar).

A part of these grain offerings was to be a contribution (*terumah*) to God. This has been translated as a *heave offering* (KJV) because the name of this sacrifice comes from a verb meaning "to raise, raise up high." This noun form of this verb, however, seems to be used for contributions in general. For example, the materials brought by the people for the building of the tabernacle were considered a *terumah*, a "contribution" (Exod 25:2, 3). This offering would belong to the officiating priest (Lev 7:14).

The one making this offering, along with others eating with him, must eat all the meat before the next morning (v. 15). Meat would not have formed a common part of their meals, and the need to eat it all before morning might mean that the meat was distributed to a larger than usual group as a public celebration of thanksgiving. This would have been a very rare treat for many people.

The next set of instructions cover a peace offering brought to fulfill a *vow* or as a *freewill offering* (vv. 16-18). In contrast to the thanksgiving offering, these offerings may be eaten the next day. However, if any is left over to the third day, it is to be burned. If it should happen that meat from this offering is eaten on the third day, it will be regarded as forbidden (NIV, *impure*). Whoever eats such meat has *desecrated what is holy to the* LORD (19:8) and is liable for punishment.

Leviticus 7:19-21 warns against contaminating the meat of this sacrifice. These instructions can be divided into three groups, answering the following questions:

1. What happens if the meat touches something unclean? Such meat is to be treated like meat that is left on the third day: it is to be burned with fire.
2. Who may eat the meat of the peace offering? The answer is simple: anyone who is ritually clean (see chs. 11-15 for the purity rules).
3. What happens if someone unclean eats the meat or even touches it? That person will be cut off (7:20-21) *[Cut Off, p. 299]*.

The penalty of being cut off, frequently mentioned in Leviticus, occurs here for the first time. The ritual for forgiveness, as we have seen, was for sinning unintentionally (4:2; 5:15). Some sins are deliberately or defiantly committed (Num 15:30-31). Being cut off is the punishment for the latter. In two passages we find that the punishment of being cut off is in addition to being executed by the people (Lev 20:2-3; also for breaking the Sabbath, Exod 31:14). Since in the present case the transgression is probably known only by the transgressor, God is the one who carries out this punishment. What being cut off means for the individual person is not clear from the text (see Hartley: 100; Milgrom 1991: 457-60). It may be that his name or lineage will disappear from Israel, an irremediable loss that was to be prevented if at all possible. Note Ruth 4:10: "To maintain the dead man's name on his inheritance, in order that the name of the dead may not be cut off from his kindred and from the gate of his native place" (NRSV).

The second part of this unit begins with a speech directed to the people (Lev 7:22-27) and concerns the proper disposal of the different cuts of meat coming from a sacrifice of well-being. The fat of animals from the flock or herd must be disposed of properly (vv. 23-25). That no fat of a herd or flock animal may be eaten is repeated from 3:17. But to this general rule is added the stipulation that if an animal dies of itself or is killed by another animal, its fat, instead of being burned on the altar, may be used for any general purpose but not eaten. For the permission to eat its meat, see 17:15.

Next come instructions concerning the blood of an animal (7:26-27). The prohibition against ingesting blood is extended from cattle—flock and herd animals—to birds. (For game animals, see 17:13.) This blanket prohibition is first found in Genesis 9:4, when Noah and all following generations are granted the right to eat animal flesh but not their blood. The punishment for this heinous crime is being cut off *[Cut Off, p. 299]*. No provision is made for any nonritual use of the blood from a dead animal.

The next collection of instructions focuses on distribution of the meat coming from a peace offering. Part of the meat must be allowed to the priests (vv. 29-36). The emphasis is that their share has been mandated by God for all time.

First, the part played by the worshiper in disposal of the peace offering's meat is described. Here we find that the layperson can handle the meat from a sacrifice, even though it is holy. The parts belonging to God must be burned on the altar, especially the fat. The worshiper is to present the chest or breast of the animal as a *wave offering* (v. 30 KJV, NIV, et al.). The exact meaning of this word is not certain. The NRSV and the NJPS translate *elevation offering*. Others consider *consecrated gift* the best translation (see *HALOT* and its discussion). After being offered, this meat is given to the priests (v. 31).

Then the right thigh of the animal is given as a contribution (as also in v. 14). The reason for this practice is that God has chosen this part; however, it is not burned on the altar but given to the priests. This rule will take effect when Aaron and his sons are inducted into the priesthood.

A Retrospective Summary of the Section on Sacrifice 7:37-38

Verses 37-38 mark the end of section 1, whose subject is sacrifices offered occasionally as well as those that must be offered daily on the altar in the courtyard. The text changes to third-person descriptive language. Even Moses is cast in third person.

The sacrifices are listed in the order of their mention in 6:8-7:36. These do not include instructions for sacrifices regulated by the calendar, such as Yom Kippur (Day of Cleansing, ch. 16), or necessary for a ceremony like the installation of the priesthood, or the inauguration of sacrificial worship at the tent of meeting (except one concerning the priestly inauguration, 6:19-23). Such instructions will follow in chapters 8 and 9. Most of the listed sacrifices here are to be brought by laypersons. It is assumed that they now have sufficient information to offer their sacrifices [*Calendar, p. 295*].

This statement also makes clear that these laws were commanded to Moses at Mount Sinai in the wilderness of Sinai. Here the Israelites were commanded how they might please God and maintain a relationship with God. This instruction is regarded as special divine revelation.

(TBC and TLC appear in the section on ch. 10.)

Leviticus 8:1–10:20

Part 1B
Inauguration of Worship

OVERVIEW

The sacrificial rituals for worship at the tabernacle are now complete. Who will perform these rituals? The priests, of course. But first the priests need to be commissioned and installed into office. This is the topic of chapter 8. With priests available, the tabernacle can be made ready for worship. The dedication of the sanctuary is described in chapter 9 *[The Tabernacle, p. 317]*.

But who can consecrate priests before there are any priests? Moses, who receives instructions from God, acts as a priest to install the first priests into office. Moses serves as a prophet in relaying God's instructions to the people, and as a priest in performing the necessary rituals. Once Aaron and his sons are established as priests, they conduct the inauguration ceremony for the tabernacle. The goal of this inauguration is reached when *the Presence of the* LORD *appeared to all the people* (9:23 NJPS) *[Aaron, p. 287]*.

Previously, God's presence was seen in a cloud (Exod 16:10). It then moved and dwelt on Mount Sinai, where it appeared on the summit of the mountain as a fire (Exod 24:16-17). Finally, the cloud of God's presence came down from Mount Sinai and enveloped the tent of meeting, which was outside the camp (Exod 40:34). Now God's presence comes and dwells among the people in the shrine amid their camp. This event is the high point of the book of Leviticus. It raises the focal question of Leviticus—how to live in the presence of God.

After God's presence resides in the tabernacle, Leviticus 10 relates the story of two priests who died because they did not perform a ritual properly in God's sacred presence. This shocking event is followed by an argument between Aaron, the high priest, and Moses, the lawgiver. What was the problem, and what went wrong? Who would want to be a priest if death could result for unknown reasons? This argument ends chapter 10 and the present unit.

The narrative of chapter 10 is resumed in chapter 16 with instructions for who, when, and how to enter the holy of holies. But before we reach chapter 16, we must learn about the purity that is necessary for worship at the tent, how it is lost, and how can it be restored. These purity instructions, in chapters 11–15, intervene before the story continues in chapter 16.

(TBC and TLC for the units in this section appear in the section on ch. 10.)

OUTLINE FOR PART 1B

The Installation of the Priesthood, 8:1-36
The Dedication of the Sanctuary, 9:1-24
A Tragic Act of Worship, 10:1-20

Leviticus 8:1-36

The Installation of the Priesthood

PREVIEW

Chapter 8 recounts the installation of the first priests and the high priest *[Leadership, p. 306]*. This historic ceremony supplies the blueprint for all future installations. The rituals used in this ceremony are found in the previous chapters (1-7), with three exceptions: the bathing and clothing rituals (8:6-9), the ritual of anointing with oil (8:30), and the inauguration ritual in which blood from the inauguration sacrifice is applied to parts of the priest's body (8:22-24).

Chapter 8 is divided into paragraphs by the repeated refrain *just as the LORD had commanded Moses*, a performance formula (NET; see vv. 4-5, 9, 13, 17, 21, 29, 34). Using this marker, we may outline the ceremony as follows.

OUTLINE

Preparation, 8:1-4
    8:1   Introduction
    8:2-3   The Command to Prepare
    8:4   The Performance Formula
Step 1: Bathing and Dressing, 8:5-9
    8:5   Introduction to the Ceremony
    8:6   Bathing the Future Priests
    8:7-9   Clothing Aaron

Step 2: Anointing, 8:10-13
    8:10-12   The Holy Things and Aaron
    8:13   Parenthesis: Clothing the Sons
Step 3: The Sacrificial Rituals, 8:14-29
    8:14-17   The Ritual for Consecrating the Altar
    8:18-21   A Ritual for Pleasing God
    8:22-29   A Ritual for Installation of the Priests
Step 4: Hallowing, 8:30-34
Conclusion, 8:35-36

EXPLANATORY NOTES

Preparation 8:1-4

8:1 Introduction

The LORD *called to Moses* has introduced God's first speech to Moses (1:1), and in 4:1 a similar phrase (*said to Moses*) also introduced a new block of material, obligatory sacrifices. It comes again in 6:8, beginning the instructions addressed to the priests. Now in chapter 8 it introduces the ceremony for the installation of the priests.

8:2-3 The Command to Prepare

In preparing for this ceremony, Moses must collect the needed people and materials. First he must bring Aaron and his sons to the tabernacle. Then he must assemble the items required for the ceremony: the priestly garments for the high priest, the oil used for anointing, three animals, and a basket of unleavened bread.

8:4 The Performance Formula

At the end of the list, Moses is also required to assemble the entire congregation. This ceremony takes place in public, but the laity are only observers. At the end of this paragraph we find a confirmation statement. Moses acted just as God had commanded, with all the congregation assembled at the tent of meeting (v. 4).

Step 1: Bathing and Dressing 8:5-9

8:5 Introduction to the Ceremony

Moses begins the ceremony with a statement of authorization; the following ceremony is commanded by God, not something invented by Moses or the priests.

8:6 Bathing the Future Priests

The first ritual is the washing of the priestly candidates and the laying aside of their old clothes. This is their first step to becoming priests. No longer laypeople, they are not yet priests. In this in-between time, Aaron and his sons are like blank sheets of paper. They have been scrubbed of their old state but have not yet entered into their new status as functioning priests.

8:7-9 Clothing Aaron

Although all the candidates have been washed, only Aaron is now dressed. (The sons will become clothed later, in v. 13.) In preparation for Aaron's new status as high priest, he is adorned with special clothing that will set him apart from the ordinary priests. (For the construction of the clothing, see Exod 28:6-39.)

Moses (1) places a *tunic* or long shirt bound by a *sash* on Aaron. Next (2), an outer garment (*robe*) is placed over the tunic, and (3) an *ephod* is placed over these as the outermost layer. The ephod was like an apron with straps going around the neck and rings attached to it. The construction of the ephod is described in Exodus 28:6-14, 25-28. (4) A band or belt (*waistband*) was tied around the ephod to attach it more closely to the body. Now the high priest was fully clothed.

A *breastplate* is now placed on top of his clothing (v. 8). It was made of the same material as the ephod and seems to have been attached to the ephod's rings (Exod 28:26-28). It was a folded piece of cloth and perhaps resembled a large pouch. Into this pouch was placed the *Urim and Thummim*. Sometimes these objects occur together (as in 1 Sam 14:41; Ezra 2:63; Neh 7:65) and sometimes alone (as in Num 27:21; 1 Sam 28:6). These two objects were used to inquire of God in order to make a choice between two alternatives: "Saul prayed . . . , 'If the fault is in me or my son Jonathan, respond with Urim, but if the men of Israel are at fault, respond with Thummim'" (1 Sam 14:41).

Next, Moses attends to Aaron's haberdashery (v. 9): (1) He places a *turban* or a wrapped headband on his head, and (2) attaches a golden "flower, or bud," to the front of this headdress (*gold plate, sacred emblem*). What this actually was is uncertain. *HALOT* and *DCH* define it as a crown or diadem since it was also associated with royalty. This golden ornament was fastened to Aaron's turban by means of a blue cord (Exod 28:36-37).

The clothing of Aaron ends with a declaration that the washing and dressing were done *as the* LORD *commanded Moses.*

Step 2: Anointing 8:10-13

8:10-12 *The Holy Things and Aaron*

This ritual begins with Moses using the oil of anointing for the first time in Leviticus (although oil has been employed as an element of grain sacrifices). He applies it to the tabernacle and all its contents. The form of anointing—sprinkling or daubing, for example—is not described. This same action is also found in Exodus 40:9. In both cases the outcome is being holy. It is a consecration ritual [*Anointing, p. 287*].

We have already encountered the verb for being holy, *qadaš*, in Leviticus 6:18, 27 (11, 20). There, an object becomes holy by touching, even accidentally, something already holy. Here, objects are made holy by the ritual gesture of anointing with oil (8:10-12). What does it mean to become holy? Primarily it signifies that these objects no longer have their natural status but have been transferred into the realm of holiness. This dedication to holiness sets holy objects apart from the profane world. It is like a table built out of wood. The raw wood is transferred into the realm of use by varnishing it. Now Moses moves from the tabernacle to the courtyard and anoints the altar, the basin (mentioned only here in Leviticus), and its stand by sprinkling them seven times to consecrate them. Finally, Moses pours oil on the head of Aaron, thereby making him holy [*Holy and Holiness, p. 302*].

8:13 *Parenthesis: Clothing the Sons*

As an appendix to this ritual, the sons of Aaron are now dressed (v. 13). This verse seems out of place since Aaron had been dressed immediately after he and his sons bathed. But his sons were not dressed then. Now the sons are clothed with a tunic bound by a sash and caps are placed on their heads. The Hebrew word translated *cap* is only used for the headdress of the ordinary priests. These three items mark the garb of the regular priests in contrast to the splendor of the high priest's garments.

Step 3: Sacrificial Rituals 8:14-29

This longer block of material describes three sacrificial rituals: (1) a ritual for purification and dedication, (2) a ritual for pleasing God, and (3) an inauguration sacrifice that also pleases God. The end result is again pleasing God.

8:14-17 The Ritual for Consecrating the Altar

Moses presents a bull for a purification ritual. As has already been noted, "sin offering" (ḥaṭṭaʾt) is a misnomer; it should be designated a "cleansing offering," since this is not an offering for sin but an offering for purification: *Moses slaughtered the bull and took some of the blood, and with his finger he put it on all the horns of the altar to purify [sterilize] the altar* (8:15; see comments in ch. 4 and *Atonement, p. 288*). The remaining blood he pours out at the base. This action makes the altar holy so that expiation can be made upon it *[Atonement, p. 288]*.

8:18-21 A Ritual for Pleasing God

Next, Moses offers up a whole burnt offering, which pleases God (see ch. 1).

8:22-29 A Ritual for Installation of the Priests

The actual ordination ritual is different from all other rituals. Blood from *the ram for the ordination* is applied to persons. Some of the blood of the animal is daubed on the right ear, right thumb, and right big toe of Aaron and his sons. The remainder of the blood is dashed on the altar. After disposing of the blood, Moses separates out the forbidden parts of the ram. To them he adds the right thigh, which is normally offered by the layperson to the priest (7:32). In addition, Moses adds three different grain offerings (see ch. 2). All of these he now places in the hands of Aaron and his sons, who in turn offer them as a raised offering to God. Moses then takes everything back and burns them on the altar (v. 28). Next, Moses takes the chest of the animal, elevates it as an offering, and takes it as his share of the offering.

Step 4: Hallowing 8:30-34

Just as the ceremony began with anointing (after washing), so it ends with Moses sprinkling Aaron, his sons, and their clothes with the oil of anointing and blood. Thus Aaron, his sons, and their clothes were made holy. (Previously, Aaron had been made holy through anointing with oil, 8:12). The ordination ceremony is now finished.

Conclusion 8:35-36

After the ceremony, Moses addresses the new priests. He gives instructions that they should cook and eat the remaining meat and bread goods of the previous sacrifice. If any remains, it must be burned. Furthermore, they may not leave the tabernacle precinct for seven days, because these are the days of ordination. Their change in status required a period of transition to move from profane to holy.

(TBC and TLC appear in the section on ch. 10.)

Leviticus 9:1-24
The Dedication of the Sanctuary

PREVIEW
Between chapters 8 and 9, seven days have passed. The priestly candidates have remained in the precinct of the tabernacle and are now ready to begin their duties. First, however, the sanctuary and its sacred things must be consecrated. Moses now gives the instructions for the consecration ceremony to the priests and the elders, respected representatives of the people (these are national elders; see *NIDB*, s.v. "Elder in the Old Testament"). Presumably each tribe would be represented by those considered elders. Once they have assembled the necessary sacrifices, Moses tells Aaron to begin the ceremony [*The Tabernacle, p. 317*].

OUTLINE
Instruction for the Consecration Ceremony, 9:1-7
The Ceremony, 9:8-22
The Blessing of the People, 9:23-24

EXPLANATORY NOTES
Instruction for the Consecration Ceremony 9:1-7
On the eighth day Moses assembles Aaron, his sons, and the elders for the dedication of the tabernacle. He then gives instructions for preparing for the consecration. Aaron is to bring a young bull for a

cleansing offering and a ram for a whole burnt offering. The people are to bring a male goat for their cleansing offering as well as a young bull and a young ram for a whole burnt offering. In addition, they are to bring a peace offering and a grain offering. This the people do.

The point of this ceremony is the coming of God's presence. Moses informs the people that God will appear to them this day (v. 4) and promises them that if they follow instructions, *the glory of the LORD may appear to you* (v. 6). "Glory" appears in Leviticus only in this chapter (here and in v. 23). The glory of God first resided on Mount Sinai (Exod 24:16). At the end of Exodus (40:34-35), it filled the tent outside the camp. Now it will reside in the tent in their midst. *Glory* is an expression indicating God's presence. Its manifestation will be described at the end of the chapter. Obviously, there could be no material symbolism representing God's presence in the tabernacle.

The wording of verse 7 is awkward. Literally, it reads *Make your cleansing sacrifice and your whole burnt offering and make for you <u>and for the people</u>. Make the offerings of the people and <u>make cleansing for them</u>* (AT, emph. added). The last sentence is redundant, and the first sentence as it now reads is inaccurate: the priestly offering makes expiation for the ones offering them, that is, the priests. The LXX, the early church's Greek Bible, reads "for you and for your house" instead of "for the people." Adopting this understanding, Aaron first makes purification for himself as high priest and then for the priests. Second, the priests then make offerings on behalf of the people *[Atonement, p. 288]*.

The Ceremony 9:8-22

Aaron now becomes the actor as he assumes the role of high priest. His first action is the slaughter of his cleansing offering. His sons present the blood, and he dips his finger into it and daubs it on the horns of the courtyard altar. In Leviticus 4:6-7, when the high priest offers a cleansing offering, he takes the blood into the tent, dips his finger into it, sprinkles some before the curtain, and daubs some on the horns of the incense altar. Here (9:8-14), Aaron is not yet prepared to enter the tent itself. Instead, he pours the rest of the blood at the base of the courtyard altar. The parts for God are then burned on the altar. The rest of the animal is burned outside the camp *[Aaron, p. 287]*.

The focus now moves to the offerings of the people (v. 15). The text only mentions the cleansing (or sterilizing) and whole burnt offerings, since they have just been described. The purpose of the former is to sterilize the altar: Aaron *performed a decontamination rite with it like the first one* (v. 15 NET; cf. 8:15). Next comes the grain offering. Aaron removes his priestly share, and the rest he turns into smoke. He offers this *on the altar in addition to the morning's burnt offering* (v. 17). A morning offering is commanded in 6:13 but commences only after Aaron is anointed.

The sacrifices end with the presentation of the peace offerings of the people (9:18-21). The blood of the ox and the ram are poured out, and the fatty parts are removed. These fatty parts are first placed on the breasts of the animal and then removed from them and burned. Next, Aaron presents the breast and the thigh as a wave (elevation) offering. In this inauguration ceremony both the breast and the right thigh are wave (elevation) offerings. This varies from the instructions given in 7:30-33, where the breast is brought by the layperson and waved by the layperson (7:30-31).

The ceremony concludes in 9:22 with Aaron, the high priest, blessing the people from the dais by the courtyard altar.

The Blessing of the People 9:23-24

Aaron then descends from the altar and, along with Moses, enters the tent. When they come out, they bless the people.

The results of this ceremony are dramatic. A fire comes from God's presence and devours all three of the offerings, signifying the active presence of God within the tent. The mention of God's fire now devouring all the sacrifices and their fatty parts seems strange since Aaron has already burned or turned into smoke the previous sacrifices as stated in verses 10, 13, 14, 17, and 20. This may be explained by assuming that the sacrifices had begun burning but had not yet been entirely consumed. After all, it would take some time to incinerate the people's whole burnt offering of a young ox and a ram, not to mention all the fatty parts that had been placed on the altar.

The whole people, seeing with their own eyes this proof of God's presence among them, cried out in joy and bowed their faces to the ground (v. 24). God indeed was present in their very midst. Their response was *joy*, not fear [*The Tabernacle, p. 317*].

(TBC and TLC for this section appear in the section on ch. 10.)

Leviticus 10:1-20
A Tragic Act of Worship

PREVIEW

Chapter 10 tells the story of two sons of Aaron who were punished by death. Why this act of divine violence? What did the two sons of Aaron do to warrant their death? What can we infer about God from this incident? Why do the purity regulations for worship follow this incident?

Chapter 10 may be divided into three parts. First, there is the event of the *unauthorized fire* or illicit fire that led to the deaths of Nadab and Abihu. After suggesting a reason for these deaths, Moses commands the removal of their corpses from the holy area and their disposal outside the camp. He also forbids Aaron and his two remaining sons to display certain mourning practices. (This event is resumed in ch. 16.)

Second, God provides additional safeguards to prevent such an event in the future. Priests are to refrain from alcoholic drinks before entering the tent. Also, priests are to distinguish between clean and unclean and to teach the Israelites the difference. This instruction is to prevent the unclean from touching the holy [Pure, p. 309].

Third, Moses reiterates the regulations for the cleansing offering. He then investigates the specific case of the people's goat for the purification ritual mentioned in chapter 9 and discovers that it was not handled properly—its meat was burned, not eaten. Finally, Aaron speaks and reaches agreement with Moses.

OUTLINE

The Narrative and Immediate Result, 10:1-7
New Instructions and Duties, 10:8-11
Review of the People's Cleansing Offerings, 10:12-20

EXPLANATORY NOTES

The Narrative and Immediate Result 10:1-7

The narrative of the strange fire is hard to understand. The first uncertainty is the actual meaning of the term *unauthorized fire* (NIV; Heb. *'eš zarah*), which is otherwise translated *unholy fire* (NRSV), *alien fire* (NJPS), and *strange fire* (NET, KJV). This last rendition might be the most literal translation of the Hebrew, but what does it mean? In a similar context, Numbers 16:40 (17:5), we find that an "unauthorized man" (AT) may not burn incense before God. Here in Leviticus 10:1 the translation is *unauthorized fire* (NIV). The two priests were newly authorized to offer sacrifices, but there is more to sacrifice than being authorized. They brought this fire to burn incense on the incense altar inside the tent, a most holy place. Although it is not said, they might have done this to create a cloud of smoke so that they could enter the holy of holies, since a cloud of smoke was needed to screen them from the holy presence of God that resided within the tent (Lev 16:12-13). While the priests were authorized to sacrifice, they were not authorized to enter the tent—and certainly not the holy of holies. So far, the high priest alone could enter the sanctuary and offer sacrifices there (see 4:3-21). This was an inconceivable act of hubris—to usurp the place of the high priest by entering the holy place and approaching the holy of holies without regard for the preparation required (see ch. 16), thus defiling the holiness of God.

The second question is the meaning of God's brief statement quoted by Moses: *Among those who approach me I will be proved holy; in the sight of all the people I will be honored* (10:3). Both verbs could be rendered as passives: *I will be sanctified* and *I will be honored*. As seen from the continuation of the story in 16:1-2, God's sanctity and honor demanded that God's very presence be approached only at certain times and in certain ways. Just as one does not enter the presence of an earthly king on a whim, so one does not enter the presence of the Sovereign of the universe carelessly.

This event happened on the same day as chapter 9. The expression *Fire came out from the presence of the LORD and consumed [them]* is the same expression as in Leviticus 9:24, at the end of the preceding chapter. All saw that God's presence was in the tabernacle and was fearsome. There was no excuse for their arrogance in overreaching their authority and approaching God improperly.

After the death of Nadab and Abihu, Moses summons two of Aaron's Levite cousins (see Exod 6:18, 20, 22-23) and commands them to remove the corpses and take them outside the camp. (Levites are rarely mentioned in Leviticus *[Levites, p. 306]*.) We are not told where outside the camp they were taken or what was done with their bodies. In addition, Moses (as a preventative against God's judgment) forbids Aaron and his two remaining sons to mourn them by letting their hair loose, becoming unkempt, or tearing their clothing. Rather, the whole camp will weep for the dead priests.

New Instructions and Duties 10:8-11

This is a momentous day for Aaron. He has entered the tent for the first time (9:23), his two oldest sons have died, and now God speaks directly to him, alone. Aaron is informed that any priest entering the tent should not drink wine or other alcoholic beverages. Priests approaching the presence of God must be sober and clearheaded so as not to act in an inappropriate manner *[Aaron, p. 287]*.

New tasks are also assigned to the priests: they are to distinguish between what is holy and what is profane, and between what is ritually clean and unclean (see "A Book of Worship and Life" in the Introduction and the essay *Holy and Holiness, p. 302*). These terms represent two different classifications. The holy and profane refer to static realms: the holy realm is the tabernacle and its courtyard. Clean and unclean represent conditions that change. People who are clean may become unclean by eating something unclean. Becoming clean again is a matter of performing the prescribed ritual (ch. 11). Only those who are pure may approach the realm of the holy. While living in the camp, the people may be unclean, but the Israelite coming before God must be clean. These new instructions point forward to chapters 11-15, in which we find the purity rituals.

Furthermore, the priests are given a teaching function. They are to teach the decrees that God has spoken through Moses. The priests need to study the Torah, the instructions of God, so that they can teach them. Study and teaching now belong to the priestly duties.

Review of the People's Cleansing Offerings 10:12-20

Moses now reminds Aaron and his two remaining sons, Eleazar and Ithamar, about the proper treatment of the priestly portions of the people's sacrifices for the cleansing of the altar. While the priests must burn up their own sacrifices entirely, they are granted a portion of the grain offerings, the peace offerings, and the offerings brought by the laity for the cleansing of the altar. Moses begins his review with the meal offering and continues with the priestly parts of the peace offering.

Moses then investigates what was done with the priestly share of the people's offerings that were offered as part of the inauguration ceremony. First, Aaron offered a priestly cleansing offering whose flesh and skin were burned outside the camp (9:11). This accords with the instructions that *the rest of the bull—he must take outside the camp to a place ceremonially clean, where the ashes are thrown, and burn it there in a wood fire on the ash heap* (Lev 4:12). Second, Aaron and the priests offered the cleansing on behalf of the people. For these offerings the rule is *The priest who offers it shall eat it* (Lev 6:26). But Moses found that the priests had entirely burned up this offering as well. Moses became angry at this mistake and asked why they had not eaten its flesh as they were obligated to do by the ritual, since *he gave it to you to bear the iniquity of the congregation, to make atonement on their behalf before the* LORD (Lev 10:17 NET). What does this statement mean, and what are its implications?

Normally, in Leviticus, persons bear their own iniquity, that is, culpability (as in 5:1, 17; 7:18; 17:16) or "sin" (as in 20:20; 22:9; 24:15). In the case of sin, the priest performs a ritual for forgiveness by offering a sacrifice for the purification of the altar on their behalf, and as a result they are forgiven (chs. 4–5). In the case of ritual impurity, a person needs to undertake a purification ritual, which may not require a sacrifice at all (Lev 17:15-16). In either type of ritual, there is no mention of the priests eating meat from the offering in order to bear guilt or sin. There is, in fact, no evidence from Leviticus that someone may bear the guilt or sin of another person in order to bring forgiveness *[Scapegoat, p. 316].*

Nevertheless, in Leviticus 10:17 we find the anomalous statement that the priests need to eat the meat from the people's offering in order to bear the people's guilt. But this statement does not make sense in the context of 9:15. There the people's goat was slaughtered to "sterilize" the altar. The verb there is not *kipper*, meaning "to cleanse" or "to purify" the altar from the effects of sin, but *ḥiṭṭeʾ*, meaning in this case "to decontaminate to make ready for holy use." Since in neither case is sin mentioned nor forgiveness given, this is not a ritual performed on account of sin but rather one to "sterilize" the altar. (See notes on ch. 16 for a discussion of the purification ritual, whose result is to restore the altar to its pristine condition.)

The phrase *to bear iniquity/sin*, however, has a different meaning when used of a second party, that is, when a person or animal "bears the guilt" of another. The ritual of the goat on the Day of Cleansing is a case in point (Lev 16:22). The high priest "cleans house" and loads all the removed contamination on the goat. The goat, as the second party, then bears Israel's (the first party's) sins, iniquities, and impurities away, removing them from the Israelite camp. In our passage in 10:17, the priests are the second party. By performing the ritual on behalf of the people, they enable the cleansing of the altar from the effects of a person's sins *[Bearing/ Removing Iniquity or Sin, p. 294]*.

How do the priests remove—bear away—the culpability of the one who trespasses? Verse 17b indicates the means: *the flesh of the cleansing sacrifice is assigned to you to eat in order to bear/remove the sins of the people through performing a cleansing ritual on their behalf before God* (AT, a difficult verse allowing a variety of interpretations; cf. NIV, *It was given to you to take away the guilt of the community by making atonement for them before the LORD*). By performing the ritual of forgiveness, which involves eating their share of the sacrifice rather than burning it up on the altar, the priests make possible the removal of guilt from the guilty party.

Moses next reminds the priests that the only exception to eating the meat of this offering is if the blood has been brought inside the tent. This regulation was given in 6:30 (23). The blood of the people's goat was not brought into the tent, so this exception does not apply to the present case.

Aaron now speaks (v. 19). He asks Moses if God would have been satisfied if the priest had eaten the meat. Aaron may have thought that since the blood of the people's cleansing offering was to be taken inside the tent (4:18-20), the meat was not to be eaten. Moses, however, holds that since the blood in the inauguration ceremony was not actually brought into the tent, presumably because it was part of a ritual sterilization of the altar, the meat of the sacrifice must be eaten. In the end, Moses and Aaron come to an understanding.

THE TEXT IN BIBLICAL CONTEXT

The Apparent Violence of God

The episode recounted at the beginning of Leviticus 10 is troubling and may even be repulsive to readers. It surely reinforces a common notion that the God in the Old Testament is an angry, touchy, and violent God. The fact that God does not act in anger makes the action seem more cold-blooded. The purpose of this brief essay is not to justify God's action here in chapter 10, but to place it within a wider canonical context in order to understand it better. A good hermeneutical principle is to understand before judging.

First, we find God striking people dead in both the Old and New Testaments. The classic example is found in Acts 5:1-11. In this narrative both Ananias and his wife, Sapphira, are accused of lying to God or testing God's Spirit; they then fall down dead at Peter's feet. In the case of Sapphira, this seems especially cruel on the part of Peter, who could have warned her about what would happen if she repeated her husband's lie. In addition, death for lying seems rather harsh.

Second, Paul in Romans 12:19 embraces God's anger (wrath) and vengeance (retribution) as forming the basis for human nonretaliation. We are not to seek retribution, because retribution is the prerogative of God. Instead, we are to do good and thus overcome evil with good (Rom 12:20-21). Our tendency is to make sure that others suffer for their misdeeds.

Third, God is a judge who is expected to judge justly, which means punishing evildoers but sparing the just. Abraham pleads with God to spare the righteous people in Sodom (Gen 18:22-33). The basis of his intercession is, "Will you sweep away the righteous with the wicked?" (18:23). This is a rhetorical question because Abraham knows the answer to another rhetorical question, "Shall not the Judge [Ruler] of all the earth do what is just?" (Gen 18:25 NRSV). Justice is God's task as ruler of the universe. God's acts of justice in the Hebrew Bible are sometimes translated "vengeance" (*naqam*), but in fact these are acts of retribution, of God meting out justice (on this verb, see Peels). Usually God's retribution brings justice to the poor and powerless, who otherwise would never see justice.

Punishing the guilty and vindicating the just does not make these judgments of God any less "violent," although we do not consider carrying out a just verdict in a court of law as necessarily practicing violence. Can retributive justice be done without violence? Would the Egyptians ever have freed the Israelite slaves if God had not intervened? As Romans 12 makes clear, such judgment is the prerogative of God, not of humans.

In the present case, Leviticus 10:1-2, we find two priests who transgressed the presence of God. Such a transgression is a capital crime (Lev 16:1-2). God defends, so to speak, the sacred holy space against unauthorized entry and defilement. God judges the trespassers as guilty of a capital crime, and they are executed for their crime. After judgment and cleanup, God's holy presence remains undefiled and can once again serve as a place of praise, feasting, and forgiveness.

Dynasty and Temple

In order to properly perform the rituals at the tabernacle, special personnel were commissioned and authorized to perform them. Aaron and his sons were those ordained into priestly office to officiate at the tabernacle. Furthermore, only these persons and their descendants could be ordained to serve at the tabernacle or in the temple. This service was their exclusive prerogative *[Leadership, p. 306]*.

The most famous case in the Hebrew Bible of a line of descent with a special or exclusive function is the line of David. However, the line of Aaron was also well known. The resumption of the priestly prerogative of Aaron's line was part of Israel's vision for the future. Jeremiah prophesies, "For this is what the LORD says: 'David will never fail to have a man to sit on the throne of Israel, nor will the Levitical priests ever fail to have a man to stand before me continually to offer burnt offerings'" (Jer 33:17-18). A few verses later, God declares: "If you can break my covenant with the day and my covenant with the night, so that day and night no longer come at their appointed time, then my covenant with David my servant—and my covenant with the Levites who are priests ministering before me—can be broken" (Jer 33:20-21).

In the time of the New Testament, we find priests offering sacrifices to God in the Jerusalem temple. Because there was no palace or Davidic ruler, the temple became the central institution for the Jewish people. People from Galilee and from the Greek and Roman world would come to Jerusalem and offer sacrifices during festivals such as Passover. Offering animal sacrifices was not strange in their world, since animal sacrifices were a regular part of religious life. (See Paul's mention of sacrifices offered to demons in 1 Cor 10:20 and his discussion of food offered to idols in 1 Cor 8.) What was different is that for Jews their sacrifices could only be offered at the Jerusalem temple.

As the central institution, the temple was the spiritual center for the people, just as Jerusalem was the holy city. Jesus announced that the Holy Spirit would come to them in Jerusalem (Acts 1:4). Jerusalem became the headquarters for the disciples (Acts 1:13-26). It is the assumed center for witness about Jesus: "You will be my witnesses in Jerusalem, and in all Judea and Samaria, and to the ends of the earth" (Acts 1:8). It is even reported that since the disciples stayed in the environs of the temple, "a large number of priests became obedient to the faith" (Acts 6:7).

The office of high priest is important for the author of Hebrews. Just as God selected Aaron to be high priest, so God selects all subsequent high priests. It was not Jesus' prerogative to become high priest, but it was God who selected him (Heb 5:4-5). It was Jesus' role as a high priest who was outside Aaron's dynasty that is significant for the book of Hebrews. The high priests in the line of Aaron needed to offer sacrifices for their own sin as well as for the people's. But Jesus, the new high priest, would no longer need to offer any sacrifices on account of sin *[Hebrews and Leviticus, p. 300]*.

The necessity of temple and priests created a crisis after the destruction of the Jerusalem temple in 70 CE. Without the temple and the rituals carried on there, how were the Jewish people to survive? We might understand the book of Hebrews as an attempt to come to terms with this loss for the Christian community. If so, even after its destruction, the temple and its priesthood remained as archetypes retaining influence for early followers of Jesus *[Hebrews and Leviticus, p. 300]*.

For the early Christians, the reality of God's presence on earth was not limited to the temple. Indeed, references such as John 1:14 indicate that the incarnation was conceptualized by using the image of God's presence in the tabernacle. Jesus, like the tabernacle, represented the presence of God. In the gospel of John we also find Jesus pointing to himself as the temple (2:19).

Paul applies this image to the Christian community or congregation. "Don't you know that you yourselves are God's temple and that God's Spirit dwells in your midst?" (1 Cor 3:16). The "you" here is the plural "you" meaning "you all." Just as the locus of God's presence was the tabernacle or temple, so also the congregation is now the place where God's presence dwells.

In Ephesians, Paul uses the metaphor of a house. The Christian congregation is like a building that can become a holy temple: "In him the whole building is joined together and rises to become a holy temple in the Lord" (Eph 2:21).

Paul also designates the body of each Christian as a temple: "Do you not know that your bodies are temples of the Holy Spirit, who is in you, whom you have received from God?" (1 Cor 6:19). Each individual believer's body is a temple for the Holy Spirit.

In the biblical tradition it seems that God's presence finds its locus on earth, whether it be in the tabernacle, in the later temple, in the person of Jesus, in the Christian congregation or church, or in the individual believer's body. Since Leviticus, the presence of God is assumed to find a residence on earth *[The Tabernacle, p. 317]*.

THE TEXT IN THE LIFE OF THE CHURCH
Specialized Functions and the Rest of Us

The inauguration of specialized personnel to perform duties that only they can do seems to be a necessary fact of organized religious life *[Leadership, p. 306]*. For Israel, within the priesthood there was also specialization: only the high priest could perform certain tasks. Although their role is not mentioned in Leviticus, Levites assisted the priests and also performed less important duties (Num 18:2) *[Levites, p. 306]*.

Although our methods of choosing people for a specialized ministry have changed, the need for specialists in the church remains. Paul names these as "the apostles, the prophets, the evangelists, the pastors and teachers" (Eph 4:11-12). God gives these gifts to individuals within the church because such gifted individuals are necessary to equip God's people and to build up the church.

Paul also uses the metaphor of the body to make this point. The congregation is likened to a body that has many members in order to perform different and specialized tasks and thereby keep the body healthy. The body cannot be reduced to one part, such as an eye or a hand. Rather, all parts are necessary, and all parts belong to the same body (1 Cor 12:22). Differentiation is a result of the Spirit's work for the good of the body (vv. 11-14). A healthy congregation has specialists whose work strengthens the whole. Leadership is necessary for a healthy congregation so as not to pluck out their eye and stumble blindly.

Sometimes there is a clash between the notion of the priesthood of all believers and the need for specialists. This notion may come from 1 Peter, where we find the Christians addressed as "a chosen race, a royal priesthood, a holy nation, a people of his own" (1 Pet 2:9 NET). The assumption is easily made that all Christians have an equal priestly status. However, this would be a mistaken idea.

The background for this claim is Exodus 19:6, where God, after claiming Israel as God's own special people from among all nations, further states that Israel "will be for me a kingdom of priests and a holy nation" (Exod 19:6). The fact that Israel is a holy nation and a kingdom of priests did not mean that Israel would have no priests. Even a "kingdom of priests" in a collective sense needs priests in an individual vocational sense!

However, the tabernacle with its priests and rituals was not the only way an Israelite related to God. Any Israelite could pray directly to God. We find Samson, the strong man, crying out to God at the end of his life (Judg 16:28). We find childless Hannah praying to God at the sanctuary at Shiloh (1 Sam 1:13-15). The first-person prayers of petition and thanksgiving in the book of Psalms point in the same direction. Through prayer, every Israelite had direct access to God (see Greenberg 1983). Prayer, however, was not a substitute for the temple, its priests, and its rituals. A religious community needed more than individual prayer. It also needed confession, forgiveness, and opportunities for praise and thanksgiving.

This is further stressed by Paul, who understands the congregation as an interdependent body. While each Christian has the Holy Spirit, the community also represents the temple of God. To this temple or body various abilities have been given in the form of individuals who have specialized abilities. The strength of a Christian community depends on the exercise of these abilities by those who have them and on the ability of others to accept these gifts. When all claim to exercise the same gifts for the good of the body or for building each other up, we find rabble and rubble rather than the temple of God's presence. (For an illustration of the destructive power of grasping for gifts not given, see esp. Num 16:8-11, the rebellion of Korah against Moses and Aaron.)

Leviticus 11:1–15:33
Part 1C
Rituals for Purity

OVERVIEW

The psalmist's question "Lord, who may dwell in your sacred tent? Who may live on your holy mountain?" (Ps 15:1) is not one we ask. "Who can enter the church building on Sunday morning and sit in the congregation of God's presence?" seems like a question meant to repel people. It is not, as we say, "welcoming." Yet the "outsider" is not the one to whom this question is addressed; the psalmist's question is for the Israelite, the insider, who is making a pilgrimage to Jerusalem to worship at the temple and wishes to enter space hallowed by God's presence.

The entrance requirements of purity may seem superfluous to us. For Leviticus, however, purity was required in order to worship God at the tabernacle. God and the sanctuary were holy, and only the pure could enter and participate in its rituals. Only here could people sacrifice and receive forgiveness, or slaughter their peace offerings for its meat. It was essential for the people to know what defiled them and what measures were needed to become pure again so they could enter the tabernacle's precinct. After all, chapter 10 is a horrifying warning to those who would transgress God's holy presence *[Holy and Holiness, p. 302; Pure, p. 309]*.

This section concerning purity rituals is distinct from the rituals prompted by sin, being separated by chapters 8–10. This symbolizes the differences between the sins in Leviticus 4:1–6:7 (5:26) and the impurities found in Leviticus 11–15. The sins mentioned in 4:1–6:7 did not make a person impure. They did not impede people from coming to the tabernacle. In the case of unknown sin, how can a person know they are not fit to worship God? In the case of known sin, they need to come to the sanctuary's altar for forgiveness. By contrast, the impurities addressed below do keep people from entering the realm of the holy, but becoming impure is not sin, and no forgiveness is needed.

This point seems obvious from the food regulations and rituals of chapter 11. Some food choices cause defilement and others do not. When the wrong choice is made, the person becomes defiled. For these impurities, they need only to launder their clothes, bathe, and wait until evening. These ritual actions are commonplace. No priests or sacrifice is required.

Impurity is unavoidable. For example, after intercourse both the man and the woman must undertake a purity ritual (ch. 15). The production of semen and intercourse are natural events. Although a necessity for human existence, semen causes impurity. The same is true for ovulation, menstruation, and childbirth (ch. 12).

Impurity may also result from abnormal conditions as described in chapters 13 and 14. Such conditions are largely, if not entirely, outside a person's control. Examples include certain skin conditions or the growth of a certain mold in a house. These impurities can occur apart from human intention; they just happen. Because of the necessity or inevitability of impurity, its contraction is not prohibited: there is no prohibition against having mold in your house. Unlike sin, impurity does not necessarily transgress God's commandments. Rather, it is an expected part of daily life.

The food regulations in chapter 11 are an exception. In contrast to chapters 12–15, Leviticus 11 does prohibit the Israelites from eating certain animals. But these prohibitions are of a different sort than those found in the preceding chapters. Like the previous material, it concerns the transgression of a divine command. Unlike in the previous chapters, no forgiveness is needed. Eating a rabbit is not a sin. The purification rituals prescribed for such disobedience are "profane": there is no mention of priests, sacrifice, or sanctuary. In this way, chapter 11 marks a transition from sin to the purity regulations.

The confusion of impurity with sin is aided by the identical sacrifice being offered in chapters 4:1–6:7. The so-called "sin offering" (*ḥaṭṭa'ṭ*) is used both in rituals for forgiveness and in rituals for the restoration of ritual purity. The transfer of the translation "sin offering" to a ritual where no sin is mentioned or has been committed is unwarranted. Not only is impurity not a sin, but its outcome is becoming clean, not forgiveness. Thus the offering should rather be titled a "cleansing offering" and the ritual a "purification ritual." In the rituals in 4:1–6:7, the altar needs cleansing on account of sin. Here the altar needs cleansing on account of an impurity. (See notes on ch. 4 for comments on the forgiveness ritual and its sacrifice. For translating the name of this offering consistently as "cleansing" sacrifice or offering in both contexts, see *Atonement, p. 288.*)

Impurity is not a disease, but it can be contagious. A pure person cannot impart purity to an impure person, but the impure can make the pure dirty. Shaking hands with a clean hand does not make someone else's greasy hands clean. Thus a potentially defiled person might be quarantined until a decision could be made concerning their purity. Purity was a state to be maintained in the camp for the sake of entering the holy.

Why the actions and states named in chapters 11–15 cause impurity is unclear. Many attempts have been made at giving rational explanations. None are entirely satisfactory: logical inconsistencies simply exist in these regulations. With large land animals and fish, a general classification suffices to divide the impure from the pure. With birds, a list of unclean ones is given, not a category. Exceptions to a rule may be listed. Gaps must be filled in to make the system coherent. As a general statement, however, purity and impurity have to do with life and death. Giving birth, menstrual and seminal discharge, intercourse, and touching a carcass—any of these can transfer impurity. (See the extensive discussion of the prohibited animals and the laws of purity in Milgrom 1991: 718–36; Douglas 1966; Frevel and Nihan: 13–43; Nihan: 311–65; for an overview of purity laws in the Hebrew Bible, see Klawans 2004. A general discussion of clean and unclean in the Bible is found in *NIDB*, s.v. "Clean and Unclean.")

(TBC and TLC appear at the end of this unit, in the section on ch. 15.)

OUTLINE FOR PART 1C

Chapter 11 stands alone as a transitional chapter. Chapter 12 is tied to chapter 15, since chapter 12 assumes the menstruation regulations found in 15:19–24. Also, they are connected by subject matter: both concern issues of the beginning of life. Chapter 12 is about birthing. Chapter 15 is about semen and ovulation. Chapters 13 and 14 form a unit and have their own internal structure. The diagnoses for blemishes on the skin appear in 13:1-46, but the ritual for purification occurs later, in chapter 14. (For a recent discussion of the structure in these chapters, see Nihan.)

Rituals for Food Impurity, 11:1-47
Birthing Rituals, 12:1-8
Rituals for Blemishes, 13:1-14:57
Rituals for Reproductive Impurities, 15:1-33

Leviticus 11:1-47

Rituals for Food Impurity

PREVIEW

What? Impurity is not a sin? The sources of impurity are common, everyday things. Becoming pure requires only common activities that can be done at home. Chapter 11 is surprising.

First, we find that priests, sacrifices, and the tabernacle are neither mentioned nor needed for these purification rituals. The priests' responsibility is to teach the laity to distinguish between the clean and the unclean (Lev 10:10-11). Laypersons are to decide for themselves whether they are impure and what they need to do to regain purity. In some cases purification requires no action at all, since the person automatically becomes pure at sunset [*Pure, p. 309*].

Second, only in chapter 11 do we find prohibitions against defilement. Chapters 12–15 assume that defilement happens in the normal course of human life and is taken for granted. But breaking a dietary prohibition results not in "sin" but in impurity.

Many animals are mentioned in chapter 11. Some can be eaten, others cannot. Some, like the pig, are well known; others are obscure and their identity is unsure. This uncertainty is reflected in the English translations, which differ in their identification of some animals. Keep in mind that the animals are classified by how they appear, not by an anatomical analysis. For example, the cloven-hoofed animals have hooves that are completely and clearly divided. The camel has such a hoof, contrary to Leviticus 11:4. However, if just looking at, not examining, their hoof, it does not appear to be divided. Likewise, rabbits are classified as animals who chew the cud. Actually, however, they are not ruminants like cows. It just appears sometimes that they are chewing a cud (11:6).

After the introductory formula in verse 1, addressed to both Moses and Aaron, and concluded with a summary, the material in this section can be divided into four parts.

OUTLINE

Introduction, 11:1-2a
Clean and Unclean Animals, 11:2b-23
    11:2b-8   Larger Land Animals
    11:9-12   Aquatic Animals
    11:13-19 Birds
    11:20-23 Insects
Rituals for Impurity: Land Animals, 11:24-31
Passive Impurity, 11:32-38
Carcass Impurity, 11:39-43
Rationale and Summary, 11:44-47

EXPLANATORY NOTES

Introduction 11:1-2a

The food laws begin with God speaking to both Aaron and Moses, commanding them both (the "you" is plural) to repeat these instructions to the Israelites. First the permitted and proscribed animals are described. These animals are grouped into five categories: (1) land animals, (2) aquatic animals, (3) birds, (4) insects, and (5) pawed animals. Within each group the differences between the clean and unclean animals are given. As related in 10:10, it is the duty of the priests to teach the Israelites these differences *[Pure, p. 309]*.

Clean and Unclean Animals 11:2b-23

11:2b-8 Larger Land Animals

The word used for "animals" in verse 2b is normally used for larger beasts such as cattle. The criteria for permitted animals in this category are that they have a completely cloven hoof and that they chew their cud (v. 3). One of these features alone will not do. This is made clear in verses 4-7 by giving examples of animals that show only one of these features. First, there are animals like the camel that chew cud but do not appear to have a completely split hoof.

Second, there are animals like the pig that have a split hoof but do not bring up cud to chew again. Verse 8 adds that in addition to not eating the flesh of these animals, the Israelites should not even touch their carcasses. The carcasses of permitted animals, by necessity, can be touched.

Instructions regarding land animals with paws instead of hooves are given in verses 27-28 below. Not having hooves, the criterion of the split hoof cannot apply to them.

11:9-12 Aquatic Animals

These may be saltwater or freshwater creatures. To be clean they must show two features: they must have both fins and scales. If they do not, they are termed detestable, not impure. We assume that "detestable" means that they too are ritually unclean. As with the land animals, forbidden fish are not to be eaten, and their carcasses are detestable.

11:13-19 Birds

The language of detesting continues with the birds. Unlike in the preceding two groups, the forbidden birds are listed rather than described. It is not clear why these birds and only these are unclean. It is generally thought that this list represents birds of prey or those that eat meat, like the stork. But the list is hardly inclusive of all such birds.

11:20-23 Insects

All flying insects that walk on all fours. (The text reads lit. *All swarming birds that walk on all fours*, but the mention of walking on all fours excludes birds.) Yet this blanket rejection of all insects is qualified by a list of permitted insects (vv. 21-22). The permitted insects must have knees, or legs with a joint so that they can hop about. The permitted insects in this category are listed. All insects not mentioned as permitted are detestable.

Rituals for Impurity: Land Animals 11:24-31

Two more categories of land animal are added to those specified in verses 3-8. Animals with paws and short-legged animals that swarm on the ground are impure. Their carcasses also carry impurity. Here in verse 24 we return to the language of impure/unclean, which was used with the land animals in verses 3-8.

What happens if a person does touch or carry the carcass of an unclean land animal? Two levels of contamination are mentioned: touching the carcass and carrying it (vv. 24-25). If a person only touches the carcass, the person is impure until evening. Time allows the impurity to dissipate. However, if they have carried the carcass of such an animal, they must first launder their clothes and then wait until evening. Carrying makes garments impure.

In the case of the short-legged land animals *that move along the ground*, all are permitted except those specifically named in verses 29-30. Verse 31 further stipulates that these impure animals only contaminate when they are dead. The impurity contracted from such a dead animal lasts until evening.

Passive Impurity 11:32-38

If a person touches or carries the carcass of a forbidden animal, that person becomes unclean. What happens if such a carcass or part of it falls on something? This passive or inadvertent contamination affects different kinds of objects differently. If the object is made of wood or leather or cloth (v. 32), it requires immersion in water. The item then becomes ritually clean at evening time.

However, if the carcass should fall into a pot made of clay, the vessel and its contents become impure. The ceramic vessel must be broken. Verse 34 seems redundant, since verse 33 declared the contents of a contaminated vessel impure. Perhaps we should understand verse 34 as applying to wetting food with water coming from a contaminated vessel. The same rule applies to ovens or stoves made of clay, which must be smashed (v. 35).

Unlike water in a container, fresh natural water does not contract corpse contamination. Such water remains ritually pure even when a carcass falls into it. However, the person who removes the carcass from the well or cistern does become ritually impure from touching the carcass.

As for seed, matters are a bit more complicated. If all or part of a carcass falls on grain that can be sown, and these seeds are dry, they remain pure (v. 37). However, if water has been put on them (for soaking), they are affected by the carcass and become impure (v. 38).

Carcass Impurity 11:39-43

Having just addressed passive impurity from accidental contact with a carcass, the text now continues with instructions for dealing with impurity from animals that die of themselves (see 7:24; 17:15; 22:8).

First, concerning the hoofed animals, which can be eaten, touching their carcasses results in impurity lasting until evening. Eating of their flesh results in the need to launder one's clothes and wait until evening. The same principle applies to carrying the carcass: the person must launder their clothes and wait until evening.

Second, verse 42 concerns the "swarmers," a group that includes snakes and centipedes. The Israelites are to have nothing to do with them because they are abhorrent.

Rationale and Summary 11:44-47

The food regulations are necessary since Israel must be a holy people because their God is holy. As we know, the impure may not touch the holy or be in the presence of the holy God. God makes Israel holy, but to remain a holy people, they must not contaminate themselves with swarmers and creepers.

These are regulations that God has the right to require since God is the one who saved them and who delivered them from slavery in Egypt. God acted on their behalf so that as a free people this liberating God would be their God. As a result, since their God is holy, God's people must be holy.

Verses 46-47 conclude the chapter with a repetition of instructions concerning the hoofed animals and birds as well as the creepers in the water and the swarmers on land. These instructions, taught to the people by the priests, will enable them to differentiate between the animals from which they may eat and those that they may not eat or touch.

(TBC and TLC appear in the section on ch. 15.)

Leviticus 12:1-8
Birthing Rituals

PREVIEW
The modern reader may wonder why a purification ritual is necessary for childbearing. After all, having a child is a joy and a time of celebration! Yet even in our modern age childbirth is a time fraught with anxiety. Mothers still die unexpectedly in childbirth. Complications may take the life of the fetus at the last moment. It is a case of "It ain't over till it's over." Life and death are central concerns of the purity rituals, and birthing is the essential act of bringing a new life into the world, but it may take life. Having come through a pregnancy and childbirth safely, certain limitations are placed on the new mother.

The outline of this chapter is based on the "if . . . then" structure of case law [Law, p. 304].

OUTLINE
Quarantine for Birthing, 12:1-5
The Ritual for Purification, 12:6-8
    12:6-7 The First Option
    12:8   A Less Costly Option

EXPLANATORY NOTES

Quarantine for Birthing 12:1-5
Obeying God's command, Moses sets out the regulations for a mother's purification after the birth of a child. The birth of a male child

is treated first (vv. 2b-4). If the child is a male, the woman is ritually impure for seven days just as she would be after her menstruation (15:19-24).

On the eighth day the male child is circumcised. Knowledge of this ritual is assumed, since circumcision is mentioned nowhere else in Leviticus. Circumcision among the Hebrews is commanded in Genesis 17:9-14. It marked the male as being in covenant with God. Males not circumcised were excluded from God's people. Upon the birth of Isaac, Abraham obediently circumcised him on the eighth day (Gen 21:2-4). Any Gentile head of a household who lived among the Hebrews and who wished to participate in the Passover must be circumcised, along with all the males in his household (Exod 12:48), since Passover is a festival held at home and includes the whole family.

However, not all Hebrew males were circumcised on the eighth day. Joshua needed to perform a group circumcision on adult Hebrew males after they crossed the Jordan into Canaan (Josh 5:3). This group circumcision took place outside a sacred precinct and without the participation of a priest. In the New Testament we find that naming a child is connected with circumcision (Luke 1:59; 2:21).

After the circumcision of her son, the woman waits for thirty-three days, the time of her purification. These thirty-three days are called her *state of blood purification* (NJPS) *[Pure, p. 309]*. Since she has not yet carried out her purification ritual, she may not enter the sanctuary or touch anything holy. Presumably she may move about camp like anyone else. (In Ghana, women must stay in the house for seven days after the birth of a child. There is a special ceremony when the child leaves the house for the first time [Wesley Bergen, correspondence to author].)

The text now turns to the case of birthing a female child (v. 5). The instructions mirror those for bearing a son, except that now the mother must remain in her post-birthing state for sixty-six days instead of thirty-three days for a son. Again, she may resume ordinary activity.

The Ritual for Purification 12:6-8

The purification rituals that follow apply to the birth of either a female or a male child.

12:6-7 *The First Option*

The woman brings a year-old lamb for a whole burnt offering (see ch. 1) and a dove or a turtledove for a cleansing offering. She brings these to the entrance of the tabernacle and presents them to a priest. The priest presents the cleansing offering to God, making purification for her that erases any effect her impurity caused to the altar. (The offering up of the whole burnt offering is not mentioned. It would have followed the purification ritual, which comes first.) The result of the ritual is that she is pure [*Cleansing Offering, p. 297*].

12:8 A Less Costly Option

Not every family can afford to offer a sheep, however. In such a case, the woman could bring two birds, either doves or turtledoves. One would serve as the cleansing offering, and the other as a whole burnt offering (see 5:7 for the offering of two birds). Again, after the purification ritual for the altar, the woman becomes pure.

Why is there a period of thirty-three days before purification for a male child and sixty-six days for a female child? The text does not say, so we do not know. But one can suppose that a longer period of uncleanness or even becoming unclean might reflect positive value (as with touching or burying a corpse). After all, for the continuation of the community, women are more important than men. (For a recent treatment of the purity laws in Lev 12 and 15 and the status of women in Leviticus considered positively, see Goldstein).

(TBC and TLC appear in this section after ch. 15.)

Leviticus 13:1–14:57
Rituals for Blemishes

PREVIEW

Does acne bar one from the sanctuary? Do some burns prohibit a person from worship? There are impurities so severe that the person cannot be allowed into the tabernacle precincts. Furthermore, some impurities are considered contagious, so the impure person must be quarantined lest they infect others. A pure person may not contact such a person or, in the case of a house, enter the house. In extreme cases, the person is even banished from the camp.

The impurities in this section are all unnatural conditions over which a person has no control. These conditions are abnormal growths, eruptions, or rashes on a person's skin or clothing, as well as on the stones in the house wall. Such abnormal appearances bring impurity with them. We should not automatically assume, however, that these unnatural conditions were brought about by disease. For example, some are caused by burns (13:24). Clothes (13:47-59) and houses (14:34-57, esp. v. 55) can become impure. The notion that we are dealing with diseases is aided by the translations. For example, the NIV uses the translation *defiling skin disease* for people (13:2, emph. added), then switches to *defiling/spreading mold* for cloth and houses (13:47, 59; 14:34, emph. added), although the same Hebrew words are used in both situations. Why not "defiling condition" for the sake of consistency?

The KJV and its successor, the NRSV, label the impurities in chapters 13–14 as *leprosy* (13:2 KJV) or *leprous skin disease* (NRSV). However, more recent translations no longer consider the condition to be leprosy. Instead, we find *scaly affection* (13:2 NJPS). The reason for this shift is the realization that in Leviticus ṣara'at is not leprosy (see *NIDB*, s.v. "Leprosy"). Exactly what this term refers to is not certain. What is sure from the text is that ṣara'at defiles people, clothing, and houses. (For a discussion of what medical conditions might be denoted by ṣara'at, see Milgrom 1991: 774-76, 816-26).

Since a person with a skin condition may be shut up for seven days or longer, we might consider this a quarantine to prevent a contagious disease from spreading. However, the menstruating woman could pass on her unclean state to things and people. Obviously, menstruation is not a disease that can be caught. It was her impurity that was contagious (15:19-20). In what follows, instead of using the circumlocution "a defiling affliction," the conditions will be referred to as "blemishes." A blemish is a mark or growth that spoils the appearance of both people and things. Although the word "blemish" (*mum*) is not used in these two chapters, elsewhere in Leviticus it refers to "defects" that disqualify a person or thing from the realm of the holy. For example, some blemishes or disabilities disqualify a priest from offering sacrifices since they would defile God's holy sanctuary (21:17-23). Laypersons with a blemish may not tender sacrifices, may not approach the holy (22:20). An animal offered for a sacrifice must *be without blemish; there must be no defect in it* (22:21 NJPS).

OUTLINE

Introduction, 13:1
Blemishes on the Skin, 13:2-46
    13:2-17   Swelling, Scabs, and Spots
    13:18-23   Boils
    13:24-28   Burns
    13:29-46   Baldness and Other Blemishes
Blemishes on Garments, 13:47-59
The Purification Ceremony for Skin Blemishes, 14:1-32
    14:2-7   Stage 1: Reentry to the Camp
    14:8-9   Stage 2: Limbo
    14:10-20   Stage 3: The Final Purification Ritual
    14:21-32   An Alternative
Blemishes in Houses, 14:33-53
    14:36-45   Diagnosis of House Blemishes
    14:46-47   The Consequences of Entering or Using a Sealed House
    14:48-53   Purification of a Defiled House
Concluding Summary, 14:54-57

EXPLANATORY NOTES

Introduction 13:1

God now addresses both Moses and Aaron concerning blemishes that defile. This speech, like the one in chapter 12, is cast in the form of case law, with instructions for variations that may occur in diagnosis. While this material is directed to Moses and Aaron, the instructions are also for the laity. They must know when a blemish must be checked by a priest to determine whether it is defiling.

Blemishes on the Skin 13:2-46

13:2-17 Swellings, Scabs, and Spots

The Vocabulary, 13:2a. The meaning of many of the words used for blemishes in verse 2 and throughout chapters 13–14 is uncertain. Some terms occur only once in the Bible, and others occur only in chapters 13–14. With such a limited set of occurrences, their meanings must be deduced from their context. This situation allows for a range of suggestions. In verse 2, most agree that the first term should be translated *swelling*, since elsewhere it can mean "lifting up, exaltation" (*DCH*). The second term has been defined as "scabs" (*DCH*), "flaking skin" (*HALOT*), *rash* (NIV, NJPS), or *eruption* (NRSV). The final term, *shiny spot*, is generally understood as a bright or shiny spot on the skin.

The Defining Case, 13:2b-3. If a person has a swelling, scab, or a bright spot on their skin that could be a defiling blemish, the person is brought to Aaron or another priest. The priest does a visual examination of the sore. If the hair in the sore is white and the sore appears to go deeper than the skin, then the case is clear cut. The priest can make a diagnosis on the spot, pronouncing the person unclean. Defiling blemishes evidently look different from nondefiling ones, since no probing or cutting is involved. It may be like separating edible mushrooms from lethal ones. Written directions on how to tell the difference are not very assuring. Having an expert look gives us the confidence to eat the ones pronounced edible.

The First Subcase: Unclear Diagnosis, 13:4-6. What if there is a white spot, but it is not deeper than the skin and its hairs have not turned white? A decision cannot be made. Rather, it is a case of watchful waiting, and the person is isolated for seven days. If after seven days there is no change, then the person goes back into isolation for another seven days. If after fourteen days the sore is dark and has not spread, then the priest declares the person clean. The person must then wash their clothes to complete the purification process. Note that the person is pronounced "pure," not "healed": the point is ritual purity.

The Second Subcase: Reoccurrence, 13:7-8. What if the person is pronounced clean but then has a relapse? The blemish must be reexamined by the priest. If the priest observes that the spot has spread, he pronounces the person unclean. It is a defiling blemish and calls for a purification ritual (see ch. 14 for this ritual).

The Third Subcase Case: Chronic, 13:9-11. If a person has a defiling blemish, is brought to a priest for examination, and the priest sees that (1) there is a white swelling, (2) its hair has become white, and (3) there is live or raw flesh in the swollen area, then the person has a chronic condition. The presence of "living" or "raw" flesh indicates that this is an enduring problem.

The Fourth Subcase: Entire Body Affected, 13:12-13. If, however, the defiling blemish spreads over the entire body, then the priest pronounces the blemish to be nondefiling. The last clause of verse 13 adds that the blemish has turned white, that is, healthy skin. In the previous case the blemish was a white swelling, not an outbreak that covered all the skin.

The Fifth Subcase: Another Relapse, 13:14-17. If raw flesh (live flesh) appears (see vv. 9-11 above), then the person is unclean and the blemish has become defiling. But in cases where the relapse reverses itself and the blemish turns white again, the priest will pronounce the person clean once more.

13:18-23 Boils

The First Alternative, 13:18-20. These cases assume that a person has had boils and they have healed. Now, if the boil is replaced by a bright whitish, pinkish spot, then the priest must examine the blemish. If the priest determines that there is a depression at the spot and it has white hair, then the boil has been replaced by a defiling blemish.

The Second Alternative, 13:21-23. On the other hand, if the boil heals and a dark or dull blemish takes its place, then the priest isolates the person for seven days. If after seven days the blemish has spread, then the person is pronounced unclean. If, however, the blemish has not spread, it is not defiling. The person is clean.

13:24-28 Burns

The diagnosis for defiling burns parallels that of boils. A spot that is deeper than the skin and has white hairs is defiling. But if there are no white hairs, the spot is not lower than the skin, and it is dark, the person is quarantined. If after seven days the blemish has spread, it is defiling. But if it has not spread and remains dark, it is the normal swelling after a burn. The person is pronounced clean.

13:29-46 Baldness and Other Blemishes

The next set of cases begins with a new formula, *If a man or woman*, although the previous blemishes could also apply to a man or a woman.

The Standard Case, 13:29-34. If a blemish is deeper than the skin and the hair in it has changed color (yellow), then it is a defiling blemish. If the blemish does not have these characteristics, the person must be *shut up* for seven days. If after seven days the blemish has not spread and does not have yellow hairs, the person is then quarantined for another seven days. If at the end of the second quarantine the blemish has still not spread and affects only the skin, the priest declares the person clean. The person then washes their clothes, and they are clean. This procedure parallels the first case in this chapter.

In Case of a Relapse, 13:35-37. If the person needs to be checked a second time, the priest looks to see if the blemish has spread. If it has, the person has a defiling blemish. On the other hand, if the priest judges that the blemish has not spread and black hair grows in it, then the blemish has healed. The person is clean.

Bright Spots Alone, 13:38-39. If a person has white spots on their skin but the priest judges them to be dull white, then it is a rash that does not defile.

Hair Problems, 13:40-46. First is the case of baldness that is not a defiling blemish (v. 40). Likewise, if the person has a receding hairline, there is no problem (v. 41). However, if a reddish white eruption should occur on the person's pate or forehead, it is a defiling blemish. The priest examines the blemish. If it is a whitish red swelling that looks like a defiling skin blemish, then the person is "defiled" (v. 44). In such a case, special regulations apply (vv. 45-46). The defiled person must (1) tear their clothes, (2) let their hair loose, (3) cover their mustache, and (4) call out, *"Unclean! Unclean!"* for as long as the condition lasts. In addition, the person is banished; that is, they must live outside the Israelite camp. What happens when a person recovers from such a defiling blemish? The instructions for purification come at the beginning of chapter 14. But before the ritual for restoration of purity, the topic changes to blemishes on clothing.

Blemishes on Garments 13:47-59

If a wool or linen garment or something fashioned from leather has a greenish or pinkish blemish, it may be defiling and must be shown to the priest. After examining it, the priest may quarantine the object for seven days. If after seven days the blemish has spread, it is a malignant or persistent blemish, and the garment must be burned (v. 52). There is no cure for this type of defilement.

On the other hand, if the blemish has not spread, the garment is washed and set aside for another seven days (vv. 53-54). After seven days the blemish is washed again, but if the blemish still looks the same, even if it has not spread, the garment must be burned (v. 55). However, if the blemish looks different after washing, if it has darkened or become dull, then the blemished spot can be torn from the garment and the garment can thus be saved (v. 56). But if the blemish reoccurs on the rescued garment, it must be burned (v. 57). In the happy event that upon washing the garment the blemish disappears instead of only becoming darker, the garment is acceptable. After a second washing it is clean (v. 58).

Chapter 13 ends with a summary statement that applies only to blemished clothing (v. 59). This summary marks verses 47-59 as a self-contained unit that was attached to regulations concerning human blemishes. The insertion breaks the continuity of 13:1-46—the diagnosis of defiling blemishes—with chapter 14, which gives the purification rituals for those pronounced defiled in chapter 13.

The Purification Ceremony for Skin Blemishes 14:1-32

The purification rituals for those who have the skin blemishes described in 13:1-46 comes in 14:1-32. This unit has no direct attachment to the surrounding material. First, we find a change in addressee. Before and after this unit, both Moses and Aaron are addressed, but here only Moses is addressed. Second, verse 2 forms an envelope with verse 32. The unit ends as it began, enclosing the unit and giving it an air of independence.

The process of purification and restoration of a person banished for impurity (13:46) proceeds in three stages (see below). After the first ritual, they are clean enough to enter the camp but not to enter their home. After the second ritual, they become clean enough to approach the entry of the tabernacle. Finally, at the end of the purification ceremony, they are fully restored.

14:2-7 Stage 1: Reentry to the Camp

The purification process begins with the person being examined by a priest. Since the defiled person must live outside the camp, the priest leaves the camp to make a diagnosis. If the priest sees that the defiling condition no longer exists, he orders that four items be brought to him: (1) *two live birds* that are pure, (2) a *piece of cedar*, (3) *scarlet* cloth, and (4) *hyssop* (v. 4).

The word translated *scarlet* actually refers to a worm (see Jon 4:7) that was used to make a crimson or scarlet dye. Here we find "two worms" understood as two pieces of cloth or yarn that could be burned in a ritual (e.g., Num 19:6).

Hyssop is a plant whose identification is unknown. It could absorb or hold liquid like a sponge. At Passover, hyssop was used to place blood on the lintel and doorposts of a house (Exod 12:22). In John 19:29 it was used to lift sour wine to Jesus' lips. In Leviticus it occurs in purification rituals, as in the present text and in the ritual for the purification of a house (see below on vv. 49-52). It is also used in the red heifer ritual (Num 19:6, 18). It occurs metaphorically in Psalm 51:7 (9), where the psalmist prays to be cleansed with hyssop.

Once these items are assembled, the priest commands the slaughter of one of the birds over or into a clay pot with fresh water. A mixture of water and blood results. This is clear from verse 51 below, where the priest dips the four items *into the blood of the dead bird and the fresh water* (14:51). This is not a sacrificial ritual, since there is no altar and the place is not holy. It all takes place outside the camp.

The priest now takes the remaining live bird, the cedar wood, the scarlet cloth, and the hyssop and dips them into the blood-water mixture. He sprinkles the person undergoing purification seven times with the blood-water mixture, most likely using the hyssop, and pronounces the person clean (v. 7). The one being purified will be pronounced "clean" several times during this ritual.

The living bird that has been dipped into the blood-water mixture is sent away, never to return. (The use of the *piel* form of the verb here connotes sending off for good.) The sending away of the live bird dipped in blood-water is part of an elimination ritual: it presumably carries off the remnants of the defilement, as in chapter 16 the scapegoat carries away sin. Now freed of defilement, the person launders their clothes, shaves off all their hair, and bathes.

14:8-9 Stage 2: Limbo

The person now enters the camp but cannot go home. They must sit outside their house for seven days. The person is in a liminal state—in between classifications. They are no longer unclean but are not yet fully purified and integrated into the community. Being shaved shows that the person belongs to a group that is easily identified as "outsider" in the process of transformation to full membership within the camp.

The end of this seven-day transition period echoes its beginning. Again the person shaves their hair, but in a very scrupulous fashion: they must shave *all* their hair, including beard and eyebrows. Once again they are clean. The person has now completed their in-between state and are ready to finish the ceremony of purification and be restored to full membership in the community.

14:10-20 Stage 3: The Final Purification Ritual

On the eighth day the person comes to the sanctuary for the final rites. The person is to bring (1) two male sheep; (2) one female sheep, less than a year old; (3) a meal offering; and (4) a measure of oil. The priest now formally places the applicant for purification at the entrance to the tabernacle. This placement indicates for whom the following ritual is being performed:

1. First, one of the male sheep is presented as a penalty offering (see 5:5-13), and along with the measure of oil, it becomes a wave offering (sometimes called an "elevation offering"; see 7:29-31).

2. The priest now slaughters the sheep and places some of its blood on the applicant's right ear, thumb, and big toe, as was done in the consecration of the priests to the priesthood (8:23-24). Next, the priest pours oil into his palm and, using his finger, sprinkles it seven times in the presence of God and daubs some of it on the person's right ear, thumb, and big toe where the blood of the slaughtered

sheep was placed. The oil that remains is placed on the head of the applicant. In this way the priest makes purification for the person before God (14:18) *[Atonement, p. 288]*.

3. The ritual concludes with the normal sequence of sacrifices. First comes the cleansing offering, which purifies the altar on behalf of the unclean person. The whole burnt offering, along with the grain offering, marks the close of the ritual.

After the whole burnt offering, the text states the result: *Thus the priest makes purification for him and he is clean* (v. 20 AT). The statement that the person is clean has occurred twice already (vv. 8-9). The first statement marks the person's entry into the camp. The second marks the transition from the camp to the entrance of the tabernacle. Now, at the end of the ceremony, the person is once again declared "clean." The person has moved from being in transition to being a normal citizen.

This new status is the result of this last ceremony, in which two purification rites have occurred: first, after the application of oil to the supplicant (v. 18), and then again after the cleansing offering (v. 19 AT), where we find the priest making *purification for the one to be cleansed from their uncleanness*. Why isn't the person pronounced "clean" at that point? Perhaps it is because the ceremony needs to be completed before such a pronouncement can be given *[Cleansing Offering, p. 297]*.

14:21-32 An Alternative

Those who cannot afford the sheep or three-tenths of a measure of grain may bring one male sheep, a tenth of a measure of grain, and two turtledoves or pigeons. The ritual actions are the same as those given above. The ritual concludes with a summary statement that echoes verse 2, which begins the instructions for purification, thus enveloping this purification ritual.

Blemishes in Houses 14:33-53

The statement on blemishes in houses begins a new unit. First, God once again addresses both Moses and Aaron. Since the Israelites will occupy stone houses only after their arrival in Canaan, the instructions given here will come into effect only in the future, unlike the previous purification rituals, which could be practiced in the desert.

Only here is God the source of an impurity: a defiling blemish in a house. The language used is similar to the language of the blessings and curses found in 26:4, 6, 11, 17, 19, 30, and 31. These curses and blessings, likewise, can occur only after the Israelites are living in Canaan [Covenant, p. 298; Blessings and Curses, p. 295].

14:36-45 Diagnosis of House Blemishes

The priest first commands that the affected house be emptied so that its contents will not be contaminated by the blemish. When the house is emptied, the priest comes to the house to inspect the blemish. If the priest finds greenish or reddish depressions, or eruptions (a word that only occurs here), that penetrate the wall, the priest seals the house for seven days.

On the seventh day, the priest checks the blemish again. If the blemish has spread, then the stones are removed, the mortar scraped, and the defiling material is dumped in an unclean place outside the village or city. We assume that if the blemish has not spread, no further steps are necessary.

The removed stones are then replaced using new mortar, and the whole house is whitewashed. It is now as good as new. However, if the blemish should break out again, the priest must come back. If the blemish has spread again, then it is a defiling blemish. The house must be destroyed and the rubble removed to an unclean place outside the village or city.

14:46-47 The Consequences of Entering or Using a Sealed House

But what about people who enter a quarantined house? If they merely enter a sealed house, they are unclean until the evening. Waiting is enough for this level of impurity. If, however, they sleep or eat in the house, they must launder their clothes as well.

14:48-53 Purification of a Defiled House

Even if the blemish has not spread after the house has been whitewashed, the house must yet undergo a purification ritual. For this ritual, two birds, a piece of cedar wood, two pieces of scarlet material, and hyssop are gathered in preparation.

The priest slaughters one of the birds into a clay pot that is located over *living water* (v. 51 AT), water from a natural spring or flowing water, not stored water. The remaining items, including the living bird, are dipped into the blood-water mixture. The priest sprinkles toward or on the house seven times. Then the priest sends away the living bird to the fields or open countryside outside the city. The house is now pure. This completes another elimination ritual that removes the house's contamination from the camp and expels it to the surrounding wilderness.

Concluding Summary 14:54-57

These verses bring chapters 13 and 14 to a close. The summary at the end of this unit echoes its beginning in chapter 13, enclosing these two chapters within an envelope *[Literary Style, p. 306]*.

(TBC and TLC appear in this section after ch. 15.)

Leviticus 15:1-33
Rituals for Reproductive Impurities

PREVIEW

As for activities that result in life and joy and are considered to be a blessing, how can they be "impure"? Remember that we are not dealing with matters of right or wrong, but with states that prohibit a person from entering the tabernacle. These are "ritual impurities" in the sense that they prevent participation in the tabernacle rituals and are removed by a ritual for purity. A person who comes to church with greasy hands that would cause others to have greasy hands has an impurity. They should undergo a ritual of handwashing before entering church and become pure. They are not sinners, but they are unclean. In fact, they may have greasy hands because they did a proper action, such as getting a car running for someone stranded on the side of the highway.

Chapter 15 returns us to the topic of chapter 12: reproduction. Chapter 15 also has an affinity with chapter 11, the food regulations, since in both of these chapters nonpriestly purification rituals dominate. Like impurity from food, impurity from natural emissions is cured by laundering, bathing, or waiting until evening (see 15:5, 6, 7, 8, etc.). In cases of unnatural emissions, a purification ritual (*ḥaṭṭaʾt*; see ch. 4) is needed (15:15, 30). With these links to the foregoing chapters 11 and 12, Leviticus 15 brings the purity regulations to a close.

The following outline shows a well-organized arrangement. For the man, unnatural seminal emissions come first, followed by regular emissions, and then intercourse. The latter, involving both men and women, forms a bridge to the discussion of female emissions. Menstruation comes first, unnatural vaginal emissions last. This inverts the order found with male seminal emissions and makes the regulations for men and women a mirror image of each other. (This structure is known as a chiasm, with intercourse at its center [*Literary Style, p. 306*].)

Chapter 15 closes with an exhortation and warning to adhere to these purity regulations lest the community and thereby the tabernacle become defiled. If this happens, God's presence will withdraw from the tent of meeting, and presumably the Israelites will then perish because of their impurities.

OUTLINE

Male Seminal Emissions, 15:1-17
    15:1-2   Introduction
    15:3-17   Male Emissions
Intercourse, 15:18
Female Emissions, 15:19-30
    15:19-24   Menstruation
    15:25-30   Abnormal Vaginal Secretion
Conclusion to the Purity Regulations, 15:31-33

EXPLANATORY NOTES

Male Seminal Emissions 15:1-17

15:1-2 Introduction

Once again God addresses Moses and Aaron, commanding them to relay the following instructions to the people. In verse 2b we get the general case to which subcases are to be appended: *When anyone has a discharge from their sexual organ, they are unclean* (AT). The word for "genital organ" literally means *flesh* (v. 2 KJV). The same word is used both for the penis and for the vagina (see v. 19 below). Since this heading includes cases for both men and women, *anyone* is a better translation than *any man*.

15:3-17 Male Emissions

Abnormal Emissions, 15:3-12. Verse 3 begins the rules concerning male seminal emissions. First comes the irregular case. The irregularity may either be a continuing leakage or a blockage so that there is no discharge at all. The person is now unclean and contagious.

Impurity can be caught by touching a bed or chair used by the impure person. Also, if the unclean person touches anyone or if he spits on someone, that person is unclean. As with a chair or bed, if an impure person uses a saddle, those who touch or carry it are contaminated. However, if the unclean person washes his hands, he does not pass on his defilement to another. Finally, as for kitchen items, if he touches something ceramic, it must be broken, presumably because it is porous (and cheap). If he touches something of wood, it can be washed and reused. In all these cases of transmitted defilement, the cure is natural: washing, laundering, or waiting until evening. No priest is involved.

Purification, 15:13-15. When the source of the man's impurity disappears and his genitals function normally, he needs to undergo a purification ritual. The procedure is much like that of a menstruating woman (see below). First he must count seven days for his purification. Then he launders his clothes, washes himself, and becomes clean. On the eighth day he brings two pigeons or two doves to the door of the tabernacle and hands them to a priest. One of the birds is sacrificed as a cleansing offering, and the other as a whole offering. Thus the priest makes purification for the person *[Cleansing Offering, p. 297]*.

Normal Emissions, 15:16-17. All seminal emissions defile a man—even natural, normal emissions. For the man himself, purification is achieved through washing and waiting until evening. Cloth or leather touched by semen must be laundered; like the person, it does not become clean until evening.

Intercourse 15:18

If a man has sexual intercourse with a woman, then both become impure: the woman because semen has also touched her. The solution is the same as for the man by himself: they both must wash and wait until evening.

Female Emissions 15:19-30

15:19-24 Menstruation

For the menstruant, her impure period lasts for seven days. During this time defilement comes through touching her or lying or sitting on furniture she has used. Purification comes through laundering, washing, and waiting until evening. In cases of a person touching her, the person becomes pure with the coming of evening (e.g., vv. 19, 23).

Finally, if a man has intercourse with a woman during her menstrual period, he becomes defiled for seven days. During this time any bed upon which he lies is also defiled. Since the regulations for purification after intercourse have been given above, we can assume that the same purification ritual was followed in this case.

We expect, but do not find, a ritual for the purification of the menstruant. This is striking since in a normal case of male seminal emission, a purification ritual is required, and even the female partner must undertake a purification process. We will notice a similar anomaly in the following case of an abnormal vaginal flow.

15:25-30 *Abnormal Vaginal Secretion*

This unit ends where it began, with an abnormal emission (or lack thereof in the case of a man). If the woman has a hemorrhage or menstruates beyond a regular time, then she becomes impure. In either of these cases, the rules for normal menstruation apply and are summarized in verse 27b. Since an abnormal flow is causing her defilement, her purification cannot begin until the abnormal flow ceases. When this happens, as in the case of the man, she is to count seven days and then will become clean.

Again, as in the case of the man, on the eighth day she is to bring two doves or pigeons to a priest at the entrance of the sanctuary. One will serve as a cleansing offering and the other as a whole offering, probably expressing thankfulness at being free from her irregularity. The priest thereby makes purification for her on account of her unclean flow [Cleansing Offering, p. 297].

What is missing from the cases of the woman is the mention of laundering and washing before the woman becomes pure. Compare verse 13: the man counts seven days, and on the eighth day he launders his clothes, washes himself, and becomes clean. In the present case, the woman counts seven days, and then she becomes pure (v. 28). No laundering or bathing is required. The absence of laundering and bathing has also been noted in the regulations for menstruation. This deviation can also be seen in the case of a man having intercourse with a menstruating woman: he is impure for seven days. He need not launder his clothes or bathe.

Several suggestions have been given to explain these anomalies. The usual explanation is that the woman can be assumed to have performed the same rituals as the man. What weighs against this suggestion is that repetition is quite frequent in Leviticus, so why would an important ritual act be omitted in these cases? This caveat is particularly weighty in verse 28: *When she is cleansed from her discharge, she must count off seven days, and after that she will be ceremonially clean.* Compare this with *When a man is cleansed from his discharge, he is to count off seven days for his ceremonial cleansing; he must wash his clothes and bathe himself with fresh water, and he will be clean* (15:13). It seems problematic that such an important part of this purification ritual would be omitted. Any such solution is a guess. The plain sense is that the woman does not need to undergo the same rituals as the man.

Conclusion to the Purity Regulations 15:31-33

The purity regulations in chapters 11-15 conclude with verses 31-33, directed to Moses and Aaron: *You must keep the Israelites separate . . .* (v. 31). The verb translated *keep separate* may also mean "to guard against" (*DCH*) and can be translated *You shall put the Israelites on guard* (NJPS). The Israelites must not regard being ritually unclean as a trifling matter, because their uncleanness could defile the tabernacle—the very dwelling place of God's presence—that is in their midst.

The clash between impurity and the holy has already been illustrated in the death of Aaron's two sons (Lev 10:1-3). Their bringing *strange* (KJV) or *foreign fire* (AT) into the tabernacle clashed with the holiness of God and caused their death. It is imperative that the Israelites be scrupulous about their purity when they approach the altar in the courtyard of the tabernacle.

Milgrom argues that in fact the defiled person does not need to come to the sanctuary to defile it (Milgrom 1991: 946). He observes that the addressee is "the sons of Israel," the entire Israelite nation, and that plural pronouns are used in this passage. The whole nation is to be on guard against defilement because the defilement of the people will lead to defilement of the sanctuary. Consequently, they, the Israelite people, will die.

How the tent and its objects could become contaminated even from a distance is unclear. In any case, the previous purification rituals have removed defilement, since cleansing blood was applied to the altar. However, some sins and defilements would be unknown but yet have their effect on the holy. The remaining influence of known sins and defilements as well as those that were unknown needed to be removed. (See Milgrom 1991: 254-61 on the effect of sins committed at a distance.)

The final two verses, 15:32-33, return to the overall topic of chapter 15: discharge from sexual organs. Verse 32 repeats verse 2 and along with verse 33 summarizes the chapter.

THE TEXT IN BIBLICAL CONTEXT
Individual Impurity but Social Consequences

The focus and central concern of these regulations is keeping the impure apart from the holy. This is not a trifling issue: it can be a matter of life and death (as in ch. 10).

The purity regulations in this section concern individuals and individual cases, but there are social effects. Individual cases can be contagious and bring about the impurity of others, as chapter 14 illustrates. Quarantine may be necessary to decrease the risk of contamination (ch. 13). Fortunately, in the most ordinary cases—becoming impure through diet or sexual relations—the process of purification is easy: normal hygiene and time suffice.

Even in the case of a man having intercourse with a menstruating woman, purification depends on time. The man becomes impure for seven days just like his partner (15:19-24). This act is one among many other sources of impurity that disqualify a person from participating in worship at the sanctuary.

It is thus very important that for the most common sources of impurity—food and sexual relations—no religious ceremony is needed. Purification is reached by some combination of bathing, laundering clothes, and waiting until evening. Otherwise, most of the people would be impure most of the time, and this would place too heavy a load on the altar and the priests there.

We find a different solution for having sexual relations with a menstruating woman. Among the prohibited sexual acts we find *Do not approach a woman to have sexual relations during the uncleanness of her monthly period* (Lev 18:19). This is an apodictic law such as we find in the Ten Commandments. There are no mitigating circumstances, no exceptions, and no punishment. Just don't do it! However, after the list of negative commands concerning sexual relationships, we find a penalty that applies to all of them: *Everyone who does any of these detestable things—such persons must be cut off from their people* (Lev 18:29). This means that the man who has intercourse with a menstruating woman must be cut off just like one who has intercourse with his mother. (Being *cut off* seems to be a divine punishment meted out to those who commit severe transgressions *[Cut Off, p. 299]*.) On the one hand, lying with a menstruating woman results in a minor impurity (ch. 15); on the other hand, in chapter 18 such impurity results in a severe punishment.

In both chapters 15 and 18 we have cases of impurity, not sin. The difference is that in chapter 15, sexual relations with a menstruant causes *ritual impurity*. Chapter 18 speaks of an *abomination* (*toʿebah* v. 26 NET), which is not contagious and for which purification is not possible. This impurity, however, does transmit impurity to the land of Israel. As a result, *the land ... will vomit you out for defiling it [ṭamaʾ, as in ch. 15], as it vomited out the nation that was before you* (Lev 18:28 NRSV; see EN on ch. 18 for a fuller discussion).

The severity of intercourse with a menstruating woman being equated with adultery or intercourse with a father's wife is also found in Ezekiel 18:6 and 22:10. In Ezekiel 18, the prophet contrasts the way of the righteous (vv. 5-9) with the way of the wicked (vv. 10-14). This context is significant. The righteous person does not practice idolatry or sexual immorality. In addition, the righteous person "does not oppress anyone, but returns what he took in pledge for a loan. He does not commit robbery but gives his food to the hungry and provides clothing for the naked. He does not lend to them at interest or take a profit from them. He withholds his hand from doing wrong and judges fairly between two parties" (Ezek 18:7-8).

The context in Ezekiel 22 is similar. A long list of Judah's sins begins with the shedding of innocent blood in the midst of the city and ends as follows: "In you are people who accept bribes to shed blood; you take interest and make a profit from the poor. You extort unjust gain from your neighbors. And you have forgotten me, declares the Sovereign LORD" (Ezek 22:12).

In the biblical tradition, sexual relations with a menstruating woman has escalated from being a minor impurity in chapter 15 to becoming a moral impurity that affects the nation's fate. The first step was taken by Leviticus 18, then in Ezekiel, God made it part of a list of sexual and social crimes. What was first a matter of ritual purity has become a moral matter on a par with lending at interest or taking a profit from the poor. The one is as morally depraved as the other. (See Klawans 2000 for the interplay of purity and sin as well as a critique of Milgrom's position. For an overview, see Klawans 2004.)

Requirements for Entering God's Presence

In the biblical tradition, the notion of prerequisites for worship was kept alive, as in Psalm 15:

> ¹ LORD, who may dwell in your sacred tent?
>   Who may live on your holy mountain?
> ² The one whose walk is blameless,

>   who does what is righteous,
>   who speaks the truth from their heart;
>   ³ whose tongue utters no slander,
>   who does no wrong to a neighbor,
>   and casts no slur on others;
>   ⁴ who despises a vile person
>   but honors those who fear the LORD;
>   who keeps an oath even when it hurts,
>   and does not change their mind;
>   ⁵ who lends money to the poor without interest;
>   who does not accept a bribe against the innocent.
>
>   Whoever does these things
>   will never be shaken.

The focus has shifted to morality. This list describes the person whom God desires as a worshiper. It may be that a church building is open to all, but who are those whom God seeks to enter for worship? Placing such a text over the entrance to a sanctuary would be honoring the notion that God has expectations of those who would worship in God's presence. It would link life with worship, as did the purity laws. Likewise, in John 4:23, Jesus states that God "seeks" those who "worship the Father in spirit and truth" (NRSV).

Psalm 50:8-15 is another text that promotes the notion of appropriate entrance into God's presence, while placing the value of sacrifice into appropriate context. God does not need sacrificial animals for food but delights in receiving thank offerings for the blessings and deliverance that God provides *[Worship and Ethics, p. 320]*.

Jesus and Paul on Ritual and Social Implications

One might think that Jesus abolished the purity laws of Leviticus or at least paid them little or no attention. However, this is not entirely correct. For example, after Jesus healed a leper, he commanded him, "Go, show yourself to the priest and offer the sacrifices that Moses commanded for your cleansing, as a testimony to them" (Mark 1:44 // Matt 8:2-4). In like manner, Jesus commanded lepers in Luke 17:14, "Go, show yourselves to the priests." Since the temple was in Jerusalem, Jesus' command could only be carried out when these lepers went to Jerusalem.

During Jesus' ministry in Galilee, there was no need to maintain the laws governing ritual purity that we find in Leviticus 11–15. It was only in Jerusalem and at the temple that purity was necessary. Thus Jesus' unconcern with purity, considered more broadly, was probably no different from that of most people living in Galilee. Indeed, there was no agreement among the Jews of Jesus' time about how to practice the law. Hillel and Shammai, the leading teachers just before Jesus, and their respective students were bitter enemies on how to be faithful to the law (see Ben-Shalom; for the extent to which Jesus' practice and teaching fell within the bounds of the Judaisms of his time, see Sanders 1985).

The notions of temple and purity became a helpful touchstone for Paul. The idea of the Christian congregation as a place of God's presence demanded a certain level of moral purity for its members. Key passages include 1 Corinthians 3:16-17 and 6:19-20, in which Paul likens the body of believers to God's sanctuary. Similarly, in 2 Corinthians 6:16, Paul posits that the local congregation and its members are God's temple. To buttress this point, he quotes from Leviticus 26:11-12: *I will live with them and walk among them, and I will be their God, and they will be my people.* The consequence is the need for purity: "Let us purify ourselves from everything that contaminates body and spirit, perfecting holiness out of reverence for God" (2 Cor 7:1). While the focus and location may have changed, Paul insists that God's presence and the need for purity are linked.

In Leviticus, ritual purity could be contagious. Moral impurity was not. But for Paul, moral impurity was also contagious: "You must not associate with anyone who claims to be a brother or sister but is sexually immoral or greedy, an idolater or slanderer, a drunkard or swindler. Do not even eat with such people" (1 Cor 5:11). Indeed, Paul urges the Corinthians to be vigilant in maintaining the suitability of the congregation for God's presence: "Expel the wicked person from among you" (1 Cor 5:13). (Resources for understanding Paul's position can be found in Lanci and in Rosner.)

THE TEXT IN THE LIFE OF THE CHURCH

The Relevance of Purity

The purity regulations found in Leviticus 11–15 may well be viewed as irrelevant. They are far removed from us in time and place and reflect different assumptions about the world. Our situation is vastly different: we no longer live around the tabernacle, with God's presence in it. The problem addressed by these laws, the contact of the impure with the holy, is not our problem. In our secular age, communion may be the only time we think about the presence of the holy in our midst. Remnant influences of these laws may exist in some Christian traditions in which some women do not take communion when they are menstruating (personal communication with author about practice among the Russian Orthodox).

We do, however, seek some explanation for this material. Surely these laws cannot just be irrational superstition. The most common way of grounding these regulations is to provide a positive rationale for them. Perhaps these commands were given for hygienic reasons: pigs carry trichinosis, so that may be why they were prohibited. Or the commands may be concerned with community health, isolating people with a contagious disease. Or there may be theological reasons, like keeping phenomena concerning life and death apart from the practices of worship. In this commentary the attempt has been to understand them, not to provide a rationale for them or to judge them.

Is not knowing the rationale for a law reason enough to ignore it? Must there be a rationale that justifies a law in order for it to be valid? *The Bible is more concerned with practice than with rationale.* Why honor father and mother, for example? We don't know what this command means in practice, but there surely must be some reason for it. Regardless of our lack of knowledge and our uncertainty about what significance it has for us, we regard it as a valid command and think it should have some bearing on relationships between parents and their children. Exodus 21:15 reads, "Anyone who attacks [strikes] their father or mother is to be put to death." We may not agree with the punishment, but we know that striking a parent is not honoring them. But *why* should children honor their father or mother? Should children agree to a rationale before they can be expected to do so? Who decides what it means for a child?

Perhaps the rationale for a command rests on a sense of community, what is best for the common good. In Leviticus, the individual Israelite was understood to be embedded in a community and as part of this community lived in the presence of God. What an individual Israelite did could affect another individual's participation in tabernacle worship and eventually affect the presence of God for the entire community. In essence, the question was not about individual behavior but about what type of community Israel would be. Would it be a community suitable for God's presence?

Paul's insight that moral impurity is contagious may well serve individuals and congregations. First, the congregation is a spiritual community in which the individual's own spiritual welfare is linked to the community as a whole. A community that seeks God's presence in worship is a necessary resource in an individualized society. How congregations define moral purity and cultivate the sense that their sanctuary is a place of God's presence may be unclear and may vary in different contexts, but in light of the biblical witness it is not an insignificant issue. In this perspective, the community is not about keeping the impure out, but as portrayed by Paul, it is about becoming a community for whom each individual is important for the spiritual well-being of the whole. If this process of transformation stalls, the community will likely decline in value as a place to experience God.

Part 2
A Hinge

Leviticus 16:1–17:16

OVERVIEW

Leviticus 16 is the capstone of the first part of Leviticus, chapters 1–15. The central question in these chapters is, How do we worship the God in whose presence we live? First, this meant bringing freewill offerings expressing joy and thanksgiving to God (chs. 1–3). Second, it meant performing purification rituals in order to receive forgiveness from sin, thus enabling and sustaining a relationship with God (chs. 4–7). Third, since only the pure may contact the holy, individuals coming to the tent needed to be cleansed from their impurities in order to approach God's presence (chs. 11–15). Lack of purity within the community affects the entire community: *You shall put the Israelites on guard against their uncleanness, lest they die through their uncleanness by defiling My Tabernacle which is among them* (15:31 NJPS).

Now in chapter 16 we learn how to cleanse the tabernacle from all accumulated sin and defilement of the people and to restore it to its pristine state, as at the time of its dedication in chapter 9. Chapter 17 is linked to the rituals of purification that preceded them, especially the cleansing found in chapter 16 (Zenger). In chapter 17 we find the explanation for what gives blood the cleansing power exhibited in chapter 16. Functioning as a supplement to chapter 16, it is tightly connected to it.

After chapter 17 we move from the realm of ritual to the realm of everyday life. How should Israel live in the presence of God? This change in subject matter clearly separates chapter 17 from what follows in chapter 18, which focuses on moral purity. Thus chapters 16 and 17 are a distinct unit and form a hinge as Leviticus swings from ritual to common life (Zenger; Seidl). What unites chapters 1–15 with 18–27 is the theme of holiness, which is found in both. However, chapters 1–15 define holiness in general as the property of things, while chapters 18–27 define holiness as an attribute of individuals (see ch. 19).

OUTLINE FOR PART 2
The Day of Cleansing, 16:1-34
Why Blood Has Power of Removal, 17:1-16

Leviticus 16:1-34
The Day of Cleansing

PREVIEW

In the absence of old-fashioned revival meetings in which people confess their shortcomings and pledge to do better, how did Israel deal with the sins and impurities of the past? The Day of Cleansing is the answer. The purpose of the extended ceremony described in chapter 16 is to cleanse the tabernacle and its furnishings from all sins and impurities and to eliminate them entirely from the camp. This housecleaning ensures the continuation of God's presence in the tabernacle and the Israelites' approach to God. A goal of this cleansing ceremony is the restoration of the tabernacle to its original state. This differs from the installation of priests and the inauguration of worship in chapters 8–9, whose goals were founding the priesthood and commencing worship at the sanctuary. That was a historic event and could not be repeated. As time went on, however, the holy became encumbered by sin and impurity. A house is built once, but it often needs to be cleaned or refurbished.

Suggestive of the difference between founding and refurbishing is the use of the verb "to cleanse or sterilize" (*ḥaṭṭeʾ*) in 8:15 and 9:15. Sterilization describes the effect of the first sacrifice ever performed on the courtyard altar (8:15) and the initial sacrifice of the people (9:15). In fact, 9:15 expressly links the two rites: *as he did with the first one* (cf. 9:15 NET). These two sacrifices transformed the altar from the profane to the holy. After this preparation, God's presence filled the tabernacle.

While the verb "to cleanse or sterilize" (*ḥaṭṭeʾ*) occurs in both founding ceremonies of chapters 8 and 9, it does not occur in chapter 16. The altar has already been sterilized and is now holy. God's presence already abides in the tabernacle, and worship there is in full swing. What is now needed is a "polishing" of what is already holy.

This difference in goal is shown by its language. In previous chapters a sacrifice purifying the altar was followed by forgiveness (4:1–6:7) or by the attainment of purity (chs. 11–15). In chapter 16 the cleansing sacrifices purge the sancta (sacred objects) of contamination caused by the people's sins and impurity as a prelude to their removal from the Israelite camp. *Forgiveness does not occur in chapter 16.*

Chapter 16 begins with a prologue and ends with an epilogue, forming an envelope around the cleansing ceremony *[Literary Style, p. 306]*. The prologue links chapter 16 to the event portrayed in 10:1-2. The epilogue converts the cleansing, elimination, and restoration ceremony into an annual event.

The restoration ceremony itself is divided into three parts: (1) the initial preparatory rituals that differentiate Aaron from his previous roles through his donning of special clothes for this ceremony; (2) the cleansing rituals of restoration and elimination, the focal point of this ceremony; and (3) the final rituals that reverse the initial rituals of differentiation: Aaron once more dons his everyday "uniform." (For a structure based on a very close reading of the text, see Jürgens: 66–72.)

OUTLINE

Prologue, 16:1-2
The Restoration Ceremony, 16:3-28
    16:3-11   Preparation
    16:12-19   The Cleansing Rituals
    16:20-22   The Elimination Ritual
    16:23-28   Concluding Rituals
Epilogue, 16:29-34

EXPLANATORY NOTES

Prologue 16:1-2

Chronologically, chapter 16 follows chapter 10, where Nadab and Abihu died for improperly entering the tent of meeting. This event triggers the instructions of chapter 16, which begins with *The LORD spoke to Moses after the death of the two sons of Aaron*. The purpose of these instructions is to enable Aaron to know when and how he may safely enter the shrine.

Given the tight connection between these two chapters, it might seem that chapter 16 should follow immediately after chapter 10. However, chapter 16 mentions the people's uncleanness and their defilement of the sanctuary, while chapter 10 charges the priests with teaching this distinction to the people (vv. 10-11). Since chapters 11-15 provide these necessary instructions concerning defilement and purity, it makes sense to break the narrative continuity in order to insert this material, which ends with a warning against defiling the sanctuary: *You must keep the Israelites separate from things that make them unclean, so they will not die in their uncleanness for defiling my dwelling place, which is among them* (Lev 15:31).

Up to now the high priest has only entered the first room of the tent in order to place blood on the incense altar (4:5-7, 16-18). However, now the priest must go into the most holy space, where God *appear[s] in the cloud over the cover* (16:2 NJPS). Such penetration into the holy of holies demands special preparation rituals.

The Restoration Ceremony 16:3-28

16:3-11 Preparation

The following instructions begin a long, complex ceremony that uses a variety of rituals and ritual gestures. First, Aaron must have on hand a young bull for a cleansing offering and a ram for a whole burnt offering. These offerings will be offered on his own behalf and that of his family. Second, he must bathe and put on special vestments. (For the normal high-priestly dress, see 8:7-9.) Third, he must receive two buck goats for cleansing rituals and one ram for a whole burnt offering from the congregation.

Fourth, Aaron offers the priests' bull as a cleansing offering, making purification for himself and his family. The point of this sacrifice is only purification of the altar since there is no mention of sin or forgiveness of sin. This prepares the courtyard altar for the coming rituals. Verse 6 is repeated in verse 11, forming an envelope around verses 7-10. This break and resumption separates the ritual gestures in verses 7-10 from the surrounding material. It also highlights their importance in the ceremony as a whole.

Fifth, Aaron casts lots over the two goats that he received from the people. Although both were originally designated as cleansing offerings, only one will serve this purpose. The goat chosen for God is designated as the goat for the cleansing ritual. The goat chosen for Azazel is left standing alive before the sanctuary. Its use is deferred until after the cleansing rituals have been completed *[Cleansing Offering, p. 297]*.

16:12-19 The Cleansing Rituals

Although it is not mentioned here, Aaron has collected the blood of the priests' offering (v. 6), which he will now apply to the tent and its furnishings. He will begin with the most holy place inside the tent and end at the courtyard altar. But in order to enter the holy of holies, he must take an additional preparatory step (v. 12). He takes a scuttle and places live coals from the courtyard altar on it. He also takes a fistful of finely ground incense. With this proper fire and smoke, he can now enter the tent.

The Ritual Begins, 16:12-15. Aaron now enters the tabernacle and stands before the ark in the holy of holies. As protection, he must place incense on the coals so that a cloud of incense screens the ark from his view. In this way he may approach the ark and not die. This cloud of incense covers the lid, or cover (*kipporet*), that protects the tablets contained in the ark. These are the stone tablets upon which Moses wrote the Ten Commandments at Sinai (Exod 34:27-29) and later placed in the ark (Exod 25:16). These commandments represented the basic stipulations or requirements of the people's covenant with God.

Mercy seat has been the traditional translation given for *kipporet*, as in the NRSV. More recent translations call it an *atonement cover* (NIV) or *atonement plate* (NET), which was set on top of the ark. It was made of pure gold and had two cherubim hammered out of the gold at each end. It was placed upon the ark and, like a lid, it covered the tablets (Exod 26:34). The notion that *kipporet* was an atonement cover arises because the word translated *cover* is derived from the word *kipper*, which is variously rendered *purge, expiate,* or *atone*. However, the simplest interpretation would be to translate it as *cover*, which is what it does (see the discussion in Milgrom 1991: 1014).

After the ark is screened by a cloud of incense, Aaron can proceed with the cleansing ritual. He takes some of the bull's blood (sacrificed in v. 6) and with his finger sprinkles it seven times on the lid of the ark and seven times before the lid. He then exits the tent and slaughters the people's buck goat that was chosen by lot to be a cleansing offering (v. 9). Aaron reenters the holy of holies with its blood and sprinkles it just as he did with the blood of the bull (v. 15) *[Cleansing Offering, p. 297].*

The Purpose of This Ritual Sprinkling of Blood, 16:16-17. The rationale for the above ritual differs in the translations. Aaron performs these rituals either to *make atonement for the Most Holy Place* (NIV) or to *purge the Shrine* (NJPS). An interpretive question arises: Does Aaron make atonement *for* the holy place, or does he do something *to* the holy place? That Aaron does something *to* the holy place—he cleanses it—is seen from three lines of evidence:

1. The first evidence is semantic. What sense does it make to atone on behalf of or for an object? What act has the ark committed for which atonement needs to be made? Elsewhere, purification is made for sins committed by people (ch. 4).

2. The second evidence is grammatical. We find summaries of this ritual in verses 20 and 23. In these summaries the tent and the altar are unambiguously designated as direct objects in Hebrew; that is, they receive the action of the verb: *When he has finished purging the Shrine, the Tent of Meeting, and the altar . . .* (v. 20 NET, NJPS). *He is to purify the Most Holy Place, he is to purify the Meeting Tent and the altar* (v. 33 NET). Something very special is taking place here. Once a year the holy place and things were purified and restored to their original state.

3. The third evidence is contextual. Reading verse 16 in light of its parallels makes contextual sense. The altar needed cleansing *because of the uncleanness and rebellion of the Israelites, whatever their sins have been* (v. 16). This purification is done *on his [Aaron's] behalf, on behalf of his household, and on behalf of the whole assembly of Israel* (v. 17b NET). Atonement, cleansing, is made for the people, not for the ark! (Note: In v. 16, *the most holy place* is not a direct object but the object of a preposition, usually meaning "on." But translating *he shall purge/atone upon the most holy place* does not make sense and does not occur in the translations cited. On v. 16, see Hartley: 240; on the word *kipper*, expiate/cleanse/atone, see Milgrom 1991: 1079-84; Sklar 2008: 22-23. For a dissenting position, see Kiuchi: 87-94. On atonement as cleansing, see the essay *Atonement, p. 288*.)

4. Finally, there is no forgiveness mentioned, which is essential to the forgiveness ritual for sin. Thus these rituals have something different in mind: cleansing.

Cleansing the Courtyard Altar, 16:18-19a. The ritual in verses 18-19 concludes the ceremony of cleansing and restoration. Aaron exits the tent and comes to the altar *that is before the LORD* (v. 18). Which altar is meant? In 4:6-7, when blood is sprinkled on the incense altar, it is identified as the altar *before the LORD in the tent of meeting* (Lev 4:7a). The courtyard altar is called *the altar of burnt offering at the entrance to the tent of meeting* (Lev 4:7b). However, since here Aaron has exited the tent, it is the courtyard altar that is called *the altar that is before the* LORD.

The Reason for the Cleansing Ceremony, 16:19b. When the ceremony of cleansing is complete, the reason for it is expressly stated: *to cleanse it and to consecrate it from the uncleanness of the Israelites* (v. 19b). The courtyard altar, along with the tent and the sacred objects in it, have been cleaned and are once again in their original holy state as they were after Moses consecrated them (8:11, 15)

16:20-22 The Elimination Ritual

The beginning of verse 20 marks the end of the previous rituals: *When he has finished purifying the holy place, the Meeting Tent, and the altar* (16:20 NET). Having completed the ritual of cleansing, Aaron now turns to the live goat that has been standing before the tent during the preceding ritual:

1. Aaron places both hands on the head of the living goat (v. 21a). Up until now, we have found the owner of the sacrificial animal placing a single hand on the animal. At 1:4 we presented the arguments for understanding this action as designating ownership. Here we find a different ritual gesture: Aaron places both hands on the goat's head, a goat that is not his but the people's goat (16:5).

2. Aaron confesses all the guilt and rebellious deeds—their sins— and places them on the head of the goat (v. 21b). The first word in this series of transgressions is often translated *iniquities*. However, it can also refer to culpability for a wrongdoing and might be translated *guiltiness* (see 5:1, 17; 7:18; 17:16; 19:8; 20:17, 19; 22:16). The goat will now bear all the guilt, or culpability, of the people.

3. The goat now carries all the sins of the people into an uninhabited wilderness (vv. 21c-22). Not only do the sins themselves seem to be borne by the goat but also the culpability for them (v. 22). The goat is sent into a cut-off place, never to return to the camp. It is like getting rid of toxic waste: removing it to a faraway place so no harm can come from it.

To ensure the permanent disappearance of the goat and its cargo from the camp, it is led away by a man ready at hand for this task. First, the goat is taken to an isolated place, and from there it is sent away to the wilderness, a place where no one dwells. The form of the verb used for *send* can mean "expel never to return," as in Genesis 3:23, when God banished the first humans from the garden.

This goat is often referred to as a *scapegoat* (vv. 8, 10, 26). But such a word does not occur in the Hebrew text. Only the function of the goat is given, never a name for the goat. What *scapegoat* means in modern English—one who is subject to hostility or bears the blame for what others did—has very little in common with the function of the goat in Leviticus. As far as we can see from the text, no hostility is shown to the goat, nor is the goat accused of doing anything. Rather, the goat is removing something from the community: it is doing them a favor. (On the confusion of the scapegoat with a sacrifice and the consequent transformation of the "scapegoat" in Christian theology, see Finlan: 34–38).

Nor does the notion that this goat is a sacrifice have any basis in the text. While the sacrificing is being done, this goat stands idly by; and after the sacrificial rituals are over, it is sent out of the camp alive. A good name for this goat might be the "lucky goat" *[Scapegoat, p. 316]*.

16:23-28 Concluding Rituals

Just as the preparatory rituals began with the rites of bathing and clothing, so the concluding rituals have these gestures, but in reverse order. First, Aaron enters the tent, strips off his clothes, and leaves them there. Next, he washes himself and puts on his regular clothing. Then he exits the tent dressed as he was before the ceremony.

Wearing his normal priestly clothing, Aaron now offers his and the people's whole burnt offerings. After the whole burnt offerings, he completes the cleansing ritual made for cleansing the tabernacle and its objects by burning the fat of the offerings on the altar. Only after the completion of the elimination ritual can the cleansing ritual be completed.

The placement of the whole burnt offerings here is unusual. Usually the sequence would be a cleansing, then a whole burnt offering (see the sequence of these rituals in the offering of the two birds in 5:7-10 and chapters 8–9). Also, after the application of blood to the altar, the cleansing offering would be burned. However, the rituals surrounding the cleansing offering in chapter 16 are unique, being part of cleansing and elimination rituals. In this ceremony there is a gap between the time the cleansing offerings were slaughtered and the time they can be burned on the altar, since the tabernacle and the altars needed to be cleansed first.

While the fat is burned on the altar, the remainder of the animals, the carcasses, is taken outside the camp and burned (16:27). The carcasses of the animals must be burned outside the camp since the blood of these cleansing offerings had been brought into the tent (see 4:10-12). This is a disposal ritual.

Both the person leading the goat from the camp and sending it away and the person burning the remains of the cleansing offering outside the camp must launder their clothes and bathe before reentering the camp (vv. 26, 28). With their reentry, the ceremony ends *[Cleansing Offering, p. 297]*.

Epilogue 16:29-34

These verses are arranged loosely in a chiastic structure and are repetitive; therefore, the explanatory comments below will be arranged by topic rather than by verse sequence *[Literary Style, p. 306]*.

This purification and restoration ceremony was commanded after the death of Nadab and Abihu (16:1), a onetime event. Now it becomes a yearly event occurring on a specific day. Every year on the tenth day of the seventh month, the high priest is to perform this cleansing ceremony. In the Hebrew calendar, the first month occurs in the spring, at the time of Passover. But the New Year occurred in the fall on the first day of the seventh month. The Day of Cleansing came ten days after the new year began *[Calendar, p. 295]*.

New features are added to this day (vv. 29, 31). First, on this day the Israelites are to humble, or humiliate (NIV, *deny*), themselves. The word "humble" (*'anneh*) can be a very strong word in Hebrew. It is used of the affliction of Israel in Egypt (Exod 1:11-12). It can refer to rape, as in Genesis 34:2. But it can also have a softer meaning, such as refraining from food (Ps 35:13). It is this latter meaning that has been applied to this passage in the course of time: to afflict oneself by fasting (Milgrom 1991: 1054).

Second, no work may be done on this day. All persons in the community, both Jew and Gentile, are to observe this day of rest. Verse 31 emphasizes that *this day is to be a Sabbath of complete rest for you* (NET, NJPS). Even today in West Jerusalem silence reigns on Yom Kippur: there are no cars, no buses, no shoppers.

The reason for the uniqueness of this day is that on this day the high priest cleansed the shrine, the objects in the shrine, and the courtyard altar. As we have seen in chapters 4 and 5, the result of the cleansing offering was forgiveness. In chapter 16, this was a Day of Cleansing (v. 33). Forgiveness is never mentioned, because the rituals here had a quite different function.

THE TEXT IN BIBLICAL CONTEXT

What Is Sin?

Sin is like coloring outside the lines—it is something that ought not to be done—or in some cases, sin means not coloring enough. Sin may be of three shades:

1. There are inadvertent trespasses, unknowingly coloring outside the line (ch. 4).

2. The second shade is murkier. A person may carelessly fail to carry out a *positive* obligation, or may have *forgotten* to carry out a positive obligation, or may have defrauded another (ch. 5). For this shade of sin we find rituals for forgiveness and a penalty payment.

3. There are also *deliberate trespasses*, stepping over the line consciously and with intent to do so (Num 15:30). These are indelible. In Leviticus, no rituals are found for forgiveness of such sins. Sometimes we find a punishment such as being *cut off* (7:20) or immediate death (20:2-6). Deliberate sins can also bring covenant curses upon the Israelites (26:14-39) *[Cut Off, p. 299]*.

In addition to what is termed *sin*, we also find what we would call a *moral impurity*, identified as an *abomination* (ch. 18). These impurities make one unclean; consequently, they can make the land unclean. Unlike the ritual impurities addressed in Leviticus 11-15, there are no purification rituals for these so-called moral impurities; like deliberate trespasses (shade 3 above), they are indelible. In some cases a nonritual impurity defiles the tabernacle, and the person responsible is to be executed (Lev 20:2-5). While we might label these moral impurities as a fourth type of sin, Leviticus does not do so. Instead, these actions cause defilement, as do ritual impurities.

Placed in a larger perspective, trespasses (i.e., sins) are actions that can break a contractual relationship with God. Wanton trespass of Israel's covenant with God not only brings punishment but eventually will also sever a relationship. At its most basic level, then, sin constitutes covenant breaking (see EN on ch. 26 and *Covenant, p. 298*). The results of deliberate sin by the individual bring about collective punishments because the covenant is between Israel and God, not between the individual and God. These punishments are listed in chapter 26.

The Effects of Sin

Sin has an effect as soon as it is committed. It contaminates the altar and the tabernacle like pollution contaminates a window. A new window is entirely clean and thoroughly transparent when installed, but as time goes by, dust, dirt, and atmospheric pollution inevitably cut down on how well the window functions. It needs a good scrubbing to function as it should. Every year the tabernacle and its "furniture" would receive a good "scrubbing." A goat then carried the filth away.

Getting Rid of Sin

A two-step process is needed to remove sin from the "window." First is the ritual of forgiveness. The blood of the sacrificed animal is daubed on the horns of an altar and poured out at the base of the courtyard altar (4:4-7; cf. 4:25). This ritual purifies the altar by removing contamination caused by a sin. Once this removal takes place, the sinner is forgiven. The immediate effect of a transgression is remedied (see EN for chs. 4–5).

The second step is the removal of the sin itself from the holy. The ceremony in chapter 16 cleanses the tabernacle and altars of all sin and restores them to their initial state. This cleansing is done by the application of blood to parts of the tent, the ark, and the altars. Once all sins have been purged from the holy things, they must be removed from the sacred precinct and from the camp. This is the function of the live goat. Unlike the blood of the animals that are killed in the forgiveness and cleansing rituals, here a living goat carries away the actual sins (see EN for ch. 16).

Beyond Leviticus, *sin can also be erased by human intercessory prayer*, as in Exodus 32:30-33, which uses the metaphor of the people being erased from God's book. Sins may also be blotted out (Ps 109:13-14). While it is said that God will punish the people for their sin (Josh 24:19-20), Jeremiah promises grace for those who survive God's judgment:

> The iniquity of Israel shall be sought,
>   And there shall be none;
> The sins of Judah,
>   And none shall be found;
> For I will pardon those I allow to survive. (Jer 50:20 NJPS)

God's grace alone is sufficient for the forgiveness and removal of sin, and even its destruction. There is no need for a sacrifice whose blood is applied to the altar.

Sin as Understood in the New Testament

An innovation in the New Testament is understanding sin as a realm as well as a deed. Sin with a capital S, so to speak, refers to a realm that has the power to enslave people. Its control is shown by individual acts of sin. Paul speaks of living in Sin's realm (Rom 6:1), of becoming slaves of Sin (vv. 6, 14, 16), of Sin reigning as a king over a person's physical body (v. 12). Of course, Paul also talks of sin with a small s like we find in Leviticus. (For Paul's understanding of sin, a concise and very helpful treatment is found in Toews: 209-11, 409-11.)

Elsewhere, we find a similar concept that seems to differentiate between "orientation" and "misdeeds." In 1 Peter 4, the Christian is "done with sin" (= Sin) because "they do not live the rest of their earthly lives for evil human desires, but rather for the will of God" (1 Pet 4:1-2). We should not expect that the person who is living for God will no longer commit sins in the sense of misdeeds. Rather, they do not *practice* sinning, because they have devoted themselves to God's will.

Sin as a realm or orientation gives people two choices. They are either slaves of God (devoted to God's will) or slaves of Sin. A person's loyalty is shown by their actions: if they continue sinning, they show themselves to be under the rule of Sin. If instead they practice justice or righteousness, they are under the rule of God. The antidote to Sin's enslavement is becoming slaves to justice or righteousness (Rom 6:18).

In this schema in which Sin can refer both to a realm and to a deed, Paul first demands a change in loyalties from Sin to God. This comes about through identification with Christ in baptism: "Don't you know that *all of us who were baptized into Christ Jesus were baptized into his death?* We were therefore *buried with him through baptism into death* in order that, just as Christ was raised from the dead, ... *we too may live a new life*" (Rom 6:2-4, emph. added).

This movement from the realm of Sin to the realm of Christ is the first basic step, which we call *conversion*. This conversion is shown by the way we live "because anyone who has died has been set free from Sin" (Rom 6:7, "Sin" capitalized) in order to become "an instrument of righteousness" or justice (v. 13).

Leviticus and the meaning of sin generally in the Hebrew Bible (Old Testament) do not fit Paul's dualistic schema. Sin is not a separate realm that has enslaved the Israelites. The Israelites were God's people by God's grace and by virtue of their covenant with God. There was no need to be converted in order to enter God's realm or rule. They were in automatically. What we find in Leviticus are not rules for *entry* into God's realm, but the rules of *membership*.

In Leviticus, sin is a trespass, an action ignoring the bounds of membership in God's people. *God could have forgiven the sins of an individual Israelite without any sacrifices or without any blood applied to the altar* (see the quote above from Jeremiah). But God chose not to do so. Instead, God gave Leviticus to Israel as a guide to being God's people. Sin was not taken lightly. The forgiveness ritual enabled a member of God's people to make amends for damages done and to maintain a good relationship within God's people. In this respect, forgiveness was not cheap in Leviticus: it was the end point of a process. This is the context of Leviticus 16.

An important point is that for both Paul and Leviticus, doing the law was not a mechanism for becoming God's people. Instead, doing came after being. Leviticus was not given to be a legalistic mechanism whereby if a person was good enough, they became part of the people of God. Rather, because they *are* part of God's people, Leviticus points out the responsibilities that go with this status.

This difference in the understanding of sin explains in part why atonement in Leviticus is so different from understandings abstracted from the New Testament. Atonement in Leviticus is a maintenance mechanism, one that maintains Israel as the people of God. The rituals in Leviticus are part of keeping God's people as God's people. In the New Testament, however, atonement becomes a necessary transfer mechanism for moving people from the rule of Sin to the rule of God. This transfer is termed *salvation*, which was unnecessary for Israel at Sinai, because they were already God's people by God's grace [*Atonement in Christian Thinking and Leviticus, p. 292*].

THE TEXT IN THE LIFE OF THE CHURCH

Forgiveness Rituals and Purification Rituals

In most churches we have fairly clear ideas of how new members enter the church. Catechism or a membership preparation class is a common rite of passage. Baptism is a ritual for marking this stage in a person's life. (For some, baptism comes first, and catechism marks full membership.) Along with first communion, this is perhaps the most celebrated event in the spiritual life of a person.

The Hebrew Bible (OT) does not give Gentiles much guidance for becoming part of the people of God. We know that the founding of Israel as a people, the liberation from Egyptian slavery, was seen as an action of God's grace. This historic event was celebrated by

Passover. But each individual Israelite who followed the generation of those liberated was born into God's people Israel. Circumcision was the sign that marked males as belonging to Israel. Male Gentiles who wished to celebrate Passover needed to become circumcised to do so (Exod 12:48). In Leviticus, resident Gentiles, Gentiles living within the nation, are taken as a given.

Leviticus states some of the membership regulations for those already in God's covenant. Leviticus 16 celebrates a restoration of purity to the tabernacle and its altars. It is a member's celebration. Do these membership regulations apply to Gentiles, non-Israelites? I think not. They are addressed to Israelites, and they are the ones commanded to keep them. They are the ones who participate in the rituals and the annual cleansing celebration in chapter 16. It is true that non-Israelites can participate in certain rituals and celebrations, like Passover. It is also true that some commands include non-Israelites. But most of Leviticus is not addressed to them.

Since chapter 16 is not addressed to the resident aliens, the Gentiles, there seems to be no requirement for them to have a yearly purification ritual. But they must observe the Day of Cleansing as a day of rest (16:29).

Some congregations have an annual covenanting ceremony in which members pledge their willingness to be an active part of the community. This ritual may mark the beginning of a new church year and be a time of planning for the future. Instead of only looking forward to the year ahead, reviewing the past year and taking stock of what was and was not done is also appropriate. This reflection might also include a group confession of where they have fallen short. Such events and rituals are maintenance mechanisms. They are not membership drives.

A personal observation: In the congregations of my youth, communion was celebrated twice a year. The Sunday before communion was a time when those wishing to participate in communion would state that they were in a right relationship with God and with their fellow believers. They also declared that if that were not so, they wanted the person who felt they had been trespassed against to come to them so they could make things right. This went beyond the Day of Cleansing ceremony, but it was a time to "purify" the congregation so that communion could also represent a new beginning with a clean slate.

Such practices have probably disappeared from most congregations, and communion is celebrated more than twice a year for many. But thinking about how to clear the slate with both God and fellow believers is a good idea. The ability to do this would be a very healthy practice for congregational relationships and dynamics. A helpful ceremony might be a rededication for a church building that would remind people of the set-apart reason for the building. Features within the building could be rededicated as media that play a part in worship. The communion table comes to mind. In many congregations its place is at the front of the sanctuary, and it is a very visible symbol of Christ's presence. In this sense, like the ark and cherubim, it points to the presence of the holy in whose presence the congregation is worshiping (Wesley Bergen, correspondence to author).

Leviticus 17:1-16
Why Blood Has Power of Removal

PREVIEW

While chapter 16 provides the capstone for the first fifteen chapters, it has left us with three sets of questions that chapter 17 attempts to answer. First, what is it about blood that gives it the power to cleanse and purify holy things? How can its application to holy things wash away the blotches of sin?

Second, where must domestic animals be killed and their blood deposited? Since blood has such power, can domesticated animals be slaughtered for meat away from the sanctuary and priests? If so, what should be done with the blood, since no priest or altar is available for its disposal? Or must all slaughter of domestic animals be done by priests at the tabernacle? (See ch. 3 for the peace offering that supplied meat for the owner and his family.)

Third, is all blood equal in its power to cleanse? What about game animals that cannot be brought to the sanctuary and offered as a sacrifice?

Chapter 17 is divided into two main parts by topic and audience. The first part has only one law, which prescribes the place of slaughter, and is addressed to the Israelites alone. The second part has four laws concerning the disposition of the blood of sacrifices and is addressed to Gentiles as well. (See Jürgens: 143-75 and Ruwe: 131-59 for detailed analyses of the structure and logic of this chapter.) A final paragraph gives the regulations for eating carrion; the blood of the animal is not an issue in this case.

Leviticus 17:1-16

OUTLINE

Introduction, 17:1-2
Place Matters, 17:3-9
    17:3-4   The Place of Slaughter
    17:5-7   The Reason Place Matters
    17:8-9   Gentiles
Prohibition of Consuming Blood, 17:10-14
    17:10-12   The Blood of Slaughtered Animals
    17:13-14   The Blood of Game Animals
Eating Carrion, 17:15-16

EXPLANATORY NOTES

Introduction 17:1-2

The following commands are addressed to Moses and repeated to the priests and the laity. The sojourner, or Gentile, will be added to the list of addressees in verse 8.

The introduction ends in verse 2b with the phrase *This is the word that the LORD has commanded* (NET). This expression also occurs in 8:5 and 9:6, introducing the ordination of the priesthood and the inauguration of worship at the tabernacle. Its repetition here may emphasize the importance of what is to follow.

Place Matters 17:3-9

17:3-4 *The Place of Slaughter*

If any Israelites—men or women—wish to slaughter a bull, sheep, or goat, they are to bring the animal to the tabernacle and slaughter it there. If the Israelite does not do this, that person will be considered a shedder of blood. The phrase *shed blood* (*šapak*; v. 4) echoes Genesis 9:6, "Whoever sheds human blood," and Numbers 35:33, "Bloodshed pollutes the land . . . on which blood has been shed." In these references, the shedding of blood refers to murder. The severity of slaughtering cattle, sheep, and goats apart from the altar at the tabernacle is compared to murder.

This command means that the person may not slaughter these animals outside the camp in the field, or even within the camp, but must bring them to the tabernacle. In fact, these animals must be presented as a gift, a peace offering. Profane slaughter is outlawed.

The Israelites must bring their animals to the tent of meeting and offer them there so that the priest can dispose of the animals' blood properly at the altar. As is the case with voluntary offerings, this will produce a pleasing odor for God. In this way the Israelites could slaughter their oxen, sheep, and goats and enjoy the meat of their animals without committing something like murder (see Lev 3).

17:5-7 *The Reason Place Matters*

This paragraph has a deliberate structure. First there is a positive command (v. 5). Its negative counterpart ends the passage (v. 7). In between, in verse 6, we find the center and focus of the passage as indicated by this structure.

The Positive Command, 17:5. This is in order that ... (NRSV) introduces reasons why all slaughter of flock and herd animals must be done at the tent of meeting. The slaughter of these animals is a holy action.

The Focus, 17:6. We know from 3:16-17 that the Israelites are not to eat the fat or blood of a peace offering. These belong to God alone. Bringing their animals to the priest and slaughtering them at the altar before the tabernacle insures the keeping of this eternal command.

The Negative Reason, 17:7. This command will prevent Israel from sacrificing to goats. The text simply says "goats," but this term refers to something beyond actual goats. English translations normally add *demons* (so NRSV). The NIV adds *idols*. The reference of this term is unknown (for speculations, see Milgrom 2000: 1462). This law is to be an eternal law for Israel throughout all generations.

17:8-9 *Gentiles*

Because of the danger of unorthodox worship in the camp, the Gentiles (non-Israelites) are also included in this prohibition. Notice that the same punishment is stated in verses 3-4 and 8-9. This extends the condition (*if*) in verse 3 to everyone. The inclusion of non-Israelites is also stated specifically in the following paragraphs, creating a link between this paragraph and what follows.

Prohibition of Consuming Blood 17:10-14

17:10-12 *The Blood of Slaughtered Animals*

Consuming blood has already been prohibited in 3:17 and 7:22-27. In the latter passage, birds are included along with herd and flock animals. In 3:17, this prohibition is given after instructions for the peace offering, presumably because the meat of this offering will be eaten by the laity outside the shrine and its court.

The general prohibition is given in Genesis 9:4: "Only, you shall not eat flesh with its life, that is, its blood" (NRSV). This prohibition, given to Noah, applies to all his descendants, to all humankind. In our text, this universal command for all humankind is restated for the Israelites (Lev 3:17). The punishment stated for this offense in Leviticus is grave: *Whoever eats any blood, . . . I will cut off that person from their people* (7:27 AT) *[Cut Off, p. 299].*

What does it mean to eat blood? It means to eat the flesh of animals whose blood has not been properly drained from it. In the sacrificial rituals, the priests would drain the blood of the animal for application on the altar. However, if the animal was slaughtered away from the altar, the blood might not be drained out before butchering. This problem has been solved by having all slaughter of herd and flock animals done by the priests. In the case of game animals (v. 13 below), their blood is to be drained onto the ground. First Samuel 14:33-34 relates that after a battle, the Israelite troops were reported to be "eating meat that has blood in it" (v. 33). Saul commanded that a large stone be rolled over to him, and the people were to bring their animals and slaughter them there. Evidently they could drain the blood from them by placing them on the stone. After draining, the meat could be eaten.

Why Not Eat Blood? 17:11. The paragraph 17:10-12 is arranged as a chiasmus *[Literary Style, p. 306].* The negative command in verse 10 is repeated in verse 12. The reason for this prohibition comes in the center, verse 11, where its position highlights its importance.

Verse 11 is the one place in the Bible where we find an explanation for why blood must not be ingested, and this explanation has become the focus of much discussion and debate. Besides theological biases, there are exegetical reasons for uncertainty about its meaning. First, the syntax of verse 11 is not straightforward and allows for differing constructions at important points. In addition, there are anomalies: this is the only reference where blood is the subject of the verb "purify" (*kipper*); it is also the only use in Leviticus of *kipper* without a mention of the cleansing offering (*ḥaṭṭaʾt*). When faced with alternative interpretations, the most likely is to be preferred above those that are less likely.

To begin, it is clear that verse 11a gives the reason for the prohibition in the previous verse, since it begins with *for* or *because* (*ki*).

The conjunction introduces a noun clause, a clause with no verb in Hebrew. In English, the translators must add a verb, *is*. Most translations read something like *the life of the flesh is in the blood* (emph. added; NRSV and NJPS are the most spare). Second, this translation assumes that the preposition *bet* before blood means "in." Elsewhere, however, this noun clause occurs without any preposition, simply stating the equivalence of blood and life, as in verse 14b, *the life of every creature is its blood*, and probably the same in verse 14a (although a slight textual difficulty does not make it certain). Elsewhere we find the straightforward equation of blood and life, as in Deuteronomy 12:23, "The blood is the life, and you must not eat the life with the meat." Genesis 9:4 uses life and blood in apposition: "with its life, its blood" (AT).

Because of these parallels, the translation of verse 11a as *the life of the flesh is the blood* (AT) recommends itself. This translation takes the preposition *bet* in its meaning as indicating equivalence (essence) rather than location (see BDB; *DCH*).

The importance of blood is that it represents life: *and I have assigned it to you for making expiation* (v. 11b NJPS). While all blood represents life, not all blood can be applied to the altar. Only the blood of herd and flock animals and birds can effect purification, and only of the blood of those that are whole and without blemish. The blood of all others, domestic or wild, cannot be used for purification *[Atonement, p. 288]*.

As verse 11 began with a reason for not consuming blood, so it ends with a second reason, again introduced by *for* or *because* (*ki*, v. 11c). In contrast to the formulation of the first reason, the order of the words *blood* and *life* is reversed, and there is a verb in Hebrew. Now blood comes first and is the subject of the verb: *because blood... purifies* (AT). However, *blood* is also the subject of a noun clause. A straightforward translation acknowledging this would be *because the blood is life it purifies* (AT). Similarly, NJPS translates *it is the blood, as life, that effects expiation*, which acknowledges the Masoretic accents (v. 11c; note also NET and its extensive notes on this verse; Hartley; Rendtorff; a dissenting position is taken by Schwartz [1991]).

The translation in the NIV, *for one's life*, does not represent what is in the text, because the term translated *one's* is not found in the original Hebrew. Nor is there any evidence in this text, or in the parallel texts cited above, for translating the preposition *bet* as "for," as if something were being done *for* someone (on the translation of v. 11c, see the translators' notes in the NET; see also the essay *Ransom, p. 312*). Thus the best translation, as suggested above, is the following:

> *Because a creature's <u>life</u> is the blood,*
> *I have given it to you on the altar to cleanse for your <u>lives</u>;*
> *because the blood is <u>life</u> it cleanses.* (AT, emph. added)

The rule in verse 10 is repeated in verse 12. All in the camp or settlement are emphatically included, no matter whether Jew or Gentile.

17:13-14 The Blood of Game Animals

The blood of sacrificial animals is placed on the altar, but the blood of wild animals cannot be so placed. Instead, the animal's blood is drained and covered over. Now their meat may be eaten.

But why should their blood be given this special treatment of being buried? It does not play a role in purification. The reason given in verse 14 is *because the life of every creature is its blood*. No less than sacrificial animals, the blood of all living animals, as life, needs to be treated respectfully. This is why God said to Israel, *You must not eat the blood of any creature* (v. 14). To ensure this obvious point is clear, the reason is stated once more: *because the life of every creature is its blood*.

Eating Carrion 17:15-16

But what about animals that are already dead? Their blood would not have been drained properly: would eating their flesh be eating blood? The answer is no. Eating the meat of such animals does not result in being cut off. Instead, the person becomes ritually impure, which can be remedied easily. They need to launder their clothes, bathe, and wait until evening, the same ritual as is used to remove impurity after eating impure meat (ch. 11).

But if a person does not perform this ritual, they bear the consequences of their neglect. Since the tent of God's presence sits in the middle of the camp and is holy, purity should reign in the camp. The realm of purity needs to be guarded by individuals so that they do not remain and live in a state of impurity. Even the casual contracting of impurity is serious and needs to be neutralized by a ritual of purification (see Lev 5:2-3).

THE TEXT IN BIBLICAL CONTEXT
Eating Blood

After the flood, God granted humans the option of eating meat: "You must not eat meat that has its lifeblood still in it" (Gen 9:4). Animal flesh was allowed, but the blood had to be drained from it before eating. Moreover, God declared of any animal or human who shed human blood that their own blood would be sought by God (vv. 5-6). God also made a covenant with Noah and all living creatures (vv. 9-10). This was God's first covenant and included all humankind, both future Jews and Gentiles. Although not stated in God's covenantal promise to Noah, the two preceding commands were likewise directed to all humankind. Thus the prohibition against eating blood applies to all humankind.

Leviticus adds five more universal laws to the two we find in Genesis 9. In the language of Leviticus, these are commands addressed to both the Israelites and the Gentiles living among them. These five universal prohibitions are found in chapters 17–24: against *eating blood* (17:11-12), *illicit sex* (chs. 18 and 20), *idolatry* (20:1-5), *blasphemy* (24:10-16), and *murder* (24:17-22).

The first command, to not eat blood, and the last, to not murder, were already commanded in the time of Noah. These two commands form bookends around the list. The middle three are the additions of Leviticus to this universal covenant.

The Noachian Laws

Over time, the list of laws that were valid for Jews and Gentiles alike became known as the Noachian laws. Of course, not all such universal laws go back to Noah. In the time of the early church, the Didache, a book found as part of the New Testament in some early manuscripts, materially agrees with the five basic prohibitions of the Noachian laws: *murder, sexual immorality, idolatry, theft,* and *blasphemy* (see Didache 3:1-6; 5:1b; Müller, 59–62). An early list in the Jewish tradition contained the following prohibitions: *idolatry, blasphemy, sexual immorality, shedding blood,* and *theft* (Tosefta, Avodah Zarah 8.4). At the final stage, the list contained the following seven commands: *establish justice* and *prohibit idolatry, blasphemy, sexual immorality, shedding blood, robbery,* and *eating blood,* defined as meat from a living animal (Sanhedrin 56a with extensive discussion; on the historical development of the Noachian commands, see Müller) *[Noachian Covenant, p. 307].*

THE TEXT IN THE LIFE OF THE CHURCH

Eating Blood in the Early Church

The most frequent topics of dissension in the early church were food and circumcision. Regarding circumcision, the question was whether Gentiles needed to become Jews to become Christian. If they did, then circumcision was necessary. But if Gentiles who became Christian could remain Gentiles, then circumcision was unnecessary. At stake was a major, perhaps *the* major sign of what it meant to be God's people. From a Jew's point of view, Gentiles were by definition sinners and had no part in the hereafter. Peter reflects this view in Acts 10:28: "It is against our law for a Jew to associate with or visit a Gentile."

The question about food was more complex. In the Hebrew Bible (OT) and Jewish tradition, the topic of food went beyond what *type* of meat a Jewish person could eat. It also concerned eating blood, and in Leviticus 17 the eating of blood is prohibited for *both Jew and Gentile* alike. But if Gentile Christians did not need to be circumcised, could they also ignore laws that both the Hebrew Bible and Jewish tradition thought necessary for them as Gentiles? Did Christian liberty set them free from all laws found in the Scriptures?

An assembly at Jerusalem was called to discuss the issue of circumcision (Acts 15:1). A range of persons were present at the assembly—perhaps from the Greek Titus (Gal 2:1) to Christian Pharisees. The initial demands were made by some of the latter Christians: "The Gentiles must be circumcised and required to keep the law of Moses" (Acts 15:5).

In light of this agenda item, the decision of the council is surprising. James, the spokesperson for the council's decision, declared first: "We should not make it difficult for the Gentiles who are turning to God" (Acts 15:19). Second, he announced, "Instead we should write to them, telling them to abstain from food polluted by idols, from sexual immorality, from the meat of strangled animals and from blood" (Acts 15:20). The issue of circumcision is not mentioned! The decision was that Gentiles do not need to become Jews to become Christian. However, the universal laws still applied to Gentile Christians just as they did to all Gentiles. To put it more plainly, Gentiles did not need to adopt the law as it applied to Jews, but they were to observe the laws that applied to Gentiles (not eating the meat of strangled animals is covered above by Lev 17:15; see Wehnert on this apostolic edict).

Comparing the list in Acts 15:20 with the universal laws in Leviticus, we find that they are almost identical. In Leviticus the universal prohibitions (applying to *anyone*) are *idolatry* (20:2-3), *sexual immorality* (18:26), *improper slaughter* (17:11-12), *murder* (24:17-22), and *blasphemy* (24:16). That blasphemy (denying God) is omitted in Acts 15 is surprising, since it is a universal prohibition in Leviticus and is also found in the Noachian laws as they were developed.

Despite the omission of blasphemy, it seems that the early church, at least at the Jerusalem conference, prohibited of Gentiles what Leviticus prohibited of them. The council did not agree that Gentiles needed to become Jews to be Christian, nor did they support the application of the whole law of Moses to Gentiles. On this last point they were supported by Jewish tradition [*Noachian Covenant, p. 307*]. (On the relevance of the Noachian covenant to Acts 15, see Flusser; Bockmuehl 1995, 2000.)

The debate over universal laws that apply to all humankind is absent from our present churches. Should Christians demand obedience to some universal laws as found in Leviticus and in the early church discussions? This is a crucial topic in today's world. Are there practices and values that all societies and political-economic systems should support and exhibit? Does the concern of Leviticus for animal life and its blood, echoed by the early church's decree, demand some safeguards on the treatment and slaughter of animals today?

Part 3

Living in Light of God's Presence

Leviticus 18:1–27:34

OVERVIEW

God calls the Israelites to be holy. How is this possible? Can people acquire holiness? How does anybody become holy? The tabernacle was holy. The altars were holy. Sacrifices were holy. The priests, keepers of the holy, were holy. But holy people?

Chapters 18–27 redefine holiness in order to apply it to life *[Holy and Holiness, p. 302]*. One becomes holy by living according to the wishes of God. This is an *accrued* holiness. It is not a granted holiness, although God begins the process by sanctifying Israel. It comes not through ritual but through life. It even comes about in the common area while living in the camp.

This holiness can exist alongside the impure because transgressing the rules for living does not make one impure or pure. As we will see in chapter 18, some acts result in moral impurity, but this impurity is not contagious, nor does it make anyone ritually impure. Rather, moral impurity results in banishment from the land (ch. 18) or death (ch. 20). Although ritual impurity bars a person from the tabernacle, lack of holiness does not. Nor does seeking holiness make one ritually pure. Moral behavior in life is a different arena. In the realm of morality, the goal is personal holiness, not ritual purity. However, moral behavior does not make ritual purity unnecessary. Both must be pursued. Holiness and purity are both marks of a life of obedience to God. Neither can be neglected.

This "practical" holiness is foreshadowed at the end of the food laws in chapter 11 (vv. 44-45). There God proclaims, *I am the LORD your God; consecrate yourselves and be holy, because I am holy.* Diet mattered because of God's holiness. It also implies that Israel can and must become holy by keeping the food laws. Here holiness rests on ritual purity.

The *moral instructions* for living a holy life are found in chapters 18–22. These chapters are shown to be a unit by the similarity between the beginning in chapter 18 and the ending in chapter 22. In both we have an allusion to or mention of the exodus, the declaration that *I am the* LORD, and the command to keep or guard the commandments (18:3-5; 22:31, 33).

However, the distinction between ritual and what we would consider to be ethics is not made in these chapters. Ritual regulations for eating the peace offering (Lev 19:5-8) are preceded by the prohibition against idol worship and followed by instructions to leave some of the harvest for the poor and the immigrant. In chapter 18, breaking the sexual prohibitions is not called a sin, but such acts make a person unclean. Thus *our distinctions between sin and purity are not those of Leviticus.*

Furthermore, what we might think are trivial instructions as opposed to significant ones are found side by side. A case in point is the command to love one's neighbor alongside a prohibition against wearing clothing constructed from a mixture of threads, or of sowing different kinds of seed in a field, or of crossbreeding cattle (19:18-19). In reading these texts the normal practice is to give importance to one command but shrug off another, depending on how serious or relevant it seems to us. But all of these commands are aspects of holy living. In these texts they all have the same weight.

Not all of these commandments are necessary for Gentiles, however. Some of them are addressed to the Israelites alone. Others are expressly addressed to both the Israelite and the non-Israelite. Some, as in chapter 18, become relevant only when they enter the Promised Land [*Worship and Ethics, p. 320*].

OUTLINE FOR PART 3

Holy Living, 18:1–22:33
Holy Time, 23:1–25:55
The Promise and Danger of Covenant, 26:1-46
Addendum: Vows, Dedications, and Tithes, 27:1-34

Leviticus 18:1–22:33
Part 3A
Holy Living

OVERVIEW
After the hinge of chapters 16 and 17, we shift to a focus on life outside the tabernacle. Obedience to the commands of God is now central and is the way to life. Although not mentioned in chapter 18, holiness becomes a thread running through these chapters. In these chapters, holiness depends on obedience, and the laity are challenged to become and remain holy. As obedience is the way to life, chapter 27 points out that disobedience is the way to death and exile.

OUTLINE FOR PART 3A
Forbidden Sexual Practices, 18:1-30
Holiness in Daily Life, 19:1-37
Holiness as Obedience, 20:1-27
Holiness for Priests, 21:1–22:33

Leviticus 18:1-30
Forbidden Sexual Practices

PREVIEW

Leviticus has instructed Israel about how to approach the God in their midst. But how should they live their daily lives in the camp? Does the holiness of God influence their behavior when they are not worshiping? This is not a trite question. Although the word "holy" does not occur in chapter 18, the chapter is bracketed by God's declaration *I am the* LORD *your God* (vv. 1 and 30). The belief that they must be completely committed to their God is the foundation of Israel's being God's people: "Hear, Israel, Yahweh is our God, Yahweh alone" (Deut 6:4 AT) is the first and greatest commandment *[Yahweh, p. 321]*. God is their master and none other. This God is holy and requires Israel to be holy (19:2).

Sexual practices are the focus of this chapter and are bracketed by an introduction and a closing statement that echo each other and point to the unity of the whole. These sexual transgressions are not labeled as sins but are sources of impurity. This provides a link with the purity regulations in chapters 11–15. A clear and stronger connection exists between the prohibition of sexual relations with a menstruating woman in verse 19 below and the purity regulations in 15:24. While in 15:23-24 there is a purification process for this impurity, there is none for it in 18:19. The moral impurities in chapter 18 are so severe as to make the land impure. For a discussion that compares the regulations of chapter 15 with those in 18, see TBC for chapter 15. In addition to the comments below, a discussion of same-sex relationships also follows chapter 20 *[Worship and Ethics, p. 320]*.

OUTLINE

Introductory Exhortation, 18:1-5
Forbidden Sexual Practices, 18:6-25
Final Warning, 18:26-30

EXPLANATORY NOTES

Introductory Exhortation 18:1-5

Chapter 18 begins with God addressing the entire people through Moses. This address begins in the first person: *I the LORD am your God* (NJPS). The word "LORD" is a substitute in English translations for the actual name of Israel's God, Yahweh. A more informative translation would read *I, Yahweh, am your God* (AT). This declaration is also found in a shortened form in verse 5, *I Yahweh am your God* (AT) *[Yahweh, p. 321]*. It is a specific God who delivered Israel from Egypt and has laid claim to them as a special possession among all nations of the earth.

But why is Israel's God identified as Yahweh and not, for example, Chemosh (Moab's god; Num 21:29)? This declaration is founded on Yahweh's act of delivering the people from Egypt. Before the exodus, God declares, "I am the LORD [Yahweh], and I will bring you out from under the yoke of the Egyptians. I will free you from being slaves to them" (Exod 6:6). Later, God states that the miracles are so "that you may tell your children and grandchildren . . . what signs I have done among [the Egyptians]—so that you may know that I am the LORD [Yahweh]" (Exod 10:2 NRSV). This act of grace lies behind the Ten Commandments, which begin with the preface "I the LORD [Yahweh] am your God who brought you out of the land of Egypt, the house of bondage:" (Exod 20:2 NJPS). Notice the colon at the end of the verse, indicating the understanding that this act of grace is the basis for what follows—an implied *therefore*. "Because I have done this for you, you will therefore . . ." It is not surprising, then, that the section of Leviticus concerning the behavior of the Israelites should be peppered with a reminder of their God's identity and grace. This identification of Yahweh as their God (and not any other), occurs more than thirty times in chapters 18–22!

Israel is not to live like either the Egyptians, whom they just left, or the Canaanites, who live in the place to which they are going. Instead, they will live according to the statutes of God, grounded in the fact that *I Yahweh am your God* (18:4 AT). These identical declarations in verses 2 and 4 separate the negative commands to not assimilate from the positive one in verse 5.

The positive command, *You will keep my statutes and practices . . .* (v. 5 AT), repeats verse 4b. However, there is also a promise: *the person who does them will live by them* (AT). Two important changes in language point to the significance of this promise. First, the language changes from second person, addressing the Israelites as *you*, to third person, *the person* who does them. Second, and reinforcing this point, the word for "person" is generic, meaning humankind in general—that is, anyone who does them. This promise is also found in Ezekiel 20:11: "I gave them my decrees and made known to them my laws, by which the person who obeys them will live." (In Ezek 20:25, God says Israel was given bad laws as punishment for disobedience to the laws by which one lives; see also 1 Kings 22:17-25.) Deuteronomy 8:3 similarly repeats this sentiment: "One does not live by bread alone, but by every word that comes from the mouth of the LORD" (NRSV). Life comes through practicing God's commands for living. Death comes through disobedience (see Sprinkle: 28–34; for more on God's concern for all people, see "What Is Sin?" in TBC for ch. 16 as well as TBC and TLC for ch. 17).

Forbidden Sexual Practices 18:6-25

The list of forbidden sexual practices is prefaced by a general statement: *No one is to approach any close relative to have sexual relations* (18:6). The following prohibited relationships are examples of this general law and cover cases in which the relationship is through blood or kinship. Thus, a man may not have sexual relations with a woman and with her daughter (by another man, v. 17), presumably because of the close relationship between a mother and her daughter. This principle also includes all incestuous relationships that are not specifically mentioned, such as a father with his daughter. Likewise, kinship, residential proximity, or frequency of contact could justify the prohibition *Do not have sexual relations with your neighbor's wife* (v. 20). The word translated *neighbor* is found only in Leviticus (apart from Zech 13:7). It has the connotation of an associate, a member of one's community (see HALOT). In Leviticus 6:2 (5:21), it is a person with whom one has business dealings. It is also parallel to "brother," someone in a person's wider circle of acquaintances (19:17).

The list of banned relationships begins in 18:6 and is constructed from a man's perspective since these are sexual relationships that are prohibited to men. The first set of prohibitions (vv. 7-17) include partners related by marriage, a stepmother (v. 8), stepsister (v. 11), or an uncle's wife (v. 14). These relationships reflect the people who would make up an extended family or household. (For discussions of the composition of this list and charts illustrating it, see Hartley; Milgrom 2000: 1537-44.)

A second grouping of forbidden practices begins with verse 18, which forbids a man from taking a wife's sister and having sexual relations with her while the first wife is alive. This law is *not* a prohibition of polygamy. What is forbidden is polygamy with sisters. (Levirate marriage obligated a man to marry the widow of his brother upon his brother's death; Deut 25:5-10. What would happen in such a case if his brother's widow was his wife's sister is not addressed.)

Included in this group is a prohibition of sexual relationship with any woman during her menstrual period. This prohibition is anomalous since it depends on the state of the woman, not on her relationship with the man (v. 19). If this happens, the man is unclean for seven days (15:24). Such a minor infraction seems out of place in this list of major infractions; however, Leviticus 20:18 rules that this infraction results in being cut off *[Cut Off, p. 299]*. (On the purity law covering this impurity, see 15:26-30 and TBC for ch. 15.)

The prohibition against offering one's child to Molek is out of place in this list (18:21; NRSV, *Molech*). An expanded version of this law occurs in 20:2-5 and includes both the Israelite and the Gentile. A list of sexual prohibitions comparable to those here in chapter 18 begins there only with 20:10. This prohibition in chapter 20 does not belong to the list of sexual transgressions. The text reads, in translation, *You shall not give one of your children to pass over to Molek* (18:21 AT). To "pass over" can have the connotation of giving to a deity: "You are to give over to the LORD the first offspring of every womb" (Exod 13:12), meaning they are God's. So this verse could be understood as transferring ownership to Molek rather than to Israel's God.

How was this done? In 2 Kings 23:10, children are passed over to Molek by fire. This suggests that children were burned up, as a burnt offering, in order to transfer them to this god. We have reason to believe that children were sacrificed to various gods, because sacrificing children to idols is specifically mentioned in Ezekiel 16:20: "You sacrificed them as food for the idols to eat" (NET). A child sacrifice is performed by the Moabite king in 2 Kings 3:26-27. The king ascended to the top of the city wall and in the sight of all offered his son as a whole burnt offering to Chemosh, the God of the Moabites (not Molek). (See Hartley: 333-37 for a discussion of Molek, also spelled *Molech*; cf. *NIDB*.)

The third group of prohibited sexual relationships are of a man with a man (v. 22) and either a man or a woman with an animal (v. 23). Lesbian relationships are not forbidden (nor in the ancient Near East in general; Milgrom 2000: 1658). The first prohibition, sex between men, is described as a totally shocking deed, a *detestable* or abhorrent action (*toʿebah*). This Hebrew word occurs only in two passages in Leviticus, in 18:22-30 and 20:13. In both cases, the context is similar. This word is used elsewhere for national characteristics. In Genesis 43:32 and 46:34 it refers to Egyptian sensibilities. It would be a horror (*toʿebah*) for Egyptians to eat with Hebrews and live with them. Egyptians just don't do this. Likewise, Israelites just don't perform these sexual acts. The second prohibition, sex between an animal and a woman or a man, is called *a perversion* (*tebel*). These special terms of approbation apply only to these last two prohibitions. Such actions bring *moral impurity*. That is, these actions cause impurity. Instead of calling them "sin," Leviticus calls them "perversion" or "horror" (for the distinction between *sin* and *moral impurity*, see TBC for ch. 16).

This entire list of forbidden sexual practices concludes with the warning *Do not defile yourselves in any of these ways* (v. 24). The word "defile" (*tameʾ*) is found most frequently in the purity laws (chs. 11-15). The defilements there were ritual defilements that precluded a person from participating in the rituals at the tabernacle. These practices of the surrounding nations are forbidden to Israelites because they will make them *morally impure* just as eating the wrong animal makes one ritually impure in chapter 11. The difference is that disobeying these moral laws, unlike disobeying the ritual laws in chapter 11, produces a moral impurity, which has no stated antidote. There is no purification ritual for transgressing any of these prohibitions. As a result of moral impurity, the land itself becomes defiled and consequently bears its "culpability," like a person in 17:16. God in turn *punished [the land] for its iniquity* (NRSV), with the result that *the land vomited out its inhabitants* (v. 25; note the past tense in this verse). The individual wrongdoer is not punished, since these acts defile the land, which in turn will affect everyone living on the land.

The common heading and ending of this list indicate that, although it is divided into three parts, it is a single topical unit. Further indication of the unity of this passage is the clear break between verses 3-5 and verse 6, which heads this list. Likewise, there is a break between verses 25 and 26. Verse 26 picks up and repeats the commands of verses 3-5 (notice the repetition of *keep* and *do*), and its tense switches to the future in order to apply to the Israelites (v. 28). These breaks also emphasize 18:6-25 as a separate unit.

It is significant that this list has a *limited scope*. In regard to adulterous heterosexual relations, with one exception (adultery with a neighbor's wife, v. 20), the list only prohibits adulterous sexual relations with a close relative (contrast Exod 20:14, which prohibits all adultery). This indicates that this list *does not prohibit adultery in general*. The limited scope in this passage raises the question, Does this list exclude any sexual relationships beyond the bounds of kinship and proximity? In the plain sense of this specific passage, the text as written, the answer is that it does not. It specifically addresses relationships between close relatives: *No one is to approach any close relative to have sexual relations* (Lev 18:6).

There are three exceptions to this general rule. First, the case of the menstruant is quite different (v. 19). This rule applies to all women *including those with whom sexual relationships are permitted*. It has to do with the *state* of the woman, not her relationship to a man. The second is bestiality (v. 24). As in the case of the menstruant, we find a *category* of forbidden partners. Animals by definition are not related by kinship and thus are not covered by the heading to these prohibitions. Relationship or proximity is irrelevant. The third is male homosexual relations. The open question is, Are the homosexual partners related by kinship, as in the proceeding prohibited heterosexual relationships, and thus prohibited because of kinship relations, or are they prohibited as a class, as in the case of the menstruant?

Final Warning 18:26-30

These practices not only morally defile their doer but also defile the land itself. As a result, the land will cast out all its inhabitants. This may seem an unfair punishment, but collective punishments are inherently unfair. A rough and inexact example would be if someone polluted a community's water supply because of a desire to punish someone for an injury done to them. All suffer the effects of the pollution, although all are not guilty. The actions of a few can affect the well-being of the whole.

Moreover, the loss of the land is not an idle threat. The nations that previously lived in the land lost it because they practiced these sexual relationships. So also Israel, in its turn, will be rejected by the land if they practice them. This leaves open the question of whether other nations in other lands also lost their land because of their sexual behavior or only those living in the land of Canaan. Here the land polluted by these practices mentions only Canaan.

While the threat is national, the individual is also punished (v. 29). Everyone who practices the previously mentioned relationships will be cut off. This punishment may mean the destruction of a person's line, a punishment executed by God. (See 7:20 for being "cut off" as well as the essay *Cut Off, p. 299*.)

The last verse in chapter 18 is a negative echo of the beginning of the chapter. The one who practices God's commandments will find life by doing them (v. 5). The one who does not keep God's regulations for life will be cut off, and the nation will be expelled by the land. This speech ends as it began: *I Yahweh am your God* (v. 30 AT).

THE TEXT IN BIBLICAL CONTEXT
The Law Gives Life

The command and promise in 18:5, *You will observe my statutes and rules. Whoever does them, by them they will live* (AT), is a universal promise. The Hebrew uses the word *ʾadam (whoever)*, which here denotes anyone or humankind as a collective (cf. Gen 1:27). This statement occurs again in Ezekiel, where God says, "I gave them my decrees and made known to them my laws, by which the person who obeys them will live" (Ezek 20:11, 13, 21; Sprinkle: 28-34).

The necessity of law for life can be put differently (as mentioned above): "One does not live by bread alone, but by every word that comes from the mouth of the LORD" (Deut 8:3 NRSV). Food may come by the command of God and is necessary for life, but it is not sufficient alone, since the words of God as found in the law are also necessary.

People often understand law as a negative burden that brings guilt and pain. However, many biblical passages joyfully proclaim God's law as positive. In Psalm 119, for example, we find "Blessed are those who keep his statutes and seek him with all their heart" (v. 2) and "I will praise You with a sincere heart as I learn Your just rules" (v. 7 NJPS).

The happiness and meaning that comes by keeping the law is expressed in Psalm 119:17: "Deal kindly with Your servant, that I may live to keep Your word" (NJPS). To live a life grounded in God's law is a joy. It is life.

Paul and the Law

Many assume that Paul regarded the law as negative or useless: "If a law had been given that could impart life, then righteousness would certainly have come by the law" (Gal 3:21). Paul's fundamental thesis is "If righteousness could be gained through the law, *Christ died for nothing!*" (Gal 2:21, emph. added; on Paul's use of Lev 18:5, see Sprinkle: 131-207).

In Romans, however, Paul seems to contradict this basic thesis: "For it is not those who hear the law who are righteous in God's sight, but *it is those who obey the law who will be declared righteous*" (Rom 2:13, emph. added). He writes of rewards and punishments: "God 'will repay each person according to what they have done'" (Rom 2:6, quoting Ps 62:12 as the warrant). Paul ends his initial argument in Romans at 3:31: "Do we, then, nullify the law by this faith? Not at all! Rather, *we uphold the law*" (emph. added).

This apparent contradiction rests on a misunderstanding of the law's function. The Jews in Paul's day, just like the Israelites in Leviticus, were part of God's people by virtue of God's grace; God delivered them from Egypt and made a covenant with them. As a part of God's people, their question was "How do I maintain fellowship with God?" rather than "How do I become Jewish, part of God's people, so I can have a relationship with God?" To put it negatively, a Gentile could obey the whole law perfectly, but that would not make that person Jewish. To become a Jew, a Gentile would need to become a proselyte, which entailed circumcision and the *intention* to keep the law—for who could live a blameless life (Eccl 7:20)?

Paul is not working with the question "How do Gentiles become Jews?" but with "How do Gentiles become included, as Gentiles, in God's people?" Paul answers that it is not through obedience to the law (or circumcision) but through Jesus' death and justification by faith. The law plays no role in becoming justified in God's sight. Doing works of the law does not make one a Christian any more than it makes a person Jewish.

Paul has made justification by faith the entrance requirement for being in Christ rather than circumcision (see Acts 15 and the rejection of circumcision as an entrance requirement). However, once a person becomes in Christ, the law is a guide for living, a maintenance requirement, just as Leviticus was for those at Mount Sinai who also had previously experienced God's grace in the exodus. Seen this way, Paul has put the law on a firmer footing. It can't "save" anyone (using our language), but it is worthy of our obedience. For Paul's converts by faith, the law points to the way of life practiced by those who are in Christ, who no longer do the works of the flesh. However, not every law applies to the Gentile Christian. Paul can agree, for example, that Gentile Christians need to keep some food laws (Acts 15) and not agree to circumcision, because it is seen as an entrance requirement but can "save" no one (Gal 5:2).

E. P. Sanders (1977) is the starting point for this understanding of law and grace. James Dunn, a major voice for this point of departure in understanding Paul, provides background and a brief review for new positions emerging after Sanders (see Dunn: 150–55, 335–40). A sharp disagreement with Sanders's view on works of the law is found in Smiles (21–25). Perhaps the biggest gain from this rethinking of Paul's position on the law is that Paul's ideas make sense in their historical context. Paul no longer needs to be seen as a strange anomaly who would have made little sense, at least to the Jews and those Gentiles associated with the Jews of his time. Paul in Romans was addressing both Jews and Gentiles, and it is assumed that he wanted to make sense to them.

THE TEXT IN THE LIFE OF THE CHURCH
Latent Anti-Semitism

It is a commonplace understanding in New Testament scholarship today that much of nineteenth- and twentieth-century scholarship was tinged with anti-Semitism and failure to appreciate the Jewish milieu and thought of Jesus' and Paul's time. Scholars saw both Jesus and Paul as engaged in a polemic against the Jews and Jewish religion (see the earlier reference to Dunn). Since Jesus was presumed to have broken with his Jewish context, any statements attributed to Jesus were inauthentic if they fit scholars' understanding of first-century Judaism. Using this approach, which easily becomes circular, it was clear to them that Jesus made a decisive break with the Jewish teaching of his time. It has become a common assumption among many Christians that Jesus' teachings are unique and opposed to Jewish thought and practice. First-century Pharisees, for example, remain to this day a foil for many sermons and are portrayed in derogatory terms as the opposite of what characterizes Christians.

Leviticus and Jesus

Following E. P. Sanders (1977), who placed Paul in his Palestinian context, many scholars have come to understand the above-mentioned way of thinking as an inaccurate and unfair picture of the Judaisms of Jesus' time. There was a diversity of viewpoints within Judaism, and the internal debates were not always peaceful. On the other hand, it also seems that Jesus and Paul were more rooted in their Jewish environment than had been previously recognized, and a consideration of their context and lives as Jews is helpful in understanding them. Neither Jesus nor Paul lived or thought in a vacuum. Jesus made some kind of sense to the Jews of his time, and Paul, a Pharisee, was embedded, it seems, in the Judaisms of his time. In summary, the notion of the law as the antithesis of grace and the depiction of a monolithic Judaism as a religion of works must be rejected. On the contrary, the law leads to life.

The laws in Leviticus 18–22 are not given to replace grace: they *presume* God's grace. Israelites did not earn their liberation from Egypt by doing the works of the law. God's very identity is linked with grace in Exodus 6:2-8. The promises of freedom and land are God's doing alone and not a reward for Israel's goodness. In Leviticus 19:36, Israel is reminded that the God who speaks the commandments is the God who has brought them forth from Egypt. God's grace is frequently mentioned in chapters 18–26 (19:34, 36; 22:33; 23:43; 25:38; 26:13, 45).

The relationship between Israel and God was envisioned as a covenant (ch. 26). In Leviticus 26:9, God declares, *I will look on you with favor and make you fruitful and increase your numbers, and I will keep my covenant with you.* The law gives life because it enables the people to live in communion with God and to express their gratitude for God's grace.

When the covenant laws are ignored, keeping them becomes an imposition, and Israel comes to despise them and they reap the punishments outlined in chapter 26. However, God yet remains a God of grace. God does not abandon them. In the end we find God saying, *I will not spurn them, or abhor them so as to destroy them utterly and break my covenant with them; for I am the* LORD *their God* (Lev 26:44 NRSV)

Keeping the law was a response to God's grace and maintained Israel's covenant relationship with God. But in order to keep the law, scholars were needed to decide *how* to practice the commands of God. For example, what constitutes *work* on the Sabbath? Guidelines were needed, such as how far one could journey on the Sabbath. We who have little reverence for the Sabbath should not scorn those who sincerely wanted to practice one of God's commandments.

We even find Jesus affirming the scholars and their task: "The teachers of the law and the Pharisees sit in Moses' seat. So you must be careful to do everything they tell you" (Matt 23:2-3). What Jesus could not tolerate was hypocrisy and an attention to minutia while "the more important matters of the law—justice, mercy and faithfulness" were neglected (23:23). This was not a debate about the validity of the law but about its practice and purpose.

Two of the most prominent teachers in Jewish history, Hillel and Shammai, lived shortly before Jesus. Hillel was lenient in his interpretation of the law, while Shammai was very strict. There were heated debates between these two schools of thought. In his ministry, Jesus was entering contested waters and was challenged on his teaching and practices by the Pharisees of both parties to see where he stood or which faction he supported. In fact, Jesus sided with the strict school of Shammai on the matter of divorce. What we may see as conflict was Jesus taking sides on differences of interpretation by his fellow Jews. (On Shammai and Hillel, see Ben-Shalom regarding the opposition between these scholars that was bitterly carried on by their students through much of the first century CE. Jesus' remarks concerning the Pharisees were mild compared to the polemics and violence carried out between these two factions.)

Practicing Christians

The church or a congregation cannot determine who is justified by faith. This depends on God, not on a committee's decision, least of all by vote. Unfortunately, many congregations and denominations spend a great deal of time deciding who is in and who is out. This may be done over doctrinal issues or over matters of piety and practice. Today, even political positions may determine the status of a person in a congregation or split denominations into opposing factions.

In this debate the proper question may be missed: What practices mark the life of a person who is responding to God's grace? What are the positive hallmarks of a believer? Instead, we decide who is a "Christian" in negative terms—by what a person is against. *Christian* has become for many a generic adjective meaning political conservative.

For Jews today, *Christian* is a polite way of saying *Gentile*—non-Jew or anti-Jew—because people by that identification have affected Jews most negatively. After all, the death camps were staffed by Christians in the Second World War. We should not be surprised that Muslims have experienced Christians in the same way through the atrocities and "collateral damage" Christians have committed in their countries. Some Christians may even view these actions positively.

Given the negative connotations of words like *Christian* and *evangelical*, perhaps we should adopt a phrase like "practicing Christian" for self-identity. Just as there are Jews and then there are "observant Jews" to differentiate between people who are Jewish by birth or nationality and those who practice being Jewish, "practicing Christian" might designate a positive way of life that in Jesus' terms is about "justice, mercy, and faithfulness." It would be a life that gives life rather than bitterness and enmity. We would ask, What practices display a concern for biblical justice and mercy?

In Paul's parlance, practicing Christians would be fruitful Christians—those whose lives show "love, joy, peace, forbearance, kindness, goodness, faithfulness, gentleness and self-control" (Gal 5:22-23) rather than "hatred, discord, jealousy, fits of rage, selfish ambition, dissensions, factions and envy" (Gal 5:20-21). As Jesus said, "By their fruit you will recognize them" (Matt 7:20).

Leviticus 19:1-37

Holiness in Daily Life

PREVIEW

Israel's God requires holiness by those who worship this God. But how does one become holy? We might think it comes through piety, such as saying prayers at mealtime or bedtime. But Leviticus makes clear that holiness is gained and maintained by following God's guidelines for holy living. Worship may be done in a holy place, but it is in life that holiness is manifested *[Worship and Ethics, p. 320]*.

Explicit instructions for holy living begin in chapter 19, and they explain what it means to live a holy life, whether in public or in private. In chapter 18 the Israelites were told what they *must not do* to remain undefiled; chapter 19 tells them what they *must do* to become holy.

The instructions for holy living are given in the form of a list of topics. Usually the commands are short, and the topics change frequently. The transition from one subject to the next may be quite abrupt, which gives the chapter a feeling of incoherence. The instructions concern attitudes and feelings as well as behavior. The form in which they are given also varies. Some commands are in apodictic form—"You shall not . . ."—like in the Ten Commandments. Some are in case form—"When this happens, then . . ." This difference in style is illustrated by verses 3-4, which are apodictic law, while verses 5-8 are case law. For these reasons it is hard to see an overall structure or coherence in chapter 19. Although coherence has been sought among the short paragraphs, one is left wondering why this follows that. The commentary below tries to explain what the associations might be, leading from one topic to another. You may find others.

We do have one helper, at least in dividing the chapter into paragraphs: the statement *I, the LORD your God, am holy* (e.g., 19:2), along with its shorter version, *I am the LORD*, occurs frequently and usually serves to end individual units of instruction. For example, verse 4, *I the LORD am your God* (NJPS), concludes a repetition of the fifth, fourth, and second commandments from the Ten Commandments. What follows in verses 5-8 obviously has a different topic: eating the meat of the peace offering.

The following outline reflects the apparent jumble of topics in chapter 19 and their various lengths. (For detailed proposals on the structure and coherence of chapter 19, see Milgrom 2000; Schwartz 1999; Milgrom's proposal builds on that of Schwartz.)

OUTLINE

Introduction, 19:1-2a
Heading: The Call to Holiness, 19:2b
Holy Actions, 19:3-36a
    19:3-4   The Ten Commandments
    19:5-8   A Digression: The Peace Offering
    19:9-10   The Imperative of Generosity
    19:11-18   Social Morality
    19:19-25   Issues of Sex and Fertility
    19:26-28   Manipulating God
    19:29-32   Miscellaneous Commands
    19:33-36a   Treatment of the Resident Foreigner
The Final Exhortation, 19:36b-37

Leviticus 19:3-36 Topics and Connections with the Ten Commandments	
The 5th, 4th, and 2nd commandments: parents, Sabbath, images	vv. 3-4
The peace sacrifice	vv. 5-8
Social justice in resources	vv. 9-10
The 8th, 9th, and 3rd commandments: stealing, falsehood, God's name	vv. 11-12
Do no harm	vv. 13-18
To the less fortunate	vv. 13-14
In dispensing justice	v. 15
In community conduct	v. 16
In personal relationships	vv. 17-18
Do not mix kinds	v. 19
The rights of a slave	vv. 20-22
The rights of a tree	vv. 23-25
Forbidden practices	vv. 26-29
Ingesting blood	v. 26
Short hair	v. 27
Defacing skin	v. 28
Prostituting a daughter	v. 29
The 4th commandment: Sabbath	v. 30
No divination	v. 31
The 5th commandment: parents	v. 32
Fairness for the immigrant	vv. 33-34
Honesty in commerce	vv. 35-36

EXPLANATORY NOTES

Introduction 19:1-2a

Chapter 19 is set apart from 18 by the beginning of a new speech addressed to *the whole congregation of the Israelites* (v. 2a AT). The *congregation* (*'edah*) is a formal assembly of the entire nation called on special occasions. The covenant at Mount Sinai was made with such a convocation (Exod 35:1), as was the assembly to witness the ordination of the priests (Lev 8:4). The phrase *the whole congregation* indicates that this is a special occasion and that what follows is especially significant.

Heading: The Call to Holiness 19:2b

The first words of this speech call for Israel to be holy. The necessity for the people's holiness is that God is holy. The adjective "holy" has multiple meanings. It can mean (1) something or someone belonging to God or the divine realm, or (2) something or someone set apart for a task. In the latter sense, it has the connotation of calling, as in the case of Jeremiah, "I consecrated you [made you holy]; I appointed you a prophet concerning the nations" (Jer 1:5 NJPS). Jeremiah was made holy for a reason. In Leviticus 21:6 we find that the priests are to be holy to God because they serve God through making sacrifices on the altar. Being in the realm of the divine requires being holy [*Holy and Holiness, p. 302*].

Holy Actions 19:3-36a

19:3-4 *The Ten Commandments*

Commandments from the Ten Commandments are scattered throughout this chapter. Three of these apodictic commands [*Law, p. 304*] initiate this section, beginning with the fifth commandment: *respect for mother and father* (v. 3a; cf. Exod 20; Deut 5). Two features in the wording of this commandment are instructive. First, mother is mentioned before father, whereas in Exodus 20:12 and Deuteronomy 5:16, father precedes mother. This reversal of order shows that both parents are to be given equal respect. Second, the Hebrew term for the NRSV's *revere* (*yareʾ*) occurs here, whereas Exodus uses the word "honor." The same deference or respect shown to the Sabbath and the temple (below in v. 30) is to characterize the respect children give their parents.

Next is the commandment to guard or keep the Sabbath, the fourth commandment. In Exodus 20:8-11, specific instructions are given for keeping the Sabbath as well as a reason for doing so: God rested on the seventh day. Deuteronomy gives a different rationale: it is a day of rest "so that your male and female servants may rest, as you do" (5:14). In Leviticus we find only the bare command followed by *I Yahweh am your God*. Keeping the Sabbath is part of being God's people.

The second commandment is echoed in verse 4 (cf. Exod 20:5-6). The people are not to have recourse to *ʾelilim*, worthless or deceptive idols (*DCH*). This is perhaps a wordplay on the Hebrew word for god (*ʾel*) and is used as a term of disparagement for other deities. This prohibition forbids casting images to represent other deities. It is a more limited command than the one we find in Exodus 20:4: "You shall not make for yourself *an image in the form of anything* in heaven above or on the earth beneath or in the waters below" (emph. added; cf. Deut 5:8-10).

From Exodus we know that God commanded the Israelites to make images and to place them in the holy of holies: "There, above the cover between the two cherubim that are over the ark of the covenant law, I will meet with you and give you all my commands for the Israelites" (Exod 25:22). The cherubim marked the place of God's presence. These creatures faced each other and had wings that were raised over the ark (25:18-20). They certainly did not represent another deity.

19:5-8 A Digression: The Peace Offering

Although *I Yahweh am your God* (v. 4 AT) marks a break before verses 5-8, these verses do continue the theme of worshiping God found in verse 4. This paragraph regulates the eating of the peace offering. The people must eat all the meat of a peace offering within two days. Any meat left until the third day must not be eaten. It is unfit for use and is no longer acceptable (*DCH*; see the parallel in 7:18). The person who violates this restriction is guilty of profaning the holiness of God and will be cut off *[Cut Off, p. 299]*.

19:9-10 The Imperative of Generosity

The peace offering was a time of generosity and celebration, and the meat from this sacrifice was shared with others. While sharing the meat of the peace offering is not commanded here, we learn from Deuteronomy 26:11-13 that the less fortunate were to enjoy the bounty of the harvest at the time of the firstfruits offering and from the tithe. Generosity seems built into the sacrificial system.

Now generosity is extended from worship into secular life. The Israelite farmer may not harvest his entire crop. The corners must be left. Likewise, what remains after harvesting should be left for gleaners (v. 9; see Ruth 2). With vineyards, the vines should not be picked clean, nor should grapes that fall to the ground be picked up (v. 10). These parts of the harvest must be left for the poor and for the immigrant.

19:11-18 Social Morality

The four paragraphs in this section command holiness in relationships between people. These commands are in apodictic form: this is how you will act, no ifs, ands, or buts about it. Sometimes a reason is given for a command, but usually it is not.

Commands regarding the Neighbor, 19:11-14. A cluster of significant words defining social relationships are used in this unit. At the end of verse 11 we find the word "fellow" (*'amit*), usually translated "one another." As an important word in this section, it occurs in verses 11, 15, and 17—also in 6:2; 18:20; 24:19; and 25:14-17. It is a Leviticus word, occurring elsewhere only in Zechariah 13:7. Another word, "neighbor," is found in verses 13, 16, and 18. Surprisingly, "brother" is used only once, in verse 17, where it is parallel to "fellow." That "brother" occurs only once in these verses suggests that the emphasis falls on social relations within Israelite society rather than only within the extended family *[Jubilee Year, p. 304]*.

This unit begins with more of the Ten Commandments in verses 11-12. First comes the *eighth* commandment, *Do not steal.* In context, stealing seems to refer to taking the whole harvest and thus stealing from the poor. If this is so, then the edges of the field and the fallen grapes rightly belong to the poor rather than represent an act of charity. The *ninth* commandment prohibits bearing false witness. Verse 12 stipulates that oaths are to be taken only in God's name, as also emphasized elsewhere: "You must revere the LORD your God: only Him shall you worship, to Him shall you hold fast, and by His name shall you swear" (Deut 10:20 NJPS). Swearing to the truth of a falsehood uses God's "name in vain" (Exod 20:7 KJV). (See examples of fraudulent oaths in Lev 6:1-2.)

The theme of doing right by your fellow is continued in verses 13-14. The prohibition against oppressing a neighbor appears often in the Bible. Deuteronomy 24:14 and Jeremiah 7:6 spell out those who are most likely to be oppressed: "You shall not abuse a needy and destitute laborer" (Deut 24:14 NJPS). "Do not oppress the foreigner, the fatherless or the widow" (Jer 7:6). Here in Leviticus 19:14, paired with concern for the oppressed, is a command concerning the deaf and the blind, examples of those who may easily be treated wrongly. Even if your victim is not aware of your harmful behavior, you must not inconvenience or harm them.

Commands against Injustice and Slander, 19:15-16. You should not act unjustly or dishonestly in dispensing justice. The weak and the powerful should receive the same attention and justice. On the positive side, you are to judge your fellow rightly or fairly. The word translated *fairly* (*ṣedeq*) occurs four times in verse 36 below. There it describes measures of weight and quantity. It is usually translated *honest.* These are measures that meet the official standard. Likewise, legal decisions must measure up to a standard of justice that transcends individual cases and their parties. What is just must be done in all cases.

One way to tarnish another person and deny them a fair hearing or rebuttal is to spread slander or gossip about them (*DCH*). Such actions give someone the taint of wrongdoing (see the ninth commandment against "false witness" [NRSV] in Exod 20:16). The axiom "Where there's smoke, there's fire" is the opposite of this verse. If a person has done wrong, show it. If not, don't keep suspicions alive by building a hypothetical fire.

The meaning of the last clause in Leviticus 19:16—*You shall not stand upon the blood of your neighbor* (AT)—is uncertain. Some find this clause to be an allusion to profiting from another's death. Others propose that it refers to doing something that endangers another's life. Another possibility, *You must not stand idly by when your neighbor's life is at stake* (NET), could be linked to the case in 5:1, where someone has seen a wrong committed but will not testify as to who actually did it. Perhaps their testimony would exonerate the accused (see Milgrom 2000: 1645). This would be the opposite of the previous verse: slander expresses what is untrue, which contrasts with the duty to speak the truth, if known. Yet this command may also be related to the sixth commandment, which prohibits murder (Exod 20:13).

Disposition toward Others, 19:17-18. These verses turn from actions to attitudes—from the external to the internal, from what can be seen to what cannot be proved—ending with the best-known command in the Hebrew Bible (OT), *Love your fellow as yourself* (v. 18 NJPS). The paragraph, however, begins with hate instead of love: *Do not hate a fellow Israelite in your heart* (v. 17). These two antithetical statements, concerning hate and love, form an envelope around the four commands found between them. This structure appears to indicate that all six commands are part of a single unit and form the immediate context for understanding the first and last commands. Specifically, the negative command in verse 17 parallels the positive command in verse 18, as shown in the following chart.

Lev 19:17	Lev 19:18
1 Do not hate a fellow Israelite in your heart.	2' Do not seek revenge or bear a grudge against anyone among your people,
2 Rebuke your neighbor [fellow] frankly so you will not share in their guilt.	1' but love your neighbor as yourself. I am the LORD.

The phrase *in your heart* stresses the mental and dispositional aspect of *You shall not hate your brother* (ʾaḥ in Heb.; AT). Hating a brother reminds us of the story of Joseph and his brothers. From the very beginning, the brothers hated Joseph in their hearts but could not act on it (Gen 37:4, 5, 8). In the end, hatred led to action. To avoid actions driven by hatred, such as vengeance, don't hate.

Don't harbor evil dispositions, like bearing a grudge. Reprove or lodge a complaint (Hartley). This is the proper response to an offense. In Genesis 21:25 we find that Abraham reproved or lodged a complaint against Abimelek about the ownership of a well. Rather than take vengeance, Abraham achieved an amicable settlement.

Incur no guilt because of him, the text continues (NJPS). Based on the command's parallel, *Take no vengeance*, reproving another would free a person from acting in hatred and bearing the guilt of vengeance and *bearing sin on his account* (AT). These commands seem to represent two scenarios. In one, hatred leads to action and bearing sin. The other leads to confrontation and avoids acting on hatred.

Do not seek revenge or bear a grudge (v. 18). Vengeance is getting back at someone, using superior power or advantage to do harm to another. An example is Lamech's boast: "If Cain is avenged seven times, then Lamech seventy-seven times" (Gen 4:24). Better to reprove another than do wrong. The verb translated *bear a grudge* is difficult since it seems to mean both (1) to keep or to guard, and (2) to be angry (*HALOT*). However, these disparate meanings may belong to two different verbs with the same spelling (homonyms), as *DCH* suggests. If so, the translation would be *You shall not be angry* (AT). This translation would form a parallel to *reprove* in its parallel clause. Instead of getting mad and getting even, don't get mad. Instead, confront the other.

Instead of hating, taking vengeance, or even holding a grudge, *Love your fellow [neighbor] as yourself* (v. 18 NJPS). The usual translation has *neighbor* instead of *fellow* (reaʿ). However, *fellow* is the better translation, as we see from Deuteronomy 4:42: "Anyone who accidentally killed someone [reaʿ] without hating him at the time of the accident . . ." (NET). *Your fellow* refers to anyone you might meet and kill, not just to killing the person who lives next door. In verse 17 you are not to hate your brother—a kinship term—perhaps because you will be most likely to hate those you are close to (e.g., a spouse is a likely suspect in murder cases). Here in verse 18, "fellow" seems to designate another person in general. You are to love everyone with whom you come in contact—as in the story of the good Samaritan

(Luke 10:30-37). Jesus was indicating how to apply this law of love to one's fellow human being.

The phrase *as yourself* has been construed in different ways. Some understand this command to say that just as you are worthy of love, so also your fellow human is worthy of love (Hartley). Preferable to deriving meaning from a psychological understanding of self-worth is placing this positive command in opposition to the preceding negative commands. Loving one's fellow is the opposite of vengeance, anger, and hatred. To love your fellow is, at a minimum, to do them no harm. As Rabbi Hillel said, "That which is hateful to you, do not do to your fellow" (Milgrom 2000: 1653).

In the New Testament we find Jesus commanding, "In everything, treat others as you would want them to treat you, for this fulfills the law and the prophets" (Matt 7:12 NET). For loving others, the minimal standard is (1) whatever I would not want done to me, I will not do to another; and (2) what I wish others would do for me in this situation, I will do for another. Love does no harm to the other, but extends help, regardless of whether one feels loved (cf. Rom 13:10). These are apodictic laws. Verse 18 ends with *I am Yahweh*, marking the end of the unit.

19:19-25 Issues of Sex and Fertility

These verses revolve around sexual behaviors and fertility practices. The unit begins with *Keep my decrees*, although a more literal translation of the Hebrew text is *My laws you will keep* (AT, emph. added), with the verb's object coming first to make laws the focus of the command. The following verses present these laws.

First, verse 19 forbids three mixtures: (1) mating two different kinds of animals, (2) planting two kinds of seed in the same plot, and (3) wearing a garment with two kinds of cloth. These prohibitions are repeated, with variation, in Deuteronomy 22:9-11. Regarding the third, a garment with two kinds of cloth, Deuteronomy defines this as cloth made with both wool and linen (22:11). This type of cloth was used in making the tabernacle. It was also used for some of the clothes of the high priest (Exod 26:1, 31; 28:6, 15). Its use for holy objects and persons has led to the notion that it was reserved for holy use alone (see Milgrom 2000: 1656-65). As for the other two mixtures, many conjecture that they were meant to maintain the order that God created (see Hartley). There is no doubt that Genesis 1 is about bringing order to chaos—separating light from darkness, water from water, land from water, and so forth. The priestly material is very concerned about order, and these commands may very well have been placed here to stress the importance of the natural order.

Leviticus 19:20-22 deals with the issue of sexual relationships with slaves. It is not a capital crime (as it would be with a free woman) for a man to have a sexual relationship with a slave girl who is promised in marriage to another if she has not been given her freedom. However, that man must pay compensation to her present owner for the women's loss of value as a mate for someone. Besides this civil penalty, the man has also incurred guilt and must bring a ram as a penalty offering. The priest will make purification on his behalf, and he will be forgiven the sin he committed.

Why is this law necessary when female and male slaves are considered to be property (chattel)? The *punishment* is not specified (v. 20), and the fine imposed on the transgressor, a ram for a penalty offering, would be a deterrent, providing at least some protection to female slaves. However, if a female slave is violated, she receives no compensation.

The commandment in verses 23-25 is intended for the future, when Israel has come into the land and planted fruit-bearing trees. When this happens, they are not to use the fruit from a tree for three years. Then, in the fourth year, the fruit is to be treated as holy, *a celebration offering for the LORD* (AT). This is an unusual expression, the word for "celebration" occurring again only in Judges 9:27: "They went out to the field, harvested their grapes, squeezed out the juice, and celebrated" (NET). In Judges, this celebration comes at the end of the grape harvest; here in Leviticus all edible produce from trees is to be celebrated. It seems to represent a type of firstfruits offering (Hartley). Finally, in the fifth year, they may eat the fruit. This might be a pragmatic command: by waiting to use the fruit of their trees, perhaps they assumed they would get more fruit during the life of the tree. Or it may be based on showing mercy to the fruit tree. (See the law in Deut 22:6-7, where a mother bird is spared if her chicks are taken. She is to be allowed to hatch any eggs on which she is sitting.)

19:26-28 Manipulating God

Readers may wonder what theme unifies the practices found in verses 26-28. The paragraph begins with *You shall not eat upon the blood* (v. 26a AT). Given what follows, Milgrom seeks to understand this verse as representing a type of divination. He refers to 1 Samuel 14:33, where eating upon the blood, he believes, refers to the blood of the animal soaking into the ground and was a form of honor for spirits (Milgrom 2000: 1685-89). Usually 1 Samuel 14:33 is understood as a command to not eat meat with its blood, which explains why Saul had the people slaughter their animals on a stone so that the blood would drain properly. In that case it would be more about purity laws than divination. (See Hartley for a variety of ways to construe this clause.)

The second half of the verse (26b) prohibits seeking or using supernatural forces to get around God or to bend God to someone's will. The practice of divination, seeking omens, or foretelling the future bypasses God, who alone determines the future and reveals it to humans. Divination practices were followed by the nations around them. But God has appointed prophets for communicating to the people when and what God wants them to know (Deut 18:14-15).

Leviticus 19:27-28 may relate to practices that try to attract God's attention, whether in mourning or in worship. The priests of Baal would slash themselves and bleed to attract Baal's attention so that he would grant their plea (1 Kings 18:28). Not so the prophets of Israel. These practices could also be a way of mourning for the dead in the hope of attracting God's attention to their miserable plight (Deut 14:1).

The restriction against cutting the hair at the side or corner of the head is practiced by Orthodox Jews who wear *peyot* (side curls). Most Amish men, although they do not wear *peyot*, do not trim their beards in order to comply with this rule.

19:29-32 Miscellaneous Commands

A variety of commands occur in the following three paragraphs (vv. 29-32), marked by *I am Yahweh* or *I Yahweh am your God*. First there is a command against the profanation or degrading of a daughter by making her a prostitute (v. 29). In 21:15 is a related command: a priest is not to profane his children. Profaning is the opposite of consecrating, making holy. In general, the people are not to practice prostitution, because then the land will become full of debauchery.

Next is the command for careful observance of the Sabbath and reverence for God's sanctuary (v. 30). These commands guard the holiness of Sabbath time and the holiness of space, the sanctuary.

Verse 31 returns to the subject of seeking information or help by unauthorized means. The Israelites are not to have recourse to those who can call up the spirits of the dead. An example is the story of Saul in 1 Samuel 28:7-14. When God did not answer Saul by any of the legitimate ways, Saul turned to a medium who could call up spirits of the dead from Sheol. The Israelites are not to soil themselves by using such means. They are to seek God alone.

The last item is respect for older people (v. 32). One is to rise before those with gray hair, that is, the aged. While Israelites were not to show honor (*hadar*, meaning favoritism) to the powerful in judgment (v. 15), they were to show honor (*hadar*, meaning respect) to the elderly.

19:33-36a Treatment of the Resident Foreigner

The basic law is that the immigrant, the resident non-Israelite (NIV, *foreigner*), must be treated as though a citizen or native Israelite. Just as the fellow Israelite is not to be oppressed or treated unfairly (25:14, 17), so too the immigrant is not to be oppressed.

There is to be no discrimination. Instead, you are to love them (19:34). This, of course, is the great commandment of 19:18 applied to all who live among the Israelites in their land. It may even be a greater commandment than verse 18, for who is more difficult to love—your fellow, your neighbor, or the foreigner, the immigrant? The reason and motivation for this love is declared: *You were foreigners in the land of Egypt* (v. 34). You know what it means to be an outsider and oppressed, living in your own ghetto in the land of Goshen. This paragraph ends with *I Yahweh am your God* (AT).

How is love shown to the immigrant as well as to citizens? Verses 35-36 speak to this. First, there is the very basic obligation: you are not to pervert justice, that is, you must *not* be *dishonest* when measuring length, weight, or liquid (v. 35). Second, you must use *accurate* and *honest* weights, dry measures, and liquid measures. Your pound should be a pound, whether you are dealing with a fellow Israelite or an immigrant (v. 36). In other words, honesty and fair practices apply to all: there should be no discrimination.

The Final Exhortation 19:36b-37

The reason and motivation for these laws is emphatic: *I the LORD [Yahweh] am your God who freed you from the land of Egypt* (v. 36b NJPS). This is the same declaration that begins the Ten Commandments in Exodus 20:2. Liberation carries with it the responsibility to live according to the will of the one who freed you. While in Egypt, you obeyed the Egyptians. Now that you have a new ruler, you must obey the rules of the one who says, "I freed you from slavery" (paraphrased).

The "therefore" that follows grace comes in the next verse: <u>*Therefore*</u> *shall ye observe all my statutes* (v. 37 KJV, emph. added). The chapter concludes in verse 37 with *I am Yahweh*. The practices commanded or prohibited are based on the sovereignty of God. God makes their laws, not the king. As the people accept the yoke of heaven, they become holy and continue to live in God's presence.

THE TEXT IN BIBLICAL CONTEXT

Love Your Neighbor

What is the greatest commandment in the Hebrew Bible? When asked this question, Jesus answered by quoting Deuteronomy 6:5, "Love the Lord your God with all your heart and with all your soul and with all your mind" (Matt 22:37). Then he added a second commandment, quoting Leviticus 19:18, "Love your neighbor as yourself" (Matt 22:39). To this Jesus added, "All the Law and the Prophets hang on these two commandments" (22:40). These two commandments are not the most important among many others, but they provide the very basis for all the rest. Remove this hook, and the rest falls to the ground like rubble.

Love for God plays a major role in Deuteronomy, where it is usually coupled with obedience: "If you carefully observe all these commands I am giving you to follow—to love the LORD your God, to walk in obedience to him and to hold fast to him" (Deut 11:22). But can the Israelite love God with heart, soul, and might? Deuteronomy says yes: God will give the Israelites the ability because God "will circumcise your hearts and the hearts of your descendants, so that you may love him with all your heart and with all your soul, and live" (30:6). The command to love God is found elsewhere in the Old Testament (e.g., Josh 22:5; 23:11; Ps 31:23). Love for God or the expression of that love is a motif in the Psalms and is confessed whenever Israel uses the Psalms.

In Luke 10:27 these commands are joined into a single command. Jesus illustrates their meaning by the parable of the good Samaritan. Jesus' ethical interpretation of the law is to show love to those in need. The operative word is *show*, as the parable demonstrates.

Paul picks up on the love of neighbor in Romans 13:8-10. The reason is that "whoever loves others has fulfilled the law" (13:8), which means "love is the fulfillment of the law" (13:10). Paul seems to be saying that if you truly love your neighbor, you will keep the law through this love. Each loving act fulfills what is in the law, just like stopping at each stop sign fulfills the law. Stopping once, fulfilling the law one time, does not do away with stop signs or the need to stop wherever they appear. So also love does not do away with the law but complies with it.

First John, of which love is the central topic, declares: "For whoever does not love their brother and sister, whom they have seen, cannot love God, whom they have not seen" (1 John 4:20; also 5:2). Love for fellow members takes on the function of a membership rule. If you don't show love to your neighbor, then how can you think that you love God with your whole being? Why would you believe that you belong to God's people and the reign of God?

Finally, note that many today believe that love and hate describe emotions and cannot be commanded: you cannot love someone because someone tells you to do so. On the contrary, as the illustration of the good Samaritan demonstrates, love means showing loving actions. Likewise, you can refuse to act in a hateful manner and can avoid emotions that do lead to sinful actions: *Do not hate a fellow Israelite in your heart* (Lev 19:17) or *bear a grudge* (Lev 19:18). Jesus also illustrates how to guard against acting from hate: don't even become angry with your fellow, because "anyone who is angry with a brother or sister will be subject to judgment" (Matt 5:22). Thus, while we cannot be forced to love, we can repress thoughts and actions that express hate. Likewise, we can encourage thoughts and actions that express love. The Bible guides us in the way of love, which flows from loving God. We are not without guidelines for what shows love.

THE TEXT IN THE LIFE OF THE CHURCH

Love for Each Other

One of the most known and repeated commands is Jesus' statement "Love one another. As I have loved you, so you must love one another" (John 13:34; also Rom 13:8; and frequently in 1 John). But it has been easier for many to love their brothers and sisters far away than to love those at home. Their faraway needs are so great, their resources are so meager, and they deserve our help. At home, we may think that poverty, homelessness, and hunger are the problem of the state. Perhaps we even think that it is not the role of government to supply food, housing, and medical care or to subsidize the living of the poor. We may assume, without evidence, that poor people suffer because they do not seek work that they could do or show initiative in getting an education. We may believe that, in general, citizens have *political* rights, such as the right to vote and the right to free speech. Yet these rights do not clothe anyone, provide medical care, help anyone in prison, feed anyone or give them something to drink, or make an immigrant feel at home (see Matt 25:35-36).

Fortunately, *love is not based on merit.* Jesus loves us not because we deserve it, but because love is extended to those who are needy. Jesus asks rhetorically, "If you love those who love you, what reward will you get? Are not even the tax collectors doing that?" (Matt 5:46). Love is demonstrated by acting in love toward those who are not of our circle, as the parable of the good Samaritan shows. Jesus commands, "Love your enemies" (5:44). If we can love even our enemies, we should be able to extend material aid to those who are not our enemies, even when we believe they don't deserve it.

This is all well known to Christians. So what is our problem? In biblical times there was comparatively little mobility, settlements were smaller, houses were smaller, and less space was available. All these factors led to people knowing their neighbors: they might well be relatives. In this context, people knew the rest of the villagers. Those who lived close to them knew them very well. In such a tight social situation, knowing others' needs was almost automatic. And those who helped others could expect the same in return.

Many of us no longer live in small villages for a lifetime, as many did in Israel. No longer do people in the West know about the needs of others through daily interactions. Learning about needs through public media may paralyze us: resources at hand are certainly too scanty to solve the social needs of a community, let alone those farther away. But love, as in the parable of the good Samaritan, does not solve a general problem, in this case the problem of banditry and its victims. Rather, it is about helping those we encounter who have needs.

The command to love is about being a loving person, not about solving a national issue or creating a loving nation. These are worthy objectives and worth striving toward. Certainly it is better to have a nation that values and expresses love more than hate. But however much we may have our eye on a larger social issue, in our life we must show love for others. Love is often a problem of will and commitment. For Leviticus, the motivation is holiness. Loving actions toward others is one way to be holy. But in Leviticus 19 it is one among many ways of being set apart as a holy people.

Leviticus 20:1-27
Holiness as Obedience

PREVIEW

Is it good to be religious? Isn't religion generally conservative, seeking to preserve rather than to improve? Many people consider the church and Christian people as opposed to values such as justice, equality, or other positive ethical values for the greater good of others. In fact, people may be surprised to find a Christian valuing or working toward a more equitable society. How much less is "holiness" seen to be a value or a concern to foster! Being holy is probably equated with being a "religious" or "pious" person quite unconcerned with larger social issues. In Leviticus, holiness is not a religious virtue, but a public virtue that shapes our "secular" lives. It is about how we live. For Leviticus, obedience, holiness, and being God's people are inseparable.

While holiness is a general theme in the previous two chapters, we now find explicit demands for holiness in Leviticus 20. First, at the beginning of the chapter, Israel is told to make themselves holy, to sanctify themselves, by careful observance of the commandments (vv. 7-8). Second, at the end of the chapter, Israel is instructed to be a separate people by keeping the statutes given by God (vv. 24, 26).

The practices for holy living in chapter 20 are somewhat repetitive of what has come before. The largest set of commandments concern sexual transgressions, which are already found in chapter 18. The biggest difference is that in chapter 20 the punishment for transgression is the death of the individual, whereas in chapter 18 the community as a whole was punished by being vomited out of the land [*Worship and Ethics, p. 320*].

Chapter 20 may be divided into two uneven parts. The first part contains two commandments and ends with an exhortation. The second part contains multiple commandments and ends in a much longer exhortation.

OUTLINE

Introduction, 20:1-2a
The Defilement of the Sanctuary, 20:2b-8
    20:2b-5   Worship of Molek
    20:6   Consulting Diviners
    20:7-8   Exhortation to Become Holy
Forbidden Sexual Relations, 20:9-21
Exhortation for Obedience, 20:22-26
Addendum: No Wizards, 20:27

EXPLANATORY NOTES

Introduction 20:1-2a

Although the chapter begins normally, the speech beginning in verse 2 starts in an unusual way. Israel, the audience, precedes the verb: *To the Israelites say* . . . (AT). This unusual wording occurs elsewhere in Leviticus only at the inauguration of worship (9:3) and the prohibition of blasphemy (24:15). It may alert us to pay attention to what follows, perhaps because the first topic is of extraordinary importance: the defilement of the sanctuary.

The Defilement of the Sanctuary 20:2b-8

20:2b-5 Worship of Molek

Two commandments are addressed to the Israelites and to the Gentiles living in Israel (v. 2b). The first states the punishment for giving one's own child to Molek (NRSV, *Molech*): *That person shall certainly be caused to die* (AT). *Be caused to die* is an expression often found in apodictic law *[Law, p. 304]*. Since the verb in this expression is passive, no subject is given, and usually no means are mentioned, as in Exodus 21:15, "Whoever strikes his father or his mother must surely be put to death" (NET). In Leviticus 20:2, however, the people carry out this sentence by pelting the guilty party with stones. The ones throwing the stones are called the *people of the land* (NRSV, NET, NJPS), meaning the community as a whole (see Exod 5:5). The responsibility for killing the transgressor falls on everyone. In addition, God also will turn against such a person and cut them off (Lev 20:3), and their line will be extinguished in Israel (see 7:20).

The very act of sacrificing a child to another deity defiles God's sanctuary and profanes God's sacred name. How does this act, performed away from the temple, perhaps in an uninhabited place, defile the temple? When a sin is committed, it evidently has an effect on the altar. Receiving forgiveness requires applying the blood of the cleansing offering to the altar on account of the results of sin (ch. 4). Once a year the shrine and its furniture are cleansed of all the sins of the people, and they are carried off into the wilderness to eliminate them from tabernacle and community. It seems that sin has an immediate effect on the altar, and a long-term residue remains that needs removal through a special ceremony (see the comments on Lev 4; 16; 15:31; and the essay *Atonement, p. 288*).

20:6 Consulting Diviners

Suddenly, the focus shifts from the worship of Molek to diviners. Two types are mentioned. First mentioned are *mediums*. These are persons who practice necromancy, who (supposedly) can raise or communicate with a dead person. Saul sought out a medium so that he could converse with Samuel (1 Sam 28:4-19). He was forced to consult a necromancer because God did not communicate with him through normal channels: by dreams, by the priestly oracle (Urim), or by prophets (1 Sam 28:6).

Consulting other sources of information about the future was forbidden because God gave Israel another way: the prophets (Deut 18:9-15). Communication began on God's end, not on the people's end. It may be significant that at the beginning of the list of forbidden divination practices in Deuteronomy we find "Let no one be found among you who sacrifices their son or daughter in the fire" (Deut 18:10). As in Leviticus 20, the prohibition of necromancy follows that of child sacrifice. Just like worshiping other gods, divination was an attempt to use another source of power to obtain what was desired.

20:7-8 Exhortation to Become Holy

The exhortation for Israel to sanctify themselves occurred previously in 11:44 after the instructions concerning pure and impure meat. Now the people are to become holy through obedience. The exhortation to holiness, *You must sanctify yourselves and be holy* (v. 7 NET), entails doing the commands of God: *You shall faithfully observe*

My laws (v. 8 NJPS). Why? *I Yahweh am making you holy* (v. 8 AT). The Israelites sanctify themselves by keeping the commands of God because obedience is God's means of making them holy.

Forbidden Sexual Relations 20:9-21

The following paragraphs concern tabooed sexual relationships, except for verse 9, which prohibits cursing parents. This same command is found in Exodus 21:17: "Anyone who curses their father or mother is to be put to death" (see also Deut 21:18-21; 27:16). The word translated *curse* can have the connotation of treating with contempt (1 Sam 3:13) and is the opposite of honoring father and mother (Exod 20:12). This command may occur here because some of the sexual acts listed below would show contempt toward father and mother.

Lack of respect also characterizes the act of having intercourse with another man's wife. The aggrieved party is described as a neighbor (*reaʿ*), not a relative. This command is also one of the Ten Commandments (Exod 20:14).

The following sexual acts describe relations between a man and his relatives, not necessarily birth relatives. For example, in verse 11 the father's wife is not necessarily the person's mother. She may be his stepmother or his father's second wife. These laws for the most part repeat those found in chapter 18. (See comments on 18:6-25 and then on the list as a whole.)

The most significant difference between the two lists (18:6-23 and 20:11-21) is the punishment for these offenses. In chapter 18, no punishments are stipulated for the individual transgressor. Rather, the punishment is collective and uniform, falling on the nation as a whole because such acts defile the land: *If you defile the land, it will vomit you out as it vomited out the nations that were before you* (18:28). The punishments in 20:11-21 are individual and vary in severity. The first set of trespasses, verses 9-16, are capital crimes. The punishments become less severe after verse 16.

Intercourse between brother and sister or a man with a woman having her menses (vv. 17-18) result in both being cut off *[Cut Off, p. 299]*. Bearing culpability is the punishment for intercourse with a sister of either one's father or mother (an aunt, v. 19). This seems like a less serious sin, although what the punishment might be is not given.

A sexual relationship with an uncle's wife or marrying a brother's wife (vv. 20-21) is forbidden. In Deuteronomy 25:5, when a brother dies without a son, then his brother is to marry his brother's wife so that she may bear an heir for her dead husband. It seems that Leviticus either assumes a divorce between a brother and his wife, not a death (Hartley), or does not know the levirate law in Deuteronomy.

Exhortations for Obedience 20:22-26

The first exhortation begins with the general appeal to carefully observe these statutes and judgments (see v. 8). If they are disobedient, the land will vomit them out (as in 18:28). Obedience to God's statutes is then contrasted with the ways of the nation that is now in the land. Their practices are abhorrent, disgusting to God, and are the reason they are being expelled from the land (18:25).

On the positive side, Israel is about to enter a land of abundance. This land is a gift of the *God who has set you apart from other peoples* (20:24 NJPS). Israel is given a blank slate on which to become God's separate people.

At Mount Sinai, Israel was reminded that God had delivered them from slavery and was bringing them to this place. As a result they made a covenant with God. If they obeyed God by keeping the covenant commands, then they would become God's treasured possession from out of all the nations on the earth. They would become God's holy nation (Exod 19:4-6). Leviticus 18–20 gives Israel instructions on how to be this holy nation separated from other nations. By their obedience, Israel becomes and remains God's holy people.

Addendum: No Wizards 20:27

Verse 27 wraps up this chapter by returning to the topic of the first paragraph and repeating the case given in verse 6. There the punishment for consulting mediums was to be cut off by God. Here a punishment by the community is stipulated. As in the case of offering children to Molek, the perpetrator is to be put to death by stoning. With this *inclusio*, the chapter comes to an end *[Literary Style, p. 306]*.

THE TEXT IN BIBLICAL CONTEXT

Is Israel Special?

This is one of those questions with both a yes and a no answer, which makes any answer complex and open to disclaimers. There is certainly ample evidence in the Bible for Israel's election by God and Israel's specialness as a result. Israel is said to have been delivered from Egypt to become God's own inheritance (Deut 4:20).

Deuteronomy has a distinctive term to express this relationship to God: Israel is God's "treasure" (*segullah*, 7:6; 14:2; 26:18), God's own "private hoard" (1 Chron 29:3 NJPS). This status of Israel is linked with their being a holy people: "For you are a people holy to the LORD your God. The LORD your God has chosen you to be his people, his treasured possession, out of all the peoples on the face of the earth" (Deut 7:6 NIV, clauses reordered). Specialness is linked with set apartness, with being a holy people. However, this specialness is conditional: "If you obey me fully and keep my covenant, then out of all nations you will be my treasured possession [*segullah*]" (Exod 19:5).

This seems to be the yin and yang of Israel's specialness: they are special for a reason that may be a hardship to them. The Israelites certainly had their problems with being holy and living as God's people. Yet as we shall see in Leviticus 26, although God will punish them for their failure to live out their specialness, in the end they will yet be God's people. Malachi, using the language of a special treasure, puts it thus: "On the day when I act, . . . they will be my treasured possession [*segullah*]. I will spare them, just as a father has compassion and spares his son who serves him" (Mal 3:17). Even after Israel's failure and judgment, they will be spared because of God's compassion for them.

In summary, Israel is said to be God's people and will remain God's people. In this sense they are special. But they are chosen for a purpose. When they do not live out their specialness, they suffer God's judgment. Being special does not mean that Israel has a blank check. They can be disobedient and fail to carry out their mission and be punished by God—even taken into captivity and become dispersed among the nations. Even here they are God's people.

Sexual Prohibitions

We find prohibitions of homosexuality and bestiality in Leviticus 18 and 20. Elsewhere in the Hebrew Bible we find two narratives that may concern homosexuality: Genesis 19 and Judges 19. In Genesis 19, the residents of Sodom first demand men. They are offered Lot's daughters. It seems that the men are not homosexuals, since they can be bought off with women instead of the male foreign guests. Rather, they seek to humiliate Lot. This exposes the degenerate character of those in Sodom.

Judges 19:22-27 is similar. First some men from the city of Gibeah ask for the male guest. But as the situation becomes more pressing, the male guest pushes his concubine out the door for their use. She is gang-raped throughout the night. Again, these men are not homosexuals, although they wish to perform a homosexual act. Rather, they are satisfied with a woman, whom they use shamefully. In any case, these two stories are not necessarily comments on homosexuality, since the women are offered not because homosexuality is wrong, but so that the men will not be violated. *Are sexual relations between men and women evil because the men violated a woman* (instead of a man)?

In the New Testament, the prohibitions of Leviticus do not play a central part in the discussion concerning homosexuality. Paul in 1 Corinthians 6:9 talks of those who practice homosexuality (cf. 1 Tim 1:10). In Romans 1:24, Paul cites idolatry as the cause of deviant sexuality in general, and in verses 26-27, these practices explicitly include homosexuality. What is not reflected in the English translations is that Romans 1:29 continues the list of vices ("who also are acting . . . ," AT) resulting from idolatry, ending in verse 32 with the notice that such people deserve to die. The hermeneutical question is, Why separate homosexuality for special censure? When unequal weight is given to different elements in a list, a consistent hermeneutic is not being applied. Some external prejudice, bias, or other factor is affecting the outcome of the process.

From the above references we can learn four things. First, unlike in Leviticus 18 and 20, in Paul's writings homosexuality is embedded in a list with other nonsexual types of sins. Second, like Leviticus, Paul does not place any special emphasis on the sin of homosexuality. Third, according to Paul, homosexuality is the result of idolatry and is its first sign. Fourth, unlike Leviticus, Paul refers to people who practice homosexuality, not to a single occurrence of homosexuality. (Also see the comments after Lev 18:25.)

THE TEXT IN THE LIFE OF THE CHURCH

The Significance of Sexual Prohibitions

In Leviticus 18:22-23 and 20:13, 15-16 we have the prohibitions against same-sex relationships and bestiality. The texts are not clear regarding their scope (see comments on 18:6-25, esp. the discussion on the third segment of this list, vv. 22-23). Consequently, their significance is a problem. First, in Leviticus the text is speaking to a single incident. If any man or woman does this once. The text does not speak of the *practice* of homosexual relations any more than in any of the other cases mentioned. One case of adultery of a man with a related woman is wrong.

Second, the social scope of the commands regarding homosexuality is not entirely clear. Does it refer only to those specified in the list of forbidden relationships as possible partners? In the case of adultery, only sexual relations with those of a specified relationship are transgressions. The text of Leviticus does not prohibit adultery outside these relationships: notice the heading in 18:6: *No one is to approach any close relative to have sexual relations.* Also note the content of 18:24-25, which together with 18:1-5 forms an *inclusio* to the list of sexual impurities. (The Ten Commandments are different: one of them forbids all cases of adultery.) Third, since these acts defile the land of Canaan, making it culpable for this uncleanness, it is the land of Canaan that spews its inhabitants forth. Does this phenomenon apply only to Canaan? Are other lands made unclean by the presence of homosexual acts? Do we expect that such lands will spew their inhabitants from the land? (See Milgrom's comments on the issue of homosexuality [2000: 1785-90].)

Today, the question of homosexuality is a hermeneutical argument, not a question of the plain sense of the text. What is done with a text usually reflects the contexts and biases of the persons using the text for a purpose. Because of the inherent dangers in such a process, one rule should govern: Can the method used be applied consistently to all similar texts? If not, why not? For example, why ignore the restriction against sexual relations with a menstruant (18:19; 20:18) and focus on the prohibition of same-sex relationships? The prohibitions and their results are the same.

Leviticus 21:1–22:33
Holiness for Priests

PREVIEW

Chapters 18–20 have addressed the need and requirements for the Israelites' holiness. But are there special holiness requirements for the priests? Are the priests to be "holier" than the layperson? The answer is yes! Because of their priestly functions made possible by consecration and their necessary participation in tabernacle rituals, their special holiness must be safeguarded. Chapters 21 and 22 place restraints on the priests to protect them from contamination and loss of holiness. In chapter 21 these restraints affect the public sphere. For example, why are priests present at some funerals but not at others? Chapter 22 begins with instructions for the priests that are more focused on priestly activity in the realm of the holy. Because of their constant contact with the holy, priests do not have the luxury of becoming impure and thereby losing access to the tabernacle and being unable to participate in its rituals. Notice that we have switched from the realm of moral purity in chapter 20 to ritual impurity in these chapters *[Leadership, p. 306]*.

The instructions in chapter 21 are given in two speeches. The first addresses the common priests (vv. 1-9) and then the high priest, who has even more restrictive boundaries (vv. 10-15).

The second speech (vv. 16-23) concerns the common priests again but is addressed to Aaron alone. The purpose of these instructions is to restrict the serving priests to those who are deemed fit. Those excluded have certain blemishes that make them ritually impure, but even blemished priests have some prerogatives: they may eat of the sacrificial meat even though they cannot perform the sacrificial rituals. In this way they are fed just like the other priests. Priestly restrictions continue in chapter 22 with a warning to be scrupulous in maintaining the purity of the offerings because holiness is at stake.

Chapter 22 brings the section (chs. 18-22) to an end. This section has regulations for living a holy life, at times repeated, and many exhortations to holiness. But have we made any progress? The answer is yes! Chapter 18 begins with an exhortation, and chapter 22 ends with one (an envelope). But these exhortations are not the same. The call at the beginning of chapter 18 is to be a different people. Israel should act neither as Egyptians nor as Canaanites but should live according to the regulations that God now sets before them. These regulations are not a reform but are the foundation of a new society, or nation. In Leviticus the Israelites are a people in formation.

At the end of this chapter, in the closing paragraph of exhortation (22:31-33), the spotlight falls on God. God is not to be profaned or dishonored. On the contrary, God will be proved holy by the Israelites: *Through those near to Me I show Myself holy* (Lev 10:3 NJPS). This holy God is now making the Israelites holy by giving them regulations for holiness. It is up to them to follow them and thereby reflect God's holiness.

OUTLINE

Restrictions concerning Death, 21:1-9
Restrictions for the High Priest, 21:10-15
Restrictions on Offering Sacrifices, 21:16-23
Everybody Heard, 21:24
Disqualified Priests, 22:1-9
Disqualified Laypeople, 22:10-16
Disqualified Animals, 22:17-30
Exhortation to Holiness, 22:31-33

EXPLANATORY NOTES

Restrictions concerning Death 21:1-9

The restrictions on common priests fall into two categories: those concerning a death in the family, and those concerning marriage and family. Regarding the dead, the general rule is that a priest may not become defiled by a corpse *for any of his people who die* (v. 1). Corpse contamination was a very severe pollution that defiled all those gathered in a tent around a corpse. Such defilement not only included a corpse but also touching bones or a grave. This contamination lasted seven days. The water of purification was made by pouring water over the ashes of a red heifer and was applied to the contaminated person (see Num 19:2, 13-21).

Given the command that a priest should not contract corpse contamination, the length of time needed for purification, and the particular nature of the cleansing ceremony, it would be expected that a priest heading toward Jerusalem, presumably for temple service, would not disobey this command of God. In the story of the good Samaritan, the priest was going away from Jerusalem ("down," Luke 10:31), so his immediate availability was not at stake. He would, however, have needed to undergo the ritual of purification when he reached home if he defiled himself by touching a corpse.

For the common priests there were certain close relatives for whom a priest could contract corpse contamination (Lev 21:2). These were his father, mother, child, brother, and unmarried sister. These relatives shared his flesh: they were related by blood. However, defilement was not permitted *for people related to him by marriage* (v. 4). Does this unusual phrase include his wife? On the face of it, it seems so. Since this seems too harsh, some propose that only the wife's relatives, not his wife herself, were included (see the modern translations).

The result of ignoring this restriction would be "defilement," a key word in this speech, occurring seven times. Here it has the sense of disrespecting and devaluing the holy by treating it as common or secular. Profaning the Sabbath meant working on the Sabbath, disrespecting its specialness and treating it as a regular workday (Exod 31:14). Practicing ordinary funeral customs that were allowed of Israelites in general would disregard the specialness of the priests and their role. They would no longer be set apart to fulfill their special duties.

In addition, priests were not to practice certain mourning rituals (v. 5). Deuteronomy 14:1 bans these mourning practices for all Israelites since Israel as a nation is holy (14:2). Here the restrictions to maintain holiness are applied to the priests alone because they offer up the food sacrifices to God (see Lev 1:13 for remarks on food offering). To disregard these restrictions would be to disrespect God by erasing the distinction *between the holy and the common, between the unclean and the clean* (Lev 10:10).

With the exhortation *They must be holy to their God* (21:6), we move to a new topic: Whom may a priest marry (v. 7)? A suitable mate is defined negatively by who is unsuitable: a sexually promiscuous woman or a divorcée. The (unmarried?) daughter of a priest may also mar the holiness of her father by becoming sexually active. Through such disgraceful action she disgraces or defiles her father. As a result, she is to be put to death by burning (v. 9).

Restrictions for the High Priest 21:10-15

Because of his special status and unique functions, additional restraints apply to the high priest. He must not shave his head (*DCH*) or tear his clothes, perhaps signs of mourning. He may not approach the corpse even of his father or mother. In fact, he should not even leave the sanctuary on account of the death of father or mother. As for marriage, he has only one choice: a virgin (vv. 13-15). He may not even marry a widow, let alone a divorcée or a sexually active woman. This may be because there should be no doubt about the paternity of his offspring, since his wife's son will succeed him as high priest.

Restrictions on Offering Sacrifices 21:16-23

The second speech is addressed to Aaron alone (v. 16). As father of all the priests and as high priest, he has a responsibility for choosing who among the priests can function as a priest—who is suitable for service in the sanctuary and who is not *[Aaron, p. 287]*.

A potential priest would be disqualified because of a physical disability. Why might physical imperfections disqualify a priest from offering food sacrifices to God? Perhaps just as a king chooses to surround himself with robust individuals, so God should be honored by having unmarred individuals perform temple service. The use of the word "blemish" (*mum*) in this chapter and the next points to this understanding, since blemished offerings are also not allowed (22:22-24). Exactly what some of these disabilities were is unsure or unknown, nor is a reason given why these disabilities and not others, such as deafness or muteness, did not disqualify a potential priest. Some disabilities, such as blindness, may be from birth; some, such as a broken leg or arm, appear to be temporary.

The first two blemishes are well known: those who are "blind and lame" are disqualified. So also are those who are "mutilated or deformed." But why are a broken leg and arm included in this list? We may assume the affected priest is disqualified only until the broken limb mends and he can resume his service.

The final two verses of this paragraph stress that anyone from Aaron's lineage who is blemished *must not come near to offer the food of his God* (v. 21). However, they may eat from the priestly share of the sacrifices—whether these are holy or most holy—offered in the courtyard or taken in part into their tent. The priests lived by these offerings.

Everybody Heard 21:24

The chapter ends with a performance statement. Moses gave all these instructions to Aaron, to his sons, and to all the Israelites. Although chapter 21 is addressed to priests, all Israel also hears these instructions. As we have seen from the beginning in chapter 1, all Israel is privy to many of the priestly regulations.

Disqualified Priests 22:1-9

The priests receive an ample share of most offerings, which represents their support. In the peace offering, the priests retain some of the meat (Lev 7:29-34). In the cleansing offering of the people, the priests retain all the meat, which must be eaten in the tabernacle's court (6:26 [19]). But may any priest, by virtue of being a priest, eat this meat?

First, the rule is that an unclean priest will desecrate the sanctified meat. Such a priest will be cut off *[Cut Off, p. 299]*. Specific cases then follow. First are those who are unclean because they have a skin blemish (see 13:44-45) or a secretion (see 15:2). The diagnosis for these contaminations and their remedies are given in chapters 13–15. These priests may not eat of the sacrificial meat until they become clean. Likewise, one who contracts corpse contamination, has a seminal emission, touches any unclean swarming thing, or even touches an unclean person is unclean until the evening. He may not eat of the sacrificial food until he bathes. When the sun sets, he may exercise his prerogatives again.

In addition, priests are not to incur uncleanness by eating from any carcass or torn animal (22:8). This contrasts with provisions for the laity in 17:15. At the end of this paragraph, the priests are again reminded to respect God's guideline so they will not bear sin (22:9). Bearing sin rather than guilt or culpability occurred in chapter 19: one should not bear sin on account of one's hatred for a fellow Israelite (19:17). Here *they do not [want to] incur sin on account of it and therefore die because they profane it* (22:9 NET). The antecedent of the last pronoun is uncertain. The NRSV believes *it* refers to the sanctuary. Other modern translations just leave it open.

Disqualified Laypeople 22:10-16

Those disqualified from eating the sacred donations are any *outsiders* (AT), usually understood as those who are not part of the priest's own family (*No one outside a priest's family*, v. 10a). Second is the *resident hireling* (AT; NIV, *hired worker*). (For a discussion of this translation with extensive argumentation, see Milgrom 2000: 1861-70.) However, a clarification must be made. If the priest bought a servant with his own money, that servant may eat sacred food. Such persons have no income by which to buy their own food and are totally dependent on their master. The same is the case for a child born to his household.

What about the daughter of a priest who has left the family because of her marriage? If she is a childless widow or divorcée and she returns home and resumes her former position as a member of the family, then she now can eat from her father's share of the sacrificial food.

Finally, what happens if someone wrongly but inadvertently eats some of a holy donation (v. 14a)? (For inadvertent sin generally, see 4:2.) In this case, because they have trespassed on the holy, they must pay an additional penalty or indemnity (5:15-16; 22:14b).

The paragraph ends with a warning to the priests, whose responsibility is to oversee the offering of sacrifices and the disposal of their parts. The priests must not allow an unauthorized person to bear guilt because that person wrongly ate of an offering (22:15-16).

Disqualified Animals 22:17-30

At the very beginning of Leviticus, the Israelites were told that their offerings must be *tamim*, whole or intact (1:3). However, this word is usually translated with a negative—*without defect* or *without blemish* (NRSV, NJPS). The problem seems to be how to describe a pure or whole animal. It is easier to describe the imperfect than to indicate the perfect.

This speech, addressed to both Israelite and Gentile, repeats 1:3. Everyone must bring whole or intact animals for a sacrifice (*tamim*, 22:19). However, here we discover blemishes that prevent an animal from being *without defect*. An animal cannot be blind or have a fracture, probably of a limb since disqualified priests had a fracture of the leg or hand (21:19). They may not be mutilated (*DCH*; 22:22 NIV, *with warts*) or have a type of rash or scabs. These blemishes disqualify all whole burnt offerings. In addition, some blemishes, such as an overdeveloped or long limb, or a stunted or short limb (v. 23), disqualify the animal from being sacrificed as a vow offering; it is obligatory. However, if the animal is a freewill offering or a regular whole burnt offering, they may have these alterations.

Next we find a list of four blemishes of the testicles—*bruised, crushed, torn or cut*—that disqualify an animal from being a sacrifice (v. 24). The last sentence in this verse may be interpreted as *You must not do this in your own land*. But if this were the case, then these genital blemishes would not exist in Israel, because this would not be practiced on any animal. Another explanation is that the sentence is redundant: you must not offer animals with these blemishes when you enter the land (although no animals raised by an Israelite should have them).

Nor may animals that have these blemishes be bought from a *foreigner* for a sacrifice (v. 25). As opposed to the non-Israelite residents and servants, the foreigner was someone who was not from Israel as a collective. If the above practices for treating testicles were not practiced by people in Israel, such animals would only be available from someone outside Israel. The phrase *as the food of your God* would refer to buying such an animal to offer as a sacrifice (sacrifices are referred to as a *food offering* in chs. 1–3).

Even though a new speech formula interrupts the flow from 22:25 to 27, it is easy to see their connection: animals invalid for a sacrifice. In the case of a newborn animal, it must be at least eight days old to serve as a sacrifice. For some sacrifices the animal must be a year old (9:3; 12:6). Also, the parent of a young animal may not be slaughtered on the same day as its offspring. This regulation may be similar in sentiment to the following: "If you come across a bird's nest beside the road, either in a tree or on the ground, and the mother is sitting on the young or on the eggs, do not take the mother with the young" (Deut 22:6). Animals were to be treated with respect.

The paragraph on animals unsuitable for sacrifice ends with a comment on the peace offering. The people who could eat of this meat were listed above in verses 10–16. Now the focus is on how long this sanctified meat can be eaten. The rule is that the meat of a thanksgiving offering must be consumed before morning. Since this meat could be taken outside the tabernacle area to be shared with family and friends, it is important not to risk its defilement. However, other types of peace offerings, such as the vow offering and the freewill offering, could be eaten over a two-day period (19:5-6).

Exhortation to Holiness 22:31-33

Keeping God's statutes is a constant refrain in chapters 18-22. It is fitting that the concluding paragraph reiterates this command: *You shall faithfully observe My commandments* (22:31 NJPS).

The central concern of chapter 22 is obedience in order that God's name or character not be made common. Instead, God says, *I will be sanctified in the midst of the Israelites* (22:32 NET). God's agenda is that the people Israel are made holy and thus reflect the holiness of their God.

God's self-identity begins chapter 18: *I Yahweh am your God* (18:2 AT; see comments there). This self-identification of God is repeated in 18:4. The deliverance from Egypt is the motivation for loving immigrants and treating them justly. But now, to this self-identification we find an addition: *who brought you out of Egypt to be your God* (22:33). The God who liberated them is the same God who is in the process of making them holy.

What right has God to demand holiness from Israel? It is because God liberated the people from slavery in Egypt (v. 33; also 19:36; with a different verb in 11:45). God did this so that Israel could become God's people. No longer would they live like others, the Egyptians or the Canaanites (18:3). Rather, they would be stamped by God as a holy people who became God's people through deliverance from Egypt.

THE TEXT IN BIBLICAL CONTEXT

Holy Things, Holy People

The nature of holiness changes in Leviticus 18-22. In chapters 1-16, objects were holy. The altar was holy, the remains of a sacrifice were holy or most holy (2:3, 10), the curtain in the tent was holy (4:6), and things or places were holy (5:15-16; 7:6). The realm of the holy was separate from secular realm of everyday life. The holiness of things comes to a climax in chapter 16. Aaron must dress in holy clothing (16:4) before conducting the ceremonial cleansing of the tabernacle and the courtyard altar and restoring it to its original holy state *[Holy and Holiness, p. 302; The Tabernacle, p. 317]*.

This type of holiness can be transmitted (6:18, 27-28). An object and people may also become holy. The tabernacle and its furniture become holy (8:10). The priests are made holy through ceremonies of consecration (ch. 8, esp. v. 30). Holiness was granted through a ritual process in order to prepare for the coming of God's presence.

The realm of the holy expands in the second part of Leviticus, chapters 18-22. This shift is foreshadowed in 11:44: *You are to make yourselves holy and be holy because I am holy* (AT; the verb translated *sanctify yourselves* means "to be or become holy"). All God's people must be holy because their God is holy.

How do people become holy? Leviticus 20:7 repeats God's demand for holiness but adds *You will keep my statutes and do them; I Yahweh am making you holy* (v. 8 AT; see also 21:8; 22:31-33). God is making them holy through their obedience to God's commands. (See 19:2, where the demand for holiness is followed by instructions in the rest of the chapter for being holy.) God specifies this condition in order that they will become a priestly nation, a holy people (Exod 19:6; Deut 7:6).

Deuteronomy announces that Israel is and must be a holy nation because of God's grace in choosing them (Deut 14:2). But holiness, because of their election, also has its obligations: "You shall not eat any abhorrent thing" (v. 3 NRSV). A holy people needs to eat an appropriate diet to avoid contamination and remain holy.

New Testament Holiness and Ethics

Christians adopted the idea that as God's people they must be holy. In 1 Peter the Christians are likened to a holy priesthood who offer up spiritual sacrifices (1 Pet 2:5). Christians are "a chosen people, a royal priesthood, a holy nation, God's special possession" (1 Pet 2:9). This text equates the Christian responsibility for obedience with that of the Israelites in Exodus 19:5-6.

Just as God commanded the Israelites, *Be holy, because I . . . am holy* (Lev 19:2), so also the church is to be holy because God is holy (1 Pet 1:16, quoting Lev 19:2). The Christians are urged not to be shaped by sinful impulses but to "become holy yourselves in all of your conduct" (1 Pet 1:14-15 NET). Holiness in the church, as in Israel, is characterized by living in obedience to God's commands. Similarly, Paul's letters reflect the necessity of holiness for Christians. Holiness is the reason for the Christian's calling: "For he chose us in Christ before the foundation of the world that we may be holy and unblemished in his sight in love" (Eph 1:4 NET; also Eph 5:27; "unblemished" brings Leviticus to mind). The Christian's calling is "to live a holy life" (1 Thess 4:7; cf. 4:3).

The connection of ethics and worship to holiness is emphasized in Paul's classic description of the holy life. In Romans, the Christians are urged to offer their bodies as a sacrifice. All sacrifices offered on the altar were holy, but Paul has in mind the life of the believer as the holy sacrifice Christians are to offer. To paraphrase Romans 12:1 slightly, they will become "living sacrifices" because it is the "logical or reasonable service of worship owed to God."

The conception of Gentile Christians living a holy life in God's service influenced Paul's understanding of his own work. He saw his mission as a priestly duty or service to the Gentiles "so that the Gentiles might become an offering acceptable to God, sanctified [made holy] by the Holy Spirit" (Rom 15:16). The Gentile Christians are Paul's freewill offering to God. In Leviticus, a sacrifice became holy when it was offered to God at the altar, but Christians become holy through the work of the Holy Spirit as they live a holy life. As holy, they can be an offering for God.

The holiness of Christians became such a common idea that Paul calls his readers "saints" (i.e., "holy ones") in his letters (Rom 1:7; 1 Cor 1:2; "holy people," NIV), just as he refers to Christians more generally as the "saints" (e.g., Rom 15:25, 26, 31 NRSV; "Lord's people," NIV). This term indicates Paul's expectation that Christians will be living a holy life. As in Leviticus, holiness is accrued through obedience.

THE TEXT IN THE LIFE OF THE CHURCH

Holy Places and Holy People

We find two types of holiness in Leviticus: the holiness of things and priests, and the holiness of common people, which also includes the priests. The priests have granted holiness, but they should also strive for acquired holiness along with all other Israelites. *Granted holiness*, like that of the priests, comes through rituals of consecration and sets them apart from the people. The *holiness of obedience* is forged through obeying God in ordinary life, away from the holy sanctuary. This acquired holiness comes to all the people, priest and common person alike, as they obey God's call to be a holy people.

In some Christian traditions, granted holiness remains. Priests and the sacraments for communion are holy, for example. The priests, because of their consecration, can endow holiness on the sacraments. Any remaining bread, for instance, should be kept in a safe place or eaten by a priest. In some situations, the priests may consecrate the bread, but it can then be taken to remote areas by those designated as "lay pastors." Some remote village people, however, refuse to take this communion because they believe it has lost its power. Lay pastors are disheartened, then, when people do not accept them as legitimate dispensers of the host.

Many times, traces of these practices endure in other Christian traditions. Who can officiate at communion? Who can baptize? Often it is the ordained clergy who must perform these services.

Where can they be performed? Sometimes they may only take place in a church.

We might think that the instructions to holiness in Leviticus 18–22 are about creating a moral society or a society in which there is a certain equality. We then become confused when we find important social norms and moral commands side by side with commands having nothing to do with justice or our sense of morality. The positive command to love your fellow and the negative one prohibiting vengeance (19:17-18) are followed by *You shall observe My laws. You shall not let your cattle mate with a different kind; you shall not sow your field with two kinds of seed; you shall not put on cloth from a mixture of two kinds of material* (19:19 NJPS).

Wearing a garment with two types of thread—what does this have to do with a moral life and the social good? What could be more irrelevant to an ethic? Yet *these laws are not about society but about individuals who wish to be God's holy people.* The stipulations are given as guides to holy living. While a holy nation might be the end point, the immediate aim of the text is for holy people.

Why such regulations make a person holy is unknown. These instructions do not come with an explanation as to *why* they produce a holy person. This is part of our modern dilemma. Unless a command makes sense to us, unless we understand why God might have given a particular commandment, it seems irrelevant. Giving the reason for a command can also be a reason for ignoring it. If we don't agree or see the relevance of the reason for ourselves, it is easy for us to dismiss a prohibition. For example, is the prohibition against eating pork irrelevant if we believe it was given to prevent trichinosis and we are not in danger of that disease?

Maybe our question should be, Is this command relevant to a holy life today? Obviously, some instructions in chapter 19 are quite strange to us. But if we consider them aimed at holiness, what are our standards of judgment for holiness? Can anybody but God know why these are part of a holy life? We don't know why God gave instructions about growing fruit trees (19:23-25). We could justify these instructions by pointing to their practical benefit, but is this chapter or group of chapters concerned with commercial success? Do we have any criteria for judging the holiness of a practice?

Jesus has some advice for us on this matter. Regarding the Pharisees who sit on the seat of Moses, Jesus told his disciples, "So you must be careful to do everything they tell you. But do not do what they do, for they do not practice what they preach" (Matt 23:3). However, Jesus went on to critique some of their teachings by arguing that they were not necessarily logical. While denouncing some of their decisions, he said, "You neglect what is more important in the law—justice, mercy, and faithfulness! You should have done these things without neglecting the others" (Matt 23:23 NET). Holy living, making choices of how to live, must be guided by justice, mercy, and faithfulness, but that does not mean ignoring the practice of other commands, such as tithing, which Jesus mentions. We may judge individual practices by the standard of justice, mercy, and faithfulness, but holiness ultimately comes through obedience.

In evaluating obedience to specific commands in Leviticus, we need to keep in mind that the audience was the Israelites, not the non-Israelites, Gentiles, or sojourners (NIV, *foreigners*, a problematic translation). When non-Israelites or Gentiles (*ger*) are included in a command, they are specifically mentioned: *whether native-born or a foreigner [ger] residing among you* (Lev 16:29) or *The whole congregation must surely stone him, whether he is a foreigner [ger] or a native citizen* (24:16 NET). Sometimes, rather, the distinction is made between the house or children of Israel and a non-Israelite, as in 17:8: *Any Israelite or any foreigner [ger]*. (For the struggles of the early church on what laws apply to Gentiles, see "Eating Blood in the Early Church" in TLC for ch. 17.)

Leviticus 23:1–25:55
Part 3B
Holy Time

OVERVIEW
Chapters 23 and 25 regulate the celebration of Israel's festivals (23) and the economic provisions of the Sabbatical Year and of the fiftieth year, the Jubilee (25). Sandwiched between these two chapters we find a case of blasphemy, along with the ensuing legal process and statements about the application of justice in general. Although holy time does not describe chapter 24, the beginning and end of this section do so.

OUTLINE FOR PART 3B
Celebrating Religious Festivals, 23:1-44
Duties and a Case of Blasphemy, 24:1-23
The Sabbatical and Jubilee Years, 25:1-55

Leviticus 23:1-44
Celebrating Religious Festivals

PREVIEW

Did the Israelites have a dreary life? Did they feel weighed down by the need to be holy? One answer is the presence of celebrations and the outpouring of joy that accompanied them. Chapter 23 focuses on national celebrations, such as Christians celebrate Christmas or Easter. These celebrations marked times of joy, either because of harvesttimes in the agricultural cycle or because of periods of great significance in the religious life of the people.

The Hebrew calendar was a lunar calendar, which meant that their twelve-month year was shorter than our solar one. A given fixed event, such as Passover, which occurred in the month of Aviv (Exod 23:15, also spelled *Abib*), would move to a different solar date each year, and after three years would be off by an entire solar month (see *ABD*, s.v. "Calendars"). Since Passover was a spring event, it could not continue to move from one solar month to the next one. To prevent this, an extra month was intercalated later in the calendar every so often to keep Aviv in the spring (our March or April). In this way the lunar month of Aviv more or less kept its alignment with the solar year. Easter likewise is aligned with the moon, which is the reason its date varies each year but is always in March or April *[Calendar, p. 295]*. As a festival calendar, Leviticus 23 is concerned with when and what rituals take place at a festival. For a full description of each, see the articles on individual festivals in

NIDB or other Bible dictionaries. The following outline is based on Milgrom (2001) and Hartley.

OUTLINE

Introduction, 23:1-4
The Spring Festivals, 23:5-22
    23:5   Passover
    23:6-8   Unleavened Bread
    23:9-14   First Sheaf
    23:15-22 Weeks (Pentecost)
The Fall Festivals, 23:23-36
    23:23-25 The New Year's Festival (Rosh Hashanah)
    23:26-32 Day of Cleansing (Yom Kippur)
    23:33-36 Booths (Sukkoth)
Concluding Remarks, 23:37-44
    23:37-38 Summary
    23:39-43 Additional Remarks concerning Booths (Sukkoth)
    23:44   Performance Statement

EXPLANATORY NOTES

Introduction 23:1-4

The festivals are introduced in verse 2: *These are my appointed festivals, the appointed festivals of the* LORD. The wording is repeated in verse 4. This repetition forms an envelope around verse 3, which concerns the Sabbath, and sets it off from the annual festivals in the following verses.

Strictly speaking, the Sabbath is not a festival, nor is it marked by the yearly calendar. It occurs weekly, every seven days, and is a day of rest, undistinguished by sacrifices or other festive actions. Here it is called a holy convocation, just like the following festivals, as if it were a gathering together of people. So although it is not annual, it is nevertheless a similar holy time. The commandment to do no work on the Sabbath is found in Exodus 20:9-10; 23:12; 31:15; 35:2; and Deuteronomy 5:12-14. The word translated *work (melaʾkah)* refers to an occupation or craft and suggests one's regular work or occupation (*HALOT*). However, in the context of this commandment, it seems to mean *any work*, since in Leviticus 23 the words for occupation (*melaʾkah*) and for work (*ʿabodah*) are used together and translated as *regular work* (23:7-8) [*Calendar, p. 295*].

The Spring Festivals 23:5-22

23:5 Passover

The Passover is to be celebrated on the fourteenth day of the first month. It is a family festival, and a lamb was to be eaten by family and friends. The instructions for keeping the Passover are given in Exodus 12:11-48 at the time of the first Passover. The Passover festival takes place in the evening: *at twilight, there shall be a Passover offering to the LORD* (Lev 23:5 NJPS).

23:6-8 Unleavened Bread

Passover is the Festival of Unleavened Bread, which was to be observed on the fifteenth day of the month, the day after Passover. The Israelites were to celebrate this festival for seven days. Only *matzah* bread, perhaps unleavened barley cakes, could be eaten (1 Sam 28:24-25). Previously, unleavened bread was used by priests in rituals, as in Leviticus 6:16-17 and 10:12. Now it was the only bread available for the people at Passover time. Try pizza with an unleavened crust!

Notice the lack of transition from the Passover to Unleavened Bread, both literarily and chronologically. The Festival of Unleavened Bread begins the very next day after Passover and is called a festival or feast, in contrast to Passover, which is not so titled. In fact, Unleavened Bread could include Passover since only unleavened bread was allowed at Passover.

Originally, it seems, there were three pilgrimage festivals in which the Israelite was to appear before God: the Festival of Unleavened Bread, in spring at the beginning of the barley harvest; the Festival of Harvest (or Weeks), at the wheat harvest, the end of the grain harvest in early summer; and the Festival of Ingathering, in the fall vintage season, at year's end (Exod 23:14-16). Over time, however, Passover became the name for the combined spring festival of Passover/Unleavened Bread. It remained a pilgrimage festival in theory, taking over this characteristic from the Festival of Unleavened Bread (see Josiah's reform in 2 Kings 23:21-23). This combined festival celebrated the deliverance from Egypt and was the most important spring festival.

The first day of Unleavened Bread was to be a holy convocation. On this day the Israelites were to do no work. On each day of the festival they were to offer a food offering to God. The seventh day was also a holy convocation in which no work was done. Thus the Festival of Unleavened Bread began and ended with an assembly and cessation from work.

23:9-14 First Sheaf

The offering of the first sheaf (v. 10) is an anomaly. It is not one of the three pilgrimage festivals, nor is it a holy convocation and day of rest, nor is it even called a *festival (ḥag)*. It has no fixed date, since the time of the barley harvest varied from year to year and from region to region. This implies that it is not national in scope but is the offering of the individual farmer at the beginning of his harvest. Like the great pilgrimage festivals, it has an agrarian basis, since the offering of the first sheaf marks the beginning of the harvest season (Exod 9:31-32).

In Leviticus, Israel is gathered around a central shrine, the tabernacle. But when they became farmers in Canaan, there were many local shrines to which the people could make a journey. Elkanah, the father of Samuel, made a pilgrimage from time to time to worship God at Shiloh (1 Sam 1:3). On the other hand, Samuel, as a priest, made a circuit, visiting various high places in order to celebrate communal sacrifices. The people would not eat of them until Samuel blessed their sacrifice (1 Sam 9:12-13). In practice, then, the first sheaf was presumably offered at a local shrine.

The farmer is to offer his first sheaf *on the day after the Sabbath* (v. 11). Is this the first Sabbath after the farmer has begun to harvest his grain? It seems so. The ritual seems straightforward. The farmer presents the first sheaf of his harvest to the priest. The priest then presents it as a raised offering to God (see 7:30-34 for the raised offering). Besides presenting the first sheaf, the farmer also offers a yearling lamb as a whole burnt offering. This offering is accompanied by a grain offering consisting of two measures of flour mixed with oil. Finally, a wine libation of *a quarter of a hin of wine*, about a quart, is made (v. 13).

Before the actual day of these offerings, the Israelites *must not eat any bread, or roasted or new grain* (v. 14). That is, from the time the farmer harvests his first sheaf until it is presented to God by the priest, they must not eat from the new harvest. The importance of this practice is stressed at the end of these instructions: *It is a law for all time throughout the ages in all your settlements* (v. 14 NJPS).

23:15-22 Weeks (Pentecost)

The Festival of Weeks is closely connected to the offering of the first sheaf: (1) it continues the speech begun in verse 9, and (2) it is dated from the day on which the first sheaf was offered. Israel is to count seven Sabbaths (weeks) from the offering of the first sheaf, fifty days in all, to determine the time of this festival (Pentecost). It is a pilgrimage festival in which the people bring their offerings from their individual settlements (v. 17) to a central sanctuary. This is the second annual pilgrimage festival (Exod 23:16), a national festival, a holy convocation, and a day of rest (Lev 23:21).

The first ritual action of Weeks is a firstfruits offering from the wheat harvest, which followed the barley harvest. Two loaves of leavened bread were made from the new grain and were brought by the pilgrims from their villages. This was offered as a wave offering (vv. 15-16).

In addition to the bread, seven unblemished yearling lambs, a yearling bull, and two rams were offered as whole burnt offerings along with their grain offerings and a libation of wine. All of this, like the whole burnt offerings of chapter 1, was a food offering that provided an odor pleasing to God (23:18).

After the whole burnt offerings, one buck goat was offered as a cleansing offering and two yearling lambs for a peace offering (v. 19) [*Cleansing Offering, p. 297*]. The yearling lambs, along with the bread, were both raised, or wave, offerings, and became the property of the priest (v. 20).

The extravagance of the animal offerings places these offerings beyond the means of an individual farmer. Rather, it is assumed that a central sanctuary to which the pilgrimage was made offered them on behalf of all assembled. This also implies a fixed date for the Festival of Weeks and thus contradicts anchoring it to the offering of the first sheaf, which did not begin on the same date every year; this was because the time of harvest would vary from Judah to Galilee. (For an extended discussion of when this festival occurred, see Milgrom's essay "The Sabbath-Week: A Resolution of a Heavy Crux" [2001: 2056–63]. Note the humility of the *A* rather than a *The* in the subtitle. That it takes seven pages to discuss the issue shows the difficulty of arriving at any certainty on this point.)

As in the case of the offering of the first sheaf, the passage ends with *This is to be a lasting ordinance for the generations to come, wherever you live* (v. 21).

A note is attached to each of these harvest festivals, reminding the Israelites of their social responsibility at harvesttime. Individual farmers are not to maximize their harvest. Rather, they are to leave grain standing at the sides of their fields, and bundles of grain left behind by the harvesters are not to be retrieved. This grain is for the impoverished and the non-Israelite (*ger*). This reinforces the harvest restrictions given in 19:9-10. Additional recipients, the orphan and the widow, are mentioned in Deuteronomy 24:19-21.

The Fall Festivals 23:23-36

23:23-25 The New Year's Festival (Rosh Hashanah)

Although there is no mention of a New Year's Day in the Bible, the first day of the seventh month is celebrated as the beginning of the new year. This festival does not mark an agrarian event like the offering of the first sheaf, nor does it celebrate a special event in the history of Israel, as does Passover. It has often been suggested that this day is significant because the number seven is significant. The first day of the seventh month represents the beginning of a Sabbath month, just as a regular Sabbath represents the seventh day of the week (see Hartley; Milgrom 2001: 2011-19; *Calendar*, p. 295).

The festival begins with a trumpet blast. The sounding of trumpets marks other festival times as well, including the one held on the first day of each month (New Moon) and at the time of sacrifices (Num 10:10). In Leviticus, however, there is no mention of an instrument, only a shout or blast, and there is no mention of specific sacrifices (23:24-25).

23:26-32 Day of Cleansing (Yom Kippur)

The purging of sin from the most sacred places, from the tent and from its altars, is the result of the ceremony in Leviticus 16 (see v. 33). This cleansing is to be done once a year, on the tenth day of the seventh month. This day is called the Day of Cleansing. As in chapter 16, the people are to abstain from work, practice self-denial, and offer a food offering to God. The offering is not specified (see ch. 16 for details).

The structure of this passage—ending with *It shall be to you a sabbath of complete rest, . . . on the ninth day of the month at evening, from evening to evening you shall keep your sabbath* (23:32 NRSV)—suggests that this day ran from evening to evening. The day began with nightfall, sunset, and continued until the next sunset. For example, the Sabbath (Shabbat) as practiced runs from Friday's sunset until Saturday's sunset, thus beginning the day with night and ending it at the end of the following day (cf. Gen 1).

23:33-36 Booths (Sukkoth)

A new speech begins in verse 33, commanding that on the fifteenth day of the seventh month the Festival of *Sukkoth*, or Booths, is to be held (NIV's *Festival of Tabernacles* is not accurate; there was only one tabernacle, and it was not a temporary shelter; *HALOT* gives "hut" as the meaning of this word; NET has *Festival of Temporary Shelters*, which is descriptively more accurate but clumsy; see its translation notes). The first and the eighth day of this celebration will be holy convocations (vv. 35-36). The eighth day seems odd because other festivals have seven days, and Booths is assumed to be a seven-day festival (v. 40). The last day is a *closing special assembly* (v. 36; also Deut 16:8; Num 29:35), which would fit with adding an eighth day for closing the festival. The term *special assembly* (only here in Leviticus) has the connotation of being ad hoc, or especially called, as in Joel 1:14 and 2 Kings 10:20.

Concluding Remarks 23:37-44

23:37-38 Summary

These festivals are God's appointed times and are to be proclaimed as holy convocations (see v. 2). They are times when the whole burnt offering, the grain offering, and the peace offering are to be performed, making a pleasing odor for God (chs. 1-3). In addition, there are to be wine libations.

All of these offerings for the festivals are in addition to those regularly offered on the Sabbath. While sacrifices on the Sabbath are not mentioned in verse 3, we know that every morning a whole burnt offering was made to ensure that a fire would always be burning on the altar (see 6:12-13; and Num 28:9-10, which prescribes a whole burnt offering on the Sabbath).

23:39-43 Additional Remarks concerning Booths (Sukkoth)

What was the reason for the Festival of Booths? First, this festival celebrates the gathering in of the earth's produce. This is its agrarian basis. On the first day of the festival the Israelites are to take the produce of the *hadar trees* (v. 40 NJPS), palm branches, leafy branches, and willows and celebrate their completed harvest for seven days (v. 41). The identification of the *hadar trees* (NIV, *luxuriant trees*) is unknown.

Second, during this time of celebration all citizens of Israel are to live in booths (v. 42). These are temporary huts like those used at harvesttime (Isa 1:8), or a temporary residence like Jonah's shelter (Jon 4:5). These booths commemorate their living conditions in the wilderness. This is the historical basis for the festival. Reenacting their history keeps it alive from generation to generation.

23:44 Performance Statement

The closing verse reports that Moses has carried out the commands of God by communicating these appointed times and how they are to be kept.

THE TEXT IN BIBLICAL CONTEXT

The Festivals in the Bible

Surprisingly, the calendrical festivals that we find in Leviticus 23 and Numbers 28-29 are rarely mentioned in narrative texts and then only late in Israel's history. The first Passover in Canaan is described in Joshua 5:10-12. The next celebration of the Passover is found in 2 Kings 23:21-23 in the time of Josiah. The writer comments, "Neither in the days of the judges who led Israel nor in the days of the kings of Israel and the kings of Judah had any such Passover been observed" (2 Kings 23:22). We find mention of the Passover again after the exile in Ezra 6:19-21.

The three annual festivals observed by Solomon were Unleavened Bread, Weeks, and Booths (2 Chron 8:13). Passover is not mentioned, although it is included in the Festival of Unleavened Bread. Hezekiah also celebrated the Festival of Unleavened Bread as a national celebration (2 Chron 30:13, 21). The account of Josiah's celebration in 2 Chronicles mentions both the Passover and the Festival of Unleavened Bread (35:17). The Festival of Booths is celebrated in Ezra 3:4 and Nehemiah 8:14-16.

By the time of the New Testament the pilgrimage festivals had caught on, and pilgrims flocked to Jerusalem to celebrate them. The Festival of Weeks (Pentecost) was marked by a great influx of pilgrims: "Now there were staying in Jerusalem God-fearing Jews from every nation under heaven" (Acts 2:5). Likewise, Paul was eager to spend the Festival of Weeks (Pentecost) in Jerusalem (Acts 20:16). However, these festivals apparently were not celebrated in the early church, although some would make the trip to Jerusalem as pilgrims.

It is in the Gospels that we find these festivals mentioned most often, especially in the gospel of John. John's gospel is punctuated by Jesus' trips to Jerusalem to celebrate Passover. Jesus' first trip to Jerusalem for the Passover included *the cleansing of the temple* (John 2:13), and the text mentions miracles that led to belief in him (v. 23). The Passover is mentioned again in 6:4 and is connected with the feeding of the five thousand. Jesus' final Passover pilgrimage to Jerusalem included the raising of Lazarus (John 11:6-12:2). Just before the Passover feast, while eating with his disciples, Jesus washed their feet (John 13:5). Obviously, the Passover celebration in Jerusalem was a prime time for Jesus to act and to teach.

In addition to Passover, Jesus attended the Festival of Booths (Tabernacles, NIV), but did so secretly (John 7:2-10), and Hanukkah (the Festival of Dedication, John 10:22). Hanukkah celebrates the dedication of the temple after its defilement by Antiochus IV. This cleansing of the altar and restoration to the worship of God occurred in October or November of 165 or 164 BCE. During this festival Jesus is found at the temple (John 10:23).

Jesus, like Jews of his time (according to John), made regular pilgrimages to Jerusalem to celebrate the great festivals. While there he taught and visited with friends in Bethany (Lazarus, Martha, and Mary, John 12:1-3). These festivals also allowed Jesus' teachings to reach those from foreign lands as well as those who were not Jews (John 12:20-21; an example of such a pilgrim is the Ethiopian, Acts 8:27).

In the early church, Jesus' last Passover was the time of the Last Supper and the foundation for the celebration of communion. In the synoptic gospels this Passover meal with his disciples took place on the evening of the first day of Unleavened Bread. It was on this day that the Passover lamb was sacrificed (Mark 14:12; Matt 26:17; Luke 22:7). In the gospel of John, this last meal took place before the Passover (John 13:1). Thus according to John, Jesus' crucifixion took place while the Passover lambs were being slaughtered in the temple (John 18:39; 19:14). For Christians, the Lord's Supper has replaced the Passover meal [Calendar, p. 295].

THE TEXT IN THE LIFE OF THE CHURCH

Festivals and the New Testament

Most of Israel's festivals were tied to historical events as well as to the agricultural calendar. In the church, two great festivals are observed, Christmas and Easter, and both are tied to events: Jesus' birth and his resurrection. The difference is that Israel's festivals celebrated events of national significance, such as their exodus from Egypt, their wandering in the wilderness, and restoration of worship under the Maccabees (commemorated by Hanukkah; see just above). These events happened to their ancestors and so are part of their story as a people. The events the church celebrates are also of theological significance. They celebrate the incarnation and the resurrection of the Messiah.

In addition to the celebration of national events, Israel also celebrated events of great individual importance, such as Yom Kippur (Day of Cleansing). This was a time of reckoning and new beginnings. In the church, baptism is an event of great importance to an individual and the congregation.

Perhaps the most overlap in festivals is connected to harvest festivals, a time of thanksgiving for crops being harvested. In some denominations or churches a harvest festival is still celebrated, but for most people in the West, Thanksgiving is a secular celebration rather than a religious one. This represents a loss. If people are not thankful, they are liable to forget that it is not only by their hard work and cleverness but also through God's grace that they have what they have. Deuteronomy has a warning in this regard that is a helpful reminder on the importance of thanksgiving:

> When you have eaten your fill and have built fine houses and live in them, and when your herds and flocks have multiplied, and your silver and gold is multiplied, and all that you have is multiplied, then do not exalt yourself, forgetting the LORD your God. . . . Do not say to yourself, "My power and the might of my own hand have gotten me this wealth." But remember the LORD your God. (Deut 8:12-13, 17-18a NRSV)

Leviticus 24:1-23
Duties and a Case of Blasphemy

PREVIEW

In what type of space is it appropriate to worship God? Tabernacle or temple? Up to now in Leviticus the worship space at the tabernacle is quite severe. In the courtyard we find the altar for sacrifices, the bare necessity for carrying out the sacrificial rituals performed there, and a bronze basin. Inside the tent is the altar for the ritual gestures performed there. Finally, in the holy of holies we find the symbols of God's presence: the cherubim and the ark of the covenant containing the Ten Commandments. This space was used only once a year (see ch. 16 for the Day of Cleansing ceremony). But according to Exodus, more items were to be found in and at the tent of meeting. There, for example, we find instructions for building a table (Exod 25:23-28), for making vessels for libations (25:29), and for building a lampstand, or menorah (25:31-39). But we have found no mention of these in Leviticus—even though libations were offered as part of the ritual for festivals (e.g., Lev 23:13) *[Calendar, p. 295; The Tabernacle, p. 317].*

Why has the furniture been omitted? Does Leviticus describe a place of worship containing only the bare necessities, the unmentioned items being peripheral to worshiping God? The more likely explanation is that Leviticus has focused on the priestly duties and rituals, not on the objects manufactured for their performance. Now we find additional priestly duties that demand additional furnishings. This additional "furniture" and the duties attached to them are described in 24:19.

But these additional elements leave the common worship space in the courtyard quite lacking in aesthetic elements. In the Christian church, where do we find the stained-glass windows, the vaulted ceilings, and the icons? Only later in the development of Christian places of worship, whose culmination is the building of great cathedrals. So too it was in Israel. See the description of Solomon's temple furnishings in 1 Kings 7:13-51. With the rise of the state and the building of Solomon's palace, we also find the temple built with all the furnishing worthy of a heavenly ruler. Which space is the better for worshiping God?

A case of blasphemy and its aftermath occupy the remainder of chapter 24 (vv. 10-23). After dealing with this special case, God discloses to Moses additional guidelines or principles for use in personal injury cases. These regulations are important for understanding the biblical laws on homicide and injury to persons.

OUTLINE

Additional Priestly Duties, 24:1-9
    24:1-4   The Light
    24:5-9   The Bread and Table
The Case of the Blasphemer, 24:10-23
    24:10-12   The Incident
    24:13-16   The Decision
    24:17-22   Supplemental Laws
    24:23   Execution of the Offender

EXPLANATORY NOTES

Additional Priestly Duties 24:1-9

24:1-4 The Light

The heading for a new speech is found in verse 1, a speech commanding obligations for the Israelites as a whole (v. 2a). First, quality olive oil is needed for a light in the sanctuary (v. 2b). The same word for light is also used in the creation account to describe the sun and the moon, the major luminaries for day and night (Gen 1:14-16). The luminary in the tabernacle is to provide a constant night light before the curtain that screens the ark from view. The stand, or candlestick, has six branches, three on each side, with a central stem. Today such a candlestick is called a menorah. Aaron as high priest is to arrange oil lamps on the each of the six branches of the menorah and its central stem. The blueprint for this lampstand is given in Exodus 25:31-37.

24:5-9 The Bread and Table

In addition to the lampstand, every week an array of bread is to be placed on a table. Aaron—the *you* here is singular—is to bake twelve loaves of bread, each made with two-tenths of a measure of flour. These are huge loaves, perhaps as much as six pounds. Once baked, these twelve loaves are to be arranged in two rows on a table inside the tabernacle, six loaves in each row. The table, as described in Exodus 25:23-28, was not constructed of pure gold. It was made of acacia wood overlaid with pure gold. Notice the difference in translation between *pure gold* (Lev 24:6 NIV) and *pure table* (NJPS). The latter follows the text in Leviticus more exactly, indicating that the table is pure, not that it is made of pure gold. The lampstand, however, is hammered out of pure gold (Exod 25:31).

Pure frankincense was then placed beside the loaves. Since these loaves were later to be eaten, they would not have had incense added to them or baked in them. Incense only went on grain or bread that was burned (Lev 2:2, 9, 16; 5:11-12; 6:15 [8]). These loaves represent a memorial token, a food offering for God. While normally a token part is burned, here the loaves as a whole represent a token offering and are not burned. Instead, they are then eaten inside the tent by the priests.

In what sense are they *an offering by fire to the* LORD (24:7 NRSV)? It was noted in the comments at Leviticus 1:9 that the term translated *fire offering* is better translated *food offering* (so NIV). None of the loaves were burned, but they represented food placed before God as an offering. In this offering God's token amount includes all twelve loaves. But if they were burned up, the priests would have had no share in this grain offering, as was normally their due (see the grain offerings in ch. 2). We might guess that God gives the entire offering to the priests as their portion; as in the case of the peace offering, God's share goes to the priests (7:34).

The Case of the Blasphemer 24:10-23

24:10-12 The Incident

A man with an Israelite mother and an Egyptian father got into a fight in the midst of the camp. During the struggle, the man with the Egyptian father blasphemed and cursed. The people hearing his curse bring him to Moses for a verdict. Moses makes no decision but has the man placed under arrest until God decides the case.

24:13-16 The Decision

God responds with a verdict: Moses is to take the blasphemer outside the camp, and the ones who heard the curse and brought the charge are to place their hands on the head of the accused, evidently signifying that this is indeed the person they witnessed cursing. On the testimony of this gesture by the earwitnesses, the entire congregation is to stone him. (On this hand gesture, see comments on 1:4.)

Verses 15 and 16 generalize the judgment given in this case to all similar cases by formulating the punishment as apodictic law *[Law, p. 304]*. Everyone who curses the name of God bears their own sin. There are no exceptions: both Gentile and native Israelite will be stoned to death by the entire congregation.

The notion of bearing sin, as opposed to bearing guilt, occurred previously in 19:17; 20:20; 22:9. Bearing sin is also linked with profaning God's name in 22:2-3. Bearing sin seems a more serious state than bearing guilt or culpability, which results from ordinary transgressions (17:16). In 20:30 the result is dying childless. Here the transgression results in death by stoning.

24:17-22 Supplemental Laws

The capital crime triggers the list of laws that follow. *Anyone who strikes a person fatally will be put to death* (AT). Parallel to this law is the case of killing an animal that belongs to someone else. For this, *restitution* is required (v. 18). The verse ends with *life for life*, which means compensation for a life, not taking another ox's life. The difference in punishment between homicide and killing an animal is starkly put in verse 21, which forms the conclusion to this list of apodictic laws: *Whoever kills an animal must make restitution, but whoever kills a human being is to be put to death* (Lev 24:21). The word translated *kills* in this verse (as in v. 17) is normally translated *strike*. The same word is used in Exodus 21:12, "Anyone who strikes a person with a fatal blow is to be put to death" (see "Homicide and Capital Punishment" in TBC below).

The laws of compensation for bodily injury are given in Leviticus 24:19-20 and operate according to the principle of *lex talionis* (the law of retaliation). The list begins with *Anyone who injures their neighbor is to be injured in the same manner* and ends with *The one who has inflicted the injury must suffer the same injury.* The text is quite explicit: no compensation can be given for causing an injury to another. In our laws, inflicting bodily harm can result in a civil case, and victims can gain monetary compensation for their injuries. In these laws, the victim gains nothing.

The law of *lex talionis* is also found in Exodus 21. There, however, the list includes cases where the victim does receive compensation. In 21:18-19, an injured party can be compensated for loss of work time. If an owner damages the eye of a servant/slave or knocks out a tooth, the person gains their freedom as compensation (21:26-27). An owner does not lose their eye or tooth.

The paragraph (Lev 24:17-22) ends by emphasizing that the same rule or law applies to everyone, the native Israelite and the non-Israelite (Gentile) alike (see above, v. 16). The grounding for equal treatment before the law is God's declaration *I the LORD [Yahweh] am your God.*(v. 22 NJPS), which proclaims God's sovereignty over Israel.

24:23 Execution of the Offender

The offender is taken outside the camp. He is then stoned by the people in accordance with God's command to Moses. This execution carried out by the people is different from mob action in which there is no judicial process to determine guilt or innocence. It might be that since the accusers of the person took a leading part in the execution, the execution was placed on their shoulders.

THE TEXT IN BIBLICAL CONTEXT

Homicide and Capital Punishment

There are many texts relating to homicide and capital punishment in the Hebrew Bible, beginning with Genesis. The first homicide is Cain killing Abel. Instead of executing Cain, God banished him (Gen 4:9-15). After the flood, God gave Noah the first law concerning homicide:

> For your own lifeblood I will surely require a reckoning: from every animal I will require it and from human beings, each one for the blood of another, I will require a reckoning for human life. Whoever sheds the blood of a human, by a human shall that person's blood be shed; for in his own image God made humankind. (Gen 9:5-6 NRSV)

This statute, based on humans representing the image and likeness of God (Gen 1:26-27; 5:2), is a concept unique to biblical law. In this essay, however, we will focus on legal texts related to Leviticus 24:17-22 and the law of *lex talionis*. (For an extensive survey of both biblical and ancient Near Eastern material on homicide, see Barmash).

The best-known law of homicide is Exodus 20:13, which is usually translated "You shall not murder." However, the traditional translation was "Thou shalt not kill [raṣaḥ]" (KJV). A basis for the traditional translation "kill" is that the verb raṣaḥ refers to anyone who kills another, even those killing accidently. For example, cities of refuge are places "to which a person who has killed someone accidentally may flee" (Num 35:11). Only after a trial would it be decided whether the killing was accidental or deliberate (Num 35:12). The verb "to kill" (raṣaḥ) includes all homicide, accidental as well as deliberate (on raṣaḥ, see Bailey: 1–25).

The law "Thou shalt not kill [raṣaḥ]" (KJV) was broken whether the homicide was accidental or deliberate (murder). We find help in Exodus 21. The general law is restated: "Anyone who strikes a person with a fatal blow is to be put to death" (Exod 21:12; cf. Lev 24:17, *Anyone who takes the life of a human being is to be put to death*). But this general rule is not applied to all cases of homicide. It first must be determined if the person *intended* to kill another. The evidence for lack of intention is that the person was not lying in wait for the victim and that it was truly an accident. On the other hand, if the person schemed to murder another by cunning, then that person is guilty of murder (Exod 21:12-14). The intention of the one striking a fatal blow modifies the punishment given (on defining the difference between manslaughter and murder, see Barmash: 120–25).

The major point to remember is that apodictic law (absolute law) may state a general principle, but refinements are needed in individual cases. Not every case of manslaughter is murder.

Other evidence is also needed for the conviction of murder. From the laws in Numbers granting refuge for those who kill, we find that there is need for witnesses: "Only on the testimony of witnesses" may a person be convicted of murder (Num 35:30). The minimum number of witnesses is two for capital punishment. Since blasphemy was a capital crime (Lev 24:14), anyone who heard the person blaspheme must bear witness to this transgression by placing their hands on the head of the person to be executed.

Within this larger context, we are better able to understand *lex talionis* as we find it in Leviticus 24:17-21 and Exodus 21:23-27. From the Exodus passage we can see that these laws were generalizations. The penalty depends on who damages whom. If a master damages the eye or a tooth of a servant/slave, the master does not lose an eye or a tooth. Instead, the master must compensate the slave/servant by granting them freedom. The allowance of compensation for physical damages illustrates how these absolute laws were modified in practice. However, no compensation is to be allowed for murder. The person who murdered another will be executed: "Do not accept a ransom [compensation] for the life of a murderer, who deserves to die. They are to be put to death" (Num 35:31).

In fact, *lex talionis* cannot be carried out in practice. If a person partially blinds another, how could the perpetrator's eye be damaged in exactly the same way, and no more or no less? Or in the case of the loss of sight in one eye, if the person causing the damage has only one good eye, that person would become blind if their only remaining eye were removed. From the beginning it seems that compensation could be given for such damages. In addition, receiving compensation for an injury would be better for the victim than would seeing the perpetrator have a hand cut off.

Jesus quotes from these texts in Matthew 5:38, but it is doubtful that his audience understood them in their literal sense. Compensation for injuries was a given. Jesus' teaching about "an eye for an eye" is not about requiring physical harm to one who injures another, but about reciprocity: if you injure me, you pay. Jesus teaches that instead of expecting or repaying tit for tat, we should turn the other cheek (see TLC below).

THE TEXT IN THE LIFE OF THE CHURCH

Humans as the Image of God

The legal texts regarding the necessity of capital punishment represent an inherent conflict regarding the value of all people being made in God's image and likeness. On the one hand, each human is of infinite value, so a murderer must be put to death. No substitution or compensation is allowed. On the other hand, each murderer also represents the image and likeness of God (Gen 9:5-6). This conflict arises from the unparalleled and *equal* value of each human being, even those executed.

The laws examined above assume that homicide cases are clear. It can be discovered whether a homicide is accidental or deliberate. It is assumed that witnesses are telling the truth. But we know that this is not always the case. Consider the blatant false testimony of witnesses in the case of Naboth. King Ahab wanted Naboth's vineyard, but Naboth could not be persuaded to part with it. To solve this problem, Queen Jezebel arranged to have Naboth convicted of a capital crime on the testimony of two false witnesses. As a result, Naboth was dragged outside the city and put to death. King Ahab got the vineyard (1 Kings 21:1-15).

In order to protect the innocent from being convicted of a capital crime, Jews drew up very rigorous safeguards against false testimony and false conviction, as found in the Mishnah. First of all, *the trial began with arguments for acquittal, not for conviction.* A jury of twenty-three heard the case. If they argued or decided for acquittal, they could not change their minds later and argue for conviction. A simple majority was needed for acquittal, but a majority of two (at least thirteen to ten) was needed for conviction. A verdict could not be given on the day of the trial but only on the next day. Once a sentence of acquittal was reached, it could not be changed; however, a guilty verdict could be changed to acquittal.

In the trial, witnesses were reminded that God created each single person and that each person is of equal value. Since all bear God's image and likeness, each should consider that the whole world was created for a single person. Witnesses were also admonished to think carefully about their testimony in a capital case because the witnesses were answerable for the blood of the accused. Just as Abel's blood cried out to heaven on account of his murder, so too would the blood of an innocent victim cry out to heaven for the person's wrongful execution.

Finally, a stay of execution was possible until almost the last moment. A man stood at the door of the courtroom with a towel, while some distance away a man sat on a horse. While the accused was on the way to be stoned, anyone of the court could change their mind. If this was the case, the man in the doorway would wave his flag and the horseman would ride to stop the procession. This might happen several times. In addition, as people proceeded to the place of execution, a herald would proclaim the names of the witnesses for conviction and would ask if anyone had something to say for acquittal. If no such deliberation or acquittal overturned the sentence, the person would be executed outside the city (see Mishnah Sanhedrin 5.3-6; Eng. translations are available in Danby and in Neusner). We do not know if these regulations—or any other like them—were in place at the time of the early church. In any case, they would be irrelevant, because murder was tried according to Roman law, not Jewish law.

In the New Testament, written when Roman law prevailed in the West, we do not find any procedures to follow in capital cases. Roman law became the standard for Western Christianity: as church and state merged, the Hebrew-Jewish legal tradition was lost. This may explain why the regulations outlined above seem so strange to us. Today, trials are weighted for conviction. False evidence and false witness are not uncommon. Even DNA evidence has been falsified, either intentionally or unintentionally because of misidentification. Yet despite all these procedural weaknesses and the difficulty of obtaining an acquittal after conviction for a capital crime even if the evidence for acquittal may be persuasive, many Christians are ardent advocates of execution. Perhaps attitudes would be different if people considered that the execution of any innocent person is murder and that in such cases God considers the false witnesses and jurors to be murderers. Even more so, what guilt do those carry who wish for a person's execution on the basis of newspaper or television accounts, gossip, and prejudicial feelings?

Leviticus 25:1-55
The Sabbatical and Jubilee Years

PREVIEW

Leviticus 25 is about ownership. Who owns land and who owns people? Answers to these questions are set out here and are based on Israel's beliefs about God. Part of their belief about the land is visible in Leviticus 25. In Genesis 2, God created man, or human, and placed this person in a garden. God did this for a reason: "He was to serve it [the common meaning for this verb] and to guard it" (Gen 2:15 AT). Humankind did not own the land; the garden belonged to God. The human was its steward, so to speak.

In Leviticus, Israel lives in the desert, with the tribes arranged around a mobile tabernacle. There is no tillable land and no private property to inherit. But when they come into the land of Canaan, they will become owners of land that will be passed on from generation to generation (inherited land). Questions of ownership and inheritance are nonissues on a journey in the wilderness, but they will need to be confronted in Canaan. The focus of chapter 25 is land, land ownership, inheritance, and servitude. We find that even here, in the realm of the secular, the need for holiness applies: *You shall hallow the fiftieth year* (25:10 NJPS). Just as God made the seventh day holy (Gen 2:3) and made Israel holy (Lev 22:32), so Israel is to make a year holy [*Jubilee Year, p. 304*].

A question behind Leviticus 25 is, How do we make the fiftieth year holy? How is this year sanctified, or set apart from, the other forty-nine years? The answers given in this chapter are based on the fundamental premise that God is the owner of both the land and each individual Israelite. From this perspective, the land does not belong to the individual who happens to be using it, nor can an Israelite person become the real property of another (see below on 25:23). God owns these assets, and God will decide how they are to be owned and passed down from generation to generation.

But before we can get to the fiftieth year, we must first have Sabbatical Years. The regulations for the seventh year will occupy the initial seven verses.

OUTLINE

The Sabbatical Year, 25:1-7
    25:1-2a   Introduction
    25:2b-7   The Earth's Sabbath
The Jubilee Year, 25:8-13
    25:8-9   When Was the Jubilee Year?
    25:10-13   What Happens in the Jubilee Year?
Regulations, 25:14-22
    25:14-19   Crops Are Sold, Not Land
    25:20-22   Food for a Jubilee Year
The Jubilee in Practice, 25:23-28
    25:23-24   The Principle
    25:25-28   Normal Practice
Two Exceptions, 25:29-34
    25:29-31   Town Houses
    25:32-34   Levite Property
The Sale of People, 25:35-55
    25:35-38   Loans to Impoverished Israelites
    25:39-43   Indentured Servitude
    25:44-46   Gentiles Bought by Israelites
    25:47-54   Israelites Bought by Gentiles
    25:55   The Rationale for the Year

EXPLANATORY NOTES

The Sabbatical Year 25:1-7

25:1-2a Introduction

The mention of Mount Sinai in verse 1 is striking since it occurs only four times in Leviticus. The expression "on [or at] Mount Sinai" occurs in Exodus 31:18, where Moses is on the mountain. Since God is no longer on the mountain (Lev 1:1), here we can translate *at*

Mount Sinai (so 25:1 NIV). Sinai first occurs in 7:38, marking the end of the first major section of Leviticus, which concerns sacrificial rituals. The other three mentions of Sinai are here in 25:1 and at the ends of chapters 26 and 27. These three occurrences seem to form an envelope around the three closing chapters. The mention of Mount Sinai at the beginning of chapter 25 may also give a special emphasis to its content.

25:2b-7 *The Earth's Sabbath*

When Israel comes into the land that God is about to give to them, the land itself must observe a Sabbath to the Lord (v. 2b). The earth is the subject of the verb, emphasizing that this is the earth's Sabbath. This will occur every seven years, just as the last day of the week, the seventh day, is a day of rest for people.

This rest year is an agricultural year, beginning in the fall, when new crops normally are planted, and ending with the final harvest (v. 3). In verse 3 the Hebrew pronoun changes from *your* vineyards to *its* (the earth's) produce. This shift in pronoun is not recognized by the translations; for example, the NIV translates *their crops* (v. 3). In the Hebrew text the earth itself is taking a rest from producing crops, which is also emphasized in verses 4 and 5. There is to be *a Sabbath of complete rest, . . . a year of complete rest for the land* (25:4, 5 NJPS). Even whatever grows from random grains left by the harvest cannot be harvested. However, whatever the land itself produces spontaneously, willingly, so to speak, may be eaten. This produce will provide food for the owner, for his male and female servants, for his hired and indentured laborers, for his livestock, and for the wild animals (v. 7).

Regulations for the Sabbatical Year are also found in Deuteronomy 15:1-11 (release of debts); Jeremiah 34:14 (release of slaves); and Exodus 23:10-11 (the impoverished eat the produce).

The Jubilee Year 25:8-13

25:8-9 *When Was the Jubilee Year?*

Several questions about the Jubilee Year are raised and answered in this introductory paragraph. Seven Sabbatical Years are counted. Why seven? Perhaps because seven is a common number in the measurement of time—the number seven dominates the calendar: seven days in a week, Sabbath on the seventh day, the seventh year is a Sabbatical Year, seven years of service for slaves (Exod 21:2), and seven years for the release of debts or debt payment (Deut 15:1-11).

A Jubilee Year is announced after seven Sabbatical Years, in the forty-ninth year of the cycle (v. 8). The fiftieth year was the Jubilee Year and, like a Sabbatical Year, begins in the fall, and a precise date is specified—month seven, day ten, which is when the Day of Cleansing is observed. This seems to assume a fall calendar in which the new year begins in the fall, but in the lunar Jewish calendar in use at the time of Leviticus, it occurs in the seventh month. The fall New Year was a holdover from another calendar system *[Calendar, p. 295]*.

The Jubilee Year is announced to the entire land by a trumpet blast (v. 9). This counting fits the symmetry of the chapter. The seventh day is the Sabbath, the seventh year is the Sabbatical Year, the seventh Sabbatical Year is the Jubilee Year, which is announced in the seventh month. But in what year is the trumpet blown and Jubilee announced? The proclamation of the Jubilee Year takes place in the fiftieth year (v. 10), and this identification is stressed in verse 11.

One way to harmonize this inconsistency is to suppose that for the Jubilee Year, seven times seven years were counted, or forty-nine years, but that it was actually celebrated in the fiftieth year. Hartley suggests that the confusion results from how we count time. For example, Pentecost comes fifty days after Easter but is celebrated on the seventh Sunday after Easter, the forty-ninth day, because we begin our count on the Monday after Easter, not on Easter itself. Including Easter as day one, the seventh Sunday is fifty days from Easter (Hartley: 434–36) *[Calendar, p. 295; Jubilee Year, p. 304]*.

Applied to the Jubilee Year, seven Sabbatical Year periods yield forty-nine years, not fifty. But if we include the last Jubilee Year in our count, we have fifty years. Seven Sabbatical Year cycles, forty-nine years, plus the previous Jubilee Year make fifty years.

After announcing a release, the text says, *[This year] shall be a jubilee for you* (v. 10). Jubilee is the English form of the Hebrew word *yobel*. Normally *yobel* refers to either the horn of a ram (Josh 6:5) or the trumpet made from it (6:4-13 frequently). The trumpet blown to announce the Year of Jubilee, however, is called a *šophar* rather than a *yobel*. Yet this trumpet was most likely constructed from a ram's horn, a *yobel*. Thus the name of the material from which the trumpet was made became the name for the fiftieth year. This presumed identification is made in every subsequent verse in this paragraph (vv. 10, 11, 12, 13).

25:10-13 What Happens in the Jubilee Year?

First, the people are to make holy the fiftieth year, or declare it to be holy (vv. 10, 11), just as God hallowed the seventh day, setting it apart from all other days. Just as the seventh day is hallowed by cessation from labor, the people hallow the fiftieth year by proclaiming a release, or liberation. The word translated *release* or *liberty* (*deror*) is rarely found in the Hebrew Bible. It may refer to a release of slaves (Jer 34:8-17), to a year of release (Ezek 46:17), or to the release of prisoners (Isa 61:1) *[Jubilee Year, p. 304]*.

Here in verse 10, release is described as a restoration:

Each shall return <u>to his holding</u>,
    <u>to his family</u> each shall return.
        (AT, emph. added; notice the chiasm *[Literary Style, p. 306]*)

For the Jubilee Year to be a release, a restoration is needed. Freeing a debtor or a slave would not really make them free. Without a means of support or a supporting community, they will remain dependent. The proclamation of a release means restoring them to their land and to their family.

This restoration does not affect every aspect of life, however. The Jubilee Year is not a year for the redistribution of wealth. Differentials in wealth will remain. Some people will naturally prosper because their land is more fertile or receives more rain or because they are better farmers. The fortunate will retain their accrued wealth. But this restoration gives the landless and impoverished a chance to start over.

The paragraph ends by echoing verse 10: the Jubilee is holy. Because it is holy, the people must not plant, reap, or gather produce but must rather eat what grows of itself. In the Jubilee, no limitations are indicated on who might eat (vv. 12-13), in contrast to the limits of a Sabbatical Year (vv. 6-7). For those returning home in the Jubilee Year, there would be no shortage of produce to sustain them on the way.

Regulations 25:14-22

25:14-19 *Crops Are Sold, Not Land*

Since title to agricultural land reverts to its original owner every fifty years, the price of land fluctuates according to the number of years the purchaser can use a piece of land. If there are only a few years left until the Jubilee, the land is not worth much. But if the purchaser can hold it for many years, the land is worth more. In reality, the purchaser buys crop years—how long they will be able to harvest crops from this land. In this system the *buyer* takes all the risk for poor crops, not the person who profits from "selling" the land.

In buying or selling crop years, neither buyer nor seller is to oppress their fellow (vv. 14, 17). The Israelites were previously commanded, *When a foreigner resides among you in your land, do not mistreat them* (19:33). So also in transactions between native Israelites, neither buyer nor seller is to take advantage of the other. Obedience to this command is grounded once again in reverence and respect for the One who declares, *I the L*ORD *[Yahweh] am your God.* (25:17 NJPS).

25:20-22 *Food for a Jubilee Year*

This paragraph is preceded by a promise: if the people are obedient, God promises, *you will live safely in the land* (v. 18). Not only that, *but the land will yield its fruit, and you will eat your fill* (v. 19). Nevertheless, the Israelites, understandably, will become anxious when two years stretch before them in which they cannot sow or reap—a Sabbatical Year (forty-ninth) and then a Jubilee Year (fiftieth). To reassure them, God promises that the sixth year will produce enough food for three years—the harvest of year six will provide for year six, and for year seven (the Sabbatical Year), and for year eight (the Jubilee Year). However, parts of four years are affected, since in the ninth year there will be no produce until they can harvest crops planted in the eighth year, the Jubilee Year. (For details, consult Milgrom 2001: 2181–83).

The Jubilee in Practice 25:23-28

25:23-24 *The Principle*

Notice the wording at the beginning of verse 23: *The land must not be sold* (v. 23). We might expect it to say "You shall not sell the land." But the land does not belong to the individual Israelite or even to the nation as a whole, because *the land is mine and you reside in my land as foreigners and strangers* (v. 23). The first principle is that an Israelite cannot sell or transfer to another what does not belong to him.

The second principle is that the Israelites must allow for redemption in all the land. The original "owner" must be allowed to repossess it. An illustration of this principle is the field that had belonged to Ruth's husband before relocating to Moab. When Ruth comes to Israel with her mother-in-law, Naomi, they have no access to land because it has been "sold," and so they must glean in the land of others. However, the "title" belongs to Naomi, who now wants to transfer its rights to another. The closest male relative has first right of redemption. Through a legal procedure at the gate, Boaz motivates the primary redeemer to yield his right. Boaz then redeems the inheritance portion of land that had belonged to Elimelek and then his sons, who are all deceased (Ruth 4:1-11).

25:25-28 Normal Practice

A case is given in verses 25-28 to illustrate how the principles just given were to be practiced. If a kinsman (lit. *brother*) becomes impoverished and sells part of his land holdings, then his closest redeemer will come (or must come) and buy what his kinsman has sold. The word for "impoverished" occurs only in this chapter (vv. 25, 35, 39, 47) and in 27:8. It is a Jubilee term and refers to a kinsman who is too poor to pay the cost of support for himself and his family (see 27:8 for one too poor to pay). As a result, he sells part of his land. When this happens, his kinsman steps forward and buys the land. In Ruth, the nearest redeemer refuses to buy back the land, so the responsibility for its redemption comes to the person next in line, Boaz, who does act to restore Ruth's ancestral land (Ruth 4:4-7).

But if no one steps up to redeem the land, the one who lost the land may later buy it back. In either case, the price of the buyback depends on how many crop years remain till the Jubilee. If the buyer, for example, paid ten shekels when there were ten years till the Jubilee (a shekel a year) but now there are only five years until Jubilee, the price of the land would be five shekels. If the original seller can pay the five shekels, then he can take possession of it. Of course, if the impoverished person has no redeemer and does not become prosperous, the buyer retains possession until the Jubilee Year. At that time the buyer must relinquish it to the seller, its original owner or clan.

Two Exceptions 25:29-34

Thus far the Jubilee legislation has concerned cropland. But not all holdings are cropland, nor is all cropland affected. The text now explains these two exceptions.

25:29-31 Town Houses

If a person sells a dwelling within a walled city, repurchase by the seller is allowed—but only for one full year from the time the house is sold (a calendar year). After this time has passed, the house may not be redeemed. The house belongs to the purchaser in perpetuity and can be passed on as if it were ancestral land.

An addendum makes clear which houses fall under this exception. Houses that are found in a settlement without an encircling wall are like open fields. These are villages in the open countryside, with arable land around them. The farmers who tilled the soil around the settlement presumably lived in these houses. A list of such villages can be found in Nehemiah 11:25-30. Such houses can be redeemed at any time and are restored to their owners at the Jubilee Year just like land.

25:32-34 Levite Property

Land and cities belonging to the Levites are the second exclusion. The use of the term "Levite" is surprising. While it occurs often in Exodus and Numbers, it occurs only in this passage in Leviticus. Elsewhere in Leviticus the word "priest" is used *[Levites, p. 306]*.

The inheritance portion of the Levites is described in Numbers 35:1-8. The Levitical city sits in the center of their holdings, with pastureland surrounding it. The houses in a Levitical city, as well as the surrounding land, represent the inheritance granted them instead of land like other Israelites. Like land, these city houses can be redeemed at any time. If not redeemed before the Jubilee, they must be returned to their owners in the Jubilee Year—contrary to the law just given that allows redemption for only one year for city houses. Also, the pastures that go with their towns cannot be sold, because they represent their permanent portion as a collective.

The Sale of People 25:35-55

25:35-38 Loans to Impoverished Israelites

After the digression of the two exceptions to the general rule of land return, the focus once again is the impoverished Israelite. We assume that the person, after selling their land, has again become destitute (see the first case above, in vv. 25-28). Now their situation is even more tenuous. *Their hand quivers* (v. 35 AT); *they are unable to support themselves* (NIV), an expression found only here in the Bible. This is the opposite of the impoverished finding financial success, which is described as *his hand reaches* in verses 26 and 28 (AT; NIV, *prospers*).

They must now live as indebted resident aliens or side by side with their lender (v. 35). The punctuation of the Hebrew text has led to different constructions. The NET translation seems to follow the punctuation best: *You must support him; he must live with you like a foreign resident* (v. 35). The person will live without land and will need to find support among his fellow Israelites, as would a resident alien.

If the destitute person borrows money or receives food, presumably for his support and that of his family, such loans are given without interest. Two types of interest are forbidden. The first is discounted interest, *a bite* (*nešek*; NIV, *interest*) taken out of the loan (vv. 35, 36). The borrower does not receive the full sum of the loan. The second type, *increase* (*tarbit, marbit*; NIV, *profit*), is accrued interest that adds an amount to the sum owed (vv. 36, 37). Generosity toward each other is encouraged because of the generosity they have received from God.

Much is unclear about this loan to an impoverished Israelite. It seems to be halfway between selling land (vv. 25-28) and selling oneself into servitude. In the latter case the person's work pays off the loan, and they go free in the Jubilee Year (see below). In the present case there is no mention of the Jubilee Year cancelling the debt. Even though there was no interest, how was the destitute borrower to pay off the loan? What happens to the borrower's land in the Jubilee? Was the loan repaid by sale of the returned land? Deuteronomy 15:1-3 commands a release of debts or their payment in the Sabbatical Year, but we find no such suggestion here.

The scope of this law is quite circumscribed. If the above conditions are met, then such a loan would be made. These personal loans for support would not include commercial loans or loans taken for investment purposes.

25:39-43 Indentured Servitude

The three cases described in this series go from (relatively) best to worse. The destitute *Israelites* now *sell themselves* to a fellow Israelite. (This legislation regulates only Israelite behavior.) The person sells himself to his master because no Israelite can purchase a fellow Israelite as a slave (v. 42). Furthermore, the Israelite is not to be treated as a chattel slave, a person who is owned by the buyer. Rather, the destitute Israelite is to be treated as a farmhand or a resident worker (the combination of farmhand and the resident worker stand in contrast to slaves in v. 6 above). The seller is the person going into service, and the purchase price is paid to him, presumably for the support of his family or to repay debts. In return for the payment, the person becomes an indentured servant whose term of service extends until the Jubilee. Unlike land, however, no explicit provision is made for an early redemption either by the person himself or by a kinsman. As an indentured laborer, the servant must work until the debt is paid, the Year of Jubilee. As with land, the price of such a worker would fluctuate according to the time left until the Jubilee. At the Jubilee, the servant and his children go free. Evidently the owner has had some type of hold over the children. The servant's wife is not mentioned. Perhaps she tended what was left of the family's possessions and was never under the master's control.

An explanation or grounding is given for this law of servitude: the Israelites are already slaves of God, the One who delivered them from slavery in Egypt. Just as the land belongs to God, so do the Israelites. Since they cannot be slaves to any human, their fellow Israelites are commanded, *Do not rule over them ruthlessly* (v. 43), which is how the Israelite slaves were treated in Egypt (Exod 1:13).

25:44-46 Gentiles Bought by Israelites

Unlike the Israelites, the non-Israelites, or Gentiles, were not affected by the regulations of the Jubilee Year. The difference between this law and the case of the Israelite slave is huge. First, they were bought; that is, they became chattel slaves. Second, there were both male and female slaves. Third, as chattel slaves, they could be bought and sold like any other possession. They could be obtained both from non-Israelites (through trade) and from Gentiles who were born in the land of Israel. These slaves became the property of the Israelite master and were not released in the Year of Jubilee. As property, they could be held for life and passed down from one generation to the next. Unlike an Israelite slave, they were unprotected from being treated harshly (v. 46).

25:47-54 Israelites Bought by Gentiles

The fourth case concerns the worst possible outcome of poverty: becoming the slave of a Gentile master. This case assumes that outsiders who are living among the Israelites will also prosper. Such a prosperous person could afford slaves, and an impoverished Israelite might end up selling himself to a prosperous Gentile. Unlike the case of an Israelite selling himself to an Israelite, the Israelite slave of a Gentile may be ransomed at any time. The net for possible redeemers is cast wide. It may be a close kinsman or an uncle or cousin or anyone related by blood. If the Israelite prospers, he may buy his own freedom.

The price of redemption is calculated just like the redemption of a field. The master has purchased so many years of labor, so the price of redemption is great if there are many years until the Jubilee Year. Likewise, the price is small if only a few years remain until the slave will be released. This is emphasized by verse 53, which explains that the Israelite slave is in fact a laborer who is hired by the year either until redemption or until the Jubilee.

The Israelite slave is not to be treated harshly by his Gentile taskmaster.

25:55 The Rationale for the Year

The chapter ends with a quotation and paraphrase from verse 42. The Israelites are God's servants, or slaves, because God liberated them from Egypt. They are never to forget that the God who addresses them and commands them is this God, and they belong to this God. As is the case with the land, so also each Israelite belongs to God. Although they may sell their labor, they cannot be bought or sold.

THE TEXT IN BIBLICAL CONTEXT

Was the Jubilee Ever Practiced?

The heart of the Jubilee legislation was a release of land and of Israelite slaves. The word used for release (*deror*, Lev 25:10) is rare, occurring in only three other passages in the Hebrew text. The first passage is Jeremiah 34:8-17 (three times), where the background is a release of slaves. The Judean king made a covenant with the people in Jerusalem to release their slaves (34:8), and they did so. But later they retook their freed slaves and enslaved them again (v. 11). God responded: "I made a covenant with the generation that came out of Egypt to set their Israelite slaves free every seven years, but the people refused to do this. Now you did proclaim a release and set your slaves free, but then reneged. Therefore you will suffer catastrophe and go into exile" (Jer 34:14-17 paraphrased). Although the word "release" is used often in this passage, it is connected to a release of slaves in the Sabbatical Year, not a Jubilee Year.

There are two other mentions of a release. Isaiah 61:1 speaks of a release of captives or prisoners. This passage looks to the future and to an action by a messenger, not to a regular release every fifty years. Ezekiel 46:17, although it also speaks of the future, seems to refer to a regular Jubilee Year and the release of land. If the king gives land to his sons, it is their inherited possession. But if the king gives land to one of his servants, it reverts to the king in the year of release. This passage does not refer to an actual year of release practiced by the Israelites but to legislation for the future when there would be a Jubilee Year. We have no direct evidence of a Jubilee Year release of slaves or land taking place. (An attempt to show the plausibility, but not the probability, of a Jubilee being practiced is found in Fried and Freedman; Milgrom 2001: 2257-70).

The Jubilee Idea

The substance of the Jubilee release in Leviticus 25 is transformed in Isaiah 61:1. Although the word "release" (*deror*) is mentioned, its meaning has been transformed. In a future time there will be a messenger who will proclaim a release to captives and a freeing of prisoners. This is quite different from the return of owners to their land and of slaves to their own land and families.

Although we have no record of a Jubilee Year being practiced in the Old Testament, we do find mention of the Jubilee in Jewish tradition. Jubilee is mentioned in the Dead Sea Scrolls (Qumran), where it can mean a fifty-year period "from the beginning of their seven-year periods up to the appointed time for Jubilee" (1QS [Rule of the Community] X, 8; AT). This quote is found in a calendar foretelling future events. Also, the key word for Jubilee, a "release" (*deror*), is said to be a release from iniquity (11Q13 [11Q Melchizedek]). Since this text is a vision of what would happen in the last days, it does not refer to an actual Jubilee release.

Did Jesus understand himself as instituting an actual Jubilee on the pattern of Leviticus 25? The basis for a positive answer is Luke 4:18. "Release/set free" (*aphesis*) occurs twice in the Greek text of Luke 4:18, but this word has a very broad range of meanings. There is nothing in this passage that would cause a reader to think of Leviticus 25. There is no indication that land is involved, as in Leviticus 25, nor are the blind, captives, or prisoners affected by the Jubilee. Perhaps it is best to say that in biblical context, we can speak of the Jubilee *idea* or Jubilee *values* that have their home in Leviticus 25 (for additional comments and bibliography, see the essay *Jubilee Year, p. 304*).

The modern concept of the use of resources and their ownership in North America is different from or, perhaps more accurately, opposed to that found in Leviticus 25. We believe in the private ownership of land that is to be used for enjoyment or profit. We may sell the land or pass it along to others. The owner alone has the right to determine how their resources are used. Land is an economic resource from which we desire to obtain the most profit. It seems that the more land a person controls, the better. It is not a resource for the sustenance of a community or even of the poor. Our practice is to harvest all of our crop in the most efficient manner. It would diminish our profit to let others also harvest some of it. (See Lev 19:8-10 for the gleaning rights of others. Interestingly, the next verse, 19:11, begins, *Do not steal*.)

A contrary concept of ownership is that it depends on use. A resource belongs to those who use it, and not necessarily to the entity specified by a legal document. If one no longer uses a resource, another may do so. Along with this concept of ownership a sense that resources are to support the community as a whole is sometimes found. Why should one person own large or many resources while others go hungry or lack adequate shelter? The regulations in Leviticus 25 are to set right such disparities. (On a comparison of economic practices embedded in Scripture with modern notions, see Yoder: 109-12.)

Social Justice and Mission

Jubilee values are an important strand in the Bible. Certainly the prophets preached these values. On the accumulation of land, Isaiah proclaimed, "Woe to you who add house to house and join field to field till no space is left and you live alone in the land" (Isa 5:8). The concentration of resources can result in a few having much and many having little or nothing. This accumulation affects the marginalized: "The LORD says, 'Do what is just and right. Deliver those who have been robbed from those who oppress them. Do not exploit or mistreat foreigners who live in your land, children who have no fathers, or widows. Do not kill innocent people in this land'" (Jer 22:3 NET).

Jesus picks up this theme when John the Baptist sends his disciples to ask Jesus whether he is the messiah. Jesus replies, "Go back and report to John what you have seen and heard: The blind receive sight, the lame walk, those who have leprosy are cleansed, the deaf hear, the dead are raised, and the good news is proclaimed to the poor" (Luke 7:22). This verse is sometimes spiritualized to say that Jesus is not talking about lame people walking but about spiritually lame people. However, the context shows otherwise. In the preceding verse Luke reports, "At that very time Jesus cured many who had diseases, sicknesses and evil spirits, and gave sight to many who were blind" (v. 21). In this context, John's disciples can see for themselves what Jesus is doing and report back to him.

Jesus ends his reply to John the Baptist's disciples with "Blessed is anyone who takes no offense at me" (Luke 7:23 NET). What is there in what Jesus is doing to cause offense? Surely everyone would be glad to see people healed and freed from their infirmities. It is the last item, "good news is proclaimed to the poor," that is problematic for some. Jesus was clearly referring to actual poor people, and good news for poor people might be offensive to others.

We forget that Jesus did not convert anyone to Christianity. Yet Christians sometimes believe this is the most important work we can do as followers of Christ. Foreign missions and overseas aid gets high priority, but home missions—work with disadvantaged people in our midst—is a poor stepchild. Overseas relief to orphans and widows draws our attention, sympathy, and support. It is hard to get excited about helping needy children from single-parent homes in our own towns or communities.

A major stumbling block is that poverty and disease are insoluble problems. We may be tempted to think, "Since we can't solve it, let's not get too excited. All we can do is apply bandages to a few, in any case." We might even quote Jesus, "You will always have the poor among you" (John 12:8). However, Jesus is quoting from Deuteronomy 15, where we find a law for the Sabbatical Year. After commanding the release of debts in the Sabbatical Year, God tells the Israelites, "There shall be no needy among you" (v. 4 NJPS). However, if despite keeping the commands of the Sabbatical Year, there are yet poor, "Do not be hardhearted or tightfisted toward them" (v. 7). Then comes Jesus' quote, "There will always be poor people in the land. Therefore I command you to be openhanded toward your fellow Israelites who are poor and needy in your land" (v. 11).

Generosity in the face of need, even incurable need, is perhaps the best way to practice Jubilee values in our time.

THE TEXT IN THE LIFE OF THE CHURCH

The Use of Resources

In Western societies, as elsewhere, debt is a major problem. People have consumer debt because of goods and services they have bought on credit. Students have debts because many need to borrow money to obtain an education. In either case the debt is incurred because something is desired that is beyond a person's resources to purchase. Leviticus does not speak to this type of borrowing or debt. Rather, the concern is with sustenance, being able to feed and house oneself and one's family.

Nor, as mentioned, is Leviticus concerned with commercial debt, borrowing in order to make money. In a sense, student loans border on commercial loans: borrowing to obtain degrees or skills so that more money can be made in the future. Perhaps the closest to this type of borrowing is indentured servitude. The debtor works to pay off a loan by service. An example of a similar situation would be students who get loans on the condition that the loans will be forgiven, at least in part, by their work for a specific institution after they graduate. Here their indentured servitude comes after they have obtained their goal, their degree. However, most students have no secure, promised jobs through which they may pay off their debt. For many, perhaps, indentured servitude might not seem so bad. What creative idea might we develop along the line of this sense of indentured servitude?

Students who borrow to prepare for ministry or other church work, such as teaching, face a particular problem: low financial return on their investment. It is worth considering ways to make it possible for those who will have meager financial rewards to get the education they need. Perhaps congregations should undertake some obligation for their debt in return for their future service.

Leviticus 26:1-46

Part 3C
The Promise and Danger of Covenant

PREVIEW

Leviticus has been about Israel living as the people of God. Israel is to live a certain way because they have contracted an agreement with God. But how is the contract they have with God understood? One answer is as a covenant or, in political terms, as a treaty. This treaty was put in place before Leviticus and is assumed by Leviticus (Exod 24:1-8). It called for obedience to God as their overlord and stipulated punishments for disobedience. The pros and cons of keeping this contract with God are listed in Leviticus 26. This reminds us that a relationship with God is a two-way street. God's responses are affected by how one responds to God's regulations for maintaining accord with God. At the end of the chapter we will find that failure and punishment are not the final word, but God's grace continues despite disobedience.

This chapter forms the proper conclusion to Leviticus, which ends with a reference to Mount Sinai. A mention of Mount Sinai concludes the first section of Leviticus, chapters 1–7 (7:38). Here it concludes chapter 26 and forms an envelope structure with chapter 25 (25:1) *[Literary Style, p. 306]*. This structure points to a relationship between the two chapters, even though chapter 26 has material in it that is quite different from anything else in the book. As we shall see, its content—blessings and curses—are covenantal features and an appropriate ending to what came before.

Obviously, however, the actual end of Leviticus comes with chapter 27, which also ends with the mention of Sinai. So it too could form an envelope construction with chapter 25. However, given its content—oaths, pledges, and tithes—it is more likely that chapter 27 is an addendum to Leviticus rather than its proper ending. (See the Preview to ch. 27 for further discussion.)

Blessings and curses make up chapter 26 and bring the book of Leviticus to its conclusion. This may seem a strange way to conclude a book of instructions and regulations that has already specified the rewards for obedience and the punishment for disobedience. However, law collections from the ancient Near East sometimes end with blessings and curses. The most striking example in the Bible is found in Deuteronomy 27-28, where we find a ceremony in which blessings are to be proclaimed from Mount Gerizim and curses from Mount Ebal. The long list of blessings and curses in chapter 28 ends with "These are the terms of the *covenant* the LORD commanded Moses to make with the Israelites in Moab, in addition to the covenant he had made with them at Horeb [Sinai]" (Deut 29:1 [28:69], emph. added). These blessings and curses conclude the covenant laws given in Deuteronomy *[Blessings and Curses, p. 295; Covenant, p. 298]*.

The language of Leviticus 26 indicates the connection of Leviticus with covenant making and keeping. The primary word for "covenant" (*berit*) has occurred only twice previously in Leviticus (2:13; 24:8), but it appears eight times in chapter 26 (three times in v. 42). The covenant connection is confirmed by verses 42 and 45, in which God promises to remember the covenant made with Israel even though Israel has not kept it.

OUTLINE

God Is Sovereign Alone, 26:1-2
The Blessings, 26:3-13
The Curses, 26:14-33
    26:14-15   Conditions Presented
    26:16-17   The Beginning
    26:18-20   Dull Students
    26:21-33   Living in Hostility toward God
Compensation for Unkept Sabbatical Years, 26:34-35
Israel's Plight in Captivity, 26:36-39
Israel's Confession and Amends, 26:40-41

God Remembers the Covenant, 26:42-45
Conclusion to the Book, 26:46

EXPLANATORY NOTES

The beginning of chapter 26 is very abrupt. There is no introductory formula indicating that these are the words of God given through Moses. The last verse of chapter 26 (v. 46) makes this claim and forms a parallel with Leviticus 25:1.

The earliest known division of the Pentateuch into segments was for public reading and includes 26:1-2 with chapter 25. This makes sense because (1) these two verses echo the first two of the Ten Commandments, and (2) in Exodus these commandments are preceded by "I am the LORD your God, who brought you out of the land of Egypt, out of the house of slavery" (Exod 20:2 NRSV). Adding Leviticus 26:1-2 to chapter 25 makes compositional sense.

God Is Sovereign Alone 26:1-2

Israel will not make images or idols for themselves (v. 1). A similar command is found in Leviticus 19:4. Three types of objects are mentioned in verse 1. They are not to erect (1) any three-dimensional image (like a statue); (2) a special memorial stone, as Jacob did (Gen 28:18) and Moses did (Exod 24:4); or (3) an engraved stone, perhaps lying flat on the ground, on which worshipers bow down or worship (Milgrom 2001: 2281-82).

Verse 2 begins with a direct object: *[God's] Sabbaths you must keep* (AT). In this verse, Sabbath refers to the seventh day; later it will refer to the Sabbatical Year in verses 34, 35, and 43. Coupled with the holy day is mention of the holy place. Israel is to reverence God's sanctuary, to treat it with the utmost respect.

The Blessings 26:3-13

The blessings and curses follow the case law form: if Israel does this, then this is what will happen. The first if-clause is in verse 3 and echoes commands given elsewhere, in Leviticus 19:37 and 20:22. This is a blanket statement covering everything for which God will hold Israel accountable. Its negative counterpart is found below, in 26:15 and 43 *[Blessings and Curses, p. 295; Covenant, p. 298]*.

The promised blessings are given in a sequence of "I" statements by God. The first promise God makes is *I will send you rain in its season* (26:4). This promise is followed by the blessing *You will eat all the food you want and live in safety in your land* (26:5). The first promise begins with the most basic need, food.

The second blessing, in verse 6, is that God will give peace not only from enemies but even from the wild animals in the land. As a result, the people will live without fear: warfare will not bother them, and Israel will be overwhelmingly successful in battle (vv. 7-8).

The third blessing is the high point of this list. God gives three consecutive promises with a final punch line: God will look with favor upon Israel, will make them fertile and numerous, and will maintain the covenant with them (v. 9).

God's covenant making with Israel is recounted in Exodus 24:3-8. First, Moses announces to the people the stipulations, or requirements, of the covenant. The people respond, "We will do it" (v. 3 AT). Moses writes the covenant on a scroll and reads it again to the people the next day. Again the people respond, "We will do it" (v. 7 AT). As described in Exodus, Israel willingly accepted God's covenant with them and promised their obedience to this "contract" between themselves and God.

Finally, God will not only be present in the tabernacle (Lev 26:11) but also promises, *I will be ever present in your midst: I will be your God, and you shall be My people* (v. 12 NJPS). This translation recognizes the continuing force of the verb form used. This verbal form echoes Genesis 3:8, "They heard the sound of the LORD God moving about in the garden" (NJPS). God will be present with them, as in the beginning with Adam and Eve.

Israel's covenant with God is a result of God's grace (v. 13) and repeats Exodus 20:2, "I am the LORD [Yahweh] your God, who brought you out of Egypt, out of the land of slavery." The foundation of the covenant lies in the past with an act of God. Its future apparently depends on the people's response.

The Curses 26:14-33

26:14-15 Conditions Presented

The list of sanctions for breaking the covenant is considerably longer than the blessings for keeping it. The first two verses, 14-15, repeat in part what is found in verse 3, at the beginning of the blessings, only this time in the negative: If the Israelites *do not obey me* (14a NET, NJPS), but *reject my decrees and abhor my laws* (v. 15a). The verb "reject" can connote an attitude of loathing or contempt (*DCH*). The second verb, "abhor," has the sense of strong negative feelings (*DCH*). The result is that the Israelites break God's covenant.

Attitudes matter because they lead to disobedience and to breaking covenant with God [Blessings and Curses, p. 295; Covenant, p. 298].

The following punishments for disobedience are somewhat repetitive and disorganized. But a narrative underlies them that increases the intensity of the punishments as the story progresses. It is a story of Israel's disobedience and God's punishment until finally they are exiled into foreign lands.

26:16-17 The Beginning

The curses begin with Israel in the land, enjoying the success of the blessings depicted in the previous section. Now there is a reversal of fortune. Instead of fertility and abundance as promised (vv. 4-5), there is disease, both for people and for the crops. The Israelites will sow their crops in vain because their enemies will eat the harvest (v. 16). Now, instead of the promised security and victory (vv. 7-9), God will turn against them. Their enemies will put them to flight. Their fear will be so great that even when there is no pursuer they will take flight (v. 17).

26:18-20 Dull Students

Despite these disasters, Israel has not yet learned its lesson. So God will continue to discipline them. There is perhaps yet hope that they will learn and change their ways if the punishments become ever more severe (v. 18). Now the strength or power of the whole nation will be broken. The earth and sky will become as hard iron and bronze. No rain will fall. The earth will become bone dry. Nothing will grow. They will exhaust themselves, but there will be no harvest (vv. 19-20). But the people will have not yet learned from their plight.

26:21-33 Living in Hostility toward God

The people are still in their own land, but if they continue their ways, not even wanting to obey God, the punishments for these attitudes will be even worse. The word "hostile" occurs only in this chapter. It is a significant word, appearing seven times, and it describes an attitude of opposition to or against (Milgrom 2001: 2309-10). The people now live in opposition to God and become the enemies of God rather than God's allies bound by a pact (v. 21).

Above, in verse 6, the wild animals were suppressed. Now the wild animals will turn against them and kill or eat their children (v. 22). This was a very real fear in Israel, as the story of children and bears in 2 Kings 2:23-24 shows. Moreover, the wild animals will destroy their livestock and make Israel few in number. This is the negation of verse 9, which promises fertility. The fear will become so great that the roads will be deserted. No one will want to leave their place of habitation (v. 22).

Now God too will act in opposition by bringing upon Israel a sword of retribution for breaking covenant. Israel will reap the results of their disobedience and rebellion against their God (v. 24).

The word often translated *avenge* or *vengeance* in verse 25 is better translated *(bring) retribution* (Peels). The punishment they receive is God's retribution upon them, their negative reward for breaking God's covenant. Verse 22 declared that the roads would be deserted. Now the people will be under siege; they will be unable to travel even if they wanted to. In these crowded conditions God will send them a disease, and they will be captured by their enemy. Famine conditions will exist. They will not have enough bread, the opposite of eating until satisfied (v. 5). It will get worse. The people will become so hungry that they will eat their children (v. 29)—as opposed to their children's earlier destruction by wild animals (v. 22).

While the people are under siege, God will destroy the high places and their incense altars. Their corpses will be strewn about upon the corpses of their idols. God will have reached the point of loathing Israel. Previously, in verse 11, God promised not to loathe the people, but the people loathed God's judgments. Now God will loathe them (v. 30). God's loathing will bring about the end of Israel. Their cities will become rubble heaps, their sanctuaries destroyed. God will no longer accept the fine odor of their sacrifices. God will make the land so desolate that even their enemies who live in the land will be appalled (v. 32). As for the people, God will scatter them among the nations (v. 33). Israel will hit rock bottom. Will Israel survive?

Compensation for Unkept Sabbatical Years 26:34-35

Since Israel will no longer be living on the land and it will lie uncultivated, every year will be a Sabbatical Year. The land is not tilled during such a year. Its spontaneous growth could be shared by all, including animals. (See Lev 25:2-7 for the regulations of the Sabbatical Year.) These Sabbatical Years will make up for the ones that Israel did not observe. The land will lie desolate, untilled, until the earth has been fully repaid for the rest years "stolen" from it.

The universal covenant made with all humankind in Genesis 9:8-17 includes not only Noah and his family, but also all the living animals. In this covenant God pledged not to destroy all life and not to devastate the earth again by a flood (v. 11). It seems to follow that God has an interest in preventing humans from doing so.

Israel's Plight in Captivity 26:36-39

How will the survivors fare in foreign lands? Not so well. Even in exile the curses will follow them. They will be filled with despair, and at the sound of a windblown leaf they will take flight as if threatened by a sword. In their flight they will fall over one another without the strength to face their enemies (v. 37). Israel will disappear among the nations who have devoured them (v. 38). There they will rot away on account of their own and their ancestors' covenant breaking (v. 39). Israel will be at an end.

Israel's Confession and Amends 26:40-41

But there is hope. If or when they confess their iniquities as well as those of their ancestors and make amends for them, there is hope. (The Heb. text of v. 40 does not begin with a conditional "if," although it is assumed by most translations.)

God Remembers the Covenant 26:42-45

After confession, submission, and paying the price for their transgressions, matters will change. After all, the earth will have been repaid for its lost Sabbaths, and Israel will have paid the price of their iniquity. Even though they rejected and abhorred God's laws, breaking God's covenant with them, God will not reject them.

Instead, God will call to mind their first covenant, which was based on God's grace. God's declaration, *I Yahweh am their God* (v. 44 AT), echoes the declaration at the end of chapter 25. The confession of the people did not erase their debts. The people have suffered for what they did. But they will not be abandoned. God will remain their God. God will be with them yet.

Conclusion to the Book 26:46

The conclusion to this chapter sums up the content of Leviticus. We found a similar summary in 7:37-38: *This is the instruction concerning the whole, grain, cleansing, penalty, ordination, and peace offerings that God commanded Moses . . . when he commanded Israel to offer their offering to God in the Sinai wilderness* (AT). Here we find a different summary:

1. The instructions (plural) are coupled with the statutes and laws. This indicates that the entirety of the commands in Leviticus are meant.
2. *God gave these between God's self and the Israelites ... through the agency of Moses* (AT). The contents of Leviticus represent a gift given by God that links the Israelites together with God (see the expansion of this point in TBC and TLC below).

THE TEXT IN BIBLICAL CONTEXT
Curses and Covenant

In the ancient Near East, curses and blessings were often part of a larger literary whole. For example, they may be found at the end of a law collection like the Code of Hammurabi (Richardson: 125–35). Blessings and curses were also a standard part of treaties between nations. In these international covenants, both parties entered into the agreement, but in cases where there was an inequality of power, the curses were formulated by the stronger nation. Preceding the curses, usually at the beginning of the treaty, the stronger party might state what they have done for the weaker. This showed the obligation of the (weaker) vassal state to abide by the stipulations of the treaty. (See the summary of treaty elements in Rothenbusch: 521–27.)

Leviticus 26 presents itself as an element of such a vassal covenant. The word "covenant" occurs here often (vv. 9, 15, 25, 42 [three times], 44, 45). We find a statement of what God, the stronger party, has done for Israel in liberating them from slavery in Egypt. This is the God of the covenant with Israel, "the Sovereign, the LORD" (Exod 23:17 NJPS). Keeping the laws, rules, and stipulations of the covenant was Israel's part of keeping their covenant with their ruler [*Blessings and Curses, p. 295; Covenant, p. 298*].

Covenant and Continuation

Regarding Israelite law as covenant law indicates its *relationship* aspect. The people are God's people, and God is the Israelites' God (Lev 26:12 and often in the laws). Breaking a law is disobedience to a *person* and diminishes one's relationship with God. If Israel not only weakens their relationship with God but also comes to loathe their covenant law and God as its author, this is a step too far. The stronger party, God, would now punish them for their behavior and attitudes.

Punishment means that the curses of the covenant come true. But despite Israel's disobedience and punishment, God says, *I will not reject them or abhor them so as to destroy them completely, breaking my covenant with them* (26:44). God's last word is *I will remember the covenant with their ancestors whom I brought out of Egypt in the sight of the nations to be their God* (26:45). God's punishment does not annul the covenant, nor does it annul God's grace and promises.

The most graphic expression of God's determination to keep covenant with Israel is found in Jeremiah 31:31-37. Since Israel has broken or annulled the previous covenant, God will act first by making a new covenant with Israel (v. 32). In this new covenant, God says, "I will put my law in their minds and write it on their hearts" (v. 33). The *new* in this covenant is that the law of the covenant will be internalized. In this future covenant, Israel will remain God's people just as God will remain as their God.

The making of a new covenant is not God rejecting Israel as a covenant partner: God will forgive and will forget their sin (Jer 31:34). God's eternal commitment to Israel is unequivocally stated as a promise by the Creator: when there ceases to be sun and moon, night and day, then and only then "will Israel ever cease being a nation before me" (vv. 36-37) *[Covenant, p. 298]*.

Jews and Christians

After Jesus' ministry on earth, what is the status of the covenant and the promises that God made with Israel? After Jesus, will God renege on the covenant made with Israel? Paul wrestled with the implications of Israel's election and covenant in Romans 9–11. The interpretation of these chapters is complex, and scholars do not always agree.

In a well-known passage in Isaiah 2:2-3, we find a vision of the Gentiles streaming to Jerusalem of their own accord, desiring to learn God's design for living because "the law will go out from Zion, the word of the LORD from Jerusalem" (v. 3). This passage ends in verse 5 with an exhortation for Israel to walk in the way of God. The hope for the Gentiles is a faithful Israel, an Israel that will keep alive the law as a witness to the Gentiles. Otherwise, why would they come to Jerusalem? Who would teach them the law?

John E. Toews has set out an insightful and persuasive explanation of Paul's understanding of God's relationship to the Jews and to the Gentiles as portrayed in Romans 9–11. He shows that the context for Paul's understanding is Isaiah 27 and 59, with its statements and promises about both Jews and Gentiles. He concludes, "Paul is confident that God will save all Israel, but he does not specify when. His accent falls rather on the inclusion of the Gentiles and the unity of the Jews and Gentiles in God's salvation promise and covenant" (Toews: 287). Toews also stresses the ambiguity of the statement in Romans regarding the Gentiles: Paul seems to declare that although all the Jews will be saved, only an unspecified, ambiguous part of the Gentiles will be saved.

THE TEXT IN THE LIFE OF THE CHURCH
Jews, Gentiles, and Christians Today

Jews, in general, do not feel the need of salvation as proclaimed by the church. They are automatically included in God's people by promise and birth. Why would they need to change religions? It is the Gentiles that have a problem. How do these people who are not God's people become God's people?

The Christians' question, on the other hand, is what to do with the Jews. The answer in history, to a greater or lesser extent, has been to do away with them. The Jews have experienced a long history of persecution by Christians, including the murdering of Jews with impunity. Christians have insisted that the church now represents the true people of God, that the Jewish people have now been superseded by Gentile Christians. This notion has in part been the motive for persecuting and killing Jews.

Because of this persecution by Gentile Christians, Christianity is seen by Jews as a renunciation of Jewish identity. A Jew converting to Christianity is regarded as joining those who would assimilate them, thus destroying the Jewish identity. In the modern State of Israel, the Supreme Court has ruled that a Christian Jew does not have the rights of a Jew to return to the land of Israel and become a citizen. A Jew can be an atheist, a Jew can be a Buddhist, but a Christian is no longer a Jew. In this they have accepted the understanding that Christianity is a threat to the Jewish people.

Indeed, in light of the Hebrew Bible and related Jewish literature, the predominant premise in Paul's time was that the Gentiles would be saved by *becoming Jews* (Toews: 286-87). However, the Jewish sages of the Mishnah (oral tradition from before the time of Jesus to about 135 CE, written about 180 CE) and the Talmud (a commentary on the Mishnah written around the fifth century) came to teach that there was no need for Gentiles to become Jews. Only Jews needed to keep all dietary laws as found in Leviticus 11, for example, because that is what God commanded *them*. All that was required of a Gentile was to become a righteous person by keeping the covenant commands given to Noah (see Müller).

As Toews points out, Paul does not blur the line between Jew and Gentile: Jews will be saved as Jews: "They [the Jews] continue to be God's people despite their refusal to believe that Jesus is the Messiah. God's grace toward Israel persists, despite the fact that it rejects this grace for the present time" (Toews: 290). Here Paul is in line with Leviticus 26:44-45 and the prophet Jeremiah in 31:31-37. (On Christian supersessionism, see Klawans 2006.)

This is a challenging issue for many Christians, especially as they remember the words of Jesus recorded in John's gospel, "No one comes to the Father except through me" (John 14:6). Whatever this statement means for Jewish people, it must mean that Jesus (and not Christians) will decide who comes to the Father.

Leviticus 27:1-34

Part 3D
Addendum: Vows, Dedications, and Tithes

PREVIEW

How are those who serve in the tabernacle supported? The priests get food from the cleansing offering and the peace offering, but how do they get cash to buy things they need in their homes? How do they get cash to buy the evening and morning whole offerings that they must provide? Places of worship and their personnel do cost money, after all. Many different resources are needed for worship and teaching (which the priests also did, Lev 10:10-11).

The final chapter of Leviticus shows us how Israel supported their worship and their priests. It discusses how the system of vows and dedications worked. Leviticus 27 begins with persons and animals who have been vowed or dedicated to God. If the person making the vow wants to retain ownership of who or what is vowed, then they can convert the vow to money and pay that instead.

The vows in verses 2-13 are in effect pledges because they promise something: "If a man makes a vow to the LORD or takes an oath of binding obligation on himself, he must not break his word, but must do whatever he has promised" (Num 30:2 NET). This type of vow seems to immediately obligate the person taking the oath. We also find conditional vows, such as the one Jacob made: "Jacob then made a vow, saying, 'If God remains with me, if He protects me on this journey . . ." (Gen 28:20 NJPS). No promises are made, no oath sworn, no obligations incurred on Jacob's part. This type of vow comes due when its conditions are met. In the case of Jacob, the Deity is to provide him with a safe journey. (On the various types of vows, see Milgrom 2001: 2409–12).

The dedication of property to God begins with verse 14. These dedications are made by declaring something holy. In these cases the valuation is set by the priest, depending on the worth of what is dedicated. The person making the dedication can buy back their property by paying its value plus 20 percent. There are exceptions. What already belongs to God cannot be dedicated to God. What cannot be used by the priests must be bought back or sold. The firstborn of unclean animals illustrates this principle (vv. 26-27). Such an animal cannot be sacrificed, so its monetary value is paid instead.

OUTLINE

Introduction, 27:1-2a
Pledges, 27:2b-13
    27:2b-8   Pledges of Persons
    27:9-13   Pledges of Animals
Dedication of Land, 27:14-25
People and Things That Cannot Be Dedicated, 27:26-29
    27:26-27   The Firstborn
    27:28-29   Banned Objects
Tithes, 27:30-33
Ending, 27:34

EXPLANATORY NOTES

Introduction 27:1-2a

After an introduction in which God commands Moses to deliver the following speech to the Israelites, the chapter launches into a discussion of pledges. This topic is presented in the form of case law.

Pledges 27:2b-13

27:2b-8 Pledges of Persons

How do we convert vowed or dedicated persons or objects to money in order to pay our vows? The short answer is that the exchange rate for persons is fixed, whereas the monetary worth of animals and land is determined by the priests. A similar process took place in previous chapters with respect to the penalty offering in which an animal brought for a sacrifice must be a certain value and could be converted into money (Lev 5:15–6:6).

The fixed valuations for vowed persons are given in verses 3-7. A man between the ages of twenty and sixty has the highest value: fifty *sanctuary shekels* (see 5:15). But a woman of the same age has a valuation of thirty shekels. The next age group is persons whose ages are five to twenty years. For a male, the valuation is twenty shekels; for a female, ten shekels. Going yet younger, between a month and five years, the valuation is five shekels for a male, three shekels for a female. At the other end of the spectrum, those sixty years old and older have the set value of fifteen shekels for a man and ten shekels for a woman.

But what if someone has pledged a person whose worth is more than they can afford? They present their pledged person to the priest, and the priest decides the value of the pledge according to how much he estimates the vowed person can afford (v. 8).

27:9-13 Pledges of Animals

If a person pledges a large animal (cow, sheep, or goat) that can be sacrificed, then the animal becomes holy and belongs to God. Since a specific animal was pledged, the owner cannot substitute either a less valuable or a more valuable one. If a switch were attempted, both animals would become holy. The vow offering of the pledged animal is a type of well-being offering (Lev 3) whose ritual is set out in Leviticus 7:16-19. In the case of vowed clean animals, no price is set, because they are sacrificed. These offerings provide additional food for the priests.

What about large animals (horses, donkeys) that cannot be sacrificed? The unclean animal is presented to the priest, who then determines its value. The one who has vowed the animal may buy it back by adding 20 percent to its price. Since the priest sets prices on the animal, it can be sold for money (shekels). In this way the coffers for the tabernacle and its servers can be filled.

Dedication of Land 27:14-25

What about real estate? Can it be pledged? The answer is yes, but different language is used. The person pledging declares a house or a field to be holy. With this declaration, the property is transferred from the profane (everyday) realm to the holy and now belongs to God. The priests will decide its value. The owner may buy it back by meeting the price and paying an additional 20 percent. The same procedure is applied to a dedicated house.

The case of a field is much more complicated, and understanding what takes place is not certain. If a person dedicates a field belonging to his inherited portion, the land will be returned in the Jubilee Year [*Jubilee Year*, p. 304]. The price for such a field is determined by the amount of seed needed to sow it. Each homer of barley seed needed to sow the field raises its price by fifty silver shekels. The larger the field, the more seed is needed and the higher the price. If two homers are needed, then the price of the land is one hundred shekels. However, since we do not know the exact amount of seed in a homer, we cannot determine how much land a homer might seed (see *NIDB*, s.v. "Weights and Measures"). All we do know is how the price was set for dedicated land.

Not only the amount of land pledged needs to be determined but also the time it will be used. If the person dedicates the field from the Year of Jubilee onward, it has its full value. If the field is dedicated after the Jubilee Year has begun, the priest calculates its price according to the years remaining to the next Jubilee release of the land (vv. 17-18). For example, if twenty-five years are left, then the person pays half of what the land would cost for the full Jubilee period of fifty years.

Two questions naturally arise. First, who receives the money? And second, who retains use of the field? In a regular case, the seller receives the money and the buyer receives ownership and works the land, accruing any money coming from its use. Yet for pledged land, who might buy it? Do the priests pay for the land? In this case they are the new owners until the Jubilee Year. A field sold from an inheritance, according to Jubilee law, can be bought back at any time by the seller (Lev 25:26-27). Here the seller can buy back his field but must add 20 percent to its price (27:19).

So far so good. But with verse 20 things become unclear. If the person does not buy back his ancestral field from the priest, does it revert to him at the time of the Jubilee Year, or does it now belong to the priests? It seems that if a person does not redeem his field before the Jubilee Year, it can no longer be redeemed and belongs to the priests. Likewise, if a person sells the field, it can no longer be redeemed, contrary to Jubilee law. But how can the person who dedicated the field and transferred "ownership" now sell what is not his, since it has been pledged to another? Perhaps since the one pledging the land must add 20 percent to the purchase price to buy it, he must also do so for its return in the Jubilee Year. The land cannot simply revert to its previous owner. Likewise, since the land fulfills the person's pledge, he cannot transfer that obligation to another. Thus the land remains under pledge that must be paid by the one who pledged it. Default means the land is forever lost. (For other speculations to solve this conundrum, see Hartley; Milgrom 2001: 2383-85.)

Despite these questions, it appears that an unclaimed field will not revert to its previous owner in the Year of Jubilee. It becomes removed from the secular domain and is now a holy field that belongs permanently to the priests (v. 21). This solution appears problematic since the landholdings of the priesthood would keep growing while those in the community would lose land.

What happens when a person dedicates a field to God that was purchased, not inherited? Again, the priest calculates the field's price by the number of crop years until the Jubilee Year (v. 23). With its purchase, the field becomes holy. In the Year of Jubilee, this field will return to its original owner. Thus the original sellers of what was for them an inheritance will not lose their ancestral land because the buyer decides to dedicate it to the temple. The buyer can only pledge its usage, not its title (v. 24).

A "footnote" in verse 25 adds that all these transactions shall be according to the holy, or sanctuary, shekel. *Twenty gerahs*, a measure, make up a sanctuary shekel. (See *NIDB*, s.v. "Weights and Measures.")

People and Things That Cannot Be Dedicated 27:26-29

27:26-27 *The Firstborn*

Some things automatically belong to God, like the firstborn of flock and herd animals. The firstborn of unclean animals, which cannot be sacrificed to God, must be sold to the sanctuary. The owner may buy the animal back, adding 20 percent to its price. If the owner does not buy it back, the animal is sold to another at its regular price.

27:28-29 *Banned Objects*

Some objects are *proscribed* (NJPS) or become permanently *dedicated* (NET) property and can never be redeemed. The words for such a banned object (*ḥerem*) and for declaring something banned (*heḥerim*) denote something given over so completely to God that it can never return to the profane realm. For example, at the time of the conquest, the city of Jericho and its contents were banned. The people were commanded to guard themselves against taking anything banned because "if you take any of it, you will make the Israelite camp subject to annihilation and cause a disaster" (Josh 6:18 NET).

The banned items belonged to God and were to be placed only in God's treasury. Outside God's realm they were lethal, and those taking them were to be burned to death (Josh 7:15). This devoting of enemies and their possessions is not uncommon in the Bible. These enemies may even be fellow Israelites (Deut 13:16-17).

However, in these verses we do not have a conflict. A person could declare a ban on animals, property, or people. As in the cases of the firstborn (see vv. 26-27), the banned items would belong to God and were most holy. They were irretrievably lost and could not be bought back or redeemed (v. 28). What happened to the banned objects and persons is not said. Presumably, they were given for the use of the priests and support of the sanctuary. (On the ban, see Milgrom 2001: 2391-96, 2417-21.)

Tithes 27:30-33

The Israelite is to devote a tenth of his crops and livestock—grain, fruit, cattle, and flocks—to God. The tithed objects are only holy, not "most holy," as in the case of the ban, and can be bought back by adding a tenth to their price. In the case of grain and fruit, a tenth can easily be measured. But how does one tithe cattle and sheep? Livestock are lined up and brought past their owner in single file. Every tenth animal is halted by lowering a staff. This tenth animal becomes a tithe. But perhaps the ninth animal is smaller or weaker and can serve just as well as a tithe. The text warns against paying attention to the animals so as to exchange or substitute a less valuable one for a more valuable one. Any attempt to exchange animals makes both animals holy to God and they must be offered without any chance at redemption.

Ending 27:34

God's speeches from Mount Sinai end with Leviticus 27:34: *These are the commandments that the* LORD *gave to Moses for the people of Israel on [at] Mount Sinai* (NRSV). A direct address to Moses at Mount Sinai begins with Leviticus 25:1. This speech comes to a close in 26:46: *These are the decrees, the laws and the regulations that the* LORD *established at Mount Sinai between himself and the Israelites through Moses.* This seems to make 27:34 redundant.

The subject matter of this second speech from Sinai also seems out of place or inappropriate for an ending to Leviticus. Some argue that it did not originally belong to Leviticus. However, others have argued that it did (see Hartley). In either case, its subject matter—vows, dedications, and tithes—does not fit smoothly with the blessings and curses in chapter 26. The position taken here is that chapter 27 is an addendum to the book, which ended properly with chapter 26.

As for its role in marking a break between Leviticus and Numbers, we need to remember that originally there were no books, only scrolls—a separate scroll for each of the first five books. These scrolls did not have titles like Leviticus or Numbers: they were called by their opening words. Leviticus was called *Wayyiqraʾ* ("and called") because that was the first word on the scroll. The scroll for Numbers was called *Bemidbar* ("in the wilderness") because it begins with God speaking to Moses in the wilderness of Sinai.

Scrolls could only be of a certain length to remain practical for regular use. Consequently, a decision had to be made as to where one scroll ended and another began. By the end of Leviticus, there was enough material for a scroll, and there was a clear disjunction between Leviticus 27 and Numbers 1. Leviticus 27 ends with God speaking to Moses at Mount Sinai, whereas Numbers 1 begins with God speaking to Moses in the tent of meeting located in the Sinai desert and with a date for the speech. The speech itself begins with a command, in the plural, to take a census. While Moses is the recipient of this speech, who will carry out the command is only mentioned later. For all of these reasons, it made sense to begin a new scroll with Numbers 1:1.

Outline of Leviticus

PART 1 RITUALS FOR GOD'S PRESENCE	**1:1–15:33**
1A Sacrificial Rituals	**1:1–7:38**
The Voluntary Offerings	*1:1–3:17*
Introduction	1:1-2a
Title	1:1a
Location	1:1b
Commission	1:2a
Rituals for Pleasing God: The Whole Burnt Offering	1:2b-17
Introduction	1:2b-c
Audience	1:2b
General Case	1:2c
Whole Burnt Offerings	1:3-17
Cattle	1:3-9
Sheep or Goats	1:10-13
Birds	1:14-17
Rituals for Pleasing God: The Grain Offering	2:1-16
The Grain Offering	2:1-13
The Uncooked Meal Offering	2:1-3
The Cooked Meal Offering	2:4-10
Further Instructions	2:11-13
Firstfruits of Grain	2:14-16
Rituals for Pleasing God: The Peace Offering	3:1-17
Heading	3:1a
If Cattle	3:1b-6
If Flock	3:7-16
Concluding Prescription	3:17

The Obligatory Offerings	*4:1–7:36*
Forgiveness Rituals: Inadvertent Sins	4:1-35
Heading	4:1-2
Individual Cases	4:3-35
The High Priest	4:3-12
The People	4:13-21
The Leader	4:22-26
The Commoner	4:27-35
Forgiveness Rituals: The Penalty Offering	5:1–6:7
Trespass by Negligence	5:1-13
The Four Cases	5:1-4
The Penalty Ritual	5:5-13
Accidental Trespasses on the Divine	5:14-19
The Case	5:14-16
Trespassing Inadvertently	5:17-19
Intentional Trespasses on the Divine	6:1-7
Trespasses against God and Neighbor	6:1-3
The Penalty Ritual	6:4-7
Priestly Instructions for Sacrifice	6:8–7:36
The Scheduled Daily Offerings	6:8-18
Introduction	6:8-9a
The Daily Burnt Offering	6:9b-13
The Daily Grain Offering	6:14-18
The High-Priestly Grain Offering	6:19-23
Additional Comments on Public Offerings	6:24–7:36
The Cleansing Offering for Forgiveness	6:24-30
The Penalty Offering	7:1-10
The Peace Offering	7:11-36
A Retrospective Summary of the Section on Sacrifice	7:37-38
1B Inauguration of Worship	**8:1–10:20**
The Installation of the Priesthood	8:1-36
Preparation	8:1-4
Introduction	8:1
The Command to Prepare	8:2-3
The Performance Formula	8:4
Step 1: Bathing and Dressing	8:5-9
Introduction to the Ceremony	8:5
Bathing the Future Priests	8:6
Clothing Aaron	8:7-9
Step 2: Anointing	8:10-13
The Holy Things and Aaron	8:10-12

Outline of Leviticus

Parenthesis: Clothing the Sons	8:13
Step 3: The Sacrificial Rituals	8:14-29
The Ritual for Consecrating the Altar	8:14-17
A Ritual for Pleasing God	8:18-21
A Ritual for Installation of the Priests	8:22-29
Step 4: Hallowing	8:30-34
Conclusion	8:35-36
The Dedication of the Sanctuary	9:1-24
Instruction for the Consecration Ceremony	9:1-7
The Ceremony	9:8-22
The Blessing of the People	9:23-24
A Tragic Act of Worship	10:1-20
The Narrative and Immediate Result	10:1-7
New Instructions and Duties	10:8-11
Review of the People's Cleansing Offerings	10:12-20
1C Rituals for Purity	**11:1–15:33**
Rituals for Food Impurity	11:1-47
Introduction	11:1-2a
Clean and Unclean Animals	11:2b-23
Larger Land Animals	11:2b-8
Aquatic Animals	11:9-12
Birds	11:13-19
Insects	11:20-23
Rituals for Impurity: Land Animals	11:24-31
Passive Impurity	11:32-38
Carcass Impurity	11:39-43
Rationale and Summary	11:44-47
Birthing Rituals	12:1-8
Quarantine for Birthing	12:1-5
The Ritual for Purification	12:6-8
The First Option	12:6-7
A Less Costly Option	12:8
Rituals for Blemishes	13:1–14:57
Introduction	13:1
Blemishes on the Skin	13:2-46
Swelling, Scabs, and Spots	13:2-17
Boils	13:18-23
Burns	13:24-28
Baldness and Other Blemishes	13:29-46
Blemishes on Garments	13:47-59
The Purification Ceremony for Skin Blemishes	14:1-32

Stage 1: Reentry to the Camp	14:2-7
Stage 2: Limbo	14:8-9
Stage 3: The Final Purification Ritual	14:10-20
An Alternative	14:21-32
Blemishes in Houses	14:33-53
Diagnosis of House Blemishes	14:36-45
The Consequences of Entering or Using a Sealed House	14:46-47
Purification of a Defiled House	14:48-53
Concluding Summary	14:54-57
Rituals for Reproductive Impurities	15:1-33
Male Seminal Emissions	15:1-17
Introduction	15:1-2
Male Emissions	15:3-17
Intercourse	15:18
Female Emissions	15:19-30
Menstruation	15:19-24
Abnormal Vaginal Secretion	15:25-30
Conclusion to the Purity Regulations	15:31-33

PART 2 A HINGE — 16:1–17:16

The Day of Cleansing	16:1-34
Prologue	16:1-2
The Restoration Ceremony	16:3-28
Preparation	16:3-11
The Cleansing Rituals	16:12-19
The Elimination Ritual	16:20-22
Concluding Rituals	16:23-28
Epilogue	16:29-34
Why Blood Has Power of Removal	17:1-16
Introduction	17:1-2
Place Matters	17:3-9
The Place of Slaughter	17:3-4
The Reason Place Matters	17:5-7
Gentiles	17:8-9
Prohibition of Consuming Blood	17:10-14
The Blood of Slaughtered Animals	17:10-12
The Blood of Game Animals	17:13-14
Eating Carrion	17:15-16

Outline of Leviticus

PART 3 LIVING IN LIGHT OF GOD'S PRESENCE	**18:1–27:34**
3A Holy Living	**18:1–22:33**
Forbidden Sexual Practices	18:1-30
Introductory Exhortation	18:1-5
Forbidden Sexual Practices	18:6-25
Final Warning	18:26-30
Holiness in Daily Life	19:1-37
Introduction	19:1-2a
Heading: The Call to Holiness	19:2b
Holy Actions	19:3-36a
The Ten Commandments	19:3-4
A Digression: The Peace Offering	19:5-8
The Imperative of Generosity	19:9-10
Social Morality	19:11-18
Issues of Sex and Fertility	19:19-25
Manipulating God	19:26-28
Miscellaneous Commands	19:29-32
Treatment of the Resident Foreigner	19:33-36a
The Final Exhortation	19:36b-37
Holiness as Obedience	20:1-27
Introduction	20:1-2a
The Defilement of the Sanctuary	20:2b-8
Worship of Molek	20:2b-5
Consulting Diviners	20:6
Exhortation to Become Holy	20:7-8
Forbidden Sexual Relations	20:9-21
Exhortation for Obedience	20:22-26
Addendum: No Wizards	20:27
Holiness for Priests	21:1–22:33
Restrictions concerning Death	21:1-9
Restrictions for the High Priest	21:10-15
Restrictions on Offering Sacrifices	21:16-23
Everybody Heard	21:24
Disqualified Priests	22:1-9
Disqualified Laypeople	22:10-16
Disqualified Animals	22:17-30
Exhortation to Holiness	22:31-33
3B Holy Time	**23:1–25:55**
Celebrating Religious Festivals	23:1-44
Introduction	23:1-4

The Spring Festivals	23:5-22
Passover	23:5
Unleavened Bread	23:6-8
First Sheaf	23:9-14
Weeks (Pentecost)	23:15-22
The Fall Festivals	23:23-36
The New Year's Festival (Rosh Hashanah)	23:23-25
Day of Cleansing (Yom Kippur)	23:26-32
Booths (Sukkoth)	23:33-36
Concluding Remarks	23:37-44
Summary	23:37-38
Additional Remarks concerning Booths (Sukkoth)	23:39-43
Performance Statement	23:44
Duties and a Case of Blasphemy	24:1-23
Additional Priestly Duties	24:1-9
The Light	24:1-4
The Bread and Table	24:5-9
The Case of the Blasphemer	24:10-23
The Incident	24:10-12
The Decision	24:13-16
Supplemental Laws	24:17-22
Execution of the Offender	24:23
The Sabbatical and Jubilee Years	25:1-55
The Sabbatical Year	25:1-7
Introduction	25:1-2a
The Earth's Sabbath	25:2b-7
The Jubilee Year	25:8-13
When Was the Jubilee Year?	25:8-9
What Happens in the Jubilee Year?	25:10-13
Regulations	25:14-22
Crops Are Sold, Not Land	25:14-19
Food for a Jubilee Year	25:20-22
The Jubilee in Practice	25:23-28
The Principle	25:23-24
Normal Practice	25:25-28
Two Exceptions	25:29-34
Town Houses	25:29-31
Levite Property	25:32-34
The Sale of People	25:35-55
Loans to Impoverished Israelites	25:35-38
Indentured Servitude	25:39-43
Gentiles Bought by Israelites	25:44-46

Israelites Bought by Gentiles	25:47-54
The Rationale for the Year	25:55

3C The Promise and Danger of Covenant — **26:1-46**

God Is Sovereign Alone	26:1-2
The Blessings	26:3-13
The Curses	26:14-33
Conditions Presented	26:14-15
The Beginning	26:16-17
Dull Students	26:18-20
Living in Hostility toward God	26:21-33
Compensation for Unkept Sabbatical Years	26:34-35
Israel's Plight in Captivity	26:36-39
Israel's Confession and Amends	26:40-41
God Remembers the Covenant	26:42-45
Conclusion to the Book	26:46

3D Addendum: Vows, Dedications, and Tithes — **27:1-34**

Introduction	27:1-2a
Pledges	27:2b-13
Pledges of Persons	27:2b-8
Pledges of Animals	27:9-13
Dedication of Land	27:14-25
People and Things That Cannot Be Dedicated	27:26-29
The Firstborn	27:26-27
Banned Objects	27:28-29
Tithes	27:30-33
Ending	27:34

Essays

AARON Along with his brother Moses, Aaron belonged to the tribe of Levi. Aaron became the high priest, and one of his sons would become high priest after his death. Aaron's other sons would become priests and officiate at the altar. The other descendants of Levi who were not sons of Aaron were designated simply as Levites and play no role in Leviticus. They are, however, mentioned in one text, at Leviticus 25:32-34, in connection with Levitical cities and land. In Numbers they become porters for the tabernacle and its guardians (Num 1:47-54). Deuteronomy erases this distinction, referring to Levitical priests in such instructions as "Go to the Levitical priests and to the judge who is in office at that time" (Deut 17:9) *[Leadership, p. 306; The Tabernacle, p. 317]*.

ANOINTING The oil of anointing is found in Leviticus 8, where it is used to consecrate the tabernacle, its objects, and the priests who will serve there. After Aaron has put on his priestly clothes and accessories, Moses takes the anointing oil and smears it on the tabernacle and everything in it. This makes these objects holy (v. 10). He then sprinkles it on the objects outside the tabernacle, such as the altar (v. 11). Finally, he pours anointing oil on Aaron, making him holy (v. 12).

As part of the installation service of Aaron and his sons to the priesthood, Moses takes the anointing oil and mixes it with blood from the installation sacrifice. He then sprinkles it on Aaron and his sons and on their clothes (v. 30). This makes Aaron, his sons, and their clothes holy. The purpose of these anointing rituals is to *induct them into a new state of being* for specialized service.

Later, other persons have oil poured out upon their heads, but the oil is not called "anointing oil" as in Leviticus. In these anointing rituals the person is *anointed for a position*, as is the case when Saul is anointed king (1 Sam 10:1). David also is anointed to be king: by Samuel (1 Sam 16:13), by the people of Judah (2 Sam 2:4), and by the elders of Israel (2 Sam 5:3). For

David, anointing was part of his public elevation to kingship, as it was for his son Solomon (1 Kings 1:34, 39). Elijah the prophet was commanded by God to anoint three people: (1) Hazael to be king over Syria, (2) Jehu to be king over Israel (the northern kingdom), and (3) Elisha to be a prophet in place of Elijah (1 Kings 19:15-16).

These are secular uses of an anointing ritual. In none of these cases does the person become holy as is the case in Leviticus. The person who anoints another could be a priest, a prophet, or anonymous.

APODICTIC LAW *See* **LAW**

ATONEMENT (*kipper*) The word "atone" in Hebrew is a verb referring to a *process* or an *action*. To atone for a wrong is to do something about it—to "make atonement." In a sense, "atone" as a verb is an empty word: it simply tells us that the necessary action was taken to bring about atonement.

Atonement is done for a reason, to atone for something. When someone says, "I atoned for my mistake," we might ask, "What did you do to make atonement?" In current English, to atone for something is "to make amends" for it (*Webster's*), that is, to set something right that was wrong. *How* we make amends is determined by what we did. The noun *atonement* indicates the *result* of a process, *not the process itself*. The result of making amends is that an earlier state has, in some way, been restored. As we shall see below, in Leviticus it means that the results of sin have been cleaned away.

The verb *kipper* is usually translated into English as *to make atonement* (see NIV, NET, NRSV, etc.) or simply *atone*. But the word *kipper* actually refers to *the process* whereby a person makes amends. To translate *kipper* as *atonement* hides what *kipper* does. The following translation note (at Lev 1:4 NET) is instructive:

> The *primary meaning of the Hebrew verb*, however, is "to wipe [something off (or on)]" (see esp. the goal of the sin offering, Lev 4, "*to purge* the tabernacle from impurities"). . . . The translation "make atonement" has been retained here because, ultimately, *the goal of either purging or appeasing* was to maintain a proper relationship between the LORD (who dwelt in the tabernacle) and Israelites. (emph. added)

The NET has substituted *make atonement* for the actual meaning of *kipper* because the translators are concerned with the *goal* of *kipper* rather than its *meaning*. This has been the practice of translations generally, unless forced by grammar or context to translate it otherwise. Translating *kipper* as *making atonement* has given readers of Leviticus a blank check to read into the text their own notion of *what is happening* and the *process used* to make atonement.

The conclusion of the NET that *kipper* means "to wipe off/purge" is based on its Akkadian cognate, *kapāru*, which is found in Mesopotamian purification rituals meaning "to wipe" or "to clean" (*CAD*), as well as from its usage in Leviticus. In the commentary, we have translated *kipper* according to its meaning: "to cleanse" or "to purify." (In Leviticus, *kipper* does not occur in its meaning to "appease," as it does in Gen 32:20 [21] NRSV, or "pacify," NIV).

The understanding of *kipper* as a cleansing or purging rests largely on the work of Jacob Milgrom, whose arguments that *kipper* means "purification" or "cleansing" have gained wide acceptance (1976; 1991: 1079–84). Consequently, in more recent English Bible versions, *kipper* is translated *to purify* (NET, REB, NLT, CEV), *make expiation* (NJPS, NEB, REB, NJB)—which means "wiping away" or "purifying"—and *to purge* (NJPS, REB). The NET translates it thus, for example, at Leviticus 16:20, *When he has finished <u>purifying</u> the holy place, the Meeting Tent, and the altar, he is to present the live goat* (emph. added; see the note in NET for this verse).

The verse just cited, 16:20, illustrates why *kipper* is best translated by *purify, cleanse*. In this verse *kipper* has a direct object, which makes the translation *atonement* awkward. Because of this construction, the NIV must translate *When Aaron has finished <u>making atonement for</u> the Most Holy Place, the tent of meeting and the altar* . . . (emph. added). First, the word *for* does not occur in this text. But even so, this translation does not make sense. In what way and for what reason must these holy objects "make amends"? What sins have they committed?

Normally, *kipper* is done *on behalf of* or *for the sake of* people. Moses commands Aaron to *make atonement [cleanse] on behalf of yourself and on behalf of the people* (Lev 9:7 NET). Aaron cleanses the altar for the people as a prelude to using the altar in the coming rituals.

Kipper is also used in rituals for restoring ritual purity (chs. 12–15). These impurities were not caused by sin but rather resulted from normal and proper actions. The result of *kipper* is that the person becomes clean, not forgiven, as in the case of sin. The ritual for a woman who gives birth illustrates this (Lev 12). At the end of her "quarantine" period, the new mother brings an offering to the priest. The priest then applies blood to the altar and offers up a sacrifice *making a cleansing [kipper] on her behalf* (v. 7 AT). Although not a sin, impurity also affects the tabernacle (15:31). The priest applies the blood to the altar, not to the person, cleansing the altar; as a result, the person becomes clean (*ṭaher*; 12:7, 8; see Lev 14:18; 9, 31, 53; 15:15, 30).

Likewise, in the moral sphere, the sanctuary was purged (*kipper*) *to cleanse [ṭaher] you* (16:30). The *objects* to which the blood is applied are purified, and the *people* thereby become *clean* (*ṭaher*). As in the cases of ritual impurity, the purpose of *kipper*—cleansing the altar—is to make the entire people clean (*ṭaher*).

But why does the altar have the cleansing blood applied to it, rather than the person who needs forgiveness or cleanness? The text does not specify what is cleaned or removed from the altar. Sin or impurity affects the altar in some way so that something needs to be fixed or removed. The text does not say what impediment the sin or uncleanness causes to the altar. But whatever it is, it must be removed before forgiveness or purity is granted.

A major difficulty with Milgrom's thesis is the question of how the holy things become contaminated in the first place. Only holy people come in contact with holy things. The high priest is the only person who enters the tabernacle, and only priests offer sacrifices on the courtyard altar. Milgrom's answer is that sin and impurity affect the holy from a distance (Milgrom 1976). Evidence for his thesis is found in a text concerning idolatry: *for by sacrificing his children to Molek, he has defiled my sanctuary and profaned my holy name* (Lev 20:3; NRSV, *Molech*). A similar statement occurs in Leviticus 15:31: *You must keep the Israelites separate from things that make them unclean, so they will not die in their uncleanness for defiling my dwelling place [tabernacle], which is among them.* Sin and ritual impurity committed outside the sanctuary can contaminate the sanctuary and its altars. (For a succinct statement of Milgrom's position and a modification of it, see Schwartz 1995; Gilders 2004; a different meaning for *kipper* is proposed by Kiuchi.)

Jay Sklar, while accepting Milgrom's basic theses, argues that the offering does more than cleanse the altar. The action of *kipper* must in some way do something to the person. He argues that *kipper* is actually derived from the Hebrew word *koper*, which can mean a "ransom payment." Hence, the meaning of the verb *kipper* is "to provide a ransom." The death of the animal not only purifies the altar but also represents a ransom payment to save the life of the sinner (Sklar 2005; 2008). However, Leviticus gives us no evidence that the "sinner" is in bondage or indebted to anyone or anything. There is no evidence in Leviticus that the sinner must be freed from some power. It is not the death of an animal that purifies the altar but its blood applied to the altar. Above, in Leviticus 16, we have seen how the blood alone effects purification and the removal of sin. The actual deposition of the animal comes later in the ceremony, after the removal of all sin and impurity by a goat sent into the desert (see Gruenwald: 180–230; Gilders 2008). Apart from the lack of evidence for this position, the extension of the meaning of *kipper* in Leviticus to mean "pay a ransom" is not likely:

1. The noun "ransom" (*koper*) never occurs in Leviticus (see comments on 17:11) and only occurs three times in Exodus through Numbers. Numbers 35:31 prohibits a *koper* (ransom) for a deliberate murderer. Exodus 21:28-32 allows a payment (*koper*) by the owner of an ox that gored another, instead of requiring the owner to forfeit their life. Exodus 30:11-16 demands a *koper* payment when a census is taken, which seems more like a poll tax than a ransom. The first two texts are legal texts, and in both cases it is obvious that the person needs to be ransomed—from capital punishment in both cases. (In any case, Sklar himself recognizes that it is improper to argue from the derivation of a word to its meaning in usage [2005: 44–45n2].)

2. Sklar's theory would mean that an inadvertent trespass (Lev 4) or becoming unclean by childbirth (ch. 12) carries with it the death penalty, from which a person needs to be ransomed. But neither inadvertent sin nor childbirth carries a death penalty. If this were the case, because of unknown inadvertent sin, no Israelites would be left in the camp.

3. This thesis does not work when the direct object of *kipper* is the sanctuary and the altar, which need no ransom and to which death cannot

apply [*Atonement as Transfer*, p. 291; *Atonement in Christian Thinking and Leviticus*, p. 292].

ATONEMENT AS TRANSFER Two traditional *Christian* views of the atonement have been supported by way of Leviticus. In the first view, substitution, the sacrifice plays the part of a substitute for the person offering the sacrifice. This assumes that a sinner deserves to die at the hands of God. It is assumed that the placing of the hand on the head of an animal indicates that the identity of the person is transferred to the animal so that when the animal dies, the guilty person "dies" and no longer stands under God's judgment. This idea finds no support in Leviticus (see below).

The second view is that the animal represents a payment on the part of the sinner. In this view, the sinner deserves to die, but by placing a hand on an animal, the sinner indicates that the death of the animal represents a payment made to God to buy their life back from God's judgment. The death of the animal removes the penalty for the sin committed by the sinner. Wenham applies this interpretation to the whole burnt offering in Leviticus 1 (Wenham: 59–62; in other places, e.g., Lev 4:25, Wenham agrees that the blood of the animal is cleansing).

The flaw with these views is that they seem to rest on theological presumptions that are not present in Leviticus. From Leviticus itself, we find that (1) many sacrifices are brought for reasons other than sin, (2) almost no sins are capital crimes and do not deserve death, and (3) blood does not always need to be shed nor does a life need to be given to obtain forgiveness—a grain offering may suffice (Lev 5:11-15).

First, the burnt offering in Leviticus 1 is not brought because of sin; rather, it is a freewill offering. All offerings for sin are compulsory, as shown by chapters 4 and 5. Furthermore, the whole burnt offering is offered after the so-called sin offering, which cleanses the altar from sin. Notice the practice described in Leviticus 8:14-17. First comes the cleansing sacrifice (sin offering), and only then are the whole burnt offerings described in chapter 1 and the peace offerings described in chapter 3. The reason for this sequence seems to be the need to "sterilize" the altar in order that it may be used in the forgiveness ritual and for other sacrifices. Note: Although Aaron and his sons place their hands on the bull to be offered, no forgiveness of sin is mentioned. Likewise, on the Day of Cleansing, hands are placed on the animal offered as a cleansing sacrifice (sin offering), but forgiveness is never mentioned in chapter 16. Indeed, sin is gotten rid of by means of an elimination ritual, not by forgiveness. (See the arguments presented in comments on Lev 1 that whole freewill offerings are brought to honor and please God.)

Second, not all sins are capital crimes and punishable by death. *God did not hold people accountable for their unknown sins*. Chapter 4 makes it clear that only when people or persons *become aware* that they have transgressed do they need to bring a sacrifice. As long as they are not aware of their sin, they cannot offer a sacrifice for it. Unless this is so, everybody would be dead.

The placing of a hand on the head of an animal to be sacrificed does not transfer guilt or the identity of a person to an animal. We find cases of transfer in Leviticus, but these occur in elimination rituals, and the animals are not sacrifices. We find an elimination ritual in Leviticus 14:48-53 for a defiled house. As part of this ritual, one bird is butchered over a pot containing water, the blood draining into the water. This mixture is sprinkled toward the house seven times. After the house is cleansed, the live bird that was previously dipped in the blood and water mixture is sent out of the camp into the countryside. *Thus he shall make expiation [cleansing] for the house, and it shall be clean* (Lev 14:53 NJPS). The inference is that the live bird has carried the impurity out of the camp. The same pattern is found in chapter 16 with the elimination of sins from the sanctuary. One goat is sacrificed and its blood is applied to the tabernacle and its sacred objects. Another goat bears the sins of the people outside the city and is set free in a wilderness place. In neither case of transfer is the animal a sacrifice *[Scapegoat, p. 316]*.

Finally, blood does not always need to be shed, but when it does, it is the blood of the animal that is effective in removing the effects or consequences of sin, not the death of an animal per se. As Leviticus 17:11 makes clear, it is the blood that is the effective agent in a sacrifice, not the sacrifice of the animal on the altar. In the cleansing offering for the inadvertent sin of the high priest or of the whole people, the blood alone is applied to the altar, and the fatty parts belonging to God are burned on it. The meat, hide, viscera, and its dung are burned outside the camp. The animal is *not* burned upon the altar (4:12, 21). This is disposal ritual, not a sacrificial one. The same is illustrated in Leviticus 16:27: *The bull and the goat for the sin offerings, whose blood was brought into the Most Holy Place to make atonement, must be taken outside the camp; their hides, flesh and intestines are to be burned up.* The blood from these animals has been used for cleansing. The animals themselves, apart from their fat, which belongs to God, are taken outside the camp and burned there. Their being burned outside the camp is extraneous to forgiveness and removal of sin.

ATONEMENT IN CHRISTIAN THINKING AND LEVITICUS Several general points for perspective need to be mentioned before entering this discussion. First, Christian theories about the atonement came relatively late in Christian thought. The early and most famous work on the atonement was Anselm's *Cur Deus Homo* (Why God Was a Man), which was written in 1098, a thousand years after the New Testament (*DCC* 73–74). From the title of this work we see that it is a response to questions about the incarnation, not the death of Jesus. How did a work on the incarnation set the agenda for later works on atonement? Anselm's short answer is that Jesus was born so he could die. God needed a perfect person's death in order to have an innocent victim die so that atonement could be made for the sins of humanity. This answer assumes that (1) all humans are sinful because of their sinful human nature, and (2) God is unable to forgive them. One might instead begin from the assumption that Jesus was born to live.

It is clear that Leviticus shares neither of these presuppositions. First, in Leviticus, sin is a deed, and a person undertakes a ritual of forgiveness to receive forgiveness for a specific deed. The individual does not need to atone for being human. Three basic facts about this ritual are significant: (1) the individual makes atonement for their own sin; (2) the blood of the sacrifice offered in this ritual cleanses the altar, not the individual; (3) the result is the forgiveness of a specific sin.

Second, in the ceremony in chapter 16 (the Day of Cleansing), *all sins and their effect on the sanctuary are purged from the sanctuary and removed from the camp*. This ceremony consists of both cleansing rituals and an elimination ritual that removes all transgression and impurities from the camp. *No forgiveness takes place on this day.* God, acting alone, is able to wipe the slate clean.

The conceptual world of the New Testament is quite different, in part because the New Testament has been influenced by apocalyptic thought (see *NIDB*, s.v. "Apocalypticism"). A few points of difference are as follows:

1. There was a cosmic realm inhabited by other forces than God. Paul speaks of being "enslaved under the basic forces of the world" (Gal 4:3 NET). The Galatians "were enslaved to beings that by nature are not gods at all" (4:8 NET). We find mention of a place "where Satan's throne is" (Rev 2:13 NET). Here evil cosmic power is given a name: Jesus speaks of Satan's "kingdom" (Matt 12:26). Satan is counted as a power that can control human beings: "after Judas took the piece of bread, Satan entered into him" (John 13:27 NET; also Acts 5:3).

Jesus came "to open their eyes so that they turn from darkness to light and from the power of Satan to God, so that they may receive forgiveness of sins and a share among those who are sanctified by faith in me" (Acts 26:18 NET). People are naturally in bondage to Satan. Forgiveness includes the sins of the past and a transfer out of Satan's domain into a new realm.

2. In this schema, original sin and the natural state of people as sinners becomes a fundamental fact. Paul writes, "Sin entered the world through one man and death through sin, and so death spread to all people because all sinned" (Rom 5:12 NET). This is the reason for Jesus: "For if, by the transgression of the one man, death reigned through the one, how much more will those who receive the abundance of grace and of the gift of righteousness reign in life through the one, Jesus Christ!" (Rom 5:17 NET). Everybody begins by being under God's judgment. Atonement is the mechanism for escaping God's judgment. (On different understandings of the atonement in the New Testament, see Driver; on the atonement, see Marshall.)

Obviously, Leviticus represents a quite different view of God. *God is God alone and unconstrained by any outside forces or factors* such as Sin or Satan. God's will is ultimate (Kaufmann; see Levenson for a critique of Kaufmann's view). This is presented as the fundamental tenet of God's own theology. God says, "Yahweh is Yahweh, a compassionate and merciful God, slow to anger and having great kindness and faithfulness, maintaining kindness for a thousand generations, forgiving iniquity, transgression, and sin, yet does not make the guilty innocent, visiting the iniquity of the fathers on children and grandchildren, upon the third and fourth generation" (Exod 34:6-7 AT). God is free both to forgive and to punish. Sin can be forgiven through prayer or through the grain offering (Lev 5:11-13).

God was known as a God of grace and mercy rather than as a God chiefly of judgment who was to be feared. The story of Jonah is a case in point. Because God is a gracious and forgiving God, Jonah does not want to go to Nineveh. He wants God to punish the people of Nineveh. But unwillingly he does go, and his worst fears are realized. The Ninevites (non-Israelites) repent, and Jonah is furious that God forgives them (Jon 4:1-3). Notice that no death is required. The Ninevites repent and change their ways. That is enough for God's forgiveness. God being God, none need die in order for God to be able to forgive the sin of the Ninevites.

Nor do persons begin life with a debt that means judgment unless they act to erase this debt. People are responsible for their own sins. (Sins, however, can have an effect long after the sinner is dead.) Although others may suffer because of a person's sin, there is no "vicarious suffering" in Leviticus—one person suffering for a sin they did not commit so that the perpetrator need not suffer. The latter certainly seems unjust. Instead, everyone needs to individually have their own sins forgiven.

However, later Christian theologians and philosophers sought to find help in Leviticus for their theological thought. So, for example, the idea of a goat carrying away sin became a helpful metaphor to explain why Jesus needed to die (although a new scapegoat was needed each year and did not die because of sin). Likewise, Christian thinking about atonement and sin led to new interpretations of Leviticus, which was understood as if Christian theories of atonement were indeed behind the rituals and their gestures. The result was that Leviticus was understood as exemplifying Christian thinking on the atonement.

In summary, although Leviticus, according to its plain sense, is irrelevant to the later Christian theories of atonement, these theories have not been irrelevant for Christians' interpretations of atonement in Leviticus. Where Leviticus has been helpful in understanding atonement is in providing metaphors to express the process of atonement, such as "cleanse from sin" or "wash away sin." In addition, Leviticus offers a process and view that reflects the power and grace of God: atonement is based on the power of God to forgive sin and on the grace of God to be willing to do so. (On the captivity of Leviticus to Christian thought and why a mistaken notion of atonement in Leviticus was necessary for later Christian atonement theory, see Finlan.)

BEARING/REMOVING INIQUITY OR SIN The word translated *iniquity* or *guilt* (*'awon*), when used with the verb *bear* (*naśa'*), is a bit slippery. It is used in two senses. In Leviticus 16:21 it occurs alongside *rebellion* and *sin* and is translated *wickedness*. There it refers to the burden that the goat will bear into the wilderness (v. 22). However, *'awon* can also mean the consequences of a trespass. Elsewhere we find that a person who does not perform a purification ritual for impurity *will be held responsible*. That is, the person bears culpability for the action (Lev 17:16; see also 5:1 and 7:18

for other actions). What happens as a result of "bearing culpability" is not specified.

The first meaning of *bear* is illustrated by the goat bearing sins and iniquity. The priest who conducts the ritual has cleansed the sanctuary and places the result upon a goat, which carries all this away. The goat has no culpability for what the people did to the sanctuary. In the second meaning of *bear*, the offender bears culpability. By the priest performing a forgiveness ritual, the culprit is forgiven and no longer bears culpability. (See Lev 10:17 regarding the failure to carry out the ritual of forgiveness properly.)

It has been argued that "bearing iniquity" is a psychological state— one bears guilt and feels guilty. However, in 5:17 we find that one who is guilty or feels guilt (ʾašam) for an unknown sin *will be held responsible*. Bearing culpability for a misdeed seems to be different from feeling guilty. Awareness leads to culpability, which is not subjective but rather is something that needs action (Schwartz 1995).

BLESSINGS AND CURSES In Leviticus, blessings and curses are based on a covenant between God and Israel. They are found in Leviticus 26 and in Deuteronomy 27–28. The blessings and curses were to stimulate obedience to the covenant by promising positive results for keeping the terms of the covenant and negative results for disobeying them. The blessings and curses in Leviticus 26 indicate that the laws in Leviticus are conceived as covenant law, founded on God's gracious actions toward Israel in the exodus *[Covenant, p. 298]*.

CALENDAR Israel's calendar is lunar, each month having twenty-nine or thirty days. The numbering of months and the counting of years is a hybrid, developed from more than one calendar system. The first month, Aviv (= Nisan), is in the spring, marking the beginning of the agricultural year. This is the month of Passover and the Festival of Unleavened Bread. However, New Year's Day occurs on the first day of the seventh month, a holdover from an earlier calendar. Since the changing of months is fixed by the moon, the first day of the first month slowly falls behind on the solar year, like the month of Ramadan in Islam. To keep Passover in the spring, an extra month must be added from time to time. These "intercalated" months keep the lunar calendar in step with the solar one. In such cases, the calendar year has thirteen months instead of twelve. (See *ABD*, s.v. "Calendars," which describes the ancient Near Eastern, ancient Israelite, and early Jewish calendars.)

The calendar of the Israelite festivals or holy times is given in Leviticus 23, along with instructions for celebrating them. The basic festivals are linked with the agricultural year but can celebrate a historical event. Passover, for example, is on the fourteenth of Aviv and celebrates the exodus from Egypt (Exod 13:4; 23:15).

The Earliest Festival Calendar Exodus 23:14-17 provides the earliest example of a festival calendar and is marked as a clear literary unit by its envelope structure (vv. 14 and 17). The Israelites are commanded to observe three festivals a year. These three celebrations are pilgrimage festivals. All males are to appear before God (see the pilgrimage of Elkanah and his family to Shiloh in 1 Sam 1:1-3). The three pilgrimage festivals in Exodus are these:

1. The *Festival of Unleavened Bread*. During the seven days of this festival, the Israelites are to eat only unleavened bread. The appointed time for this event is the month of Aviv because in this month, Israel left Egypt in haste. No dates are given for its celebration, but Exodus 12:2-3 places the original event at the tenth day of the first month. It is at the beginning of the barley harvest, with barley being the first grain to ripen and its firstfruits offered.
2. The *Harvest Festival*. This festival celebrated the firstfruits of the wheat harvest. No time is specified and no historical event is mentioned.
3. The *Festival of Ingathering*. This fall harvest festival celebrated the gathering in of the fall harvest.

The last two festivals celebrate major events in the life of the farmer. Exodus 34:18-26 repeats this calendar, and the Sabbath is incorporated into it as in Leviticus (Lev 23:3). The work forbidden is agricultural work: plowing or harvesting.

The Calendar in Deuteronomy 16:1-17 Three festivals are also listed in Deuteronomy, but with variation and elaboration:

1. *The first festival is now called the Passover*. Besides Passover proper, the people must eat unleavened bread for seven days. This can be done in their villages. The Festival of Unleavened Bread and Passover now refer to the same festival.
2. *The Festival of Weeks* now joins the festival calendar. It is observed seven weeks after the beginning of the barley harvest and thus came to be called Pentecost. The new harvest is celebrated by giving an offering of firstfruits to God from the harvest.
3. *The Festival of Booths* (Tabernacles, NIV) is the fall harvest festival. It is to be celebrated at the shrine for seven days. No historical event or time is connected to this festival in Deuteronomy.

These three festivals are the major national pilgrimage festivals in Israel.

The Calendar in Leviticus 23 The calendar we find in Leviticus 23 gives the final shape of Israel's festival calendar, adding festivals and providing fixed dates for all the festivals:

1. *Sabbath* is mentioned first, although it is weekly, not annual (23:2-3).

2. *Passover* is dated to the fourteenth day of the first month (23:5).

3. The *Festival of Unleavened Bread* begins on the next day, the fifteenth, and is celebrated for seven days. The first and last day of Unleavened Bread are holy convocations, and work ceases (23:6-8).

4. The *offering of the first sheaf* is celebrated on the day after the Sabbath that follows Unleavened Bread. The people may not eat bread, parched grain, or new grain until the rituals for this day are completed (23:9-14).

5. The *Festival of Weeks* comes seven weeks, or fifty days, after the offering of the first sheaf. Leavened bread is brought as a wave offering to God, celebrating the new crop (23:15-22).

6. A new festival takes place on *New Year's Day*, the first day of the seventh month. It is marked by a trumpet blast and is a day of rest (23:23-25).

7. The *Day of Cleansing* falls on the tenth day of the seventh month (23:26-32). The rituals for this day are given in Leviticus 16.

8. The *Festival of Booths*, beginning on the fifteenth of the seventh month, lasts for eight days. It celebrates the ingathering of the fall harvest and memorializes the people's sojourn in the wilderness. The people live in huts or booths during this festival (23:33-43).

Numbers 28 and 29 provide the most detailed festival calendar in the Bible. It specifies what offerings are to be brought for each observance. Its calendar also lists the morning and evening offerings found in Leviticus 6:8-13. (For an overview of biblical festivals mentioned in the New Testament, as well as some reflection on their use in the church, see TBC and TLC for ch. 23. For a full description of each festival, see the articles in *NIDB*.)

CASUISTIC LAW *See* **LAW**

CLEAN AND UNCLEAN *See* **PURE**

CLEANSING OFFERING Jacob Milgrom's work on Leviticus and the priestly material more generally suggest that atonement results from a process of purification *[Atonement, p. 288]*. Milgrom has also suggested that the sacrifice normally called a sin offering (*ḥaṭṭaʾt*) is better understood as a cleansing offering because this is what it does—cleanses the altar (1991: 253–69, 1079–84). The case rests on the following points:

1. First, the so-called sin sacrifice is offered in rituals where no sin was committed and no forgiveness is sought. The purification rituals in chapters 12–15 illustrate this point. In these chapters, this sacrifice occurs in rituals for cleansing the altar, thereby restoring purity to a person who has become impure.

2. Second, the blood cleanses objects. Moses takes the blood from this sacrifice and places it on the horns of the altar, thereby cleansing or sterilizing the altar to hallow it (8:15; cf. 9:15). Likewise, on the Day of Cleansing, Aaron's application of the blood from a sin offering, a *ḥaṭṭaʾt* sacrifice, is to *cleanse it and to consecrate it from the uncleanness of the Israelites* (Lev 16:19). This cleansing of the altar is an end in itself; no impurity or sin of an individual is mentioned.

3. Third, the noun *ḥaṭṭaʾt* (cleansing [traditionally, "sin"] offering) comes from the *piel* form of the verb *ḥaṭaʾ*, which in that form most often means "to purify, cleanse," as in the references above. The blood of the purification or cleansing sacrifice is applied to the altar to make cleansing of the altar possible (Lev 8:15; *DCH*). Moses *purifies* (*ḥiṭṭeʾ*) the altar by using the blood from a *cleansing* (*ḥaṭṭaʾt*) offering. In this reference, no sin is mentioned nor is forgiveness its aim. It is about cleansing. So also in 9:15.

4. Fourth, the so-called sin sacrifice (*ḥaṭṭaʾt*) almost always occurs in conjunction with the verb *kipper* (to cleanse or purge) in Leviticus 1–16 (see the exceptions in 8:15 and 9:15). Because of this coupling with *kipper*, this sacrifice (*ḥaṭṭaʾt*) provides the necessary blood for cleansing the altar *[Atonement, p. 288]*.

In this commentary, when the *ḥaṭṭaʾt offering* is used either in a ritual of forgiveness, such as in Leviticus 4:1–5:13, or in a ritual for purification, such as in Leviticus 12–15, it is called a *cleansing offering* or *cleansing sacrifice*. For purging rituals, which do not have to do directly with specific human sins or ritual impurities—notably the installation of the priesthood (ch. 8), the dedication of the sanctuary (ch. 9), and the Day of Cleansing (ch. 16)—the term *cleansing ritual* is used.

COVENANT A covenant is a contract between two parties. It may be between two people, as in the case of Abraham and Abimelek (Gen 21:25-32), or between nations, as in the case of Solomon and Hiram (1 Kings 5:12 [26]). Covenant as a contract can also metaphorically represent the theological relationship between God and individuals, nations, or humankind.

The first covenant was with Noah (Gen 6:18). After the flood, God's covenant with Noah was extended to include all humankind as well as all creatures on earth (9:9-17). God also made a covenant with Abram (15:18). These covenants were *promissory contracts* in which God, the stronger party, promised to do something for a weaker party.

Besides promissory covenants there are *obligatory covenants* in which the stronger party contracts what the weaker party will do. God, the stronger party, makes such a covenant with Israel, the weaker party (Exod 24:1-8). God first gives the stipulations of this contract to Moses, who then relays them to the people: "Moses . . . told the people all the LORD's words and laws" (Exod 24:3a). The people agree to these stipulations: "All the people answered with one voice, and said, 'All the words that the LORD has spoken we will do'" (Exod 24:3b NRSV). The terms of their contract with God have been accepted, and obedience to them has been accepted.

After the people's agreement to this covenant, Moses writes down the *stipulations* and prepares for the ratification of this covenant by the people; he builds an altar for sacrifice and sets up stone pillars that will *witness* the ceremony. Moses commissions young men to offer peace offerings. He then reads the words of the covenant to the people, and again they wholeheartedly agree to accept the terms of the contract. Then Moses seals the covenant by dashing the blood of the covenant on the people.

Frequently in ancient Near Eastern treaties, the stronger party will list *what has been done for the weaker*. This list of good deeds apparently provides a rationale for the stipulations that the stronger party has placed on the weaker and validates the justice of the treaty to the gods. However, even without the agreement of the lesser party, the stronger party can impose codes of behavior on the weaker (Altman: 19–42).

In Israelite covenants with God, we find mention of what gives God the right to demand obedience. The Ten Commandments, for example, are prefaced by "I am the LORD your God, who brought you out of Egypt, out of the land of slavery" (Exod 20:2; Deut 5:6). In Leviticus we find similar expressions in 26:45-46, which grounds God's covenant and its stipulations on God's deliverance of Israel from slavery and thus God's right to stipulate the regulations for their relationship.

Covenants in the ancient Near East contained *blessings and curses*. We find them in the covenants appearing in Leviticus 26 and in Deuteronomy 27–28. The blessings and curses are to stimulate obedience to the covenant by promising positive results for keeping the terms of the covenant and negative results for disobeying them. The blessings and curses in Leviticus 26 indicate that the laws in Leviticus were conceived as covenant law founded on God's gracious actions toward Israel in the exodus.

Seen as covenant law, the instructions in Leviticus are a response to God's grace, not a means of earning it. As argued in this commentary, the sacrificial rituals in Leviticus 1–16 are given to maintain a positive relationship with God rather than to earn one. Likewise, in Leviticus 19–25, holy living is to strengthen the relationship between God and the people: a holy God relates to a holy people.

CUT OFF A punishment mentioned in Leviticus and elsewhere. Usually the verb is passive, as in Leviticus 7:20, *That person shall be cut off from his kin* (7:20 NJPS). An agent is not mentioned with the passive verb, but usually, as here, the person is cut off from their people (see 7:21, 25, 27; 17:4). It is assumed that God is the agent because when the verb is active, God is the subject: *[the one] who eats blood, . . . I will cut them off from the people* (17:10; cf. 17:4). However, in one case, Leviticus 26:22, wild animals who will *cut off your cattle* (AT) are the subject and indicate the destruction of the Israelite flocks and herds (NIV, *destroy your cattle*). Here, applied to cattle, it clearly refers to their death.

In Leviticus 20:1-3, it appears that God's declaration, *I myself will set my face against him and will cut him off from his people*, is in addition to the execution of the person. In this reference the subject of "cut off" is God, but in verse 3 the people put the person to death. It may be argued that these are two different punishments.

Milgrom suggests a harmonization between the acts of being cut off and being stoned to death (Lev 20:1-3). The expression of having a name *cut off from the people* means "his name will ... disappear [be cut off] from among his family or from his hometown" (Ruth 4:10). Boaz marries Ruth so that a son will be born to carry on the lineage of Ruth's first husband. Consequently, the punishment of being "cut off" might mean the end of the person's lineage in future generations (although "name" is not used in Leviticus). In which case, the culprit himself would remain available for execution, as in Leviticus 20:1-3. It is his lineage that will disappear.

However, from Ezekiel's use of this expression in 14:8, "I will cut him off from the midst of My people" (NJPS), it seems Ezekiel used the expression meaning "to terminate," since this person will now become a symbol "and a byword" after their death. Despite Leviticus 20:1-3, the expression "cut off" refers to cutting off the life of the culprit.

FORGIVENESS In Leviticus, forgiveness can be likened to a triangle. One point of the triangle is the one who has sinned, is aware of it, and decides to do something about it. Another point of the triangle is what the sin does. It seems to defile the altar, like making a streak on a window. The third point is the purification of the altar, removing the effects of sin on it. Once this is completed, the transgressions are forgiven (see Lev 4).

Sinners must begin the process of forgiveness by bringing their sacrifice to the priests. Since chapter 4 concerns an individual's sin, it is the responsibility of the individual to seek forgiveness. In many cases, presumably, no one else would know of the person's transgression. It is the sinner who comes to realize that they have sinned *when they realize their guilt* (4:22, 27). In other cases their transgression is made known to them (4:23, 28 NJPS; see EN there).

In some cases of deliberate trespass on a third party, the sinner must first make restitution for damages done and pay a fine as a prerequisite to undertaking a forgiveness ritual (see 5:15-6:7).

HEBREWS AND LEVITICUS The book of Hebrews presents a revisualization of the tabernacle and priestly duties as found in Leviticus (see Heb 9:1-10 for their formulation in Hebrews). The earthly tabernacle and priesthood, which centered on sacrificing and cleansing the sacred, was an earthly realization of a pattern whose blueprint remained in heaven (8:5-6). In this heavenly tabernacle Jesus is both a cleansing sacrifice and the high priest. The contrast between the earthly tabernacle and the heavenly one changes the nature of sacrifice and the function of the high priest. The cleansing sacrifice of Jesus need only be done once, and Jesus, as high priest, is not involved in the earthly rituals portrayed in Leviticus (9:18-28). Rather, the role of the high priest is now one of intercession (7:25). The role of sacrifice for believers is now reconfigured as prayer (13:15).

What triggered this shift from an earthly tabernacle to a heavenly one? From a high priest who annually performs rituals to cleanse the tabernacle to a heavenly high priest whose role is intercession? Scholarly opinion is fragmented, but usually a reason for the writing of Hebrews is found in its audience and the problems encountered in the early Christian community. (For a review of scholarship, see Koester: 41-79.) However, there is no consensus on either the makeup of the audience, the problems facing the community, or the identity of the author and the stream of early Christianity reflected in Hebrews (Philip: 61).

The destruction of the temple in 70 CE was the most significant event for the Jewish community in the first century. Many Jews were slaughtered or enslaved, and the temple was razed. This disaster affected Jews not only in Judea but also in the Diaspora. No more pilgrimage festivals to Jerusalem and sacrifices, no more daily offerings in the temple, no more sacrifices for vows. With the destruction of the temple, the community was faced with questions of identity. If the temple is not restored or at least the Levitical practices renewed, what will become of us? What will replace Leviticus? For what became the normative stream of Judaism, post-temple Jewish life and practice was founded on the teachings of the great rabbis as found in the Mishnah (ca. 135-170 CE) and as discussed in the Talmud (ca. 500 CE).

The early Christian community in Jerusalem was dominated by Jews and continued Jewish practices. Many Christians were priests: "a large number of priests became obedient to the faith" (Acts 6:7). Paul himself offered sacrifices in the temple: "Now after some years I came to bring alms to my nation and to offer sacrifices" (Acts 24:17 NRSV). Earlier, Acts says that "Paul took the men, and the next day, having purified himself, he entered the temple with them, making public the completion of the days of purification when the sacrifice would be made for each of them" (21:26 NRSV). Paul did this to show something to the Jerusalem Christian community: although he was teaching that circumcision was unnecessary for Gentiles, he as a Jew maintained Jewish religious practices. Notice that in Galatians 2:3, Titus, a Gentile, was accepted at Jerusalem without circumcision. However, Paul recruited Timothy to assist him and circumcised him since he had a Jewish mother (Acts 16:3).

The Christians, then, would also have been affected by the destruction of the temple in 70 CE. What does the loss of temple mean for God's plan as set out in God's covenant with Moses and Israel and for the practices God mandated in Leviticus as part of this covenant?

The answer Hebrews gives is that earthly temple practices no longer matter, because the earthly temple system has been succeeded by a heavenly temple. The efficacy of the earthly temple is now, after 70 CE, replaced by the efficacy of the heavenly temple. The relationship between the tabernacle and ritual system in Leviticus and Hebrews is diachronic, not synchronic. The earlier sacrificial practices were necessary and effective, but being earthly, they needed to be repeated continually. In the heavenly temple, sacrifices are no longer necessary, because only one sacrifice and one high priest are needed. One did not replace the other, but followed it.

Thus, in Hebrews, the Levitical material gets a sympathetic reading. As Mayjee Philip writes, "The sacrificial system in Hebrews, based entirely on the Levitical system, is transformed into one that is required, but completed once and for all, both for the present and the future. The author's ingenuity in reinterpreting the Levitical sacrificial system without discounting it in disparaging terms is the hallmark of his hermeneutical and exegetical expertise" (Philip: 58). (See *The Tabernacle*, p. 317; on the messianic priest tradition, see Mason; *NIDB*, s.v. "Hebrews.")

HOLY AND HOLINESS Leviticus sets forth two aspects of "holy." In the first section of the book, chapters 1–16, *holiness is a quality or state achieved through ritual*. The altar, for example, is made holy (8:15) through a sterilizing ritual (*ḥiṭṭeʾ*, "to purify"). We find the priests and high priest made holy through ritual. They do not become holy by touching holy people or holy objects. The same is true of purity. Purity is not contagious, caught by touch, but comes as the result of a purification ritual. Some impurities, however, are catching and cause the pure to become impure.

We do find several cases of the transmission of holiness. In 6:18, 27 (11, 20) we find that a person or thing touching the flesh of a sacrifice or being spritzed by its blood becomes holy. Holiness could also be defiled. In 20:3, a person who gives one of their children to Molek *has defiled my sanctuary and profaned my holy name*. Or the people in general could do so by defiling God's sanctuary through their uncleanness (15:31).

In the second section of Leviticus we find acquired holiness. The Israelites have been set apart to be holy: *You are to be holy to me because I, the LORD, am holy, and I have set you apart from the nations to be my own* (20:26). Through obedience, Israel becomes holy (20:7-8; 22:9).

The relationship of holiness and purity as a quality is straightforward, although they belong to different categories: being pure and being holy are not the same thing. However, they are related: only the pure may come in contact with something holy. For example, only the pure person may eat of food from an offering placed on the altar (7:20-21). In the case of the peace offering (ch. 3), those eating the meat are not holy, nor do they become holy by consuming meat from the offering. But they must be pure to eat holy meat.

Likewise, the rituals for purity in chapters 11–15 restore the quality of purity to a person but do not make them holy. The rituals only give them a "ticket" to enter the holy tabernacle precinct and eat what is holy.

Where holiness is acquired, as in the second part of Leviticus, the holy obviously are those who are obedient, and they rub shoulders in the camp with those who are disobedient. But contacting nonholy people does not affect one's holiness. Consequently, those who have sinned are not impure and may enter the sanctuary, as sinners, to receive forgiveness. Their sin has not forfeited their purity. A "pure" sinner may enter the holy area by choice.

Thus we have three independent systems of classification. The following chart indicates by a broken line where persons in given moral and ritual states have or do not have access to the holy realm. The moral state does not affect a person's access to the holy. If a person is ritually pure, that person may enter the holy realm.

Moral State	Sinner	
Realms	Holy (tabernacle)	Common (the camp)
Ritual States	Pure	Impure

Only impurity can affect the state of another by making that person impure. Holy people, such as priests, can become impure as they live in the camp, but they remain holy. Thus a holy priest may be pure or impure; he may be a sinner or be forgiven. What must not happen is for an *impure person*, priest or layperson, to enter the holy realm of the tabernacle and its surrounding area. Thus we have restraints on priests to keep them from becoming impure (ch. 21).

There are some trespasses for which there is no forgiveness ritual. These transgressions result in *moral impurity*. Moral impurities have no purification ritual that can restore a person to moral purity. We find this type of transgression in chapters 18 and 20. These sins may be punished immediately or after delay, or punishment may be extended over a lifetime. In some cases, moral impurity never affects the individual, although the nation as a whole suffers (ch. 18). *Although not forgivable, these acts do not make a person ritually impure. They may continue to come to the tabernacle courtyard and receive forgiveness and cleansing for their offenses and defilements.* As in the chart below, all who commit moral violations may enter the sanctuary if they are ritually pure. Moral violations do not remove the person from the territory of the community or its worship. The following chart illustrates the distinction between two types of moral violation and ritual violations.

Type	Source	Effect	Resolution
Moral Violations	**Sin**, e.g., inadvertent, negligence, fraud (Lev 4:1–6:7)	*Defilement* of the altars and tabernacle *Not contagious* Terms: *sin* (ḥaṭṭaʾt), *culpable* (ʾašam), *trespass* (maʿal)	Forgiveness rituals (ḥaṭṭaʾt, cleansing offering)
	Impurity, e.g., idolatry, sexual transgressions, spiritism (chs. 18, 20)	*Defilement* of the culprit, land, and sanctuary *Not contagious* to people *Contagious* to the land Terms: *impure* (ṭameʾ), *abomination* (toʿebah), *pollute* (ḥanap)	No resolution No forgiveness rituals No purification rituals for moral impurity
Ritual Violations	**Impurity**, e.g., bodily flows, contact with corpse (chs. 11–15)	*Defilement* of persons, altars, tabernacle *Some contagious* Term: *impure* (ṭameʾ)	Purification rituals (ḥaṭṭaʾt, cleansing offering)

Being holy is being different, but being different for a purpose. In the case of the altar, it is made holy so it can function as an instrument of purification and forgiveness (8:11). For Israel, it means being God's people. Holiness is not an end in itself. *Sanctify* and *sanctification* have been used in the past for "be or becoming holy" and "holy." Thus, Daniel Kauffman heads his discussion of holiness with the title "Sanctification," which he defines thus: "The primary use of the word sanctification is that of a setting apart or consecration to some special work, cause, or purpose" (Kauffman: 303). He further comments: "In no case would the meaning of the sentence be changed very materially if the word 'separate' or 'set apart to' were substituted for the word 'sanctify.'" Being different is not an end in itself. What counts is dedication to "some special work, cause, or purpose" (ibid.).

JUBILEE YEAR In Leviticus 25 we find a release year called the Jubilee Year. This year occurs once every fifty years (see comments on 25:10-17). The word *jubilee* comes from the name of a ram or its horn (*yobel*) that is blown to sound an alert (Josh 6:5, 8-13). However, in Leviticus 25 it is used as the name of a year: *That year will be your jubilee* (*yobel*; Lev 25:10 NET). The Jubilee Year was actually announced by a "trumpet (*šophar*) blast" in verse 9.

Jubilee gives us the name of the year, but what happens in this year? In this year a release (*deror*) is proclaimed in the land (v. 10). Agricultural land is given back (released) to its original owner, and Israelite slaves are freed (released). The Hebrew word *deror* is linked to the Akkadian word *andurāru*, which refers to a release of debts, slaves, and land (*CAD*). Periodic releases can be proclaimed by a king, or the king can issue a written text announcing a social and economic reform (*mīšarum*; for such a text, see *ANET* 526-28; also see Otto; Lemche). The provisions of the Israelite release are found in Leviticus 25, from verse 10 to the end of the chapter. Unlike other nations, Israel's release is fixed by calendar rather than initiated by a royal proclamation.

There is also a Sabbatical Year release (Deut 15:1-11). This release is a remission (*šemiṭṭah*) of debts. The Sabbatical Year in Exodus 23:10-11 and Leviticus 25:3-7, however, is one of rest for the land, a year in which the Israelites are not to till the land: *When you enter the land I am going to give you, the land itself must observe a sabbath to the* LORD (Lev 25:2). (For excellent discussions of the biblical material, see *NIDB*, s.v. "Jubilee"; Lemche; C. Wright: 197-212; Ollenburger.)

LAW Two general categories of law have been distinguished in the Hebrew Bible: casuistic law and apodictic law. *Casuistic law* presents a specific case, as illustrated by the slave law in Exodus 21:2-4 (italicized words highlight references to specific circumstances):

When you acquire a Hebrew slave, he shall serve six years;
    in the seventh year he shall go free, without payment.
If he came single, he shall leave single;

> *if* he had a wife, his wife shall leave with him.
> *If* his master gave him a wife, and she has borne him children,
>   the wife and her children shall belong to the master,
>   and he shall leave alone. (NJPS, emph. added)

The first verse (v. 2) presents the simple case. The following verses explain what to do in more complex cases. What happens if the slave is part of a married couple? What happens if the owner gives the slave a wife? What happens if there are children? Casuistic law does not cover all circumstances that might occur. For example, if a slave marries a wife that the master does not give him, does she leave with him? If they have children, do their children leave with the parents or stay? An example of casuistic law in Leviticus is the sequence that begins chapter 4. The heading for the law is given:

> *When* a person unwittingly incurs guilt in regard to any of the Lord's commandments about things not to be done, and does one of them . . . (Lev 4:2 NJPS, emph. added)

After this general heading regarding inadvertent sin, we have the case of the high priest (v. 3), the whole people (v. 13), the ruler (v. 22), and the commoner (v. 27). All these "ifs" hang from the general heading in verse 2 (see Rothenbusch).

Apodictic law is a law without stated cases or extenuating circumstances.

> Whoever strikes his father or his mother must surely be put to death. (Exod 21:15 NET)

There are no mitigating circumstances. A positive command may also be apodictic, as in the second part of Leviticus 19:18:

> You must not take vengeance or bear a grudge against the children
>   of your people,
>   but you must love your neighbor as yourself. I am the Lord. (NET)

The distinction between apodictic law and case law is not always clear cut, such as in Exodus 21:12-14. Verse 12 is an apodictic law:

> He who fatally strikes a man shall be put to death. (NJPS)

This is an unconditional command, we might think. But we would be wrong. The following verse (13) adds extenuating circumstances to this absolute law:

> If he did not do it by design, but it came about by an act of God,
>   I will assign you a place to which he can flee.

This example shows that apodictic commands should not be taken at face value; they may be modified according to circumstances or other laws.

LEADERSHIP Because Leviticus, especially in the first sixteen chapters, focuses on the priests and their duties, one might think of them as leaders. On the one hand, they are cultic functionaries. This means they are servants of God, of the tabernacle, and of the people. They need to keep fire burning on the altar. They need to take out the ashes. They need to inspect houses for impure molds. They need to offer sacrifices. Their life seems rather well defined, and their role of priest or high priest is hereditary. Israel itself did not have hereditary political leaders until the rise of the monarchy. Moreover, priests seem to be under the control of the laity at times (Judg 18:14-20).

On the other hand, besides their ritual duties, the priests were charged with teaching the people, which was vital for their living in the camp as God's holy people (10:8-11; 11:43-44). In this regard the priests were indirectly responsible for the people living a life of purity and holiness outside the tabernacle area. They also affected the daily lives of the people since they were also the judges of impurity in people, clothing, and housing. This deep reach into the life of the people made them of great importance for all Israelites.

Secular or political leadership was in the hands of Moses and the elders. Moses ordains the priests. He relays the words of God to the people. The elders serve as the official representatives of the people (4:15; 9:1). They are to be honored by the people: *You must stand up in the presence of the aged, honor the presence of an elder* (Lev 19:32 NET). Many translate *old* rather than *elder*. But there seems to be a difference between *gray haired* (*śebah*, 1 Sam 12:2) and *elders*, who would not necessarily be gray haired or old—although *zaqen* (elder) can also mean old.

Leviticus focuses on the holy, the priests, and the high priest. Although secular leadership is outside its interest, it presents the leadership provided by the holy priesthood.

LEVITES The Levites are descendants of Levi who make up the tribe of Levi. The brothers Aaron and Moses are Levites who are called to a special function. Moses is to serve as Israel's leader from Egypt until they stand on Jordan's bank, ready to enter Canaan. Aaron, who has accompanied Moses from the beginning of his mission (Exod 4:14-17), has become the first high priest, and his sons serve as priests at the tabernacle (Lev 8).

The remaining members of the tribe of Levi are devoted to the service of the tabernacle and its rituals. This includes packing, unpacking, and moving the tabernacle as porters and carrying it when the camp moves (Num 1:49-50). Since their activity does not begin until after the book of Leviticus, they are mentioned only in connection with the regulations for the Levitical cities at the time of the Jubilee Year (Lev 25:32-34).

LITERARY STYLE How an author uses language shows the literary style. This includes vocabulary, grammatical structures, and patterns of expression found in a passage.

In the case of *vocabulary*, the frequency of the term "holy" and "be or become holy," and how both are used—all these distinguish chapters 1–15 from chapters 19–25. In 11:44-45, "holy" and "becoming holy" refer to a lifestyle—eating only the allowed living creatures, for example. Previously, the word "holy" has referred to a place (e.g., 6:16, 26, 27 [9, 19, 20]). The use of "holy" to refer to lifestyle is found in chapter 19 (see 19:2, where it prefaces commands for holy living). This difference in word usage sets the style of Leviticus 1–15 apart from the ethical regulations found in chapters 19–25.

For a comment on the significance of *grammatical structure* in the Hebrew text, see the EN on Leviticus 20:2. Here the audience, Israel, precedes the verb "to speak": *To the Israelites say* (AT), breaking the normal pattern in which Israel follows the verb of speaking.

The most frequent *literary pattern* found in Leviticus is the *inclusio*, which we have referred to as an "envelope" structure. These terms define passages that begin and end with the same or similar words. See the EN on 20:27. Chapter 20 begins and ends with the same topic, forming an *inclusio*, or envelope, around chapter 20. This sets the chapter apart from what precedes and what follows it.

Another pattern is *chiasm*. This term refers to a mirror relationship between the first part of a passage and its second part. Sometimes a chiasm has a "hinge" that marks the point at which the passage begins to fold back or repeat itself. Such a hinge marks the focus of the chiasm and of the passage. See the EN on 17:10-12, where verse 11 forms the hinge of the chiasm and points to the significance of this verse for the passage and for Leviticus.

While such matters of style may be obscured by the translations, they are important markers for understanding a text.

NOACHIAN COVENANT The commands and covenant that God made with Noah in Genesis 9 are called the Noachian covenant in Jewish tradition. From Genesis 9:1-6, two rules were derived by the Jewish sages: (1) the command against eating blood, also found in Leviticus 17; and (2) the law against murder, because God will bring retribution on any human or animal that takes the life of a human being.

The Noachian covenant is valid for all humankind, since all humankind descends from Noah. This covenant contrasts with the Mosaic covenant, which was made only with the Israelites. The first covenant (Gen 9), in ancient Jewish tradition, regulates the behavior of Gentiles, while the second (the Mosaic law) regulates conduct of the Jews.

When the sages developed a list of laws that are universal, applying to both Jews and Gentiles, this list was known as the Noachian laws. (See TBC and TLC for ch. 17.)

PLAIN-SENSE INTERPRETATION Only within the last 150 or so years have the contemporary languages, literature, and history become available, as well as archaeology from the time of the Hebrew Bible (OT). Previously, this contextual and textual information was unknown, and interpretations were constructed from within a contextual vacuum. During this period, unhistorical interpretations, such as typological and allegorical approaches, flourished (and are alive even now). The interpretation of the Bill of Rights in the U.S. Constitution is a vivid example of how law may be interpreted out of the context in which it was written. It now means what the Supreme Court says it means. For the Bible it was the Church.

Into this interpretive desert, around the eleventh century, as learning moved from the Islamic lands (including Spain) to Europe and was initiating the Renaissance, awareness of Jewish biblical scholarship and learning increased among Christians. Concerning the interpretation of the Old Testament, eventually a polemic developed between Western Jewish scholars, who obviously used the Hebrew text, and church authorities who did not. In their efforts to refute Jewish claims, Christian scholars influenced by the Renaissance sought to base their conclusions on the original Hebrew text, rather than on the Vulgate, a Latin translation. This meant learning Hebrew, which led them to Jews, thus also acquainting them with Jewish scholarship and interpretation.

A Jewish scholarly tradition of plain-sense interpretation was developing and expanding during this time. An early and its most influential practitioner was the scholar known as Rashi, who resided in France. What Rashi had was a Hebrew text, and he sought to explain it from itself. He attempted to distinguish between the plain sense of a text and its derived senses, such as midrashic interpretations (reflections and often expansions), which had grown up around the text (see Halivni).

Through contact with Jewish scholars and debates with them, a budding tradition of Christian scholarship was heavily influenced by Rashi's method and his tradition of plain-sense interpretation. These scholars compared the text of the Hebrew Bible with the Vulgate and developed their own plain-sense tradition as Bible scholars in their own clergy cloisters (Smalley: 83–195). (For Rashi, see the groundbreaking work of Sarah Kamin [1986]; for the relationship between Jewish and Christian interpreters of this time, see Kamin 1991: 1–68 Eng., 1–99 Heb.; see also *DBI*, s.vv. "Rashi," "Hugo of St. Victor," "Andrew of St. Victor," and "Richard of St. Victor." For rabbinic interpretation more generally, see Halivni.)

Today the historical, cultural, and literary contexts have become important elements in biblical interpretation, but they are not sufficient. A careful reading and understanding of the text as a text (Leviticus according to Leviticus) is necessarily fundamental to all else. It is this text that we seek to understand by the use of external contextual clues, which by nature are speculative in the case of Leviticus. However, some guesses are more reasonable than others, and these limit what the plain sense of a text might have been in its external context.

When the dating, the audience, and the immediate setting of a book are uncertain and disputed, as in the case of Leviticus, it seems wise to base an interpretation on what is in the text first of all rather than on suppositions, some of which are undoubtedly wrong, about what is around the text and forms the external context of the text. In the case of ritual texts and laws, this is even more so the case. The book of Jonah is a good example of interpretations that depend on an overemphasis on contextualization. The historical context of Jonah is speculative, so the understandings of scholars have been quite varied. For a discussion of differing interpretations that find little or no support in the text (or perhaps are even contradicted by the text), see the careful study in Simon (vii–xlii).

In the modern era of biblical studies, plain-sense interpretations draw on what is known from cognate languages and literatures, tools such as the study of literary genres, the structure of a passage and of the text, the evaluation of the composition of the text, and sources used, as well as what is known from contemporary historical sources. They draw much less on reconstructed lines of development, such as the idea that a text must be late or must be exilic because its concepts or recommendations were not possible in a former time and place (see Greenberg 1995a).

Amid all types of readings of a text from various points of view, it is important to distinguish between what we may *suppose* the text might mean and what we can know. What we know we can show, which is far less than what we can suppose (cf. the essay *The Traditional Western Method of Exegesis, p. 318*).

PURE The term for pure (*taher*) is used to denote persons, animals, and things that may approach or touch the holy. Impure (*tame'*) is the opposite and denotes what may not approach or touch the holy. Impurity is contagious (among living things), while purity is essentially not—just as greasy hands can make clean hands greasy but clean hands cannot make greasy hands clean. (For degrees of how contagious an impurity may be, see D. Wright 1991; Nihan.)

Impurity is not a sin. In some cases no sacrifice is needed for regaining purity (ch. 11), whereas sin always requires a sacrificial ritual for forgiveness (ch. 4). In the case of impurity, the result of the ritual is becoming pure, as in chapter 12.

Most impurities in Leviticus are *ritual* impurities, since the impure person may not approach the tabernacle (the holy place), participate in rituals performed there, or eat the meat of a sacrifice. A ritually impure person must undertake a purity ritual to become clean of their defilement. These rituals may be simple everyday tasks such as washing a garment or bathing, or just waiting until evening. Or they may require a waiting period, preliminary rites, and a sacrifice.

The layperson learns the purity regulations from the priests and in simple cases can determine for themselves if they have become impure. The food laws in Leviticus 11 give an example of lay discretion. In other cases, such as for certain skin blemishes, the layperson must consult a priest, as in Leviticus 13.

In addition, we find "moral" impurities in Leviticus 18. There are no rituals for restoring purity to those who have committed these defiling actions. Eventually such actions are transmitted to the ground of Palestine, and in the end they will result in the expulsion of Israel from the land (Klawans 2000).

Impurity and *sin* are different matters in most of Leviticus. Chapters 1-16 contain most of the uses of the word "sin" in Leviticus. Leviticus 18-27 rarely uses it. In 19:22 it refers to the act of violating a servant girl, and in 26:18, 21, 24, and 28 it occurs in the plural, referring to Israel's sins generically, which broke covenant with God.

What is surprising is that sin (*ḥaṭṭaʾt*) does not occur in the list of misdeeds in chapters 18 and 20. The grave sexual misconducts listed in Leviticus 18 are labeled "uncleanness" eight times and called "horrors" rather than "sin." Elsewhere in these chapters, uncleanness refers mainly to ritual uncleanness, as in chapters 1-16.

However, we suggest that since a ritual is needed for removing an impurity or removing the contamination of the altar by sin, both are part of a ritual system. *Thus it seems impossible to separate a moral realm and a ritual realm.* Ritual is the cure for both, and both sins and impurity are removed from the temple on the Great Day of Cleansing, as explained in Leviticus 16.

PURIFICATION *See* **CLEANSING OFFERING**

RADICAL REFORMATION AND MENNONITE USE OF LEVITICUS Early leaders of the Radical Reformation *used* Leviticus instead of *understanding* it. In doing so, they took no notice of its actual sense or the larger context of a passage. The use made of Leviticus 11 illustrates their practice. Thomas Müntzer writes, "The temporal lords and princes are the eels, as is figuratively represented in Leviticus (ch. 11:10-12)" ("Sermon before the Princes," *SAW*: 63). How does one arrive at such an interpretation? To all appearances the chapter is about food, not symbolic language for rulers. In *The Ordinances of God*, Melchior Hoffmann maintains that all of God's words, if properly understood, are of equal weight, "because to explicate the Scripture is not a matter for everybody ... but only for those to whom God has given the power." Thus the meaning of the "cloven claws and horns" are to be decided by those to whom God has given the power to understand these words. The differences between clean and unclean animals (Lev 11) were often used by early Anabaptists (*SAW*: 202-3n42).

However, use was also made of Leviticus when interpreting the New Testament. Hans Denck, in *Whether God Is the Cause of Evil*, uses Leviticus 18:5 to understand Romans 10:5. The Jews, he writes, only obey the law externally and live without internalization of the law (*SAW*: 93). However, in Leviticus 18:5, Moses is talking about life and living, not just external obedience: doing the law brings life.

Menno Simons went a step further and cited Leviticus in support of his own practices. An example would be his requirements for leadership in the church: "Those who are comprised in the doctrine, ordinance, and life of our Lord Jesus Christ, and unblamable in all things." He then cites 1 Timothy 3:2; Titus 1:6; Leviticus 21:7; and Ezekiel 44:21 as his biblical warrant, even though Leviticus 21:7 refers to Israelite priests (Menno: 303). He also uses Leviticus to support a point he is making about the New Testament. On James 3, he writes concerning the tongue, "Take heed, brethren, take heed that you allow no defamer among you, as Moses taught. Lev. 19" (Menno: 412).

Menno also used the Old Testament to answer troubling questions, such as why polygamy is forbidden when Abraham, Isaac, and Jacob practiced it. His answer was that Leviticus forbids to marry two sisters (ch. 18), although previously practiced. He also pointed to Genesis, where a marriage consisted of two persons, Adam and Eve, and which practice was also commanded by Jesus in Matthew 19, based on the example of Adam and Eve (Menno: 560).

His argument that the command of Jesus in Matthew 5:33-35 prohibited all oaths represents a fairly sophisticated use of the Old Testament based on its plain sense. Against Martin Micron in the *Epistle to Martin Micron* (1556), who argues that Jesus meant to prohibit only unconsidered or false oaths, Menno answers: On the one hand, we know that Moses's law already prohibited such oaths. On the other hand, we all know also that Moses commanded Israel to swear in God's name, citing Leviticus 19:12 and Deuteronomy 10:20. Thus Jesus must be referring to the latter practice and forbidding the swearing of all oaths (Menno: 922-23).

When we jump to the twentieth century, we find in Daniel Kauffman's *Doctrines of the Bible* (1928) an understanding of the plain sense of Leviticus. However, his presuppositions and conclusions do not necessarily reflect the plain sense of a passage. For example, he maintains, "There was a system of Sabbaths, having both a literal and a *symbolical use and significance*" (183, emph. added). The plain sense of the Jubilee was "the year of Jubilee—every fiftieth year—a summary of Sabbaths, so to speak, in which time there was opportunity for the poor to redeem their lands, for the redemption of servants, a year of grace for all the oppressed and distressed" (ibid.). However, in a spiritual sense, these Sabbaths pointed "forward to the Christian Sabbath, the divinely appointed day of rest and worship in the present dispensation" (ibid.). This use of Leviticus posits two meanings for its texts. There is the plain sense, which governed the people of Israel. There is also a spiritual sense, which in hindsight points toward the institution of Sunday, the first day of the week, being the day of rest and worship.

His understanding of oaths is similar to that of Menno. Previously there had been oaths, some permitted, some prohibited (Exod 20:7; Lev 19:12; Num 30:2; Deut 5:11). However, Jesus forbids the taking of all oaths (Menno: 517). One of Menno's prooftexts against taking any oath is Leviticus 5:4-5, which he understands as forbidding oaths in situations where a person does not know what they might entail (Menno: 526). However, this is not the plain sense of this text (see comments on 5:4-5).

To summarize, Kauffman maintains that we find both a plain sense and a spiritual sense in Old Testament texts. This latter is an anachronistic interpretation, read back into the text in light of the need to support the church and Christian practices. This we saw in the case of Sunday, the shifting of the day of worship and rest from the seventh day, as commanded in the Old Testament, to the first day, Sunday, which became the church's day of rest and worship.

A representative of a much more sophisticated use of the Old Testament is *Israel's Scripture Traditions and the Synoptic Gospels* by Willard Swartley (1994). First, Swartley's aim is not to interpret passages in Leviticus but to use them as helpful background for understanding gospel texts. An example is his discussion of the antitheses in Matthew 5:33-48, where he cites Leviticus 19:12 as the background for Jesus' renunciation of oath taking, Leviticus 24:19-20 as background for *lex talionis* (an eye for an eye), and Leviticus 19:18 for the command to love one's fellow (71n72).

A different use of Leviticus is illustrated in Swartley's discussion of the Jubilee theme introduced in Luke 4:16-19. He points to the use of the word "release" twice in this passage to affirm the importance of this notion for Jesus' ministry (76–78). As evidence that the word "release" in Jesus' quotation has at least Jubilee connotations, he cites the use of "release" in Leviticus 25 and 27 (78). Leviticus here is used to illuminate how the gospel writers or their audience might have understood the quotation from Isaiah 61:1-2a. In a sense, Leviticus becomes a tool for interpreting the New Testament.

In sum, Swartley has no need to depart from the plain sense of the text in Leviticus, since he assumes Jesus' contemporaries so understood the texts he cites from Leviticus. Using later anachronistic interpretations would have defeated his use of Leviticus because they would not have been available to the readers of Leviticus in Jesus' time. Understanding the plain sense of Leviticus now becomes the first step in understanding how it shaped the synoptic gospels.

RANSOM The word for ransom, *koper*, is used in Exodus 21:30 for a payment made by a negligent owner of an ox known to gore. When such an ox kills someone, the victim's family may accept payment (*koper*) instead of the owner being put to death. We find a similar payment in Exodus 30:12, where it looks like a census tax: everyone counted in the census must make a payment to spare themselves from a plague sent by God. This payment is also called "an offering" in Exodus 30:13-14. In verse 15 this payment is made "when you make the offering to the LORD to atone [make purification] for your lives." The presentation of a gift of money makes it appear parallel to the case of the goring ox, cited above (*HALOT*). In cases of a deliberate murder, a ransom cannot be given, nor can it be accepted to shorten a sentence in a city of refuge (Num 35:31-32).

On the basis of these references it is argued that the verb translated *atone* in Leviticus should be understood as a ransom paid to God by sinners to save themselves from death. There are several reasons to question this transfer.

First, the noun "ransom" (*koper*) does not occur in Leviticus. Instead, when Leviticus discusses the idea of a ransom, it uses different vocabulary, such as *he may ransom it according to its conversion value and must add one fifth to it, but if it is not redeemed*... (Lev 27:27 NET). The word translated *ransom* in Leviticus is the Hebrew word *padah*, which can be used of God in the sense of God redeeming people. In Leviticus it is used only of *commercial transactions.* For these transactions Leviticus never uses the verb *kipper* (to purify, cleanse).

Second, this interpretation presupposes that all sinners deserve death, regardless of their trespass. This does not fit Leviticus. Nowhere do we find that sinners *in general* deserve death. In cases in which a sinner should be executed, the text says so, as in a case of idolatry (Lev 20:2) or for cursing God (24:14-16). In these cases no ransom is allowed.

Neither those who have sinned inadvertently nor those who have sinned deliberately are threatened with death. Instead, once a year all sin is removed from the camp on the Day of Cleansing, and the people may begin the next year with a clean slate. On this day, *atonement [cleansing] is to be made once a year for all the sins of the Israelites* (Lev 16:34, emph. added). The God of Leviticus is a gracious God, granting Israel remission from its sins. This God does not need to take the lives of those who have transgressed, nor do sinners need to pay God to remain alive *[Atonement, p. 288].*

SACRIFICIAL SYSTEM IN LEVITICUS There are three main types of sacrificial rituals in Leviticus: occasional, fixed, and ceremonial. *Occasional offerings* are sacrifices that arise according to circumstances. The *voluntary offerings* of chapters 1-3 by nature fall into this category. These include the *whole burnt offering*, the *grain offering*, and the *peace offering*. These offerings occur in rituals for pleasing God, but each has its own regulations on how the sacrifice is treated. The *obligatory offerings* are rituals triggered by sin or impurity. For sin, there are the *cleansing offerings* (ch. 4) and the *penalty offerings* (5:1–6:7). The purification rituals to address *impurity* are found in chapters 12-15.

The *fixed offerings* are set by time or calendar. These include the offerings made every morning and evening to keep the fire on the altar burning (Lev 6:8-13) and the sacrifices made on the Day of Cleansing (ch. 16). Tithes and firstfruits offerings also fit here, since they are offered at harvesttime, as do the Sabbatical and Jubilee Years and various annual festivals.

The *ceremonial offerings* are used in rituals for special national events. These are found in the *ordination ceremony* of the first priests in chapter 8. The ritual of *anointing with oil* functions to make people and altar holy so they may serve in or occupy holy space (8:10-12) *[Calendar, p. 295].* For examples and discussion of these sacrifices, see the comments at the cited references.

The Sacrificial System		
Occasional Sacrifices		
Voluntary		Whole burnt (NIV, *burnt offering*), ch. 1
		Grain (NIV, *grain offering*), ch. 2
		Peace (NIV, *fellowship offering*), ch. 3 Thanksgiving and vow, 7:11-21, 29-35
Obligatory		For sin: cleansing sacrifice (NIV, *sin offering*), 4:1-35 Penalty sacrifice (NIV, *guilt offering*), 5:1–6:7 (5:1-26)
		For impurity: cleansing sacrifice (NIV, *purification*), chs. 12–15
Fixed Sacrifices		
		Continuous sacrifice morning and evening, 6:8-13 (1-6)
		Daily grain offering, 6:14-18 (7-11)
		The high-priestly grain offering, 6:19-23 (12-16)
		Yearly Day of Cleansing, ch. 16
		Daily oil, Sabbath bread, 24:1-9
		Tithes, 27:30-33

		Annual festivals, ch. 23
		Spring festivals, 23:5-22
		  Passover, 23:5
		  Unleavened Bread, 23:6-8
		  First Sheaf (NIV, *firstfruits*), 23:10-14 (2:14-16)
		  Weeks (Pentecost), 23:15-21
		Fall festivals, 23:23-36
		  New Year's Festival (NIV, *trumpets*), 23:24-25
		  Day of Cleansing (NIV, *Day of Atonement*), 23:26-32 (ch. 16)
		  Booths (NIV, *Tabernacles*), 23:39-43

		Sabbatical and Jubilee Years, ch. 25
Ceremonial Sacrifices		
		Installation sacrifice, 8:22-29
		Anointing with oil, 8:10-12, 30

It is difficult for modern readers to appreciate the scope and the effectiveness of these rituals. We may believe that the prophets were opponents of them and suggested moral behavior as their replacement. But this is a misguided notion. In Isaiah 1:10-17 we find a substantial critique of sacrifices and celebrations. But if we look closely, it is actually a critique of the worshipers. First of all, consider the range of worship practices that are included in this list: Sabbath, the pilgrimage festivals like Passover, and prayer. It does not seem likely that God wanted the Israelites to abandon these practices. Rather, it is because "your hands are full of blood!" (Isa 1:15). What God desires of these worshipers is that they cease to do evil, and do justice (vv. 16-17). Apparently Isaiah is placing morality as a precondition of worship. In general, this is the position of prophets. As Micah 6:8 puts it, "To act justly and to love mercy and to walk humbly with your God." This does not replace the sacrificial system, but it points again to the primacy of morality. It might be said that Leviticus 18-25 is the priestly response to these charges since here too we find a demand for the moral life [*Holy and Holiness*, p. 302].

Sacrifice Terminology in Leviticus

Commentary	Hebrew Term	Milgrom	NIV	NRSV	NJPS	NET
(whole) burnt offering	ʿolah ch. 1	burnt offering	burnt offering	burnt offering	burnt offering	burnt offering
grain offering	minḥah ch. 2	cereal offering	grain offering	grain offering	meal offering	grain offering
peace offering	šelamim ch. 3	well-being offering	fellowship offering	well-being offering	well-being offering	peace offering
cleansing offering (sin and impurity)	ḥaṭṭaʾt chs. 4, 12–15	purification offering	sin offering	sin offering	sin offering	sin offering
penalty offering	ʾašam 5:14–6:7	reparation offering	guilt offering	guilt offering	guilt offering	guilt offering
contribution	terumah 7:14	contribution	contribution	gift	gift	contribution
vow offering	neder 7:16	votive offering	result of a vow	votive offering	votive offering	votive offering
freewill offering	nedabah 7:16	freewill offering	freewill offering	freewill offering	freewill offering	freewill sacrifice
ordination offering	milluʾim 7:37	ordination offering	ordination offering	ordination offering	ordination offering	ordination offering
libation	nesek 23:13	libation	drink offering	drink offering	libation	drink offering

SCAPEGOAT The word *scapegoat* was invented by William Tyndale for use in his English translation of 1530. He used it to refer to the unnamed goat in Leviticus 16:8 that is sent away into a deserted place. Tyndale needed to coin a new word because this living goat has no name in the Hebrew text.

The ritual indicated involves two goats. One is sacrificed. The other, the scapegoat, is the living goat that is sent away. In Hebrew it is called the goat *for Azazel* (Lev 16:8 so transcribed in NET). The fate of this goat is contrasted to God's goat, which is to be sacrificed. The scapegoat is described as *the live goat*, since it is spared from being sacrificed (Lev 16:20). Aaron places both hands on the head of this living goat and confesses over it the sins of the people. These sins are transferred to the goat's head. The goat, now bearing all of Israel's transgressions, is led out of the camp and sent away to a deserted place.

Should we call this goat "the one for Azazel," "the living goat," "the sin-bearing goat" or "the goat sent away"? Tyndale solved this problem by giving the goat a name: *scapegoat*. In time, the word no longer referred to the "sent-away, sin-bearing goat" in Leviticus 16 but became free floating and unattached to its original meaning.

Today the word *scapegoat* has a different meaning. Now a scapegoat is someone blamed for the mistakes of others and who bears the punishment they should bear. Today a scapegoat is a victim who suffers in place of the real culprits.

This new meaning of the term is now read back into Leviticus 16, and it is assumed that the scapegoat mentioned there plays the same role as someone we now call a scapegoat. But this is an anachronistic reading. The scapegoat in Leviticus is not blamed for the sins of the people but acts to remove the people's sins from the sanctuary and camp. The scapegoat is not punished for the sins of the people but is an elimination vehicle. In fact, at the end of the day, the scapegoat is living, and the other goat has been slaughtered, drained of blood, and burned. If any goat suffered for the sake of the community, it would be this goat, not the one left alive.

If we follow the course of events in Leviticus 16, we find that the scapegoat is chosen by lot. There are two goats, one chosen for sacrifice, the other chosen to remain alive. The second goat is not a sacrificial goat: it is not killed; its blood is not applied to the altar, nor is its flesh burned. To serve its purpose, the scapegoat must remain alive. The living goat is in fact *defiled*; it does not cleanse, as does a sacrifice. The person who leads the goat away from the tabernacle and camp needs purification because contact with the scapegoat has *contaminated* him. He needs to launder his garments and bathe before reentering the camp.

There are parallels between the goat in chapter 16 and the use of birds in Leviticus 14:6-7. In this ritual of cleansing, two birds are used. One is slaughtered, and its blood is placed on the living bird and on the person being cleansed. The slaughter of the first bird and the manipulation of its blood do not amount to a sacrificial ritual. The action takes place outside the camp, and the blood is applied to the living bird and the person, not to an altar. The living second bird is sent away into the wilderness, thus eliminating the impurity, and the person becomes clean. (For the history of the word *scapegoat* in Eng., see Dawson. For a discussion of Greek material that supposedly contains a scapegoat and its comparison with Lev 16, see Douglas 1993: 121–41. That the sent-away goat is part of an elimination ritual is argued by D. Wright [1987: 8–73] and by Milgrom [1991: 1040–45]. Kiuchi's arguments are similar [144–59].)

SIN *See* TBC on Leviticus 16, p. 160.

SIN OFFERING *See* **CLEANSING OFFERING**

THE TABERNACLE The following diagram shows the structure and features of the tabernacle.

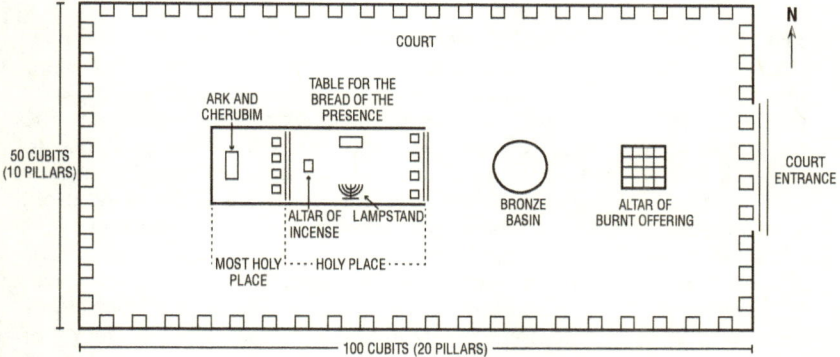

For the presentation of these features and a discussion of tabernacle theology in the Old Testament, see Waldemar Janzen, *NIDB*, s.v. "Tabernacle."

In Leviticus there is variation about naming what we call the "tabernacle." In its opening verse Leviticus speaks of a "tent of meeting" (*'ohel mo'ed*). This is also the name given to the just-completed tabernacle in Exodus 40:35. This same verse also speaks of it as "the dwelling place" (AT), usually translated as "tabernacle" (*miškan*). This latter term, although used frequently in Exodus and Numbers, is rarely used in Leviticus (occurring four times, in 8:10; 15:31; 17:4; 26:11). Instead, Leviticus restricts itself largely to "tent of meeting" (thirty-seven times). While this name for the tabernacle is also frequent in Exodus and Numbers, it is rarely used in other books; it is not used at all in Deuteronomy and appears only four times in Joshua through Kings. In summary, "tabernacle" and "tent of meeting" refer to the same structure. What we are not told is how this tent of meeting came to be located in the center of the camp.

Perhaps Leviticus prefers "tent of meeting" because of its concern with the presence of God and how the Israelites are to conduct themselves, both outside the tent of meeting and when they come before God with their sacrifices. God does not live in this tent. Only God's glory or presence is there.

TABOO The noun *taboo* may be defined as "a prohibition imposed by social custom or as a protective measure" (*Webster's*, meaning no. 2). Taboos may also carry a sense of danger because of divine or supernatural sanctions if the taboo is transgressed (*Webster's*, meaning no. 1). The word "perversion" occurs in Leviticus 18:23 and 20:12; and "detestable" in 18:22, 26, 27, 29, 30; 20:13. Both Hebrew terms occur only here in Leviticus, in contexts of forbidden sexual acts. These terms seem to denote actions that are abhorrent. For Israel they are taboo; that is, they are disgusting and are to strike an Israelite with horror. An example from many Western countries is incest, which can carry an emotional impact of disgust and aversion. How incest is defined may vary from country to country and from time to time within the same country. Thus it is a social custom or protective measure. Brother-sister marriages also carry emotional freight in many societies.

THE TRADITIONAL WESTERN METHOD OF EXEGESIS Certain fundamental questions are normally posed in Western scholarship and summarized in introductions to commentaries. These are questions of context, who wrote the book, when was the book written, what was the social-historical setting (of the book, its author, and the audience to whom it was written), and the purpose of the writing (what the author was hoping to achieve). Such are essential questions of interpretation, since understanding is contextual and scholars hope to understand a text in its native context. There has been a shift away from lengthy discussions of these issues. Compare Ernest Burton, who writes twenty-three pages on the location of the Galatian churches—north or south Galatia?—with Hans Betz, who ignores the issue. Instead, Betz focuses on the genre of Galatians, a matter of defining what type of literature it is. Here clues in the text support a hypothesis.

These essential questions, however, can lead to a circular methodology. The text is read for possible clues to these historical questions. Once the interpreter has posited hypothetical answers to these introductory contextual questions, the text is then interpreted in light of the presumed context. The ensuing interpretation usually substantiates the assumptions of the author. Putting these matters in the introduction to a commentary casts a long shadow over it. However, in many cases, the assumed context, purpose, and author are far from certain. One need only look at commentaries on the book of Jonah to see the amazingly different results from this methodology. (For a discussion of differing interpretations that find little or no support in the text, see the careful study in Simon: vii–xlii.)

The author of Leviticus is unknown. The text speaks of Moses in the third person rather than the first. Summary statements reflect a later time. In 7:38 the preceding commandments are those *which the* LORD *commanded Moses on Mount Sinai, when he commanded the people of Israel to bring their offerings to the* LORD, *in the wilderness of Sinai* (NRSV, past tense). Likewise, at the end of the book we find statements indicating that Leviticus was composed after Moses received these commands (Lev 26:46;

27:34). How long after Mount Sinai were these words written and by whom? There are no statements in the text of Leviticus to answer these questions.

However, scholars have read the book of Leviticus meticulously in order to find clues as to authorship, date of writing, and purpose. Some observations are more convincing than others. On the matter of authorship, it seems evident that there are two types of material in Leviticus. Thus 11:44-45 reads, *For I am the LORD your God; sanctify yourselves therefore, and be holy, for I am holy. You shall not defile yourselves with any swarming creature that moves on the earth* (NRSV). This language sticks out like a sore thumb in the context of chapters 1–15. However, it represents the rhetoric and vocabulary of chapters 18 and following. For example, the exodus from Egypt is mentioned only here in chapters 1–15, but ten times in chapters 18–26. It is a short step from this data to the assumption that there are two traditions represented in Leviticus. One focuses on the presence of God, purity, and rules for worship, called P for Priestly source, found in Leviticus 1–16. The other source, found mainly in chapters 18–27, focuses on a morality that leads to an attained holiness; as a result, this source is labeled H for Holiness Code.

Who transmitted these different materials, when, and who finally wrote them down is a matter of conjecture on which there is no scholarly agreement. Some argue that the P material was committed to writing first and the H material was committed to writing later. The intrusion of H material into Leviticus 1–16 would point in this direction (see example above). Others argue the reverse, perhaps because ritual material must come late while moral concerns must be early. Some think the P and H materials were put into writing in the exilic or postexilic period. Others argue that at least one tradition was written down during the monarchy. With such disparate assumptions being used to understand Leviticus, it is quite risky to use one or the other as a grid through which to interpret the text. For example, the material in H might be seen as a priestly reaction to the ethical concerns and polemics of the eighth-century prophets. Its material might then be interpreted in light of the message of these prophets. If it was postexilic, however, it might be seen as an example of Jewish exclusivism dating from the time of Ezra and Nehemiah. These chapters then became a marker of Jewish exclusivism and legalism. So are they positive response to the prophetic material, or are they late Jewish legalism? Which assumption is chosen certainly affects how the text of Leviticus is understood.

The late dating of Leviticus, which seems assumed by most scholars (in informal assessment), rests in part on theological biases and anti-Semitism. Ever since Julius Wellhausen, the Protestant understanding of the Hebrew Bible has been influenced by his thesis that the Prophets preceded the Law. The Law, Leviticus in particular, was considered a late document attesting to the decadent development of Judaism from the high point of prophecy, which represented the living religion of the Old Testament. Wellhausen describes religion after the exile and the rise of the Pentateuch as follows:

It is estranged from the heart; its revival was due to old custom, it never would have blossomed again of itself. It no longer has its roots in childlike impulse, it is a dead work, . . . that heathenism in Israel against which the prophets vainly protested, . . . and the cultus, after nature had been killed in it, became the shield of supernaturalistic monotheism. . . . The ideal of holiness governs the whole of life . . . [and] separates the Jew from the natural man. (Wellhausen: 425, 499)

On the other hand, some Jewish scholarship points to the early origins of the legal material (in part by citing ancient Near Eastern analogues), and especially of the book of Leviticus. See the foundational work of Yehezkel Kaufmann, as translated and condensed by Greenberg (Kaufmann: 153–211). This Hebrew publication, begun in 1937, was a response to Wellhausen's literary historical analysis and an extended critique of Wellhausen's arguments. Kaufmann's eight-volume work has never been translated into English. Although this material became familiar to most Western scholars only since the early 1960s, it has been largely ignored by non-Jewish scholars. However, Kaufmann's work has provided a beginning point that has been explored, fleshed out, and exploited by scholars at Hebrew University in Jerusalem. This includes Jacob Milgrom, a professor at the University of California at Berkeley, who has dated the material in Leviticus early.

How much the ideological, theological, and social contexts bias how Leviticus is contextualized is an open question. But obviously its marginalization in Christian circles and its centrality in Jewish circles (it is the traditional beginning point of study for a budding Jewish student) influences how the material is understood and evaluated. Is Leviticus the center of the Torah, or does it represent a late legalism that produced the Judaism we believe we see depicted in the Gospels?

Historically, most agree, the first five books, the Pentateuch, formed the earliest canon and became the foundational criteria for later material as it subsequently was expanded. The law of Moses, as the original canon, was Scripture with a large S for the Jews, including Jesus, who did not come to abolish the law (Matt 5:17-20), and Paul, who came not to do away with the law but to "uphold the law" (Rom 3:31 NRSV). This follows in the footsteps of Leviticus, which states, *So you must keep my statutes and my regulations; anyone who does so will live by keeping them. I am the* LORD (Lev 18:5 NET). For the contemporary reader, a helpful question is, How does Leviticus promote life?

To answer this question, it seems best to understand Leviticus from within its text rather than to place it in a hypothetical social-historical context or on an ideological line of devolution (see Greenberg 1995b).

WORSHIP AND ETHICS Leviticus can be divided into two major parts connected by a hinge (chs. 16–17). The first part, chapters 1–15, centers around worship at the sanctuary. The God who is worshiped there is a holy God, and the sanctuary is also holy. People must come to worship in a state of purity, with reverence for God's holiness. The worship at the sanctuary is characterized by praise, thanksgiving, and the forgiveness of sins.

In the final major part of Leviticus, chapters 18–25, we find regulations for daily life. The purpose of these was for Israel to be a holy people. We might say that the holy God who was worshiped in the sanctuary was demonstrated to be holy through the holy lives of the people. Although lack of holiness did not prevent people from entering the sanctuary, holiness was expected of those worshiping a holy God. Notice the "entrance requirements" we find listed in Psalm 15 after the questions "LORD, who may dwell in your sacred tent? Who may live on your holy mountain?" (Ps 15:1). God's holiness requires purity in worship and holiness in life (see TBC for ch. 15).

YAHWEH Yahweh is the personal name of Israel's God. Gods in the ancient Near East had names because in polytheism, gods needed names to distinguish them from one another. For example, the god of the Moabites was Chemosh. We do not know what other gods they had. Israel, of course, was not polytheistic, but their God still had a personal name: Yahweh.

God's personal name was held in such reverence that in the course of time it was no longer pronounced. Instead, when Jews came to the consonants YHWH (Yahweh) in the Bible, they instead would say the Hebrew equivalent of "LORD" (*'adonay*). Translators have followed this tradition and, to securely indicate God instead of some human lord, use small caps for the last three letters: LORD.

In Leviticus, God, when speaking in the first person, uses God's own personal name, Yahweh. The usual translation uses LORD: *Be holy because I, the LORD your God, am holy* (Lev 19:2). Translating the text as written would read, *You will be holy because I, Yahweh, your God, am holy* (AT). This more personal identification may give more emphasis to the sentence.

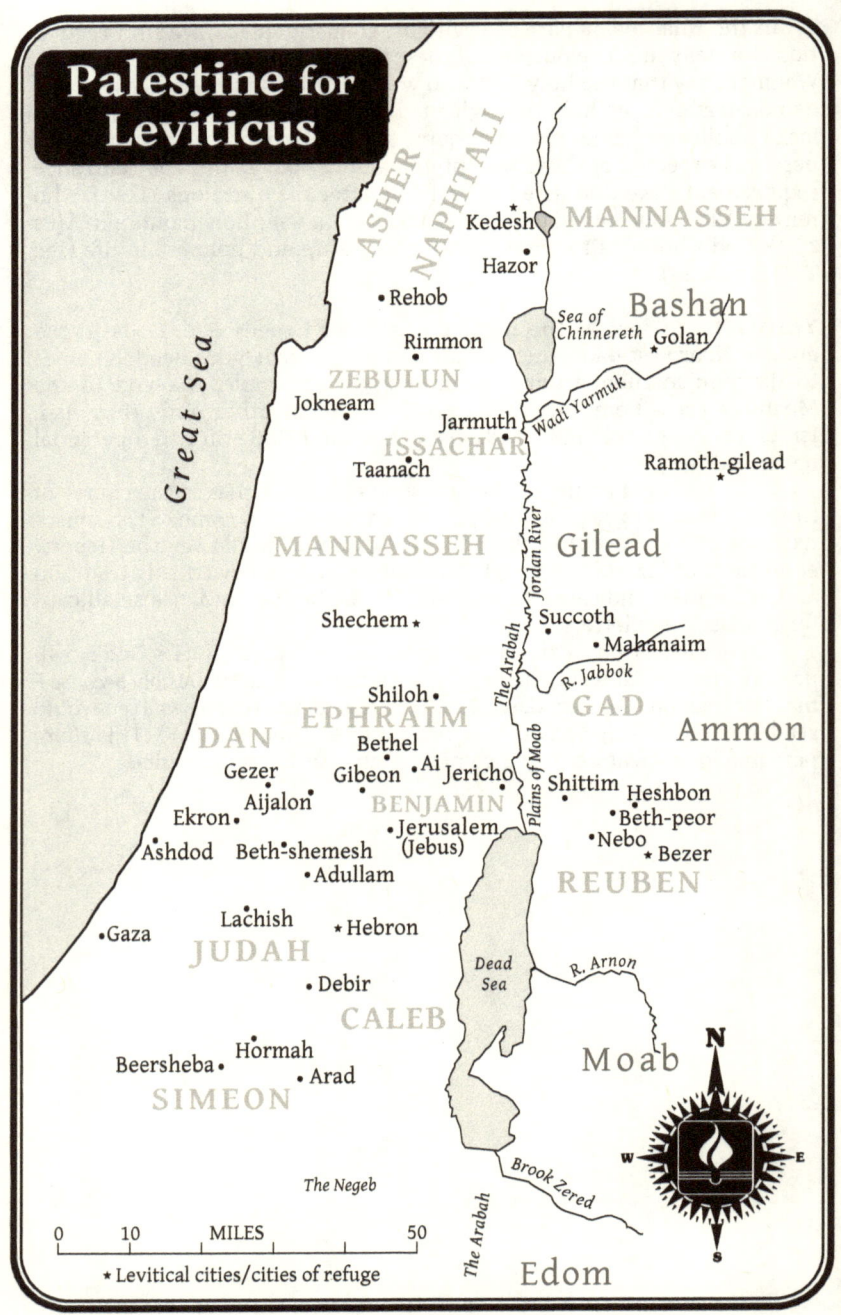

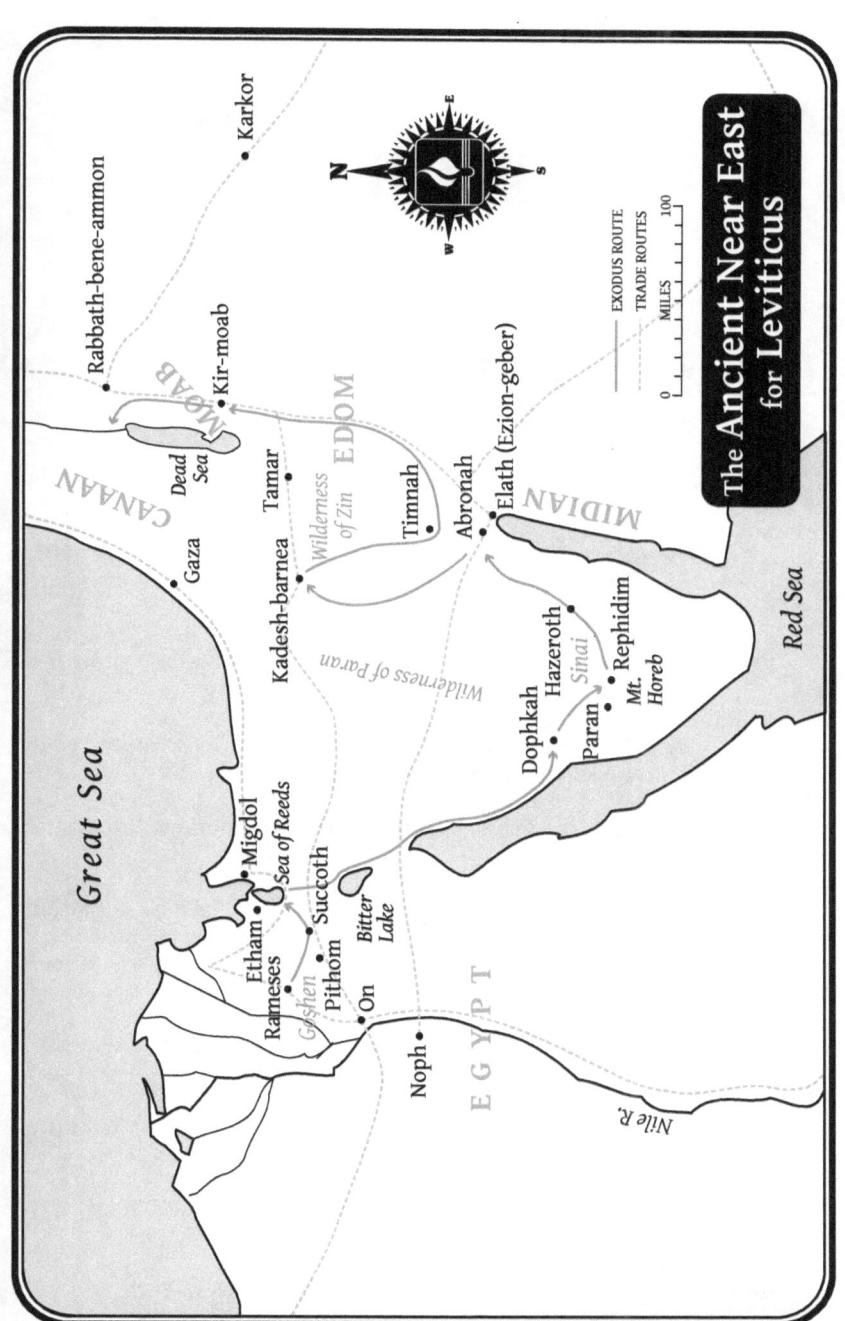

Bibliography

Altman, Amnon
    2004   *The Historical Prologue of the Hittite Vassal Treaties: An Inquiry into the Concepts of Hittite Interstate Law*. Ramat-Gan: Bar-Ilan University Press.

Anderson, Gary A.
    1992   "Sacrifice and Sacrificial Offerings: Old Testament." In *Anchor Bible Dictionary* 5:870–86. New York: Doubleday.

Bailey, Wilma A.
    2005   *"You Shall Not Kill" or "You Shall Not Murder"? The Assault on a Biblical Text*. Collegeville, MN: Liturgical Press.

Barmash, Pamela
    2005   *Homicide in the Biblical World*. Cambridge: Cambridge University Press.

Barrett, C. K.
    1995   "The First Christian Moral Legislation." In *The Bible in Human Society: Essays in Honour of John Rogerson*, edited by M. Daniel Carroll R., David J. A. Clines, and Phlip R. Davies, 58–66. JSOTSup 200. Edinburgh: T&T Clark.

Bell, Catherine
    1997   *Ritual: Perspectives and Dimensons*. Oxford: Oxford University Press.

Ben-Shalom, Israel
    1993   *The School of Shammai and the Zealots' Struggle against Rome* [in Heb.]. Jerusalem: Ben-Zvi.

Bergen, Wesley J.
    2005   *Reading Ritual: Leviticus in Postmodern Culture*. JSOTSup 417. London: T&T Clark.

Berlin, Adele, and Marc Zvi Brettler, eds.
    2004   *The Jewish Study Bible: Tanakh Translation*. New York: Oxford University Press.

Bibliography

Betz, Hans Dieter
    1989   *Galatians.* Hermeneia: A Critical and Historical Commentary on the Bible. Mineapolis: Fortress.

Bibb, Bryan D.
    2009   *Ritual Words and Narrative Worlds in the Book of Leviticus.* New York: T&T Clark.

Bockmuehl, Markus
    1995   "The Noachide Commandments and New Testament Ethics, with special reference to Acts 15 and Pauline Halakhah." *Revue Biblique* 102:72–101.
    2000   *Jewish Law in Gentile Churches: Halakhah and the Beginnng of Christian Public Ethics.* Edinburgh: T&T Clark.

Burton, Ernest De Witt
    1921   *A Critical and Exegetical Commentary on the Epistle to the Galatians.* London: Charles Scribner's Sons.

Cross, F. L., and E. A. Livingstone, eds.
    1997   *Dictionary of the Christian Church.* 3rd ed. Peabody, MA: Hendrickson.

Danby, Herbert
    1933   *The Mishnah: Translated from the Hebrew with Introduction and Brief Explanatory Notes.* Oxford: Oxford University Press.

Dawson, David
    2013   *Flesh Becomes a Word: A Lexicography of the Scapegoat, or the History of an Idea.* Studies in Violence, Mimesis, and Culture. East Lansing: Michigan State University Press.

Douglas, Mary
    1966   *Purity and Danger: An Analysis of the Concepts of Pollution and Taboo.* London: Routledge & Kegan Paul.
    1993   "The Go-Away Goat." In *The Book of Leviticus: Composition and Reception*, edited by Rolf Rendtorff, 121–41. Leiden: Brill.
    1993-94   "Atonement in Leviticus." *Jewish Studies Quarterly* 1:109–30.
    1999   *Leviticus as Literature.* Oxford: Oxford University Press.

Driver, John
    1986   *Understanding the Atonement for the Mission of the Church.* Scottdale, PA: Herald Press.

Dunn, James D.
    1998   *The Theology of Paul the Apostle.* Grand Rapids: Eerdmans.

Eberhart, Christian A.
    2011   "Sacrifice? Holy Smokes! Reflections on Cult Terminology in the Hebrew Bible." In *Ritual and Metaphor: Sacrifice in the Bible*, edited by Christian A. Eberhart, 17–32. Atlanta: Society of Biblical Literature.

Elliger, Karl
    1966   *Leviticus.* Handbuch zum Alten Testament. Tübingen: Mohr.

Finlan, Stephen
    2005   *Problems with Atonement: The Origins of, and Controversy about, the Atonement Doctrine.* Collegeville, MN: Michael Glazier.

Flusser, David A.
    1986   "Die Aposteldekret und die Noachitischen Gebote." In *"Wer Tora vermehrt, mehrt Leben": Festgabe für Heinz Kremers zum 60. Geburtstag*, edited by Edna A. Brocke and Hans-Joachim Barkenings, 173–92. Neukirchen-Vlyn: Neukirchen Verlag.

Frevel, Christian, and Christophe Nihan
    2013   *Purity and the Forming of Religious Traditions in the Ancient Mediterranean World and Ancient Judaism*. Dynamics in the History of Religions 3. Leiden: Brill.

Fried, Lisbeth S., and David N. Freedman
    2001   "Was the Jubilee Year Observed in Preexilic Judah?" In *Leviticus 23-27*, by Jacob Milgrom, 2257–70. Garden City: Doubleday.

Gane, Roy E.
    2008   "Privative Preposition מן in the Purification Offering Pericopes and the Changing Face of 'Dorian Gray.'" *Journal of Biblical Literature* 127:209–22.

Gane, Roy E., and Ada Taggar-Cohen, eds.
    2015   *Current Issues in Priestly and Related Literature: The Legacy of Jacob Milgrom and Beyond*. Atlanta: SBL Press.

Gilders, William K.
    2004   *Blood Ritual in the Hebrew Bible: Meaning and Power*. Baltimore: Johns Hopkins University Press.
    2008   "Blood as Purificant in Priestly Torah: What Do We Know and How Do We Know It?" In *Perspectives on Purity and Purification in the Bible*, edited by Baruch J. Schwartz et al., 77–83. London: T&T Clark.

Goldstein, Elizabeth W.
    2015   "Women and the Purification Offering: What Jacob Milgrom Contributed to the Intersection of Women's Studies and Biblical Studies." In *Current Issues in Priestly and Related Literature: The Legacy of Jacob Milgrom and Beyond*, edited by Roy E. Gane and Ada Taggar-Cohen, 47–65. Atlanta: Society of Biblical Literature.

Gorman, Frank H., Jr.
    1997   *Leviticus: Divine Presence and Community*. International Theological Commentary. Grand Rapids: Eerdmans.

Grabbe, Lester L.
    1993   *Leviticus*. Old Testament Guides. Sheffield: JSOT Press.

Greenberg, Moshe
    1983   *Biblical Prose Prayer*. Berkeley: University of California Press.
    1995a   "Reflections on Interpretation." In *Studies in the Bible and Jewish Thought*, edited by Moshe Greenberg, 227–34. Original article, 1979. Philadelphia: Jewish Publication Society.
    1995b   "To Whom and for What Should a Bible Commentator Be Responsible?" In *Studies in the Hebrew Bible and Jewish Thought*, 235–43. Original article, 1990. Philadelphia: Jewish Publication Society.

Gruenwald, Ithamar
    2003   *Rituals and Ritual Theory in Ancient Israel*. Leiden: Brill.
Halivni, David Weiss
    1991   *Peshat and Derash: Plain and Applied Meaning in Rabbinic Exegesis*. Oxford: Oxford University Press.
Hartley, John E.
    1992   *Leviticus*. Word Biblical Commentary 4. Dallas: Word.
Houston, Walter
    1993   *Purity and Monotheism: Clean and Unclean Animals in Biblical Law*. Sheffield: JSOT Press.
Janzen, David
    2004   *The Social Meanings of Sacrifice in the Hebrew Bible: A Study of Four Writings*. Beihefte zur Zeitschrift für die alttestamentliche Wissenschaft 344. Berlin: de Gruyter.
Jüngling, Hans-Winfried
    1999   "Das Buch Levitikus in der Forschung seit Karl Elligers Kommentar aus dem Jahr 1966." In *Levitikus als Buch*, Bonner biblische Beitrage, edited by Heinz-Josef Fabry and Hans-Winfried Jüngling, 1–45. Berlin: Philo.
Jürgens, Benedikt
    2001   *Heiligkeit und Versöhnung: Levitikus 16 in seinem literarischen Kontext*. Freiburg im Breisgau: Herder.
Kamin, Sarah
    1986   *Rashi's Exegetical Categorization in Respect to the Distinction between Peshat and Derash* [in Hebrew]. Jerusalem: Magnus.
    1991   *Jews and Christians Interpret the Bible* [in Heb.]. Jerusalem: Magnus.
Kauffman, Daniel
    1928   *Doctrines of the Bible: A Brief Discussion of the Teachings of God's Word*. Scottdale, PA: Herald Press. Reprinted 1992.
Kaufmann, Yehezkel
    1960   *The Religion of Israel: From Its Beginnings to the Babylonian Exile*. Translated and abridged by Moshe Greenberg. Chicago: University of Chicago Press.
Kim, Jin-Myung
    2011   *Holiness and Perfection: A Canonical Unfolding of Leviticus 19*. Bern: Peter Lang.
Kiuchi, N.
    1987   *The Purification Offering in the Priestly Literature: Its Meaning and Function*. JSOTSup 56. Sheffield: JSOT Press.
Klawans, Jonathan
    2000   *Impurity and Sin in Ancient Judaism*. New York: Oxford University Press.
    2004   "Concepts of Purity in the Bible." In *The Jewish Study Bible*, edited by Adele Berlin and Marc Zvi Brettler, 2041–47. New York: Oxford University Press.
    2006   *Purity, Sacrifice, and the Temple: Symbolism and Supersessionism in the Study of Ancient Judaism*. New York: Oxford University Press.
    2008   "Methodology and Ideology in the Study of Priestly Ritual." In

Perspectives on Purity and Purification in the Bible, edited by Baruch J. Schwartz et al., 84–95. London: T&T Clark.

Klingbeil, Gerald A.
    2007   *Bridging the Gap: Ritual and Ritual Texts in the Bible*. Bulletin for Biblical Research, Supplements 1. Winona Lake, IN: Eisenbrauns.

Knohl, Israel
    1995   *The Sanctuary of Silence: The Priestly Torah and the Holiness School*. Minneapolis: Fortress.

Koch, Klaus
    1999   "עון *'āwōn*." In *Theological Dictionary of the Old Testament*, edited by G. Johannes Botterweck et al., 10:546–62. Grand Rapids: Eerdmans.

Koester, Craig R.
    2001   *Hebrews: A New Translation with Introduction and Commentary*. Anchor Bible 36. New York: Doubleday.

Lanci, John R.
    1997   *A New Temple for Corinth: Rhetorical and Archaeological Approaches to Pauline Imagery*. New York: Peter Lang.

Lemche, Niels
    1976   "The Manumission of Slaves—the Fallow Year—the Sabbatical Year—the Jobel Year." *Vetus Testamentum* 26:38–59.

Levenson, Jon D.
    1985   *Creation and the Persistence of Evil: The Jewish Drama of Divine Omnipotence*. San Francisco: HarperSanFrancisco.

Levine, Baruch A.
    1989   *Leviticus*. JPS Torah Commentary. Philadelphia: Jewish Publication Society.

Lienhard, Joseph T., ed.
    2001   *Exodus, Leviticus, Numbers, Deuteronomy*. Ancient Christian Commentary on Scripture 3. Downers Grove, IL: InterVarsity.

Marshall, Christopher D.
    2003   "Atonement, Violence and the Will of God: A Sympathetic Response to J. Denny Weaver's *The Nonviolent Atonement*." *Mennonite Quarterly Review* 77:69–92.

Mason, Eric F.
    2008   *You Are a Priest Forever: Second Temple Jewish Messianism and the Priestly Christology of the Epistle to the Hebrews*. Leiden: Brill.

Menno Simons
    1956   *The Complete Writings of Menno Simons, c. 1496-1561*. Translated by Leonard Verduin. Edited by J. C. Wenger. Scottdale, PA: Herald Press.

Milgrom, Jacob
    1976   "Israel's Sanctuary: The Priestly 'Picture of Dorian Gray.'" *Revue Biblique* 83:390–99.
    1991   *Leviticus 1–16: A New Translation with Introduction and Commentary*. Anchor Bible 3A. New York: Doubleday.
    2000   *Leviticus 17–22: A New Translation with Introduction and Commentary*. Anchor Bible 3B. New York: Doubleday.

2001   *Leviticus 23-27: A New Translation with Introduction and Commentary.* Anchor Bible 3C. New York: Doubleday.
2004   *Leviticus: A Book of Ritual and Ethics.* Continental Commentary. Minneapolis: Fortress.
2007   "The Preposition מִן and the חטאת Pericopes." *Journal of Biblical Literature* 126:161–63.

Müller, Klaus
    1998   *Tora für die Völker: Die noachidischen Gebote und Ansätze zu ihrer Rezeption im Christentum.* 2nd ed. Berlin: Institut Kirche und Judentum.

Neusner, Jacob
    1998   *The Mishnah: A New Translation.* New Haven: Yale University Press.

Nihan, Christophe
    2013   "Forms and Functions of Purity in Leviticus." In *Purity and the Forming of Religious Traditions in the Ancient Mediterranean World and Ancient Judaism*, edited by Christian Frevel and Christophe Nihan, 311–67. Leiden: Brill.

Ollenburger, Ben C.
    2001   "Jubilee: 'The Land Is Mine; You Are Aliens and Tenants with Me.'" In *Reclaiming the Old Testament: Essays in Honour of Waldemar Janzen*, edited by Gordon Zerbe, 208–34. Winnipeg, MB: CMBC Publications.

Otto, Eckart
    1998   "Soziale Restitution und Vertragsrecht: Mīšaru(m), (An)-durāru(m), Kirenzi, Parā Tarnumar, Š^{e}miṭṭa und D^{e}rôr in Mesopotamien, Syrien, in der Hebräischen Bibel und die Frage des Rechtstransfers im Alten Orient." *Revue d'assyriologie et d'archéologie orientale* 92:125–60.

Peels, Hendrik G. L.
    1995   *The Vengeance of God: The Meaning of the Root NQM and the Function of the NQM-Texts in the Context of Divine Revelation in the Old Testament.* Leiden: E. J. Brill.

Philip, Mayjee
    2011   *Leviticus in Hebrews: A Transtextual Analysis of the Tabernacle Theme in the Letter to the Hebrews.* New York: Peter Lang.

Poorthuis, Marcel, and Joshua Schwartz
    2000   "Purity and Holiness: An Introductory Survey." In *Purity and Holiness: The Heritage of Leviticus*, edited by Marcel Poorthuis and Joshua J. Schwartz, 3–26. Leiden: Brill.

Rendtorff, Rolf
    1995   "Another Prolegomenon to Leviticus 17:11." In *Pomegranates and Golden Bells: Studies in Biblical, Jewish, and Near Eastern Ritual Law and Literature*, edited by David P. Wright et al., 23–28. Winona Lake, IN: Eisenbrauns.

Richardson, Mervyn E. J.
    2000   *Hammurabi's Laws: Text, Translation and Glossary.* Sheffield: Sheffield Academic.

Rogerson, John W., ed.
    2014   *Leviticus in Practice*. Dorset, UK: Deo.

Rosner, Brian S.
    1994   *Paul, Scripture, and Ethics: A Study of 1 Corinthians 5-7*. Leiden: Brill.

Rothenbusch, Ralf
    2000   *Die kasuistische Rechtssammlung im "Bundesbuch" (Ex 21,2-11.18-22,16) und ihr literarischer Kontext im Licht altorientalisher Parallelen*. Münster: Ugarit-Verlag.

Ruwe, Andreas
    1999   *"Heiligkeitsgesetz" und "Priesterschrift": Literaturgeschichtliche und rechtssystematische Untersuchungen zu Leviticus 17.1-26.2*. Tübingen: Mohr Siebeck.

Sanders, E. P.
    1977   *Paul and Palestinian Judaism: A Comparison of Patterns of Religion*. Philadelphia: Fortress.
    1985   *Jesus and Judaism*. Minneapolis: Fortress.

Schertz, Mary H., and Perry B. Yoder
    2001   *Seeing the Text: Exegesis for Students of Greek and Hebrew*. Nashville: Abingdon.

Schwartz, Baruch J.
    1991   "The Prohibitions Concerning the 'Eating' of Blood in Leviticus 17." In *Priesthood and Cult in Ancient Israel*, edited by Gary A. Anderson and Saul M. Olyan, 34-66. Sheffield: JSOT Press.
    1995   "The Bearing of Sin in the Priestly Literature." In *Pomegranates and Golden Bells: Studies in Biblical, Jewish, and Near Eastern Ritual Law and Literature*, edited by David P. Wright et al., 3-21. Winona Lake, IN: Eisenbrauns.
    1999   *The Holiness Legislation: Studies in the Priestly Code* [in Hebrew]. Jerusalem: Magness.
    2000   "Israel's Holiness: The Torah Tradition." In *Purity and Holiness: The Heritage of Leviticus*, edited by Marcel Poorthuis and Joshua J. Schwartz, 47-59. Leiden: Brill.

Schwartz, Baruch J., Naphtali S. Meshel, Jeffery Stackert, and David P. Wright, eds.
    2008   *Perspectives on Purity and Purification in the Bible*. London: T&T Clark.

Seidl, Theodor
    1999   "Levitikus 16—'Schlussstein' des priesterlichen Systems der Sündenvergebung." In *Levitikus als Buch*, edited by Heinz-Josef Fabry and Jans-Winfied Jüngling, 219-48. Berlin: Philo.

Simon, Uriel
    1999   *Jonah*. The JPS Bible Commentary. Philadelphia: Jewish Publication Society.

Sklar, Jay
    2005   *Sin, Impurity, Sacrifice, Atonement: The Priestly Conceptions*. Sheffield: Sheffield Phoenix.
    2008   "Sin and Impurity: Atoned or Purified? Yes!" In *Perspectives on Purity and Purification in the Bible*, edited by Baruch J. Schwartz et al., 18-31. London: T&T Clark.

Smalley, Beryl
    1964   "The Victorines" and "Andrew of St. Victor." In *The Study of the Bible in the Middle Ages*, 83–195. South Bend, IN: University of Notre Dame Press.

Smiles, Vincent M.
    1998   *The Gospel and the Law in Galatia: Paul's Response to Jewish-Christian Separatism and the Threat of Galatian Apostasy.* Collegeville, MN: Liturgical Press.

Sprinkle, Preston
    2008   *Law and Life: The Interpretation of Leviticus 18:5 in Early Judaism and in Paul.* Wissenschaftliche Untersuchungen zum Neuen Testament. Tübingen: Mohr Siebeck.

Swartley, Willard M.
    1994   *Israel's Scripture Traditions and the Synoptic Gospels: Story Shaping Story.* Peabody, MA: Hendrickson.

Toews, John E.
    2004   *Romans.* Believers Church Bible Commentary. Scottdale, PA: Herald Press.

Warning, Wilfried
    1999   *Literary Artistry in Leviticus.* Biblical Interpretation 35. Leiden: Brill.

Watts, James W.
    1999   *Reading Law: The Rhetorical Shaping of the Pentateuch.* Biblical Seminar 59. Sheffield: Sheffield Academic.
    2007   *Ritual and Rhetoric in Leviticus: From Sacrifice to Scripture.* Cambridge: Cambridge University Press.
    2011   "The Rhetoric of Sacrifice." In *Ritual and Metaphor: Sacrifice in the Bible*, edited by Christian A. Eberhart, 3–16. Atlanta: Society of Biblical Literature.

Wehnert, Jürgen
    1997   *Die Reinheit des "christlichen Gottesvolkes" aus Juden und Heiden: Studien zum historischen und theologischen Hintergrund des sogenannten Aposteldekrets.* Göttingen: Vandenhoeck & Ruprecht.

Wellhausen, Julius
    1885   *Prolegomena to the History of Israel.* Edinburgh: Adam and Charles Black. Kindle edition, 2009.

Wenham, Gordon J.
    1979   *The Book of Leviticus.* New International Commentary on the Old Testament. Grand Rapids: Eerdmans.

Williams, George H., and Angel M. Mergal, eds.
    1957   *Spiritual and Anabaptist Writers.* Library of Christian Classics. Philadelphia: Westminster.

Wright, Christopher J. H.
    1995   *Walking in the Ways of the Lord: The Ethical Authority of the Old Testament.* Downers Grove, IL: InterVarsity.

Wright, David P.
    1987   *The Disposal of Impurity: Elimination Rites in the Bible and in Hittite and Mesopotamian Literature.* Dissertation Series 101. Atlanta: Scholars Press.

1991 "The Spectrum of Priestly Impurity." In *Priesthood and Cult in Ancient Israel*, edited by Gary A. Anderson and Saul M. Olyan, 150–82. Sheffield: JSOT Press.

Yoder, Perry
1987 *Shalom: The Bible's Word for Salvation, Justice, and Peace*. North Newton, KS: Faith & Life.

Zenger, Eric
1999 "Das Buch Levitikus als Teiltext der Tora/des Pentateuch: Eine synchrone Lektüre mit kanonischer Perspektive." In *Levitikus als Buch*, edited by Heinz-Josef Fabry and Jans-Winfied Jüngling, 47–83. Berlin: Philo.

Selected Resources

Helpful Commentaries

Berlin, Adele, and Marc Zvi Brettler, eds. 2004. *The Jewish Study Bible: Tanakh Translation*. New York: Oxford University Press. The *Tanakh Translation* is the NJPS translation referred to in this commentary. This is a one-volume commentary on the Hebrew Bible (OT), with extensive essays at the end. As customary with Jewish commentaries, and most study Bibles, the text and its comments occur on the same page, greatly aiding understanding besides being convenient.

Gorman, Frank H., Jr. 1997. *Leviticus: Divine Presence and Community*. International Theological Commentary. Grand Rapids: Eerdmans. A short, topical commentary on Leviticus. An easy read.

Hartley, John E. 1992. *Leviticus*. Word Biblical Commentary 4. Dallas: Word. A standard reference consulted and referred to often in this commentary. Hartley's comments and brief essays on topics are long enough to be informative yet short enough to be read quickly. A good reference commentary.

Levine, Baruch. 1989. *Leviticus*. JPS Torah Commentary. Philadelphia: Jewish Publication Society. A non-Milgrom commentary, but very good. Another case where it is wonderful to read text and comments on the same page. Highly recommended as the initial commentary to read.

Milgrom, Jacob. 2004. *Leviticus: A Book of Ritual and Ethics*. Continental Commentary. Minneapolis: Fortress. A shorter Milgrom commentary and quite readable. Read this for the "essential Milgrom." It is not a commentary on each individual verse but on representative or important passages.

Helpful Resources

Anderson, Gary A. 1992. "Sacrifice and Sacrificial Offerings: Old Testament." In *Anchor Bible Dictionary* 5:870–86. New York: Doubleday. An overview of what we find in the Hebrew Bible generally about sacrifice, providing a broader perspective on what we find in Leviticus.

Bergen, Wesley J. 2005. *Reading Ritual: Leviticus in Postmodern Culture*. JSOTSup 417. London: T&T Clark. A short introduction to ritual theory and an application to modern activities. Reference is made to Leviticus throughout. An educational and fun read.

Gane, Roy E., and Ada Taggar-Cohen, eds. 2015. *Current Issues in Priestly and Related Literature: The Legacy of Jacob Milgrom and Beyond*. Atlanta: SBL Press. Essays on going beyond the work of Milgrom and applying some of his findings to broader issues. An important collection for those looking to see what questions and issues modern scholars find worth exploring.

Grabbe, Lester L. 1993. *Leviticus*. Old Testament Guides. Sheffield: JSOT Press. A splendid introduction to the study of Leviticus. A good first read to get your bearings and form a horizon and perspective to begin studying Leviticus.

Kim, Jin-Myung. 2011. *Holiness and Perfection: A Canonical Unfolding of Leviticus 19*. Bern: Peter Lang. A brief introduction to regulations for holy living, with a focus on chapter 19 and its wider influence. A good guide for those who automatically turn to Leviticus 19 when they think of Leviticus.

Rogerson, John W. 2014. *Leviticus in Practice*. Dorset, UK: Deo. Shows how scholars would make use of topics or passages in Leviticus for readers today. Each chapter is on a different theme, with two chapters on Jubilee.

Three Works for Digging Deeper

Janzen, David. 2004. *The Social Meanings of Sacrifice in the Hebrew Bible: A Study of Four Writings*. Beihefte zur Zeitschrift für die alttestamentliche Wissenschaft 344. Berlin: de Gruyter. Although a monograph written for scholars, it is readable and coherent. A good first read for those who want to go beyond what they find in the commentaries. It is both helpful and illuminative.

Klawans, Jonathan. 2008. "Methodology and Ideology in the Study of Priestly Ritual." In *Perspectives on Purity and Purification in the Bible*, edited by Baruch J. Schwartz et al., 84–95. London: T&T Clark. A very informative work and a good introduction to Klawans, who has been a critic of Milgrom. As its title shows, it is beneficial for those interested in methodology.

Watts, James W. 2007. *Ritual and Rhetoric in Leviticus: From Sacrifice to Scripture*. Cambridge: Cambridge University Press. An introduction to Watts, who has applied the analysis of rhetoric to Leviticus. Another lens through which to see Leviticus.

Secondary Readings on Topics Raised in the Commentary

Finlan, Stephen. 2005. *Problems with Atonement: The Origins of, and Controversy about, the Atonement Doctrine*. Collegeville, MN: Michael Glazier. A basic read for understanding how Christian atonement theories work and what these understandings have meant for the captivity of Leviticus to Christian thought. It illustrates how misunderstanding Leviticus was necessary to support these theories, or how Leviticus was misunderstood by assuming a Christian theory of atonement.

Marshall, Christopher D. 2003. "Atonement, Violence and the Will of God: A Sympathetic Response to J. Denny Weaver's *The Nonviolent Atonement*." *Mennonite Quarterly Review* 77:69–92. The careful discussion of a dissenting opinion on the atonement—within the context of the received atonement theories. A modest compromise is reached.

Philip, Mayjee. 2011. *Leviticus in Hebrews: A Transtextual Analysis of the Tabernacle Theme in the Letter to the Hebrews*. New York: Peter Lang. A work that I found helpful and a resource for my understanding of the book of Hebrews. It presents the thesis that Hebrews was a successor to Leviticus, not a replacement. The Platonic ideal in heaven does not replace the earthly shrine.

Index of Ancient Sources

OLD TESTAMENT

Genesis
.... 25, 311
1 199
1:14-16 238
1:26-27 241
1:27 185
2:3 246
2:15 246
3:8 264
4:9-15 241
4:24 198
5:2 241
6:18 298
9:1-6 307
9:4 .... 91, 170–71
9:5-6 .... 172, 241, 243
9:8-17 266–67
9:9-10 172
9:9-17 298
14 60
15:18 298
17:9-14 124
18:22-33 109
19 211

21:2-4 124
21:25 198
21:25-32 298
28:18 263
28:20 272–73
32:13 51
32:20 289
34:2 159
37:4-5 198
37:8 198
43:32 183
45:18 57
46:34 183

Exodus
.... 25, 253, 317
1:11-12 159
1:13 255
3–4 42
4:14-17 306
5:5 207
6:2-8 188
6:6 180
6:18 106
6:20 106
6:22-23 106

9:31 54
9:31-32 230
10:2 180
12:2-3 296
12:11-48 229
12:22 132
12:48 .... 124, 163
13:4 295
13:12 182
16:10 93
19:3 42
19:4-6 210
19:5 211
19:5-6 .... 26, 42, 222
19:6 .... 112, 222
19:20 42
20 194
20:2 . 180, 202, 263–64, 299
20:4-6 194
20:7 .... 196, 311
20:8-11 194
20:9-10 228
20:12 .... 194, 209
20:13 242
20:14 .... 209, 213

Index of Ancient Sources

20:16 197	28:15 199	11:2 71
21 241	28:42 85	11:10 23
21:1-4 44	29:37 87	11:33 23
21:2 .... 44, 248	29:38-39 85–86	14:19-20 .... 68, 70
21:2-4 304–5	29:40-41 86	15:10 48
21:2-11 28	30:11-16 290	15:25-26 68
21:12 240	30:12-14 312	15:27-30 62
21:12-14 .... 242, 305	31:14 216	15:28 68
21:15 .... 146, 207, 305	31:15 228	15:30 160
21:17 209	31:18 247	15:30-31 90
21:23-27 242	32:10-12 23	16:8-11 113
21:28-32 290	32:30-33 161	16:40 105
21:30 312	34:6-7 294	18:2 .... 21, 112
22:24 23	34:9 .... 68, 70	18:12 53
23:10-11 .... 248, 304	34:18-26 296	18:13 54
23:12 228	34:22 .... 50, 54	18:19 53
23:14-16 229	34:26 .... 50, 54	19:2 216
23:14-17 295	34:27-29 155	19:6 132
23:15 .... 227, 295	35:1 193	19:13-21 216
23:16 .... 54, 231	35:2 228	19:18 132
23:17 268	40:9 98	21:7 71
23:19 54	40:34 .... 42, 93	21:29 180
24:1-8 .... 261, 298	40:34-35 102	27:21 97
24:3-8 .... 24, 264	40:34-38 25	28–29 .... 234, 297
24:4 263	40:35 .... 41, 317	28:4-8 86
24:16 .... 42, 102		28:9-10 233
24:16-17 93	**Leviticus**	29:35 233
25:2-3 90	Not indexed, see	30:2 .... 272, 311
25:8 25	contents	30:8 70
25:16 155		31:50 45
25:18-20 195	**Numbers**	35:1-8 253
25:22 .... 41, 195	.... 25, 253, 317	35:11-12 242
25:23-28 .... 237, 239	1:1 .... 25, 278	35:30 242
25:29 237	1:47-54 287	35:31 .... 243, 290
25:31 239	1:49-50 306	35:31-32 312
25:31-37 238	1:53 23	
25:31-39 237	5:6-8 80	**Deuteronomy**
26:1 199	5:7-8 76	.... 25, 317
26:31 199	7:13 45	4:20 210
26:34 155	8:7 65	4:42 198
28:6 199	10:10 232	5 194
28:6-39 97	11:1 23	5:6 299

5:8-10 195	29:1 261	28:4-19 208
5:11 311	30:6 203	28:7-14 201
5:12-14 228		
5:14 194	**Joshua**	**2 Samuel**
5:16 194	5:3 124	2:4 287
6:4 179	5:10-12 234	5:3 287
6:52 203	6: 4-13 249	
7:6 .... 211, 222	6:5 304	**1 Kings**
8:3 .... 181, 185	6:8-13 304	1:34 288
8:12-13 236	6:18 276	1:39 288
8:14 60	7:14 277	4:22 51
8:17 60	18:1 317	5:12 298
8:17-18a 236	19:51 317	7:13-51 238
10:20 .... 76, 196, 311	22:5 203	8:4 317
11:22 203	23:11 203	8:50 70
12:23 170	24:19-20 161	8:63 82
13:16-17 277		18:28 201
14:1 201	**Judges**	19:15-16 288
14:1-2 216	9:27 200	21:1-15 243
14:2 .... 211, 222	16:28 113	22:17-25 181
15 259	17:1-2 74	
15:1-3 254	18:14-20 306	**2 Kings**
15:1-11 .... 248, 304	19:22-27 211-12	2:23-24 265–66
15:4 259		3:26-27 182
15:7 259	**Ruth**	7:1-16 51
15:11 259	2 195	7:16 53
16:1-17 296	4:1-11 251-52	10:7 47
16:8 233	4:10 .... 91, 300	10:20 233
17:9 287		20:12 51
18:14-15 201	**1 Samuel**	23:10 182
21:18-21 209	1:1-3 296	23:21-23 .... 229, 234
22:6 220	1:3 230	23:22 234
22:6-7 200	1:13-15 113	
22:9-11 199	2:21 317	**1 Chronicles**
24:14 196	3:13 209	29:3 211
24:19-21 231	9:12-13 230	
25:5 209–10	10:1 287	**2 Chronicles**
25:5-10 182	12:2 306	8:13 234
26:11-13 195	14:33 200–201	13:5 53
26:18 211	14:33-34 169	30:13 234
27:16 209	14:41 97	30:21 234
27–28 ..... 261, 295, 299	16:13 287	35:17 234

Index of Ancient Sources

Ezra
.... 319
2:63 97
3:4 234
6:19-21 234

Nehemiah
.... 319
7:65 97
8:14-16 234
11:25-30 253

Psalms
15 143–44
15:1 .... 114, 321
31:23 203
35:13 159
50:8-15 144
51:2 27
51:7 132
62:12 186
66:15-17 58
66:16 59
107:22 58
109:13-14 161
119:2 185
119:7 185
119:17 185

Proverbs
29:17 48

Ecclesiastes
7:20 186

Isaiah
1:8 233
1:10-17 314–15
2:2-5 269
27 269
59 269
61:1 .... 250, 256–57
61:1-2a 312

Jeremiah
1:5 194
5:1 70
5:7 70
7:6 196
22:3 258
31–33 70
31:31-37 .... 269, 271
31:34 70
33:8 70
33:17-18 110
33:20-21 110
34:8-17 .... 250, 256
34:14 248
36:3 70
50:20 .... 70, 161

Ezekiel
4:3 52
14:8 300
16:20 182
18:5-14 143
20:11 .... 181, 185
20:13 185
20:21 185
20:25 181
22:10 143
22:12 143
44–48 17
44:19 86
44:21 310
46:17 .... 250, 256

Hosea
2:8 61

Joel
1:14 233

Jonah
.... 309, 318
4:1-3 294
4:5 233
4:7 132

Micah
6:8 315

Zechariah
13:7 181

Malachi
3:17 211

NEW TESTAMENT

Matthew
5:17-20 320
5:22 204
5:23-24 .... 59, 81
5:33-35 311
5:33-48 312
5:38 243
5:44 204
5:45 61
5:46 204
6:14-15 71
7:12 199
7:20 190
8:2-4 144
12:26 293
18:15-20 16
18:22 81
19 311
22:37 203
22:39–40 203
23:2-3 188–89
23:3 224
23:23 .... 189, 225
25:35-36 204
26:17 235

Mark
1:44 144
11:25 71
14:12 235

Luke
1:59 124
2:21 124
4:16-19 312
4:18 257
5:14 59
6:31 72
7:21-23 258–59
10:27 203
10:30-37 199
10:31 216
11:4 .... 71, 82
17:14 144
22:7 235

John
1:14 .... 26, 33
1:29 26
2:13 234
2:19 111
2:23 234
4:23 144
6:4 234
7:2-10 235
10:22 235
10:23 235
11:6–12:2 234
12:1-3 235
12:8 259
12:20-21 235
13:1 235
13:5 235
13:27 293
13:34 204
14:6 271
18:39 235
19:14 235

19:29 132

Acts
1:4 110
1:8 111
1:13-26 110
2:5 234
5:1-11 109
5:3 293
6:7 .... 111, 301
8:27 235
10:28 173
15 .... 60, 186–87
15:1 173
15:5 173
15:19-20 173–74
16 234
16:3 301
18:9-15 208
21:24-26 59
21:26 301
24:17 301
26:18 293

Romans
1:7 223
1:23 61
1:24 212
1:25 61
1:26-27 212
1:29-32 212
2:6 186
2:13 186
3:31 .... 186, 320
5:12 293
5:17 293
6:2-4 162
6:7 162
6:13 162
6:18 162
9–11 269–70
10:5 310

12 109
12:1 .... 61, 222
12:19 109
12:20-21 109
13:8 204
13:8-10 203
13:10 199
15:16 223
15:25-26 223
15:31 223

1 Corinthians
1:2 223
3:16 111
3:16-17 145
5:11 145
5:13 145
6:9 212
6:19 111
6:19-20 145
8 110
10:20 110
12:11-14 112
12:22 112

2 Corinthians
6:16 145
7:1 145

Galatians
.... 318
2:1 173
2:3 301
2:21 186
3:21 186
4:3 292
4:8 293
5:2 187
5:20-23 190

Ephesians
1:4 222

2:21 111	**OT APOCRYPHA**	**MESOPOTAMIA, ANE**
4:11-12 112		ANE 241, 304, 320
5:27 222	**1 Maccabees**	Code of Hammurabi
	4:52–59 235	 268
1 Thessalonians		purification rituals
4:3 222	**DEAD SEA SCROLLS**	 288
4:7 222		
	11QMelchizedek	
1 Timothy	11Q13 257	
1:10 212		
3:2 310	**Rule of the Community**	
Titus	1QS X, 8 257	
1:6 310		
	RABBINIC SOURCES	
Hebrews	 308	
5:4-5 111		
8:5-6 300	**Mishnah**	
9:1-10 300	 270–71	
	Sanhedrin 5.3-6 ... 244	
James		
3 310–11	**Rabbis**	
5:15 71	Hillel 145, 189, 199	
	Shammai 145, 189	
1 Peter		
1:14-15 222	**Talmud**	
1:16 222	.... 82, 270–71, 308	
2:5 222	Sanhedrin 56a 172	
2:9 .... 26, 112, 222		
4:1-2 162	**Tosefta**	
	Avodah Zarah 8.4 .. 172	
1 John		
.... 204	**APOSTOLIC FATHERS**	
4:20 204		
5:2 204		
	Didache	
Revelation	3.1-6 172	
2:13 293	5.1b 172	

The Author

Perry B. Yoder was born in Portland, Oregon, and graduated from Western Mennonite High School. After matriculation at Hesston College (Kans.), he graduated from Goshen College (Ind.) with a BA in sociology. He studied at the University of Pennsylvania in the department of Ancient Near Eastern Studies with a major in Semitic Literatures and Languages. During his graduate studies he spent a year in Israel at Hebrew University. He received his PhD in 1970.

His first teaching position was at Bluffton College in Bluffton, Ohio. After seven years of teaching, he and his family spent two years traveling and teaching in Mennonite settings in the United States and Canada. After this assignment, he taught at Bethel College in North Newton, Kansas. He spent the last twenty years of his teaching career at Associated Mennonite Biblical Seminary in Elkhart, Indiana. Now Emeritus Professor of Old Testament from that institution, he lives in Ely, Minnesota, with his wife, Elizabeth. They have two grown sons.

Throughout his career the topic of Bible study has occupied his attention. *Toward Understanding the Bible: Hermeneutics for Lay People* (Faith & Life), which grew out of his experiences as an itinerant Bible teacher in Mennonite congregations, was followed by *From Word to Life: A Guide to the Art of Bible Study* (Herald Press). He coauthored *Seeing the Text: Exegesis for Students of Greek and Hebrew* (Abingdon) with Mary Schertz, a New Testament scholar. Thematically, his abiding interest has been justice and peace. Two books represent his major contributions to this topic: *Shalom: The Bible's Word for Salvation, Justice, and Peace* (Faith & Life) and *The Meaning of Peace* (Westminster John Knox), which he coedited with Willard Swartley.

"Perry B. Yoder's clear and approachable study of Leviticus works with the most recent scholarship to unlock key theological ideas such as atonement, the holiness of an ethical life, and divine grace. This commentary will be of enormous help to both pastors and educated laypersons seeking to understand what can seem like a puzzling but fascinating biblical book." —*David Janzen, associate professor of Old Testament, Durham University*

"Perry B. Yoder teaches readers that Leviticus is not a book of ancient, cryptic rules but rather an invitation to encounter a gracious and holy God. Throughout his commentary, Yoder adeptly narrates Leviticus for followers of Jesus today. Yoder's insightful, well-researched, and pastoral commentary will be a gift to preachers and students who seek to understand one of the Old Testament's most underestimated books." —*Melissa Florer-Bixler, pastor, Raleigh Mennonite Church*

"Focusing on the text of Leviticus raises the question, How do people live with a holy God? Perry B. Yoder guides the reader to consider obedient purity requisite for knowing and worshiping God. Reading with the text leads to the surprising discovery that God is gracious, not angry; friendly, not an exacting bookkeeper." —*Lynn Jost, professor of Old Testament and preaching, Fresno Pacific Biblical Seminary*

"Perry B. Yoder is a consummate teacher, with a singular gift for illuminating the biblical text, and with an eye to how it informs the church today. That gift is very much evident as he leads us into Leviticus, revealing a holy, gracious, and forgiving God, with directions for how to worship and live." —*Gerald Gerbrandt, president emeritus and professor emeritus of Bible, Canadian Mennonite University*

"Perry B. Yoder provides an engaging study of Leviticus for the serious Bible student and the practicing Christian, disclosing a gracious God who invites obedience as well as sacrifice as a response of gratitude to God's love. Yoder provides a measured approach to key New Testament texts and the doctrine of atonement." —*Robert W. Neff, president emeritus, Juniata College, and professor emeritus of Old Testament, Bethany Theological Seminary*

www.ingramcontent.com/pod-product-compliance
Lightning Source LLC
Chambersburg PA
CBHW030520230426
43665CB00010B/701